THE UMBRELLA ACADEMY™

GERARD WAY & GABRIEL BÁ

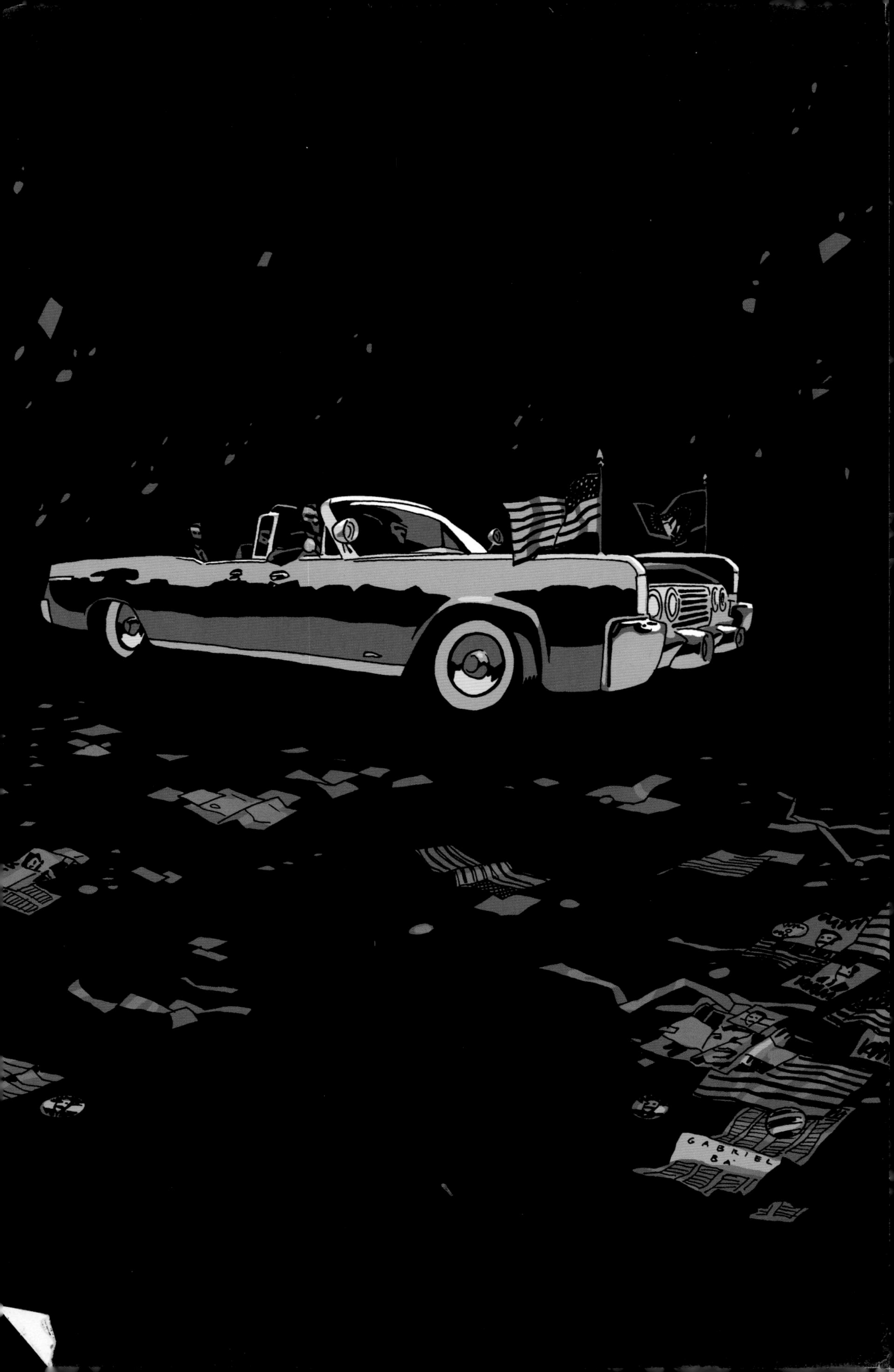
GABRIEL
BÁ

THE UMBRELLA ACADEMY™

VOLUME 2: DALLAS

STORY	**GERARD WAY**
ART	**GABRIEL BÁ**
COLORS	**DAVE STEWART**
LETTERS	**NATE PIEKOS of BLAMBOT®**

COVER ARTIST	**GABRIEL BÁ with DAVE STEWART**

DARK HORSE BOOKS®

PRESIDENT & PUBLISHER **MIKE RICHARDSON**

EDITOR **SCOTT ALLIE**

ASSOCIATE EDITOR **SIERRA HAHN**

ASSISTANT EDITOR **FREDDYE LINS**

COLLECTION DESIGNER **TONY ONG**

Colors to original series covers #2, #3, #4, and #5 by Dave Stewart.

Special thanks to Jim Krueger, Jonathan Rivera, and Stacy Fass.

Song lyrics to "The World Is Big Enough Without You" by Gene Ripley Jr.

NEIL HANKERSON Executive Vice President • TOM WEDDLE Chief Financial
Officer RANDY STRADLEY Vice President of Publishing • MICHAEL MARTENS Vice
President of Business Development • ANITA NELSON Vice President of Marketing, Sales,
and Licensing • DAVID SCROGGY Vice President of Product Development • DALE
LAFOUNTAIN Vice President of Information Technology • DARLENE VOGEL Director
of Purchasing • KEN LIZZI General Counsel • DAVEY ESTRADA Editorial Director
SCOTT ALLIE Senior Managing Editor • CHRIS WARNER Senior Books Editor, Dark
Horse Books • DIANA SCHUTZ Executive Editor • CARY GRAZZINI Director of Design
and Production • LIA RIBACCHI Art Director • CARA NIECE Director of Scheduling

THE UMBRELLA ACADEMY™
VOLUME TWO: DALLAS

This volume reprints the comic-book series *The Umbrella Academy: Dallas* issues #1–#6,
and a story from *MySpace Dark Horse Presents* #12, "*Anywhere but Here,*" published by
Dark Horse Comics.

Published by
Dark Horse Books
A division of
Dark Horse Comics, Inc.
10956 SE Main Street
Milwaukie, OR 97222

darkhorse.com

To find a comics shop in your area, call the Comic Shop Locator Service toll-free at
(888) 266-4226.

First edition: October 2009
ISBN 978-1-59582-345-8

10 9 8
Printed in China

INTRODUCTION

I was on the radio. It was the day after I'd won the Newbery Award, and I'd just been hustled into a tiny NPR studio somewhere in New York. I hadn't slept for more than three hours in a couple of days, had flown across the country the day before to spend four desperate minutes on the *Good Morning America* sofa that morning, and I was, by this point, only barely tracking with reality. Everything had become very unlikely.

The show was *Talk of the Nation*, and people were calling in asking questions. Someone from somewhere in America comes on with his question. He says, "What comics are you reading? What's good?"

My head is completely blank. I know that I must have read some comics in the last twenty-five years. I have shelves full of them in the basement. I could distinctly remember having read a comic. There were years in which I had read almost nothing but comics. In truth, if you asked me that question now I could rattle off dozens of titles I've enjoyed in the last few months, talk about creators whose work I love and am following. But there, in that radio studio, and then, in that strange media wasteland, someone had asked the question and all I was certain of was that I could not have named a single comic with a gun to my head. I even knew what was going to happen next. There was going to be a long moment of dead air, followed by me going "ummmmm . . . ," and I was never going to be invited back to National Public Radio ever again.

It was then that I heard my voice talking, using my mouth independently. It had circumvented the normal brain-to-voice-box-to-lips method of communication, and had struck out on its own. "*Umbrella Academy*," it was saying, confidently. "Written by Gerard Way. It's really good." Or words to that effect. And I sighed, the sigh of relief you can only sigh when a great burden is lifted from you. While I was not certain I had anything to do with the choice of comic, or the utterance over the radios of the nation, it was one of which I wholeheartedly approved.

I don't feel that old. When I think of, say, Grant Morrison, I'll as often think of the Grant I knew when we were both twenty-five, when we were trying to figure out how to do this comics thing we'd wanted to do our whole lives: mop-headed, gawky, shy lads with our heads filled with dreams. Sometimes it seems unlikely that we've been doing this comics thing for almost a quarter of a century, that we've had any effect on the world. I've seen it before. And then I get to read something as assured and as smart as *The Umbrella Academy*, and I feel as excited as I did when Grant Morrison's run of *Doom Patrol* first started going off into strange and uncharted places, back before your mother and father met and fell in love in that comic-store signing line, back in those far-off halcyon days before every University had a course on The Graphic Novel.

Those comics that, simply, make me happy are few and far, and you are holding one of them.

Rereading the stories in this book yesterday, I realized that most of what I enjoy is the mixture of joy and of assurance in the voice of the author. As Roger Zelazny once pointed out, it isn't the story (although the story is beautifully constructed), but the way that the story is told. The best thing about being young and smart and making comics, especially when you've spent your whole life wanting to write comics, is that everything is new. Each panel transition, every thing you ask an artist to do is being asked for the first time, which brings with it a joy and a delight: the joy of the new. At the same time, this is assured and beautifully crafted work: the beats and the rhythms of the story are the beats and rhythms of someone who understands that comics have their own unique virtues, and is determined to exploit them all, not to miss a trick. Gerard Way knows when to shout and when to whisper and when simply to sing.

The Umbrella Academy has the virtue of being uniquely itself. It is funny and smart, often exciting, sometimes silly, in a fine and sensible way: I trust that more landmarks will come to life in opening flashbacks. I care about the characters, even the dead ones: especially the dead ones, although they do not stay dead for long. This is comics, after all, and if there is one thing that Gerard knows, it's his comics.

And comics are never just the writing, otherwise we'd just print the scripts: Gabriel Bá's art walks the tightrope of being comic and serious at the same time, and then begins to bounce on the tightrope, and dance on it, and cartwheel and somersault and flip: it's the point you find yourself grinning at the monstrous, caring about people who are, if the truth be known, merely lines on paper. There's a lightness to the lines, and to the people and worlds that they describe, that makes me happy.

I am grateful to my voice for getting me out of a tight place on *Talk of the Nation* that afternoon. If it hadn't, I would not have had this opportunity of being the announcer and introducer for *The Umbrella Academy: Dallas*. In which the assassination of John F. Kennedy will be prevented and ensured and rumored, in which Hazel and Cha Cha will gain their cookie recipe and serve as an example for all of us of the dangers of sugar abuse, in which the secret history and future of Number Five will be revealed. Also, I'm sorry to say, in which a nuclear device will be detonated, destroying the Earth completely.

But before any of those things happen, Abraham Lincoln is on the attack. Quickly. Turn the page. It's starting, and you wouldn't want to miss a single panel . . .

NEIL GAIMAN
May 2009

For my brother, Mikey Way, and all the Saturdays spent reading comics, firing laser guns, and saving the world.

GERARD WAY

To my dear friend, founder of Terra Major, writer of *Roland: Days of Wrath* (my first professional comic-book work), great enthusiast of historical fictions, and, above all, the man responsible for my first trip to San Diego in 1997. If it weren't for him, I wouldn't have known about Comic-Con International, wouldn't have discovered so many different possibilities that comics had to offer me, and wouldn't have become the professional I am today. If you are reading this comic, it's because of a guy called Shane Amaya.

GABRIEL BÁ

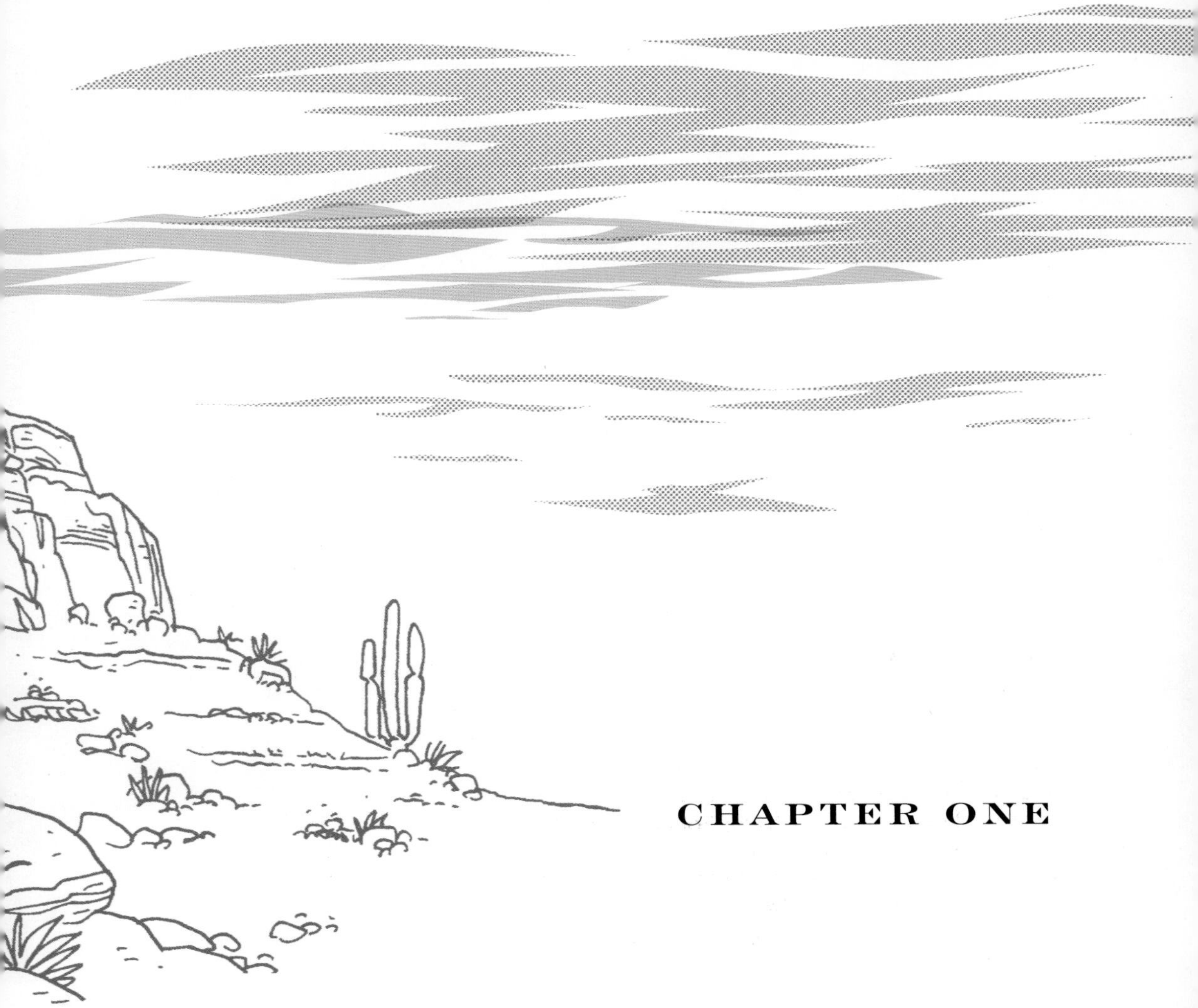

CHAPTER ONE

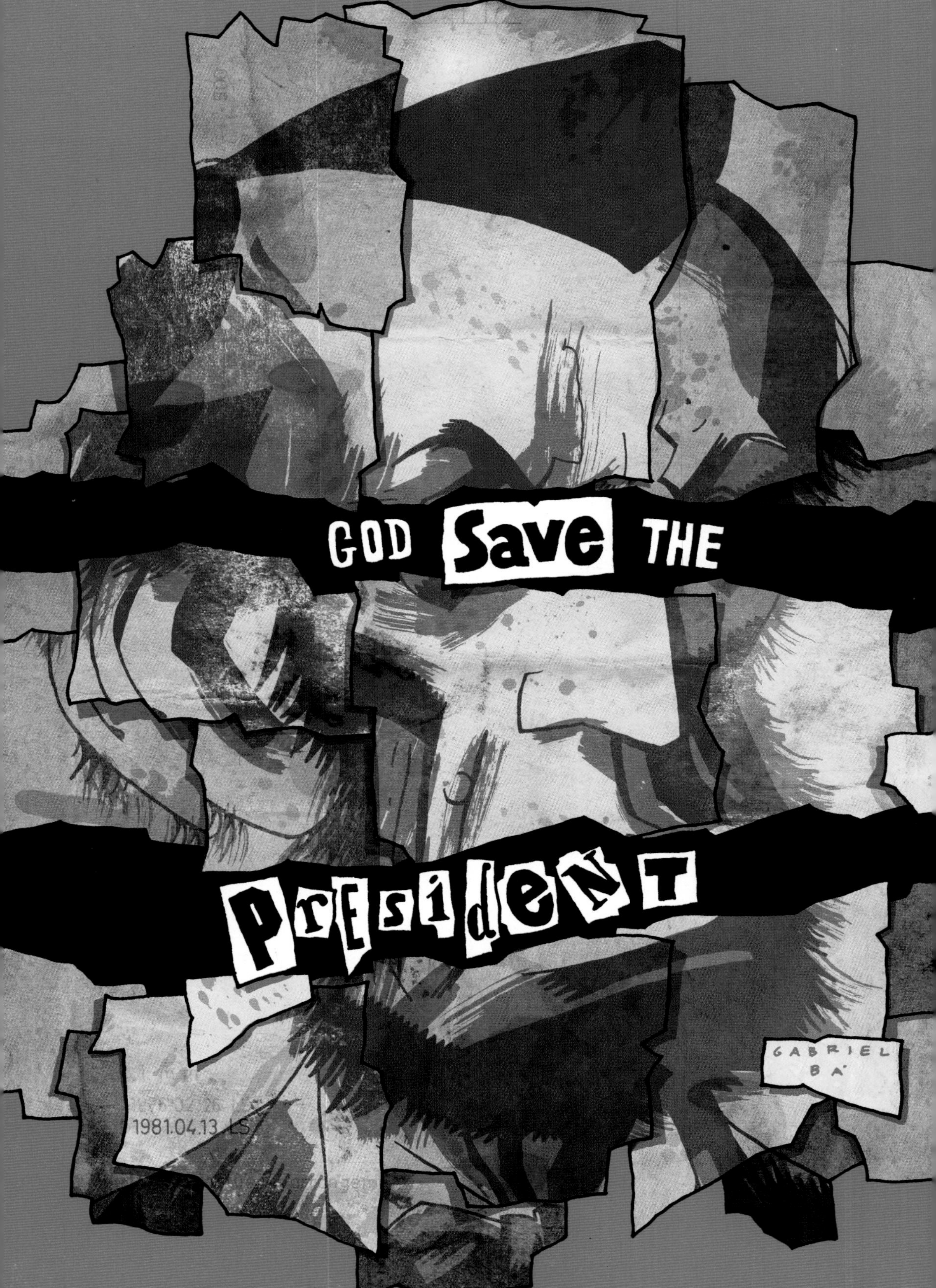
GOD Save THE
PRESIDENT
GABRIEL BÁ
1981.04.13 LS

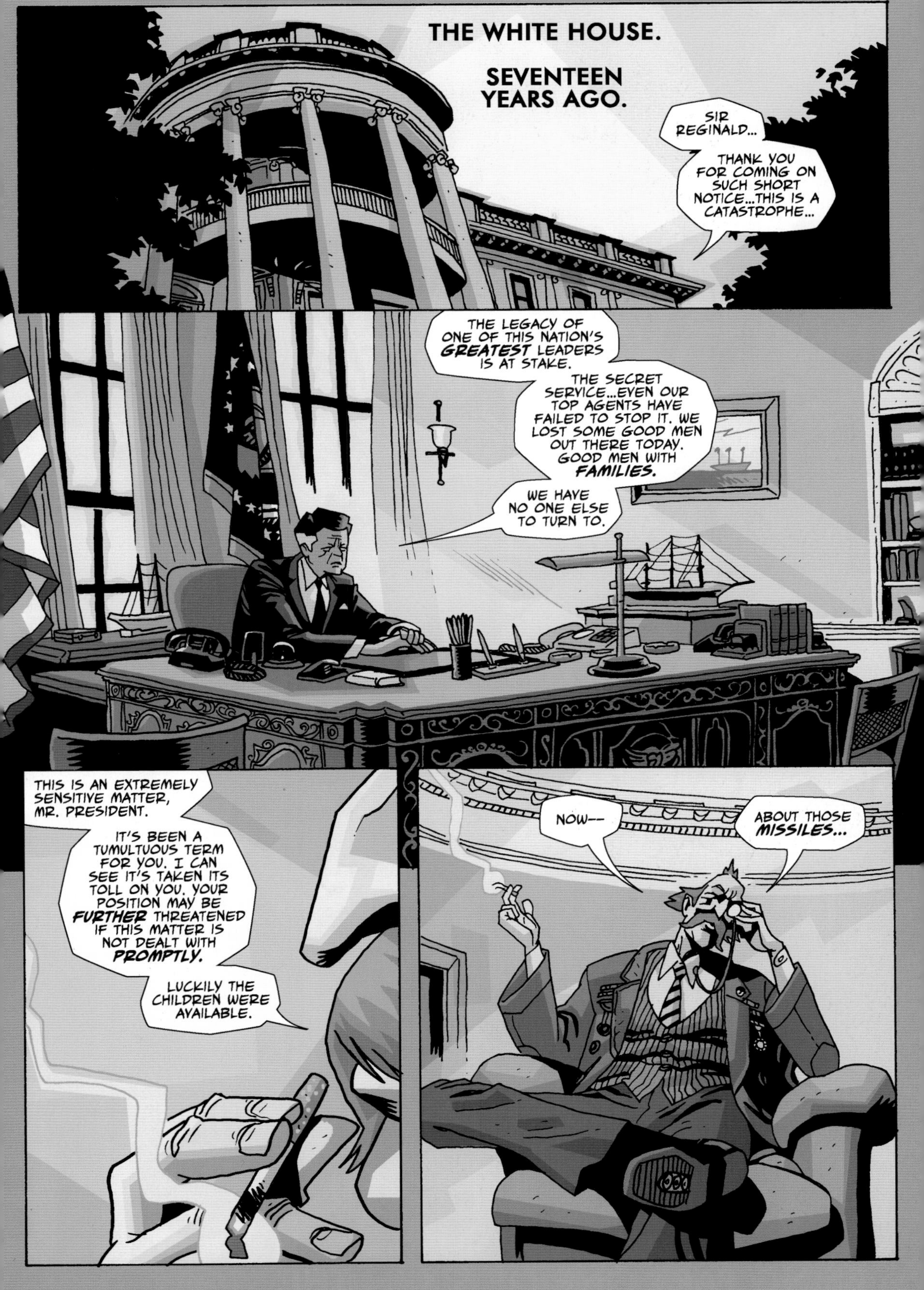
THE WHITE HOUSE.
SEVENTEEN YEARS AGO.
SIR REGINALD...
THANK YOU FOR COMING ON SUCH SHORT NOTICE...THIS IS A CATASTROPHE...
THE LEGACY OF ONE OF THIS NATION'S GREATEST LEADERS IS AT STAKE.
THE SECRET SERVICE...EVEN OUR TOP AGENTS HAVE FAILED TO STOP IT. WE LOST SOME GOOD MEN OUT THERE TODAY. GOOD MEN WITH FAMILIES.
WE HAVE NO ONE ELSE TO TURN TO.
THIS IS AN EXTREMELY SENSITIVE MATTER, MR. PRESIDENT.
IT'S BEEN A TUMULTUOUS TERM FOR YOU. I CAN SEE IT'S TAKEN ITS TOLL ON YOU. YOUR POSITION MAY BE FURTHER THREATENED IF THIS MATTER IS NOT DEALT WITH PROMPTLY.
LUCKILY THE CHILDREN WERE AVAILABLE.
NOW--
ABOUT THOSE MISSILES...

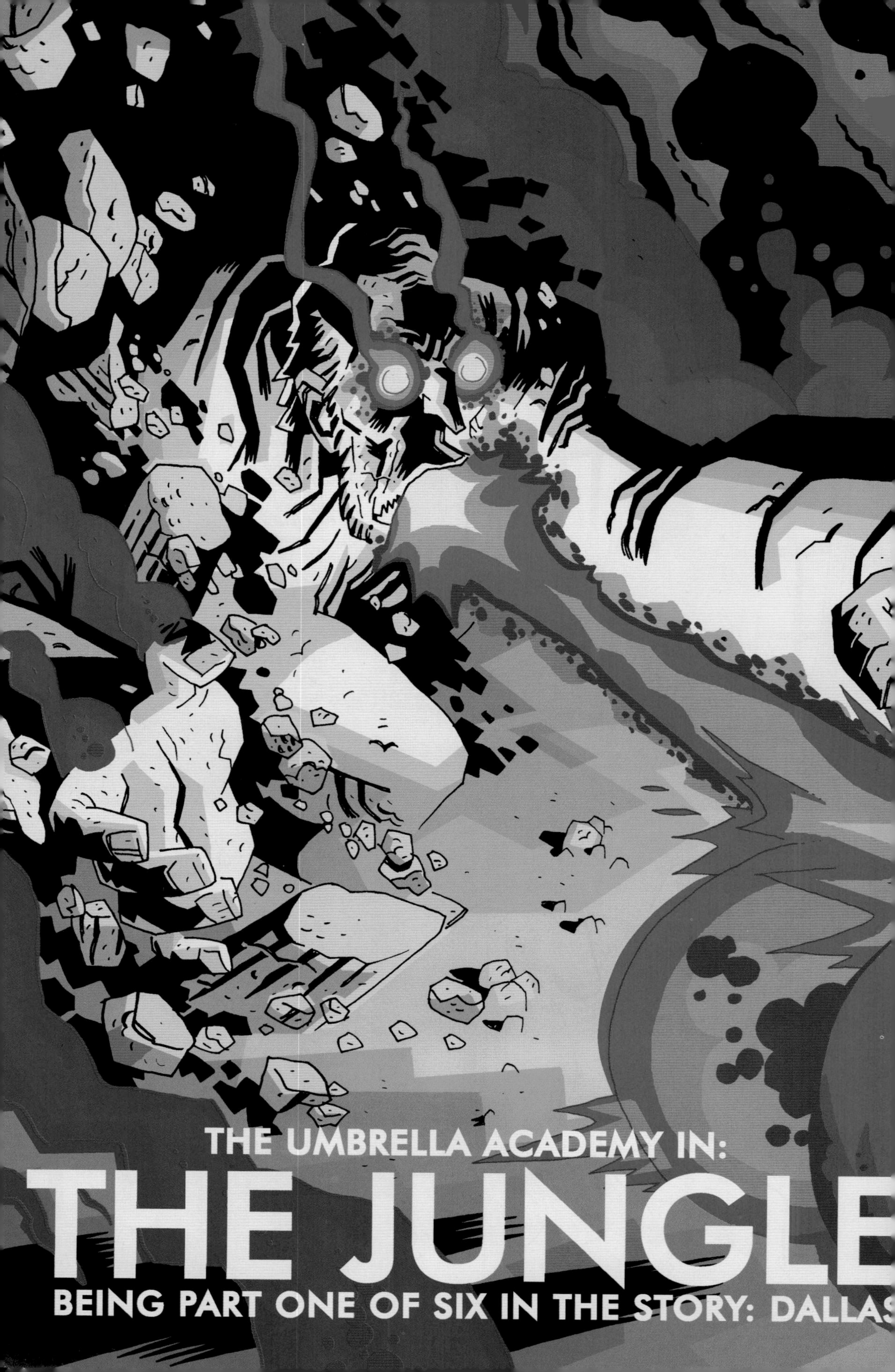
THE UMBRELLA ACADEMY IN:
THE JUNGLE
BEING PART ONE OF SIX IN THE STORY: DALLAS

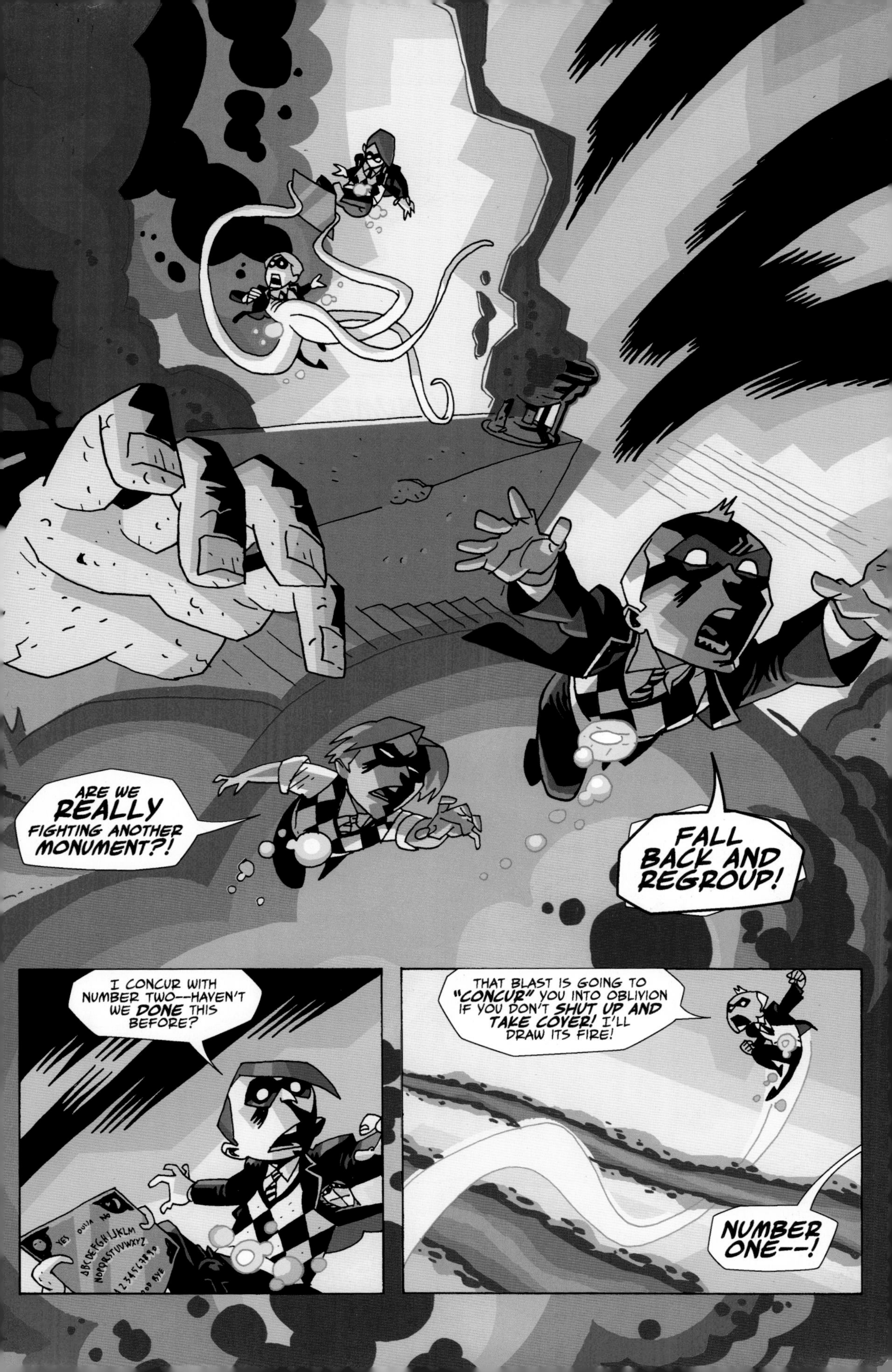
ARE WE REALLY FIGHTING ANOTHER MONUMENT?!
FALL BACK AND REGROUP!
I CONCUR WITH NUMBER TWO--HAVEN'T WE DONE THIS BEFORE?
THAT BLAST IS GOING TO "CONCUR" YOU INTO OBLIVION IF YOU DON'T SHUT UP AND TAKE COVER! I'LL DRAW ITS FIRE!
NUMBER ONE--!

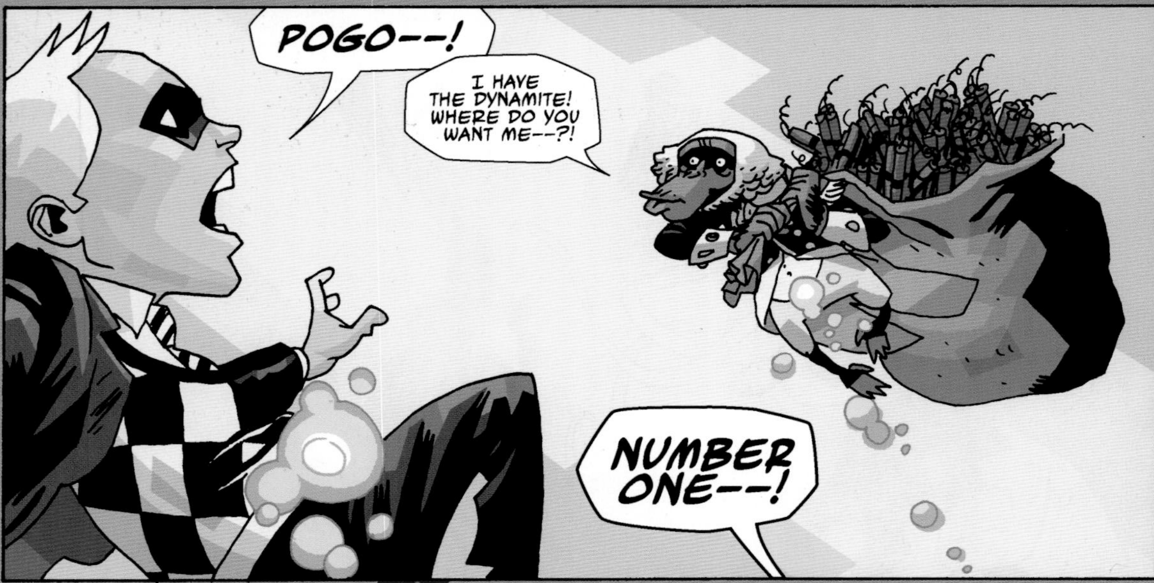
POGO--!
I HAVE THE DYNAMITE! WHERE DO YOU WANT ME--?!
NUMBER ONE--!

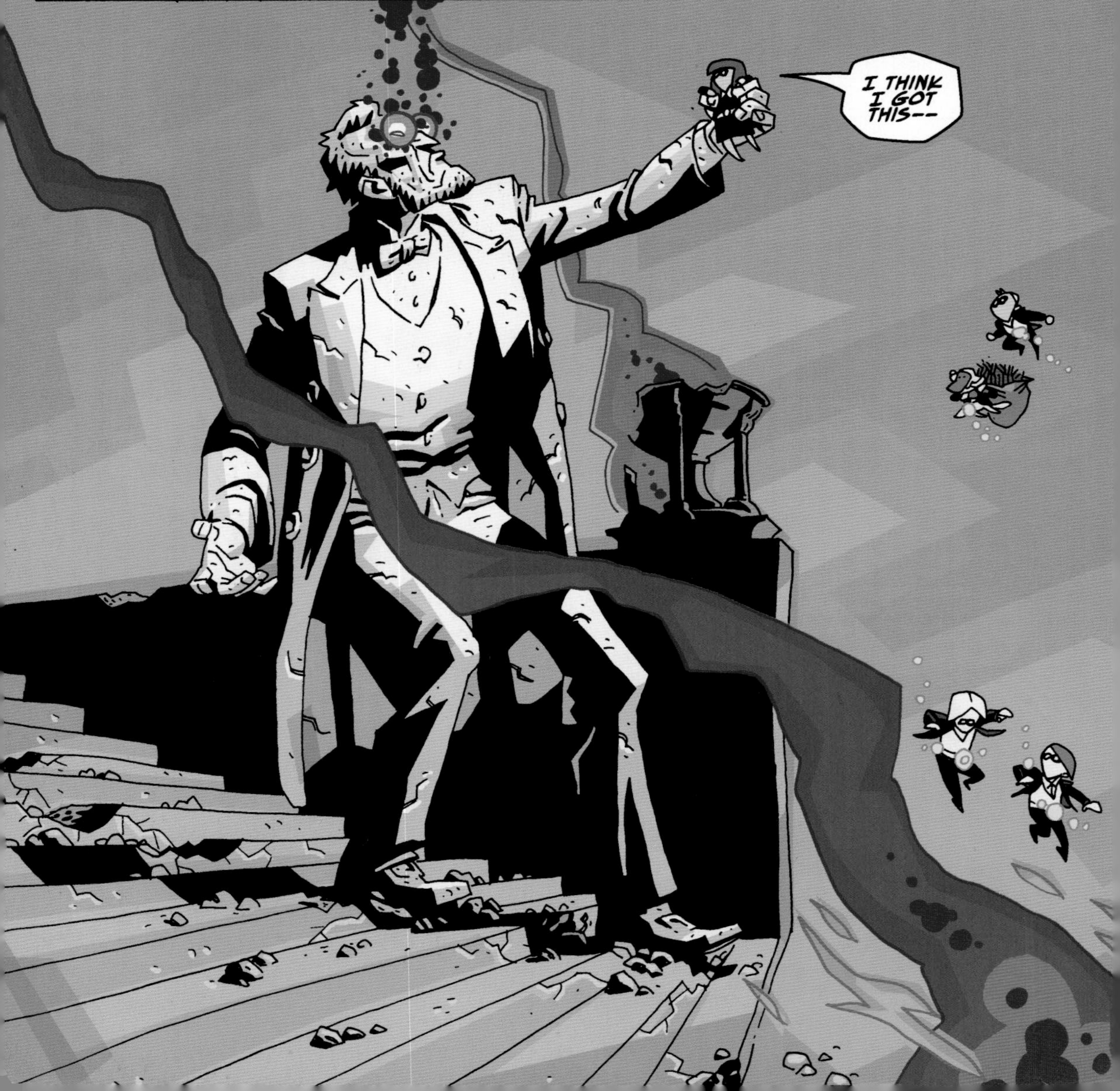
I THINK I GOT THIS--

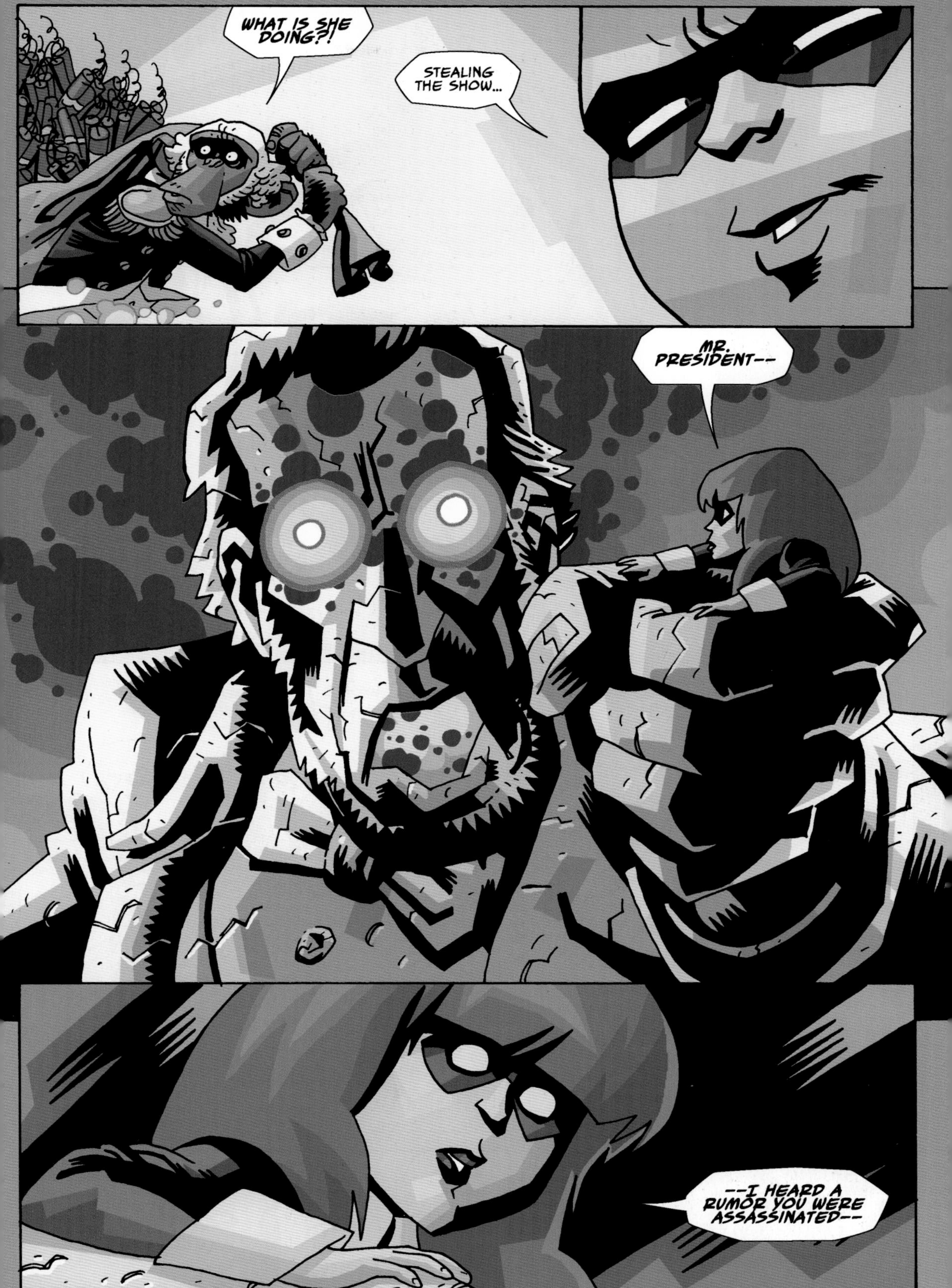
WHAT IS SHE DOING?!
STEALING THE SHOW...
MR. PRESIDENT--
--I HEARD A RUMOR YOU WERE ASSASSINATED--

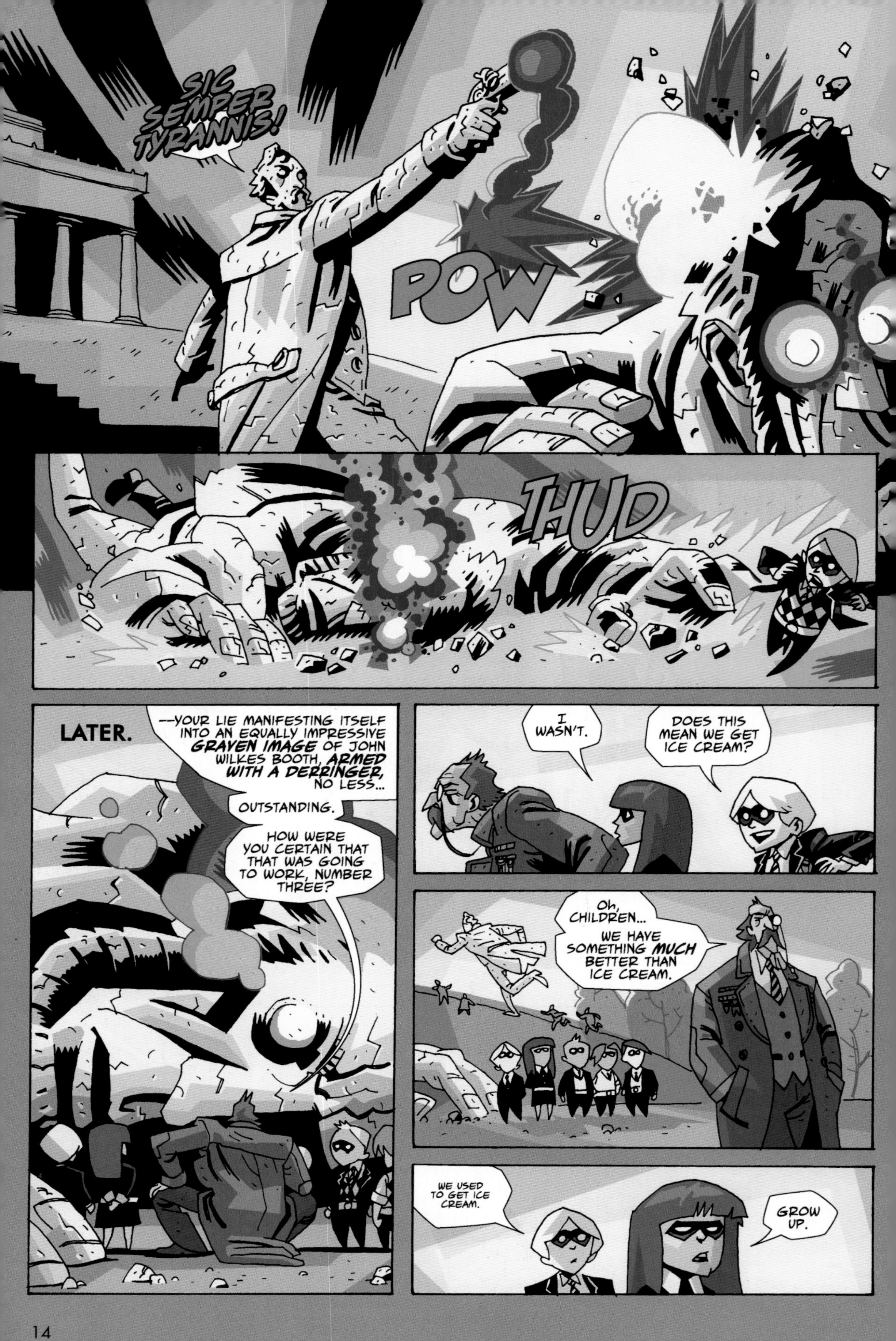
SIC SEMPER TYRANNIS!
POW
THUD
LATER.
--YOUR LIE MANIFESTING ITSELF INTO AN EQUALLY IMPRESSIVE GRAVEN IMAGE OF JOHN WILKES BOOTH, ARMED WITH A DERRINGER, NO LESS...
OUTSTANDING.
HOW WERE YOU CERTAIN THAT THAT WAS GOING TO WORK, NUMBER THREE?
I WASN'T.
DOES THIS MEAN WE GET ICE CREAM?
Oh, CHILDREN...
WE HAVE SOMETHING MUCH BETTER THAN ICE CREAM.
WE USED TO GET ICE CREAM.
GROW UP.

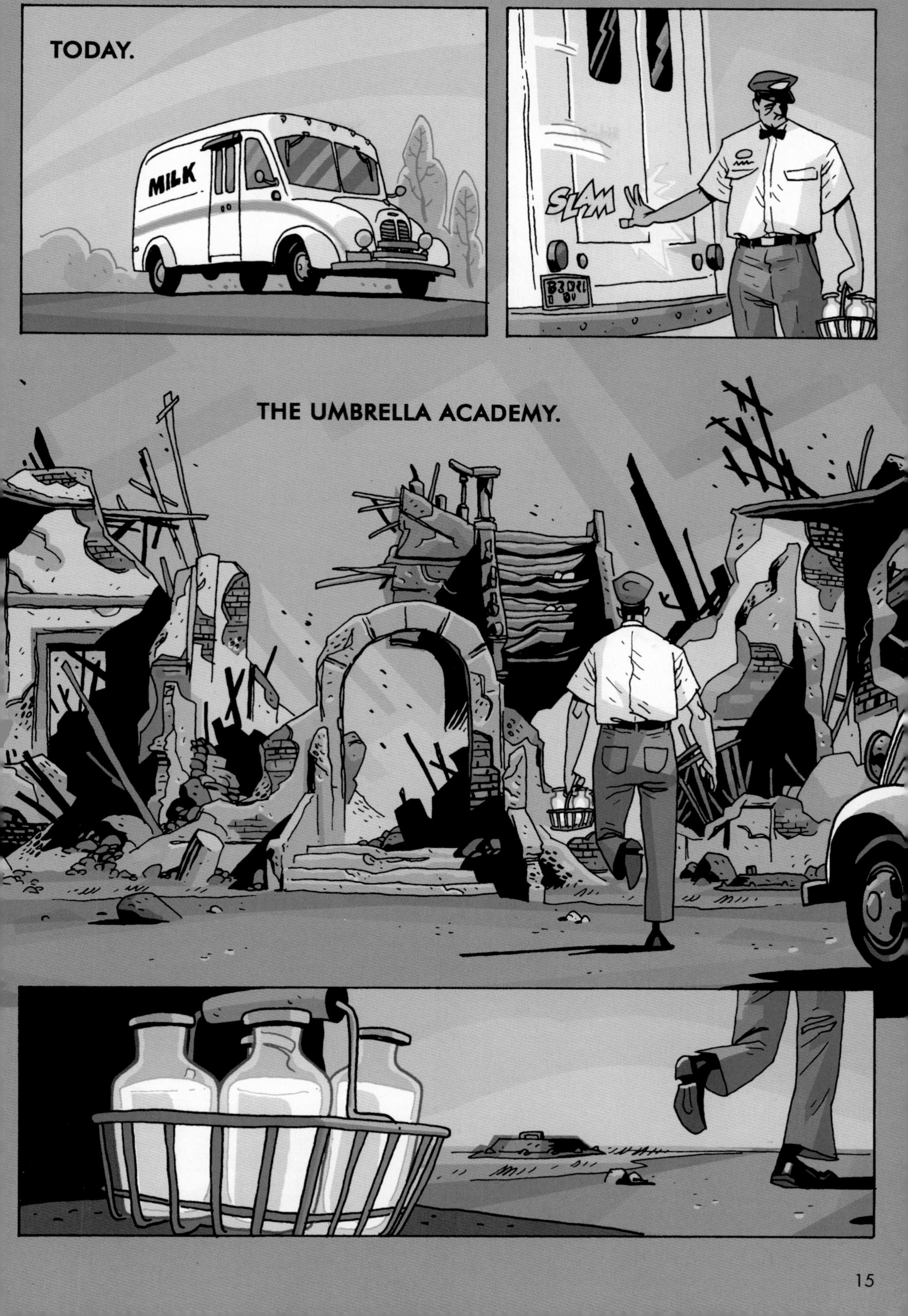
TODAY.
MILK
SLAM
THE UMBRELLA ACADEMY.

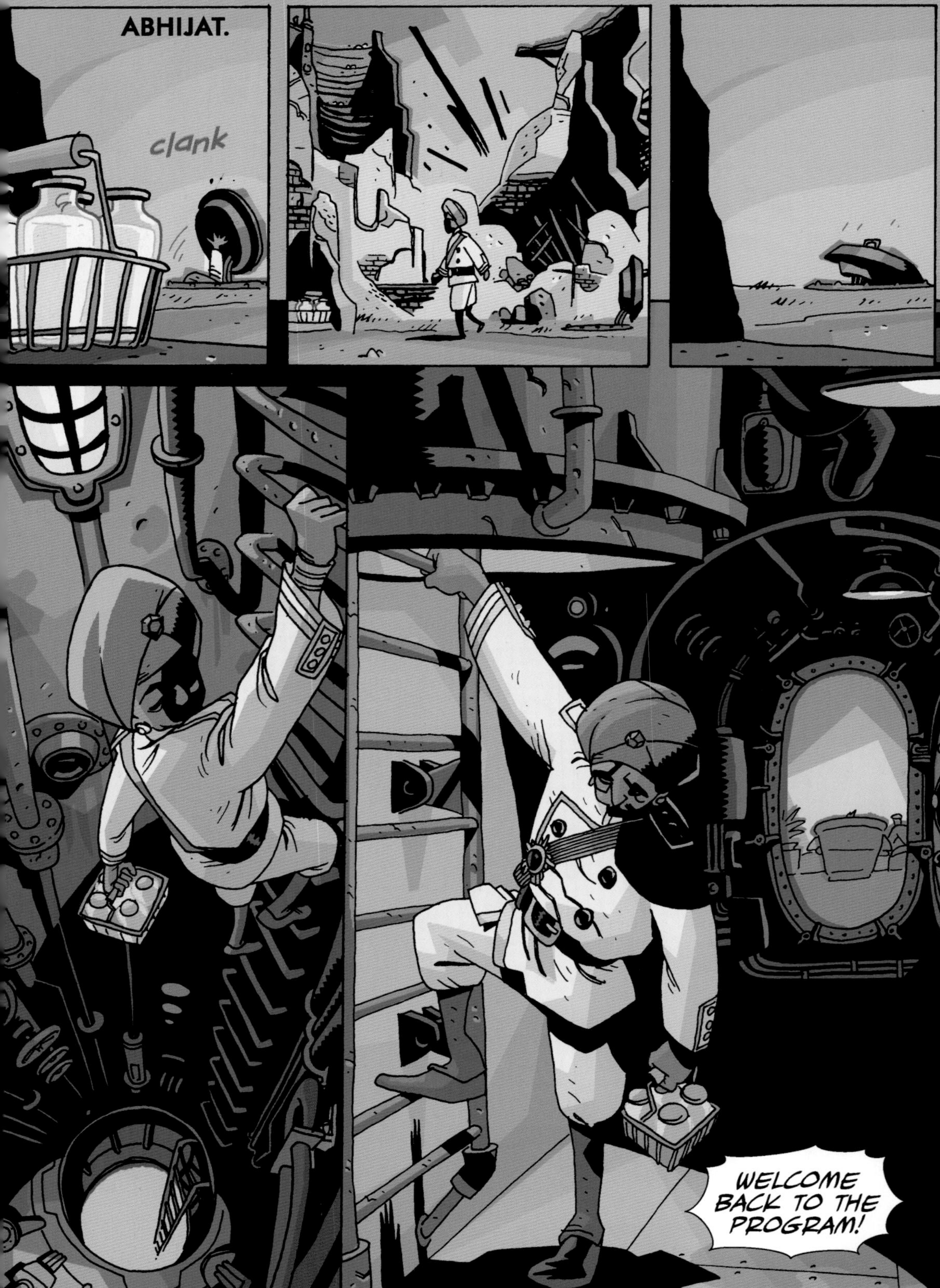
ABHIJAT.
clank
WELCOME BACK TO THE PROGRAM!

IN JUST A FEW SHORT MOMENTS, OUR HOMELY CONTESTANT WILL BE FREED OF HER SHAPE-ALTERING, CHEMICAL-BURN MASK--

--AND READY TO FACE THE WORLD LIKE IT HAS NEVER SEEN HER BEFORE!

RIGHT HERE ON CELEBRITY SURGERY!

OUR WORLD-FAMOUS CADRE OF DOCTORS HAVE COMPLETED A GRUELING NINE-WEEK SERIES OF OPERATIONS--

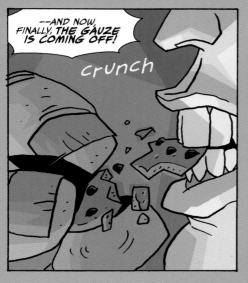

--AND NOW, FINALLY, THE GAUZE IS COMING OFF!

crunch

DR. GROSSMAN IS HANDING HER A MIRROR...

POP

17

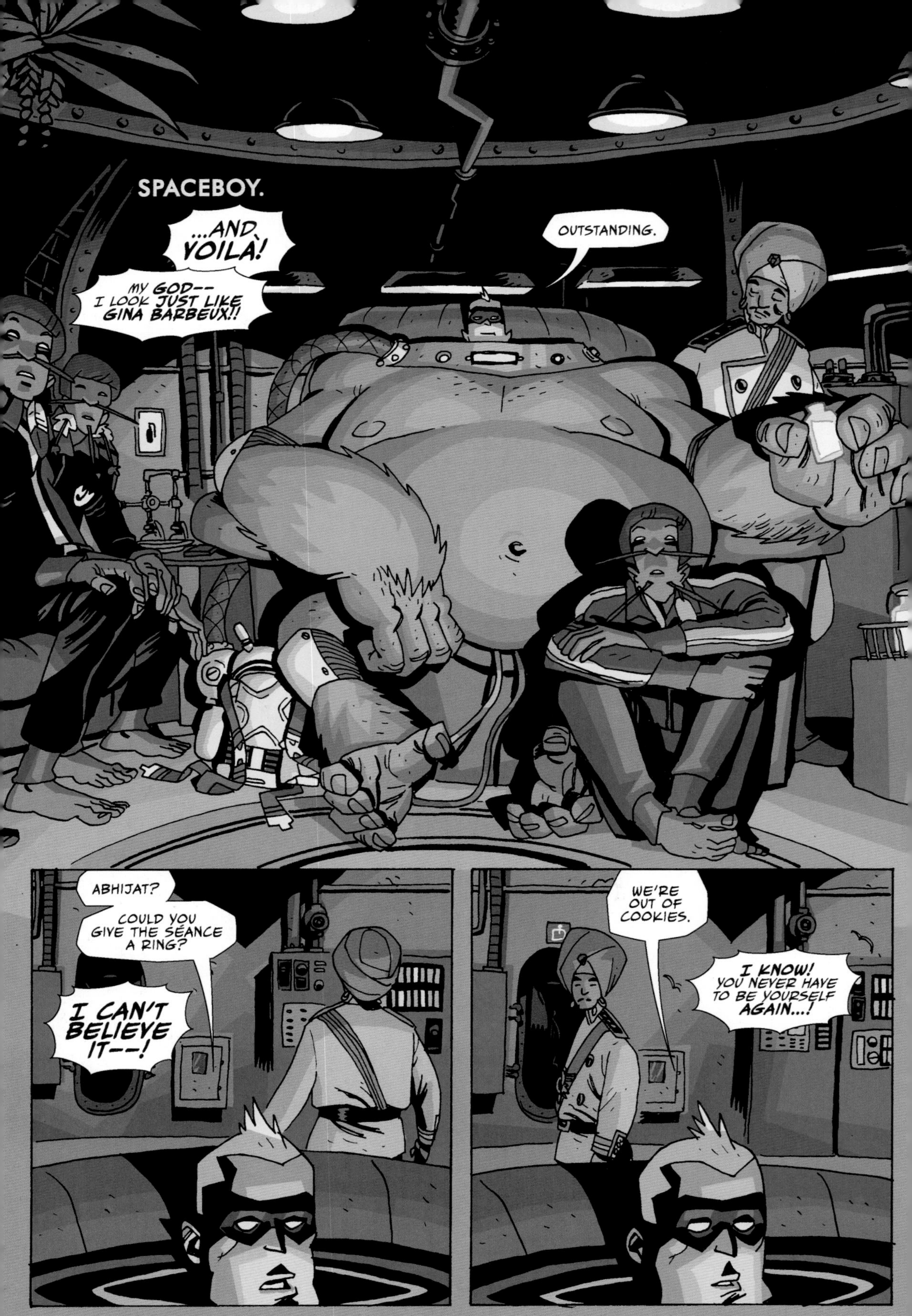
SPACEBOY.
...AND VOILÀ!
MY GOD-- I LOOK JUST LIKE GINA BARBEUX!!
OUTSTANDING.
ABHIJAT?
COULD YOU GIVE THE SÉANCE A RING?
I CAN'T BELIEVE IT--!
WE'RE OUT OF COOKIES.
I KNOW! YOU NEVER HAVE TO BE YOURSELF AGAIN...!

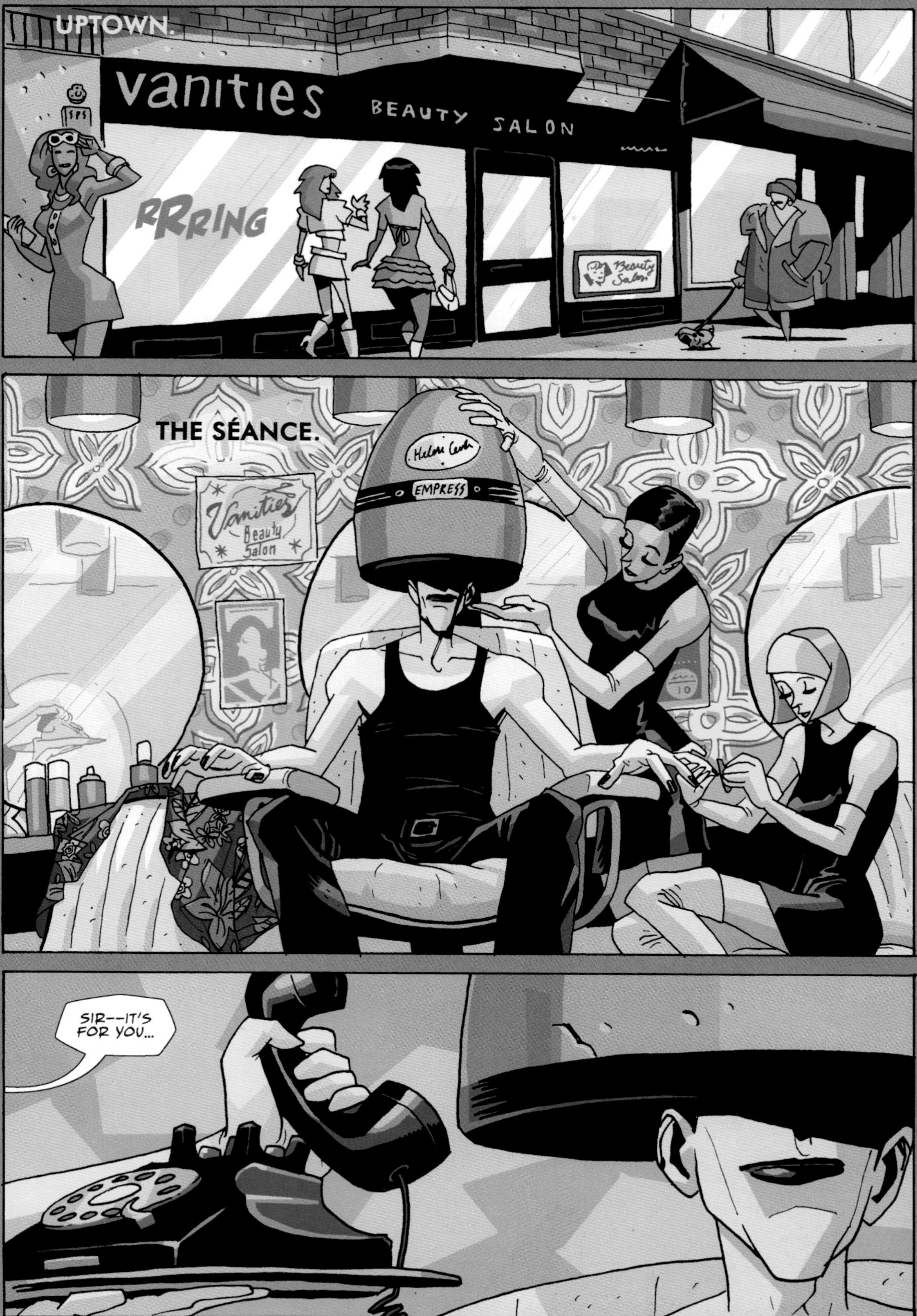
UPTOWN.
vanities
BEAUTY SALON
RRRING
Beauty Salon
THE SÉANCE.
EMPRESS
Vanities Beauty Salon
SIR--IT'S FOR YOU...

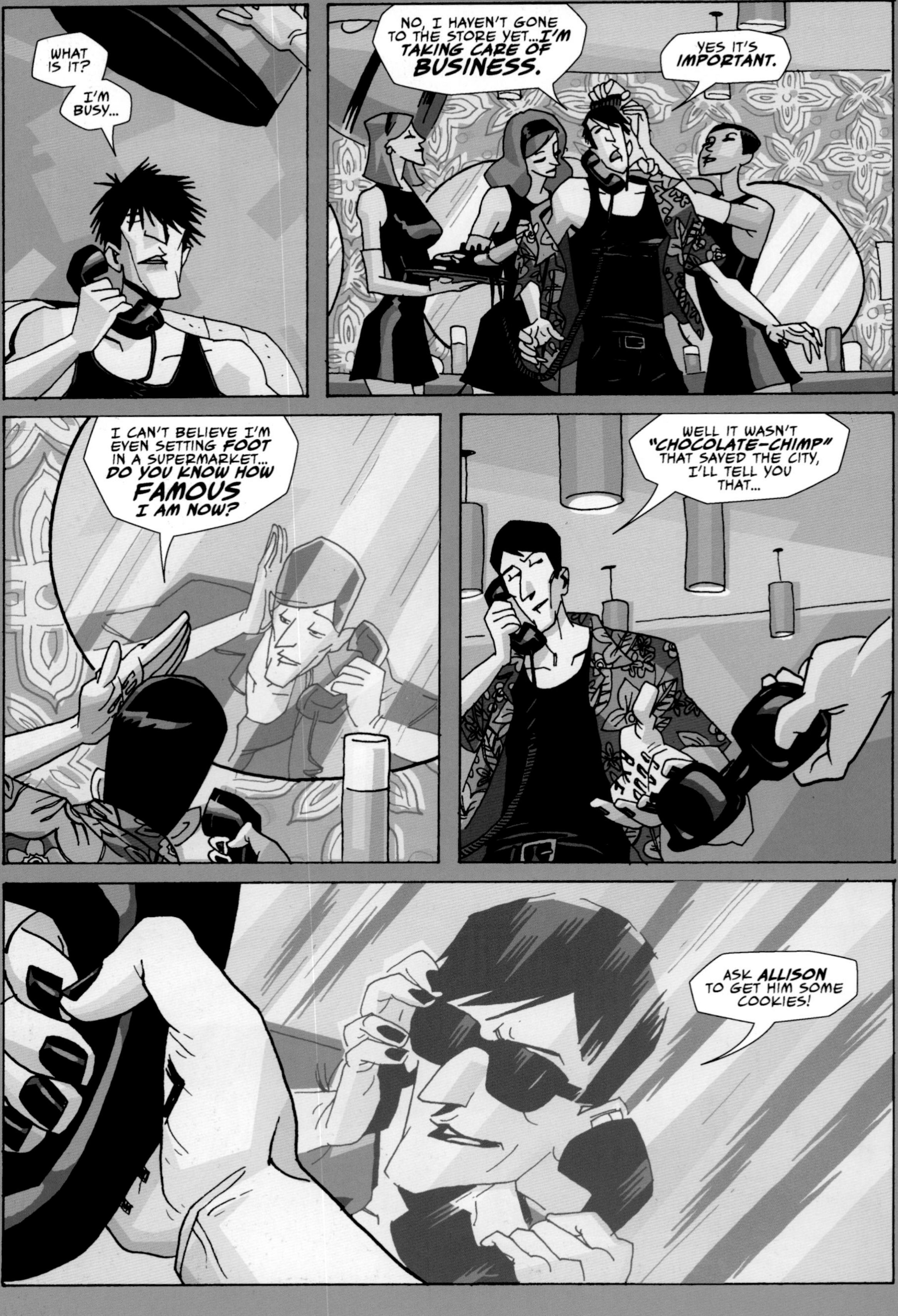
WHAT IS IT?
I'M BUSY...
NO, I HAVEN'T GONE TO THE STORE YET...I'M TAKING CARE OF BUSINESS.
YES IT'S IMPORTANT.
I CAN'T BELIEVE I'M EVEN SETTING FOOT IN A SUPERMARKET... DO YOU KNOW HOW FAMOUS I AM NOW?
WELL IT WASN'T "CHOCOLATE-CHIMP" THAT SAVED THE CITY, I'LL TELL YOU THAT...
ASK ALLISON TO GET HIM SOME COOKIES!

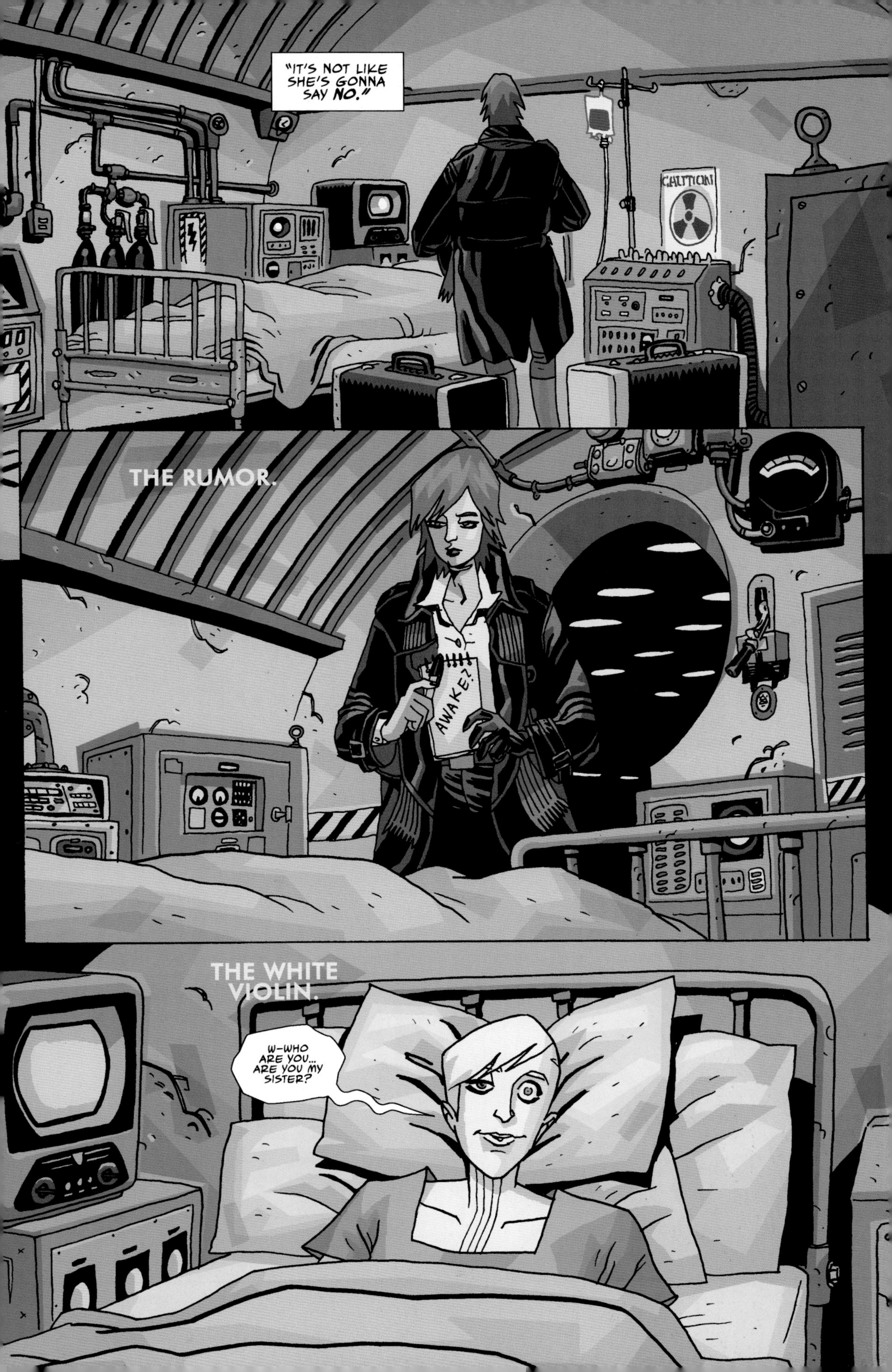
"IT'S NOT LIKE SHE'S GONNA SAY NO."
CAUTION
THE RUMOR.
AWAKE?
THE WHITE VIOLIN.
W-WHO ARE YOU... ARE YOU MY SISTER?

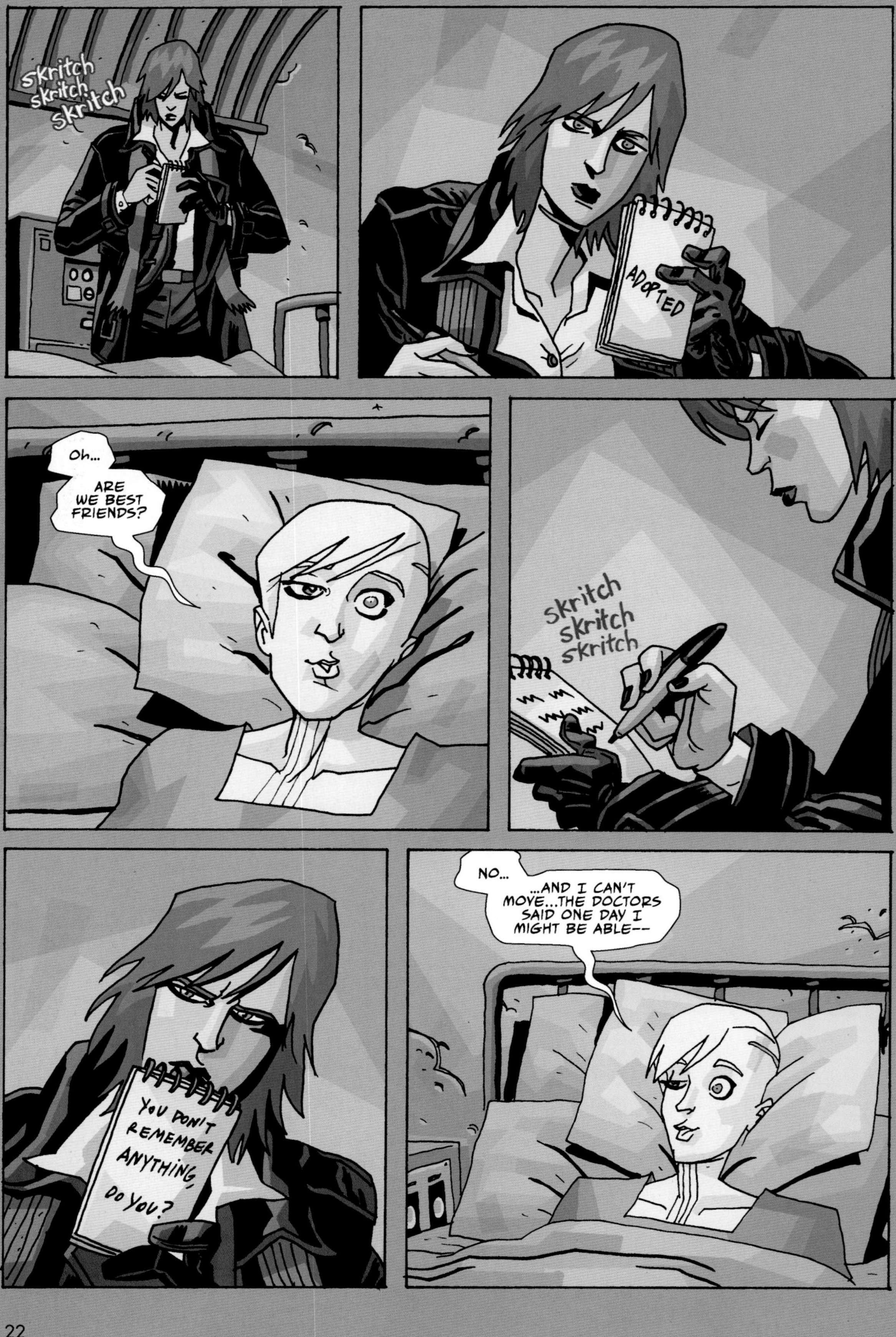
skritch skritch skritch
ADOPTED
Oh...
ARE WE BEST FRIENDS?
skritch skritch skritch
YOU DON'T REMEMBER ANYTHING, DO YOU?
NO...
...AND I CAN'T MOVE...THE DOCTORS SAID ONE DAY I MIGHT BE ABLE--

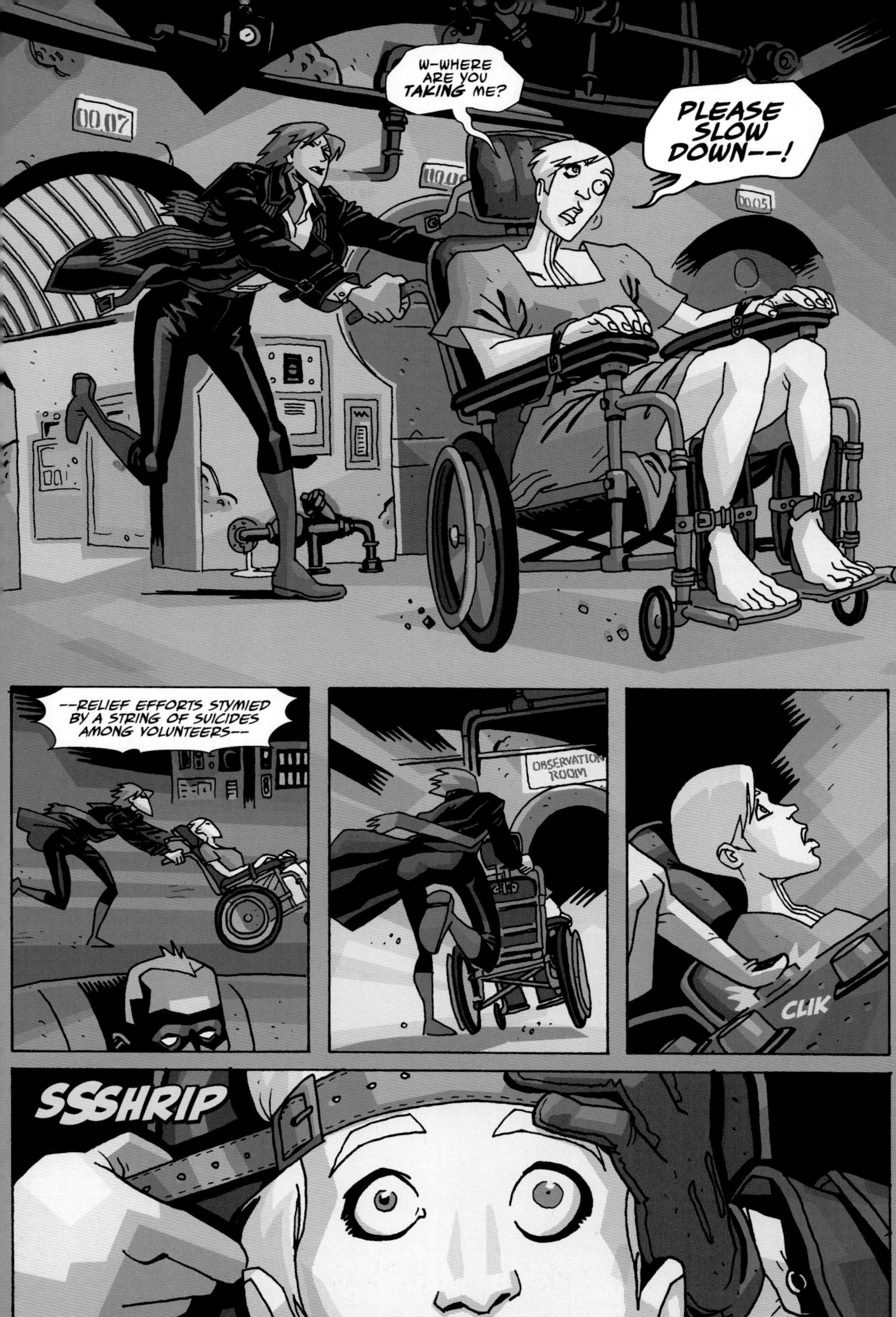

00.07
W-WHERE ARE YOU TAKING ME?
PLEASE SLOW DOWN--!
00.05
--RELIEF EFFORTS STYMIED BY A STRING OF SUICIDES AMONG VOLUNTEERS--
OBSERVATION ROOM
CLIK
SSSHRIP

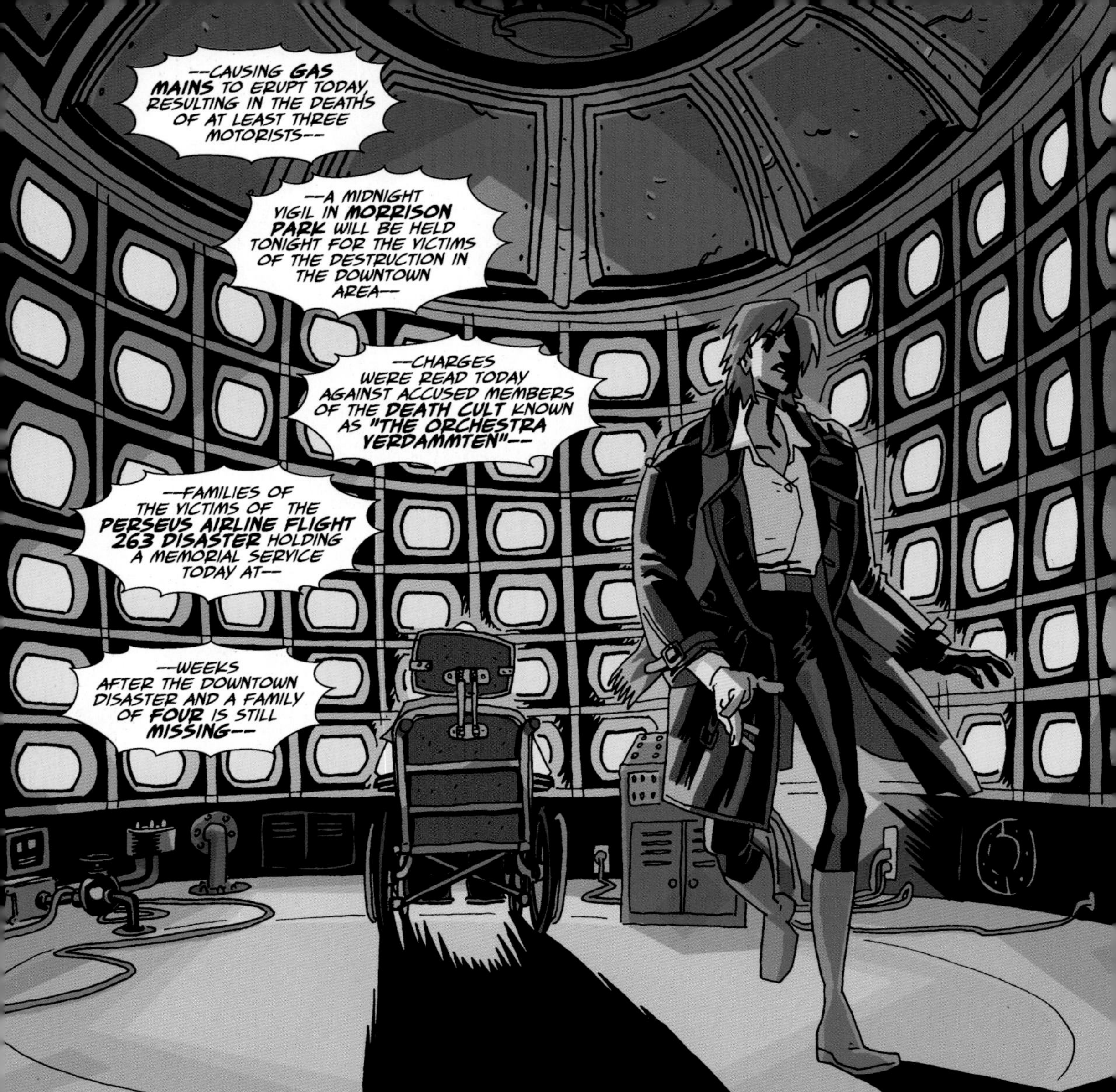
--CAUSING GAS MAINS TO ERUPT TODAY, RESULTING IN THE DEATHS OF AT LEAST THREE MOTORISTS--
--A MIDNIGHT VIGIL IN MORRISON PARK WILL BE HELD TONIGHT FOR THE VICTIMS OF THE DESTRUCTION IN THE DOWNTOWN AREA--
--CHARGES WERE READ TODAY AGAINST ACCUSED MEMBERS OF THE DEATH CULT KNOWN AS "THE ORCHESTRA VERDAMMTEN"--
--FAMILIES OF THE VICTIMS OF THE PERSEUS AIRLINE FLIGHT 263 DISASTER HOLDING A MEMORIAL SERVICE TODAY AT--
--WEEKS AFTER THE DOWNTOWN DISASTER AND A FAMILY OF FOUR IS STILL MISSING--

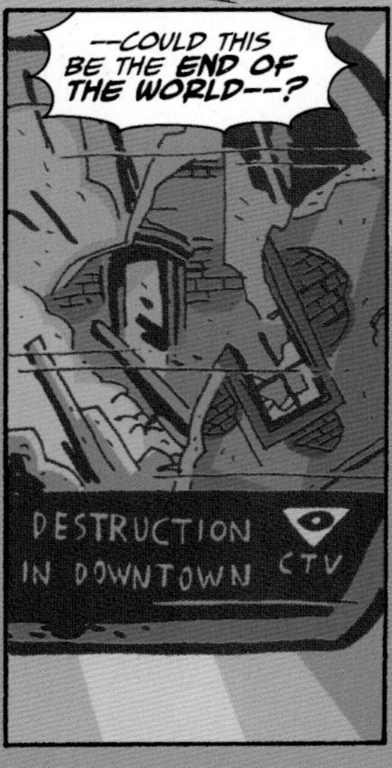
--COULD THIS BE THE END OF THE WORLD--?
DESTRUCTION IN DOWNTOWN
CTV

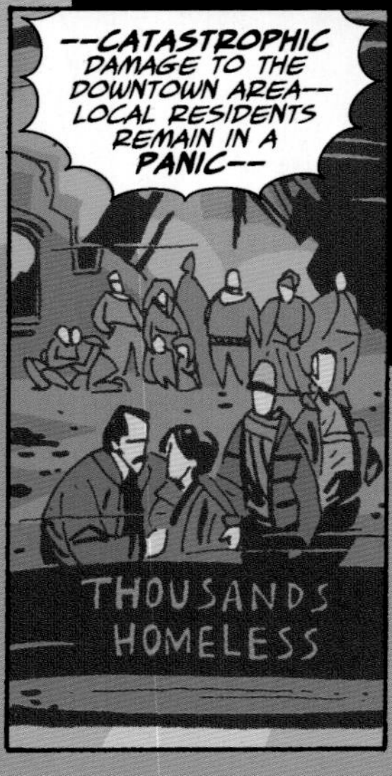
--CATASTROPHIC DAMAGE TO THE DOWNTOWN AREA--LOCAL RESIDENTS REMAIN IN A PANIC--
THOUSANDS HOMELESS

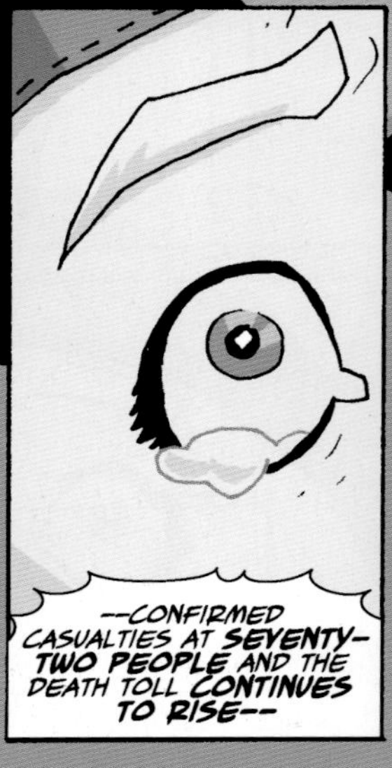
--CONFIRMED CASUALTIES AT SEVENTY-TWO PEOPLE AND THE DEATH TOLL CONTINUES TO RISE--

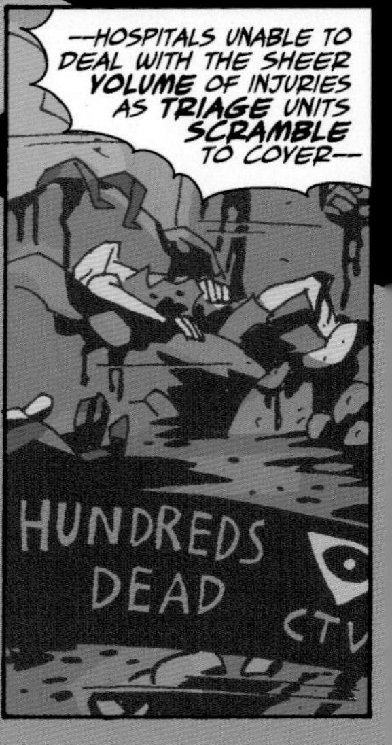
--HOSPITALS UNABLE TO DEAL WITH THE SHEER VOLUME OF INJURIES AS TRIAGE UNITS SCRAMBLE TO COVER--
HUNDREDS DEAD
CTV

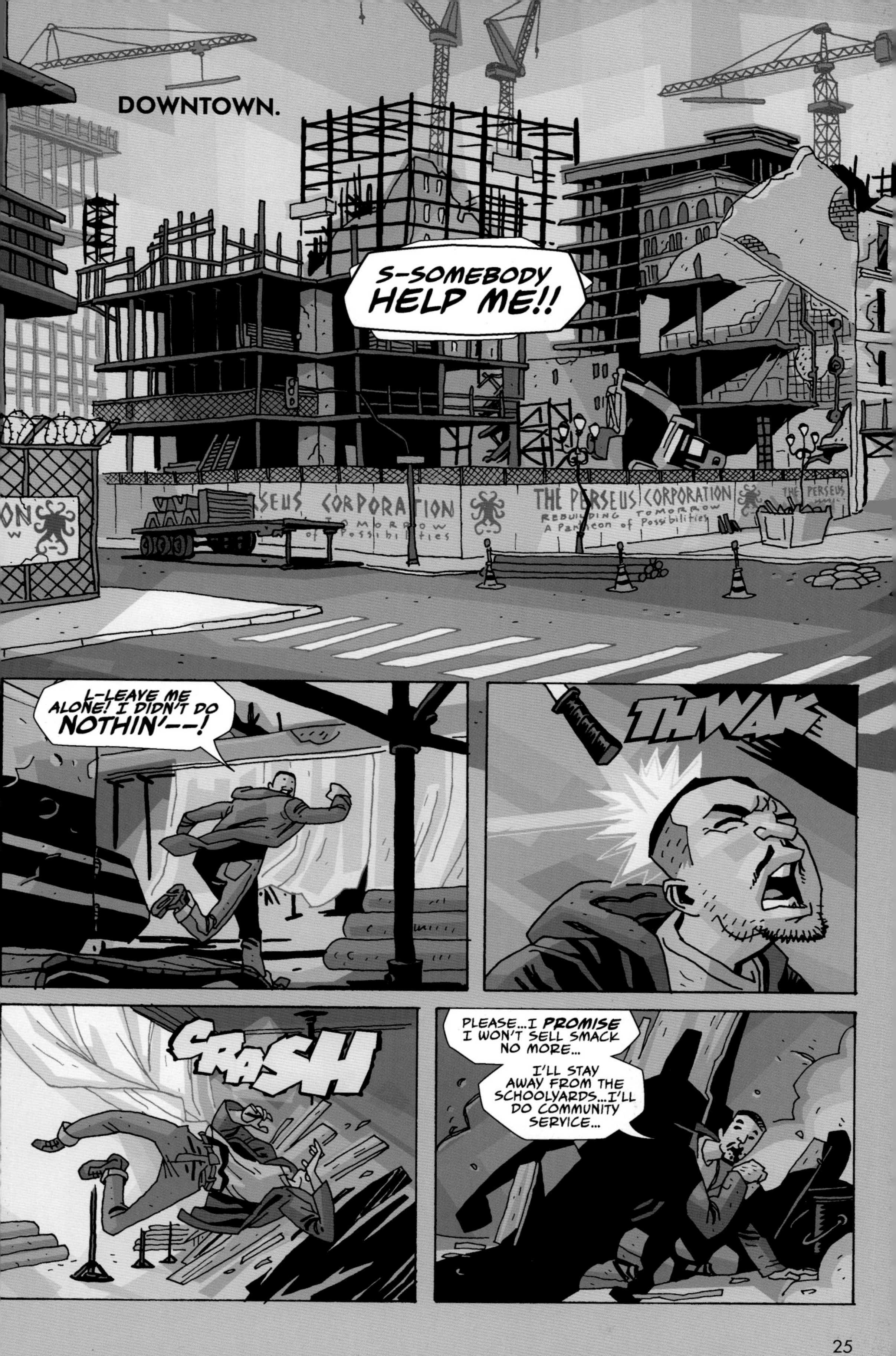
DOWNTOWN.
S-SOMEBODY HELP ME!!
THE PERSEUS CORPORATION
REBUILDING TOMORROW
A Pantheon of Possibilities
L-LEAVE ME ALONE! I DIDN'T DO NOTHIN'--!
THWAK
CRASH
PLEASE...I PROMISE I WON'T SELL SMACK NO MORE...
I'LL STAY AWAY FROM THE SCHOOLYARDS...I'LL DO COMMUNITY SERVICE...

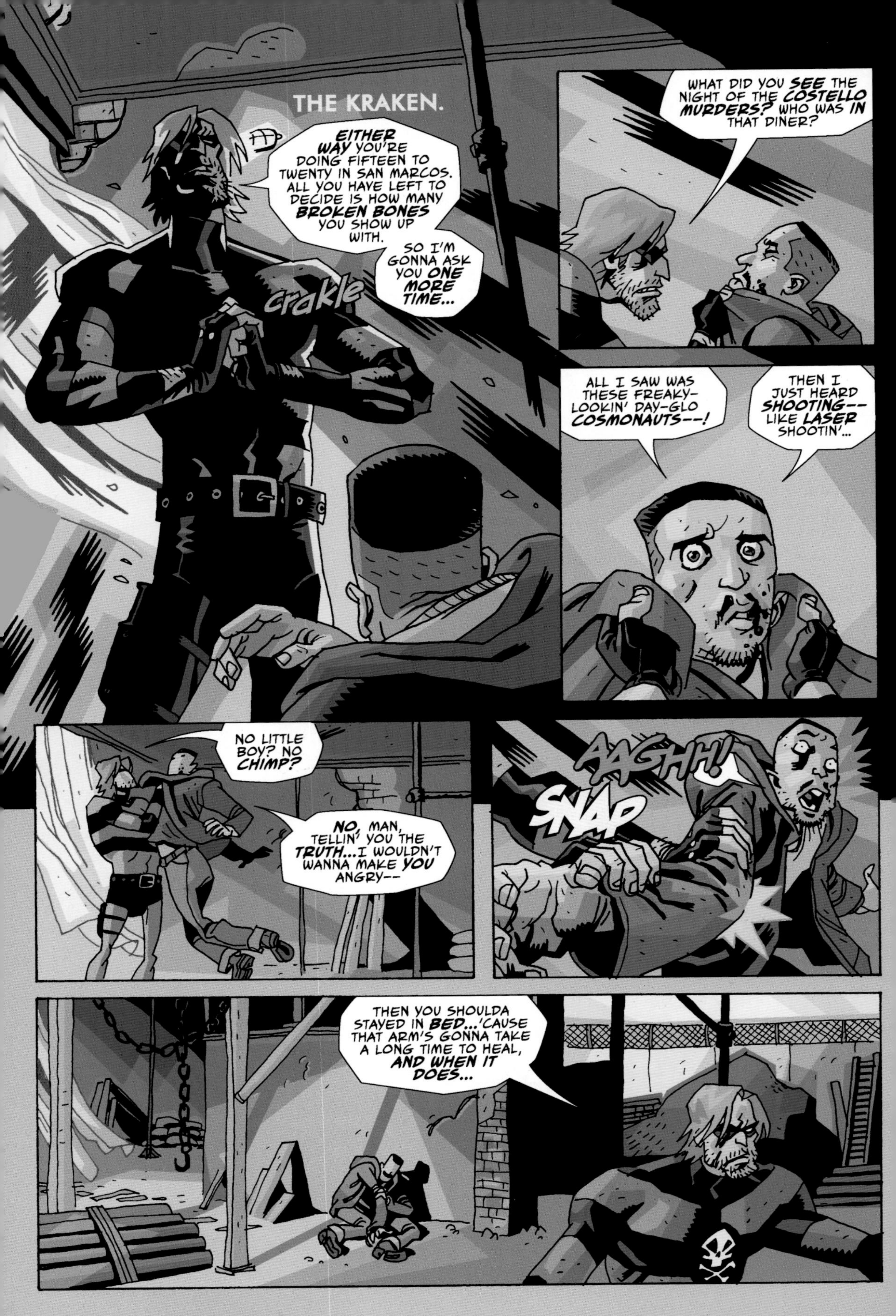
THE KRAKEN.
EITHER WAY YOU'RE DOING FIFTEEN TO TWENTY IN SAN MARCOS. ALL YOU HAVE LEFT TO DECIDE IS HOW MANY BROKEN BONES YOU SHOW UP WITH.
SO I'M GONNA ASK YOU ONE MORE TIME...
crakle
WHAT DID YOU SEE THE NIGHT OF THE COSTELLO MURDERS? WHO WAS IN THAT DINER?
ALL I SAW WAS THESE FREAKY-LOOKIN' DAY-GLO COSMONAUTS--!
THEN I JUST HEARD SHOOTING--LIKE LASER SHOOTIN'...
NO LITTLE BOY? NO CHIMP?
NO, MAN, TELLIN' YOU THE TRUTH...I WOULDN'T WANNA MAKE YOU ANGRY--
AAGHH!
SNAP
THEN YOU SHOULDA STAYED IN BED...'CAUSE THAT ARM'S GONNA TAKE A LONG TIME TO HEAL, AND WHEN IT DOES...

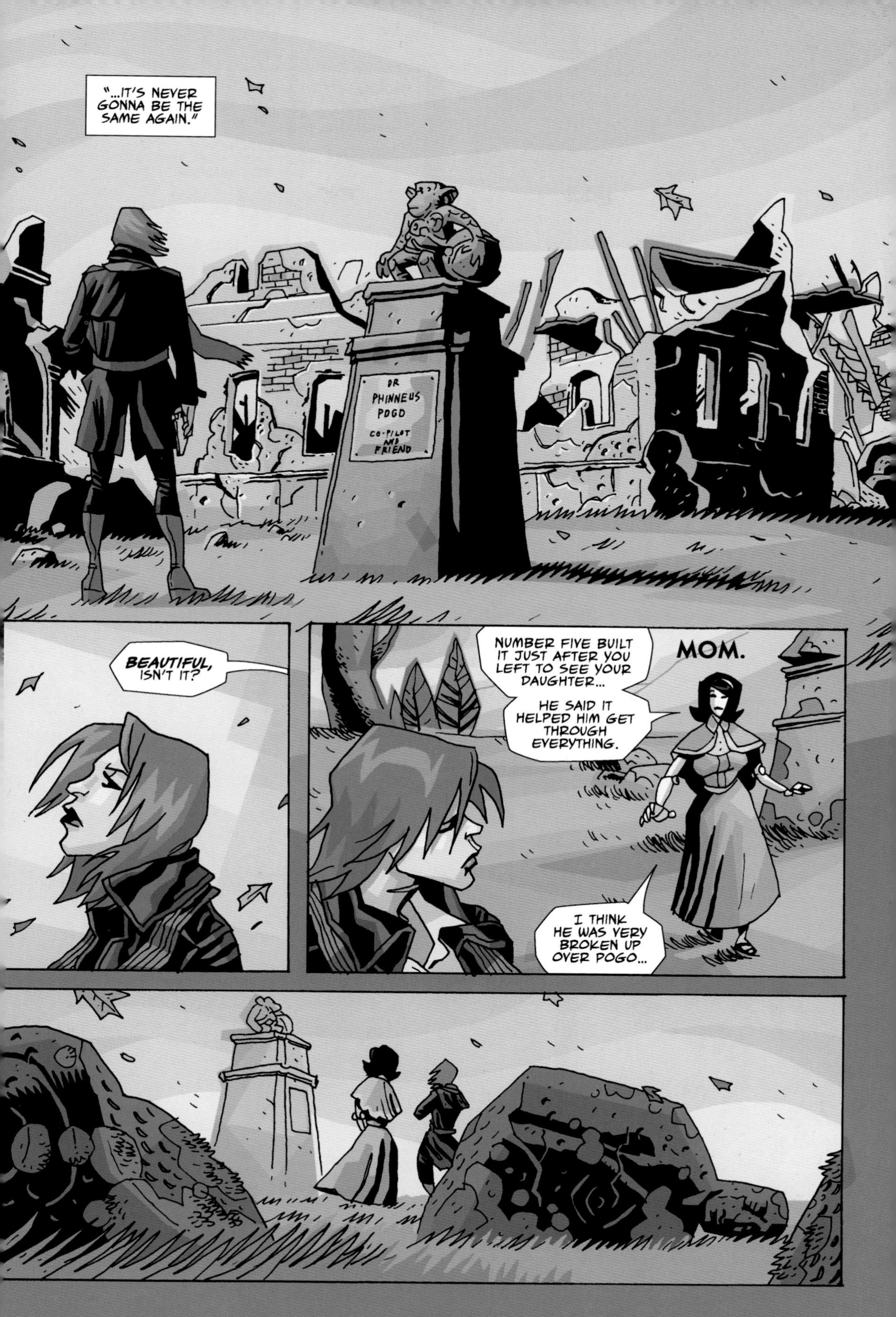

"...IT'S NEVER GONNA BE THE SAME AGAIN."
DR PHINNEUS POGO CO-PILOT AND FRIEND
BEAUTIFUL, ISN'T IT?
NUMBER FIVE BUILT IT JUST AFTER YOU LEFT TO SEE YOUR DAUGHTER...
HE SAID IT HELPED HIM GET THROUGH EVERYTHING.
MOM.
I THINK HE WAS VERY BROKEN UP OVER POGO...

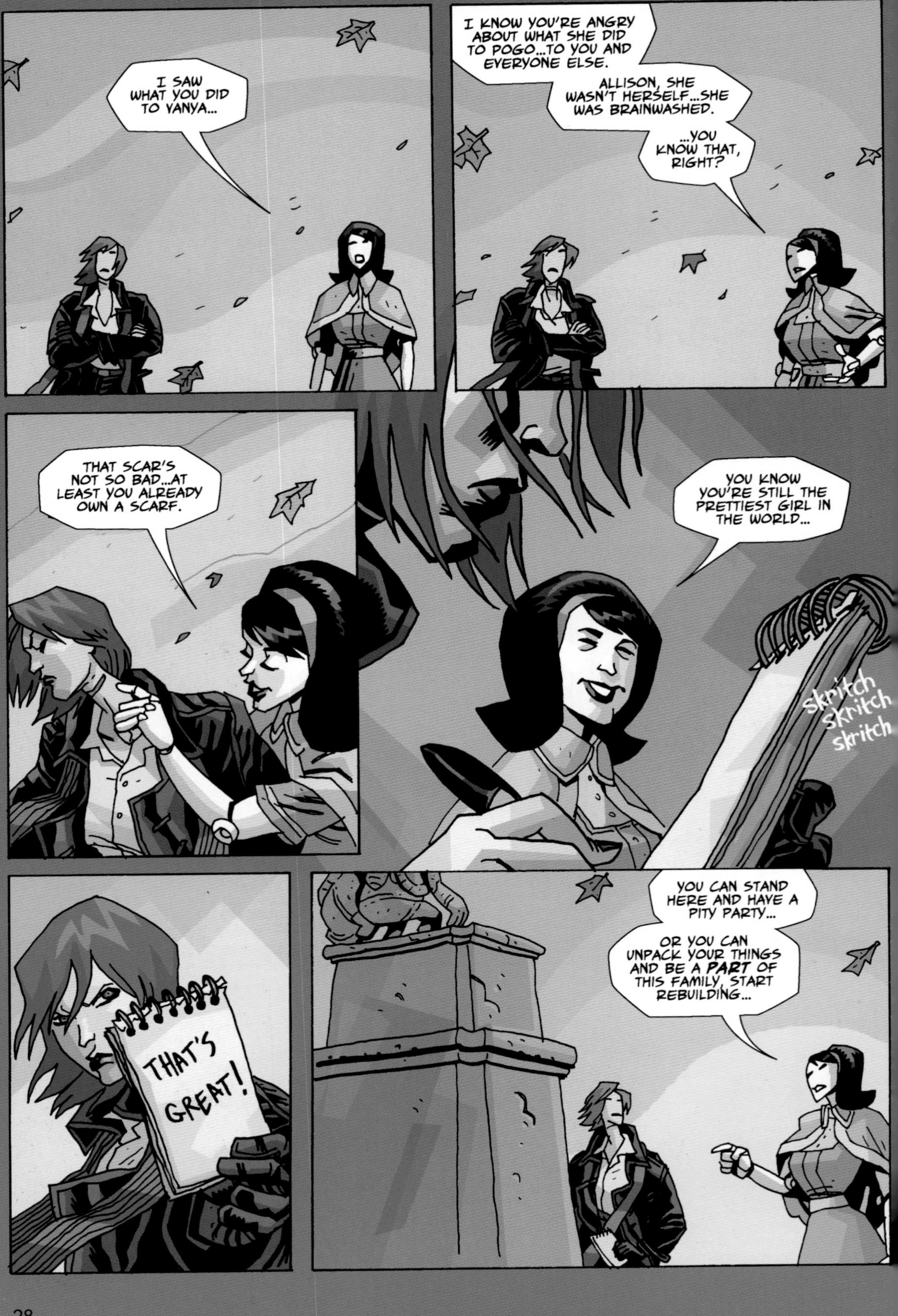
I SAW WHAT YOU DID TO YANYA...
I KNOW YOU'RE ANGRY ABOUT WHAT SHE DID TO POGO...TO YOU AND EVERYONE ELSE.
ALLISON, SHE WASN'T HERSELF...SHE WAS BRAINWASHED.
...YOU KNOW THAT, RIGHT?
THAT SCAR'S NOT SO BAD...AT LEAST YOU ALREADY OWN A SCARF.
YOU KNOW YOU'RE STILL THE PRETTIEST GIRL IN THE WORLD...
skritch skritch skritch
THAT'S GREAT!
YOU CAN STAND HERE AND HAVE A PITY PARTY...
OR YOU CAN UNPACK YOUR THINGS AND BE A PART OF THIS FAMILY, START REBUILDING...

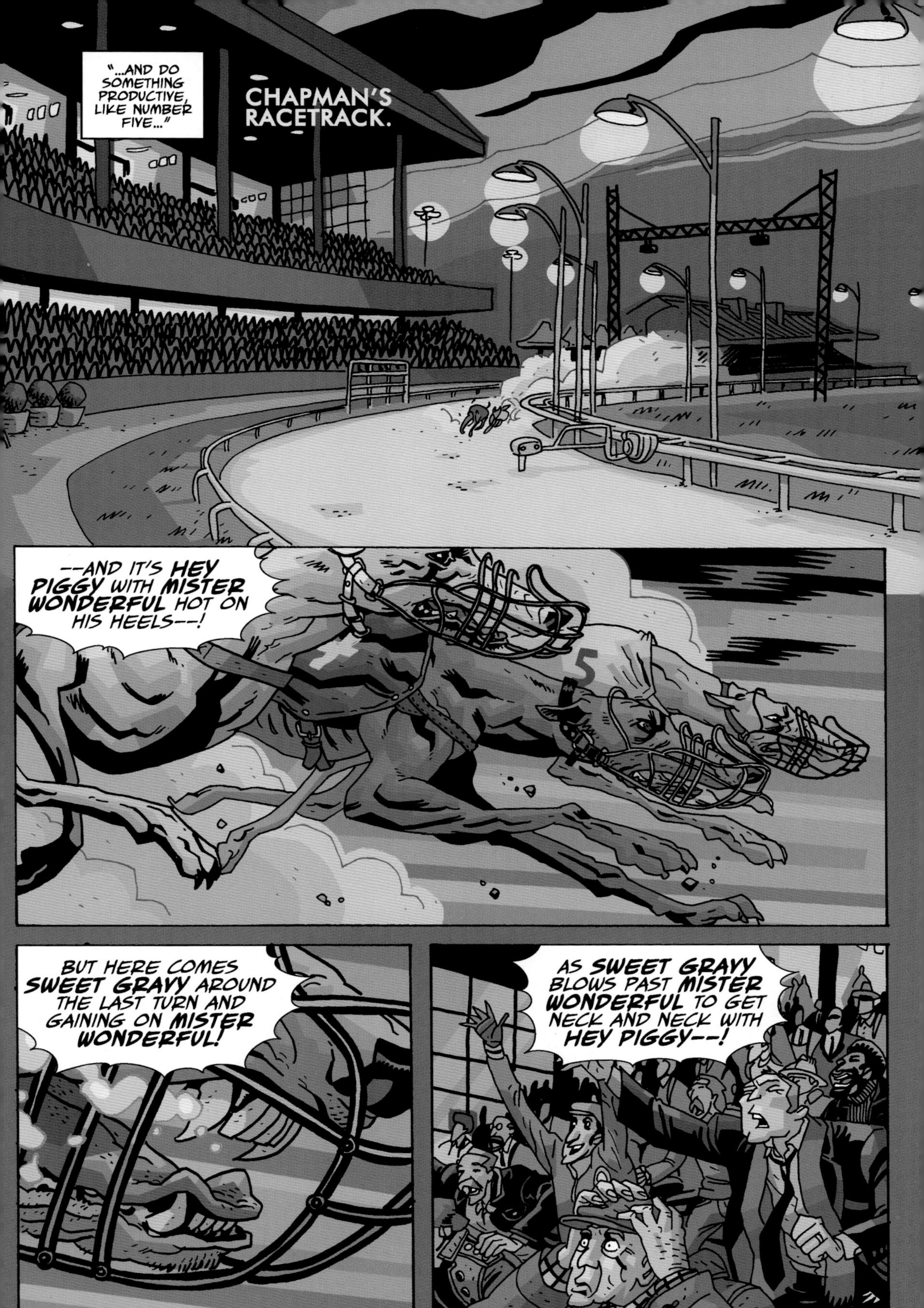
"...AND DO SOMETHING PRODUCTIVE, LIKE NUMBER FIVE..."
CHAPMAN'S RACETRACK.
--AND IT'S HEY PIGGY WITH MISTER WONDERFUL HOT ON HIS HEELS--!
BUT HERE COMES SWEET GRAVY AROUND THE LAST TURN AND GAINING ON MISTER WONDERFUL!
AS SWEET GRAVY BLOWS PAST MISTER WONDERFUL TO GET NECK AND NECK WITH HEY PIGGY--!

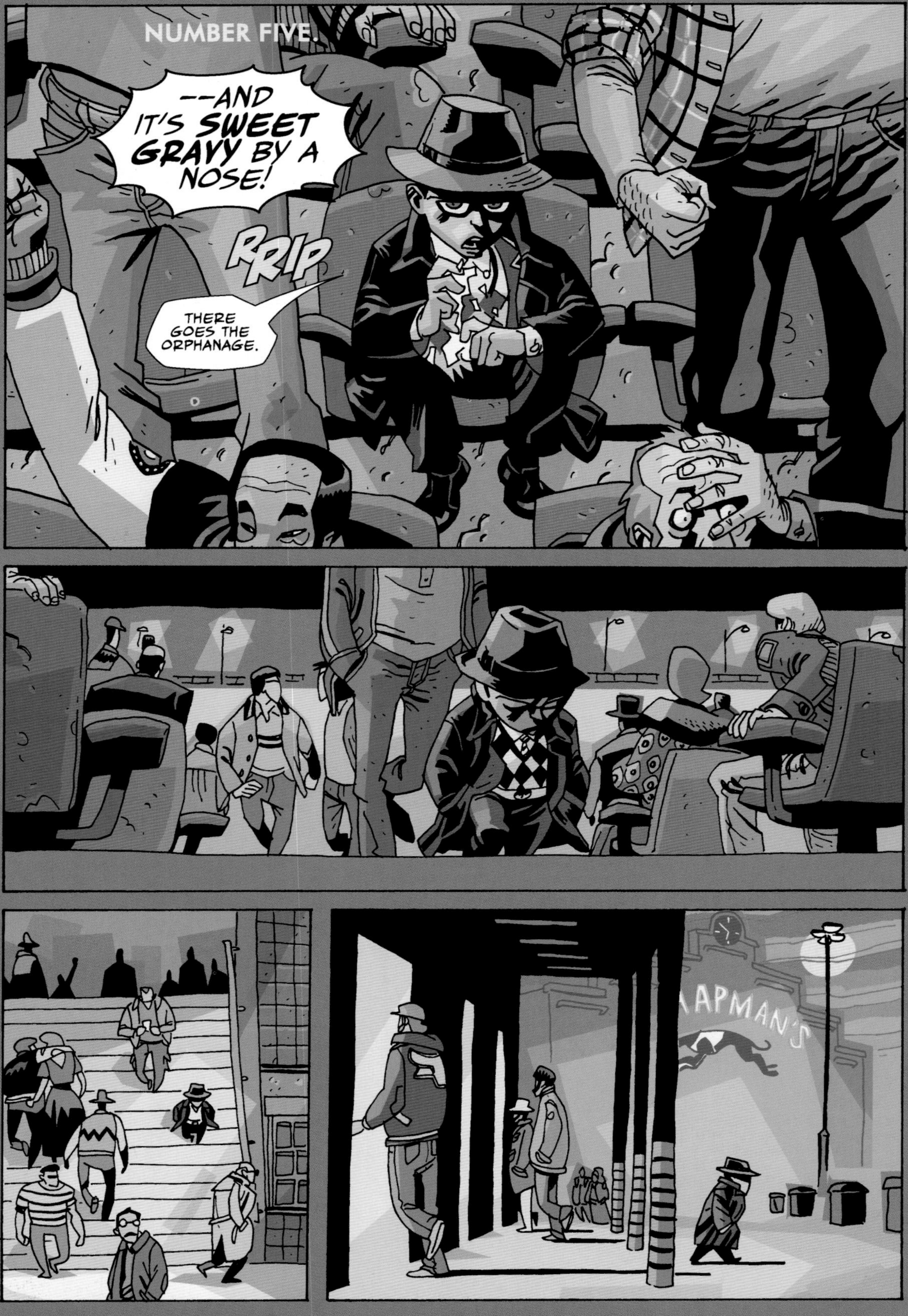
NUMBER FIVE.
--AND IT'S SWEET GRAVY BY A NOSE!
RRIP
THERE GOES THE ORPHANAGE.
APMAN'S

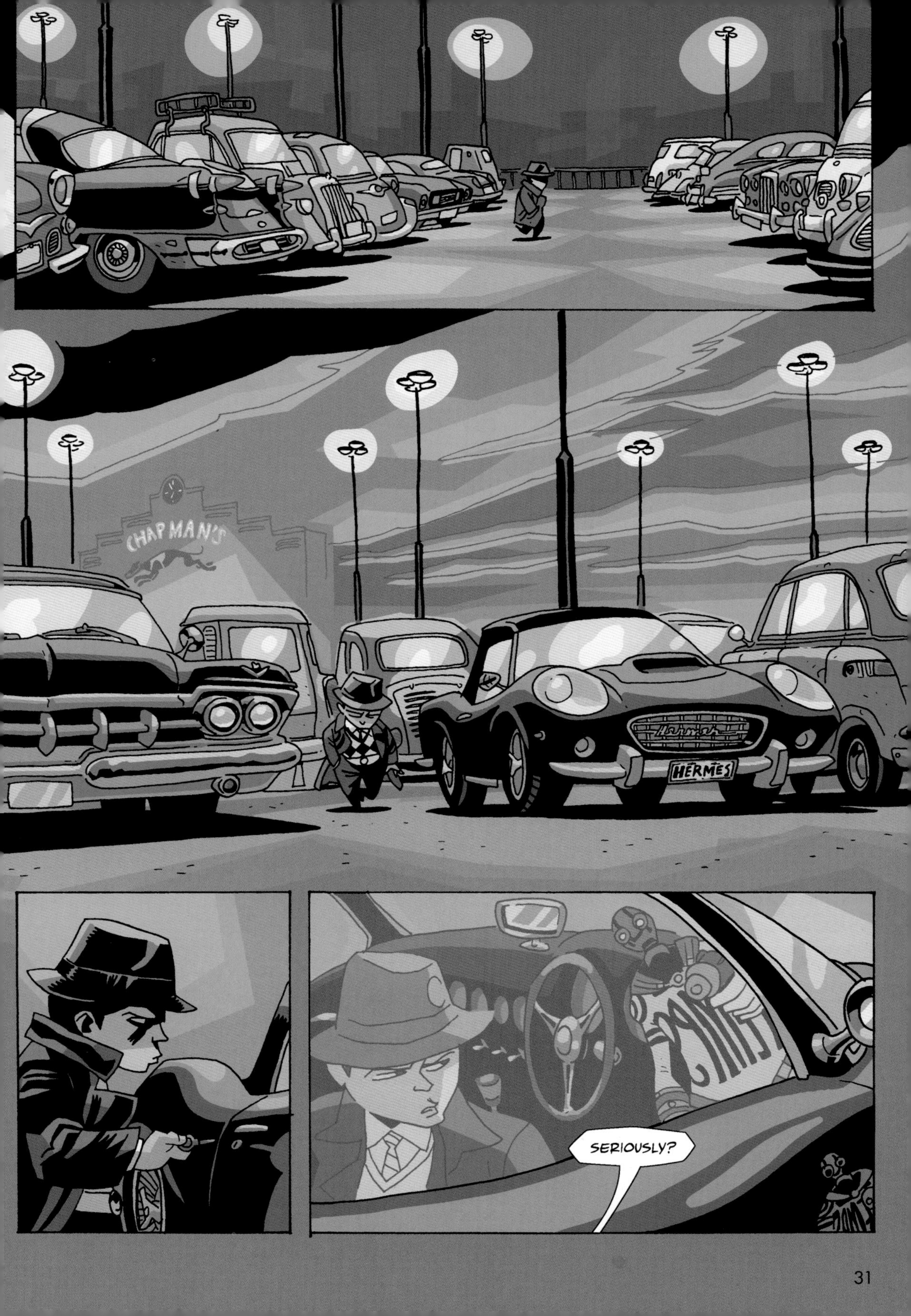
CHAPMAN'S
HERMES
SERIOUSLY?

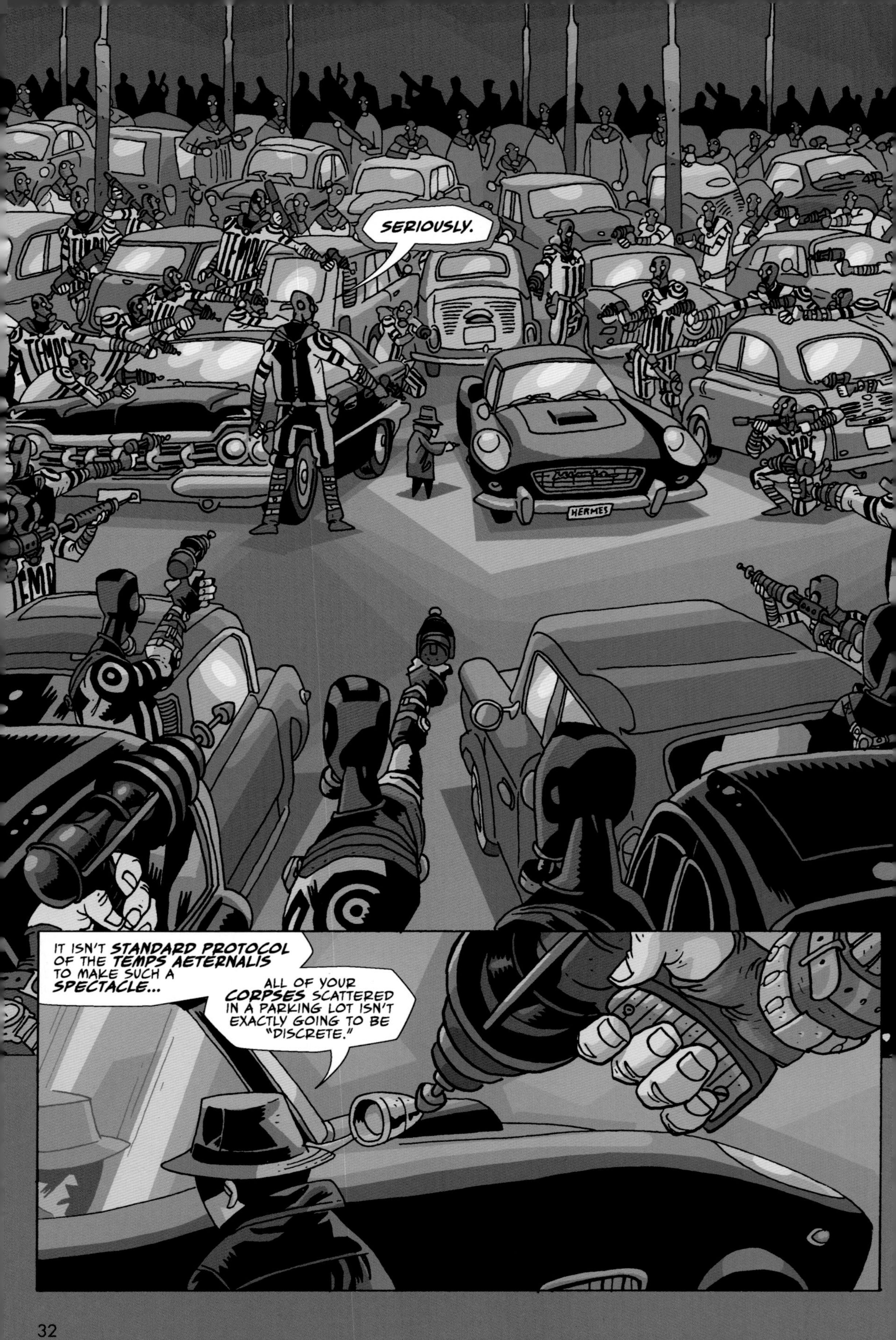
SERIOUSLY.
HERMES
TEMPS
IT ISN'T STANDARD PROTOCOL OF THE TEMPS AETERNALIS TO MAKE SUCH A SPECTACLE...
ALL OF YOUR CORPSES SCATTERED IN A PARKING LOT ISN'T EXACTLY GOING TO BE "DISCRETE."

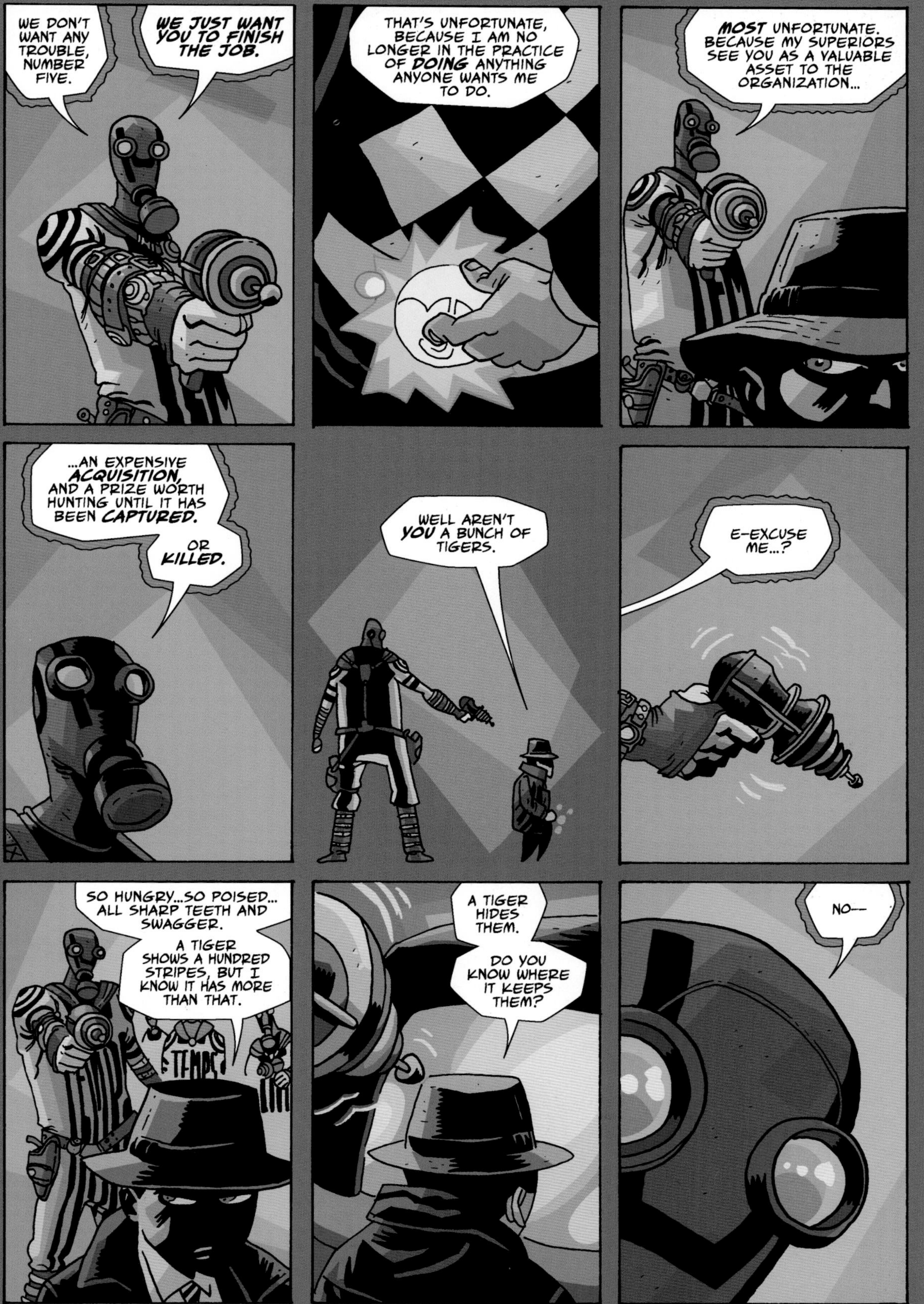
WE DON'T WANT ANY TROUBLE, NUMBER FIVE.
WE JUST WANT YOU TO FINISH THE JOB.
THAT'S UNFORTUNATE, BECAUSE I AM NO LONGER IN THE PRACTICE OF DOING ANYTHING ANYONE WANTS ME TO DO.
MOST UNFORTUNATE. BECAUSE MY SUPERIORS SEE YOU AS A VALUABLE ASSET TO THE ORGANIZATION...
...AN EXPENSIVE ACQUISITION, AND A PRIZE WORTH HUNTING UNTIL IT HAS BEEN CAPTURED.
OR KILLED.
WELL AREN'T YOU A BUNCH OF TIGERS.
E-EXCUSE ME...?
SO HUNGRY...SO POISED... ALL SHARP TEETH AND SWAGGER.
A TIGER SHOWS A HUNDRED STRIPES, BUT I KNOW IT HAS MORE THAN THAT.
A TIGER HIDES THEM.
DO YOU KNOW WHERE IT KEEPS THEM?
NO—

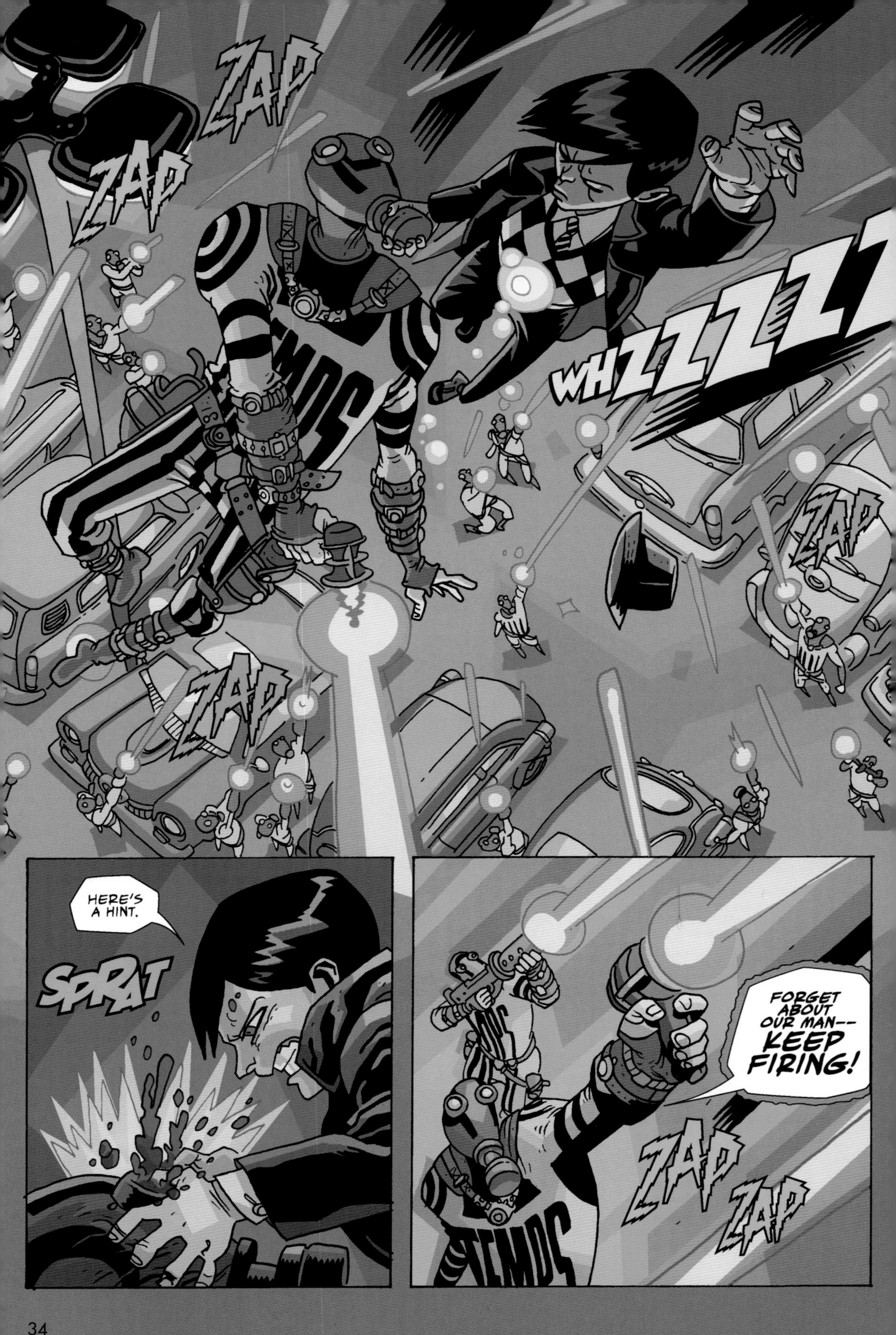
ZAP
ZAP
WHZZZZZ
ZAP
ZAP
HERE'S A HINT.
SPRAT
FORGET ABOUT OUR MAN-- KEEP FIRING!
ZAP
ZAP

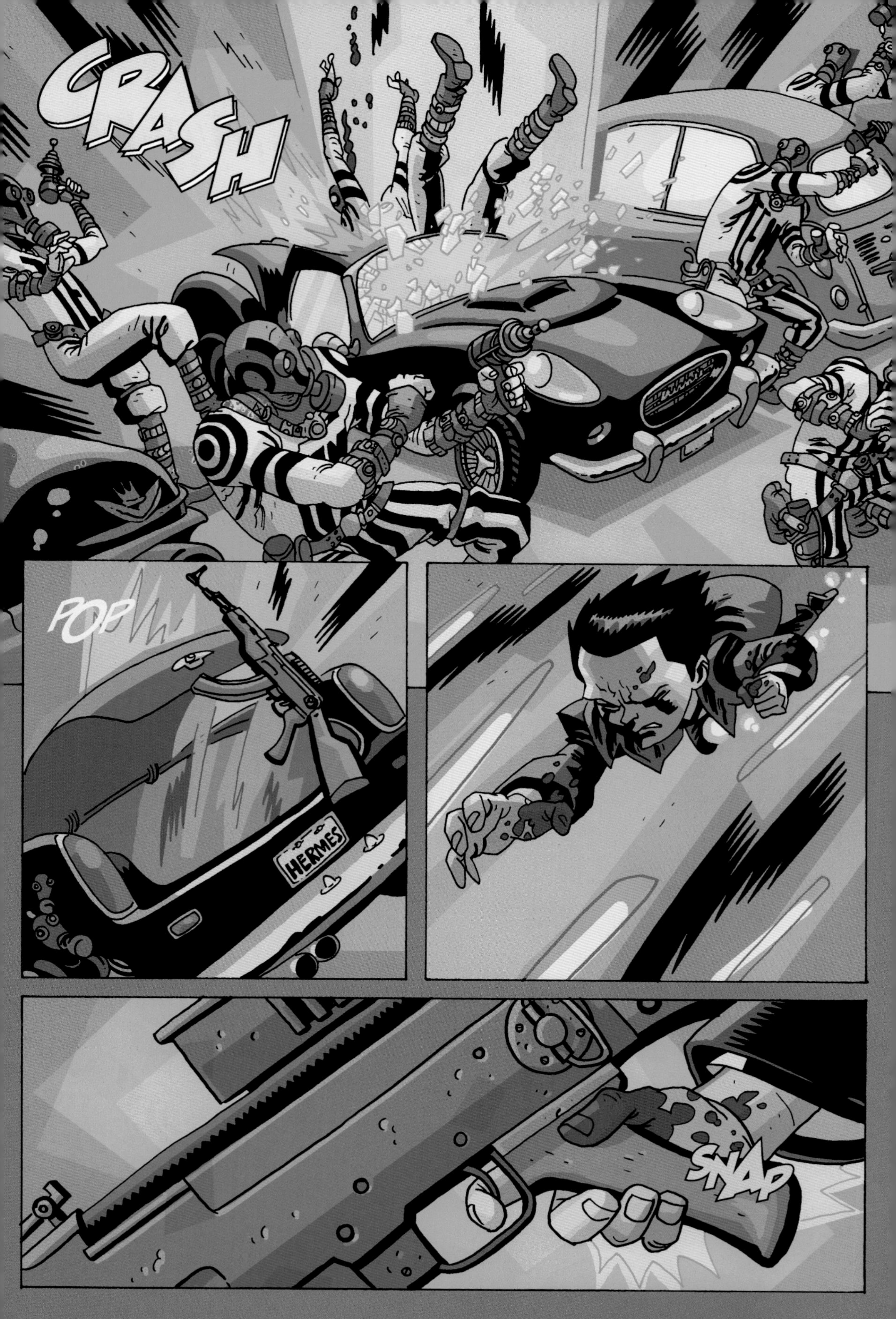
CRASH
POP
HERMES
SNAP

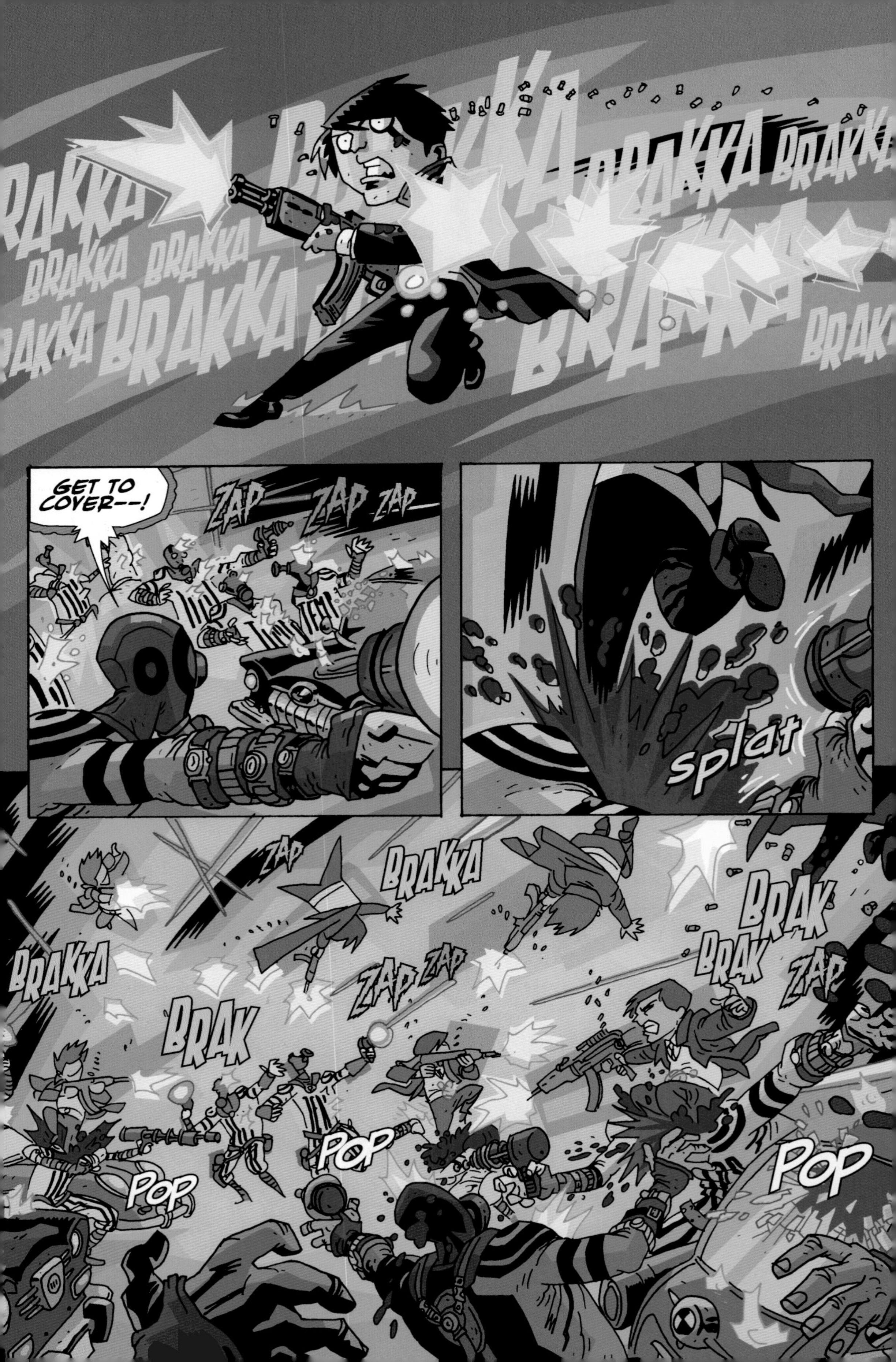
BRAKKA
BRAKKA
BRAKKA
BRAKKA
BRAKKA
BRAKKA
BRAKKA
BRAKKA
GET TO COVER--!
ZAP
ZAP ZAP
splat
ZAP
BRAKKA
BRAK
BRAKKA
BRAK
ZAP ZAP
ZAP
BRAK
POP
POP
POP

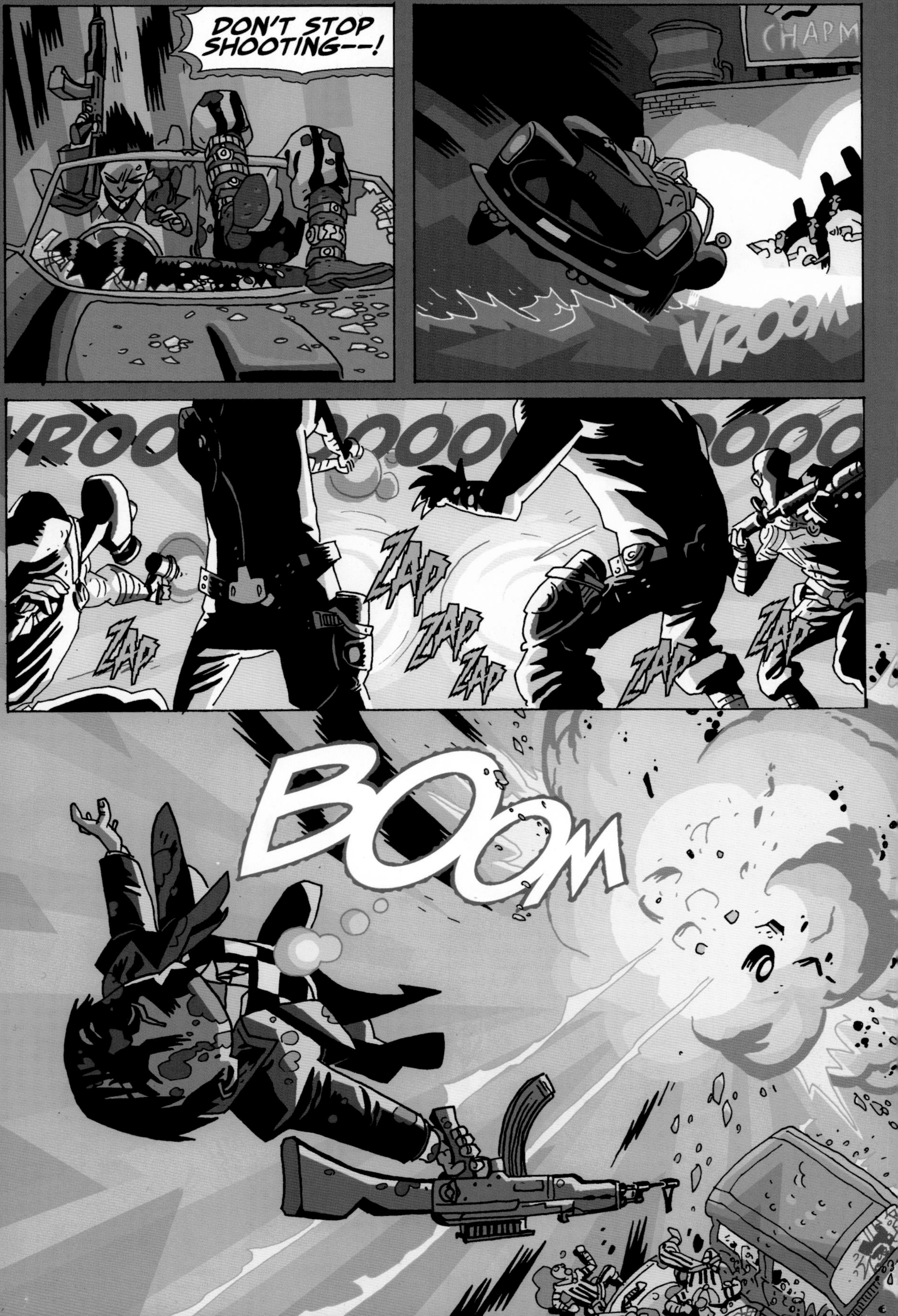
DON'T STOP SHOOTING--!
CHAPM
VROOM
VROOOOOOOOOOOO
ZAP
ZAP
ZAP
ZAP
ZAP
ZAP
BOOM

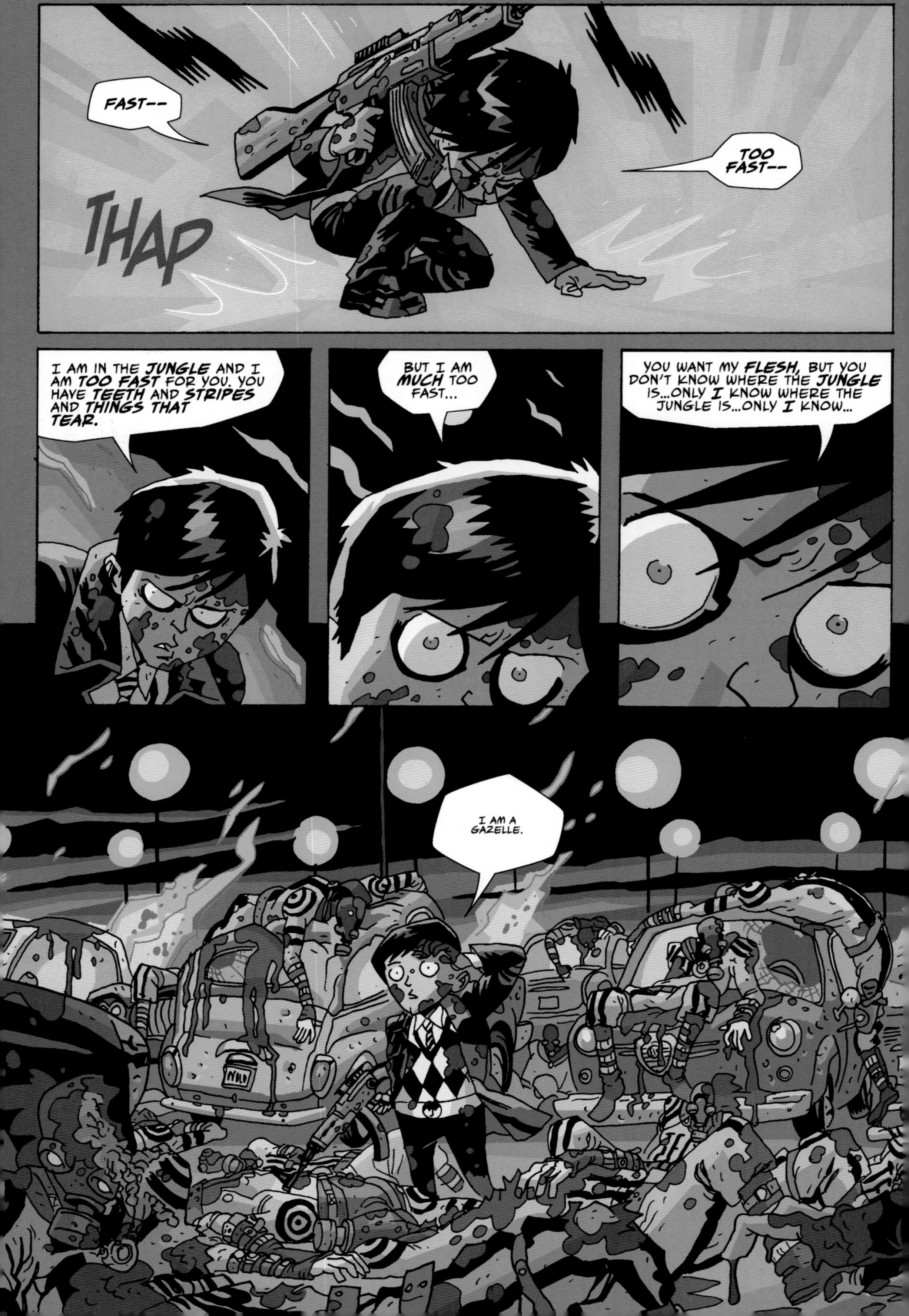
FAST--
TOO FAST--
THAP
I AM IN THE JUNGLE AND I AM TOO FAST FOR YOU. YOU HAVE TEETH AND STRIPES AND THINGS THAT TEAR.
BUT I AM MUCH TOO FAST...
YOU WANT MY FLESH, BUT YOU DON'T KNOW WHERE THE JUNGLE IS...ONLY I KNOW WHERE THE JUNGLE IS...ONLY I KNOW...
I AM A GAZELLE.

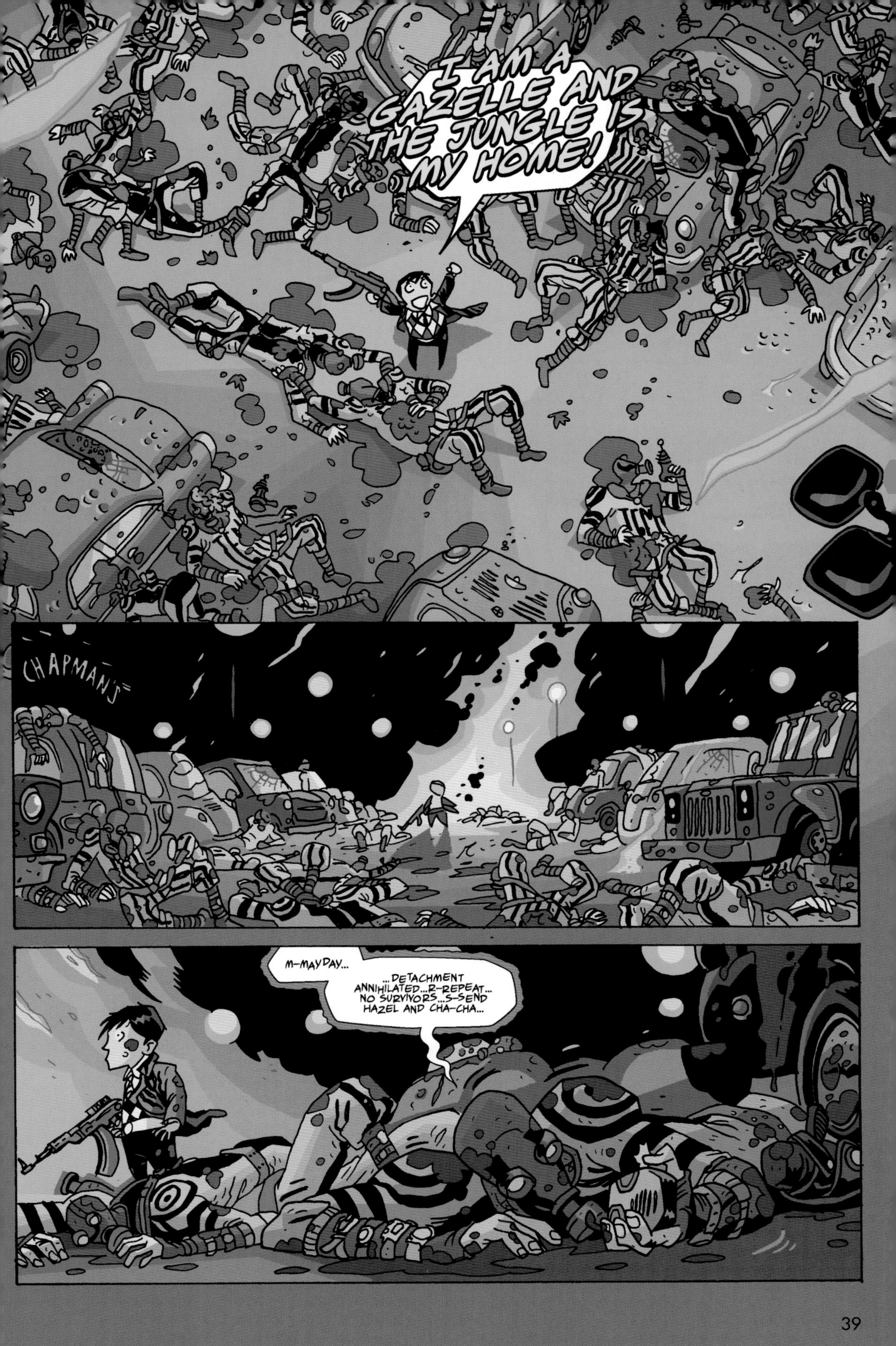
I AM A GAZELLE AND THE JUNGLE IS MY HOME!
CHAPMAN'S
M-MAYDAY...
...DETACHMENT ANNIHILATED...R-REPEAT... NO SURVIVORS...S-SEND HAZEL AND CHA-CHA...

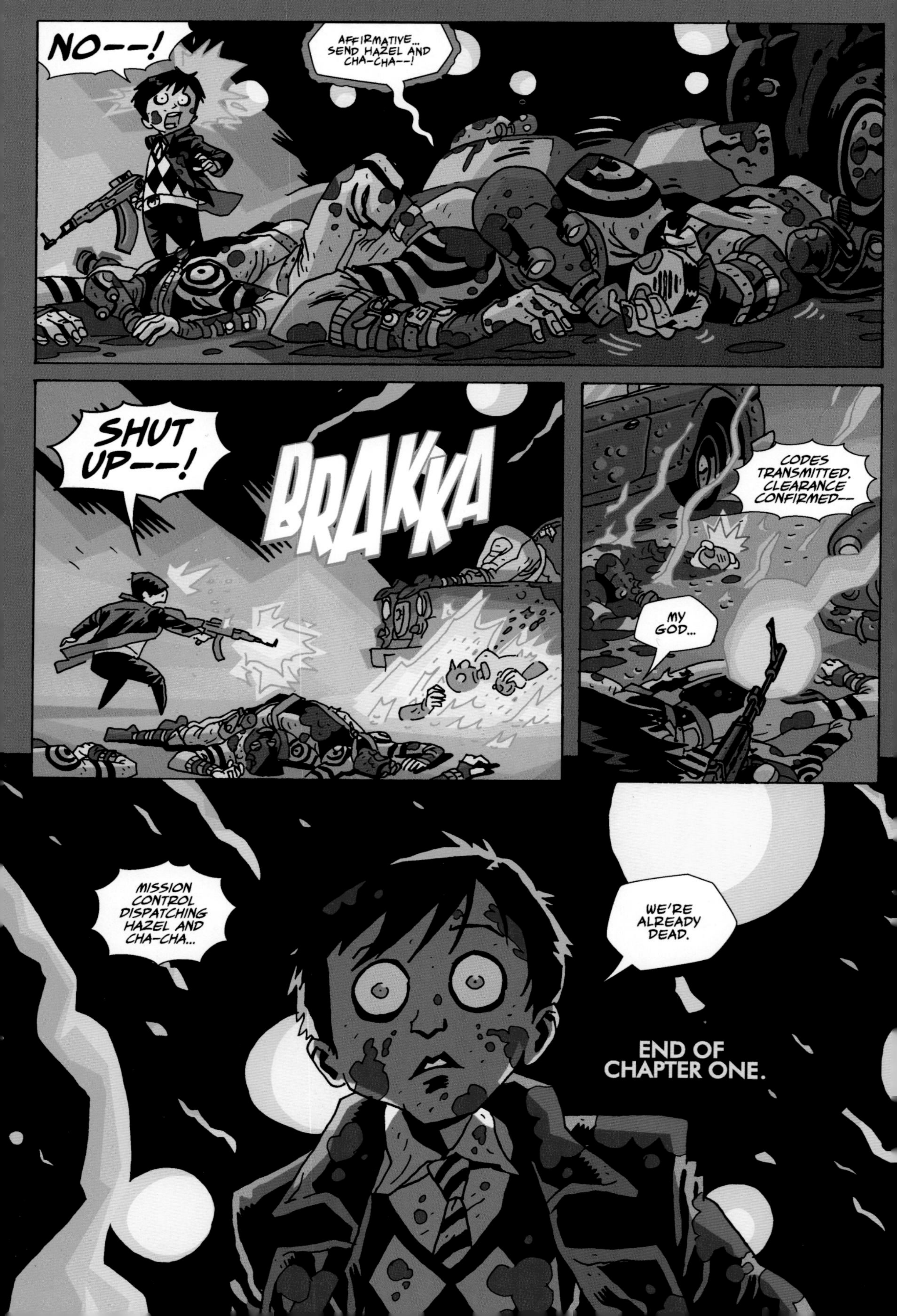
NO--!
AFFIRMATIVE... SEND HAZEL AND CHA-CHA--!
SHUT UP--!
BRAKKA
CODES TRANSMITTED. CLEARANCE CONFIRMED--
MY GOD...
MISSION CONTROL DISPATCHING HAZEL AND CHA-CHA...
WE'RE ALREADY DEAD.
END OF CHAPTER ONE.

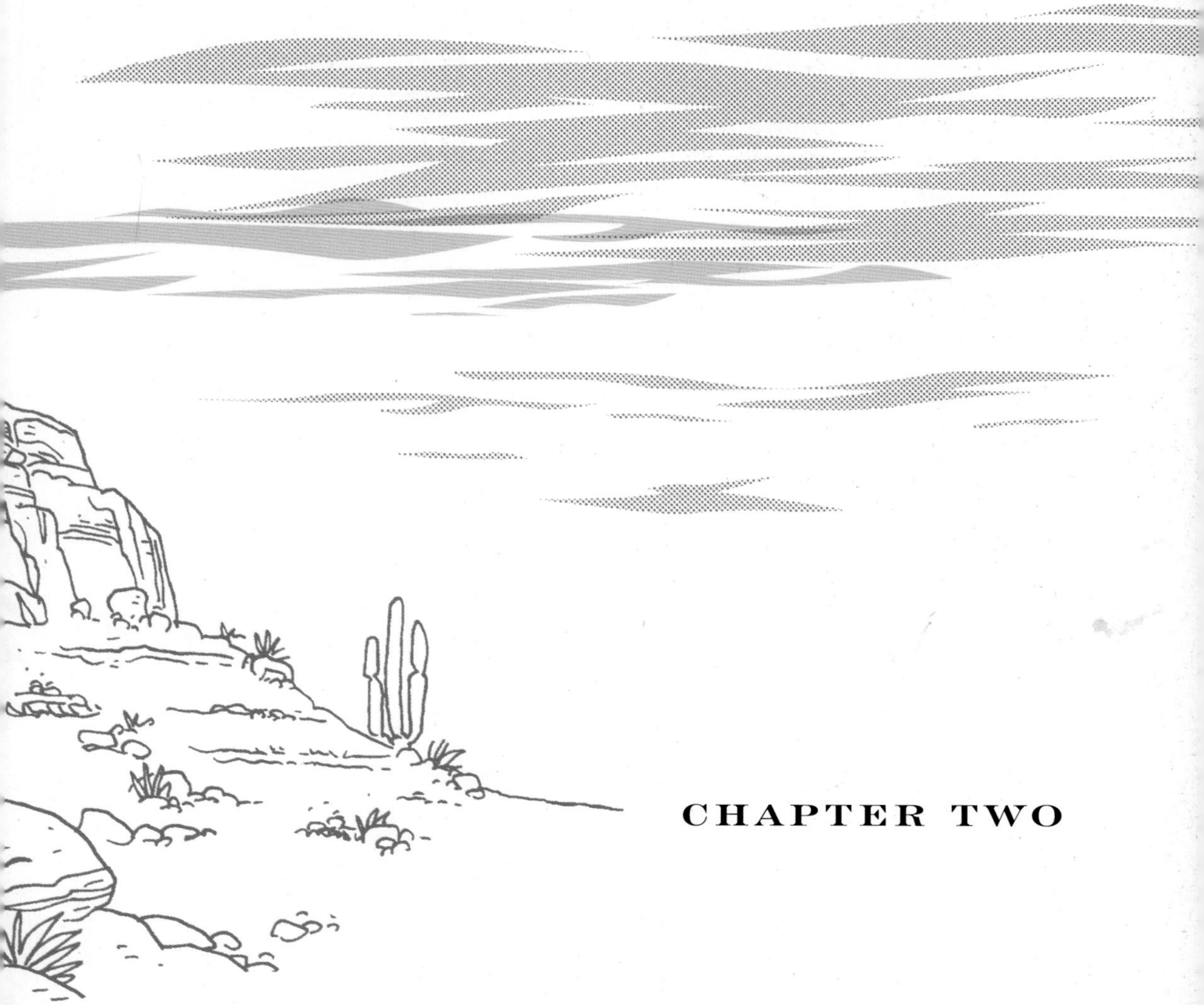

CHAPTER TWO

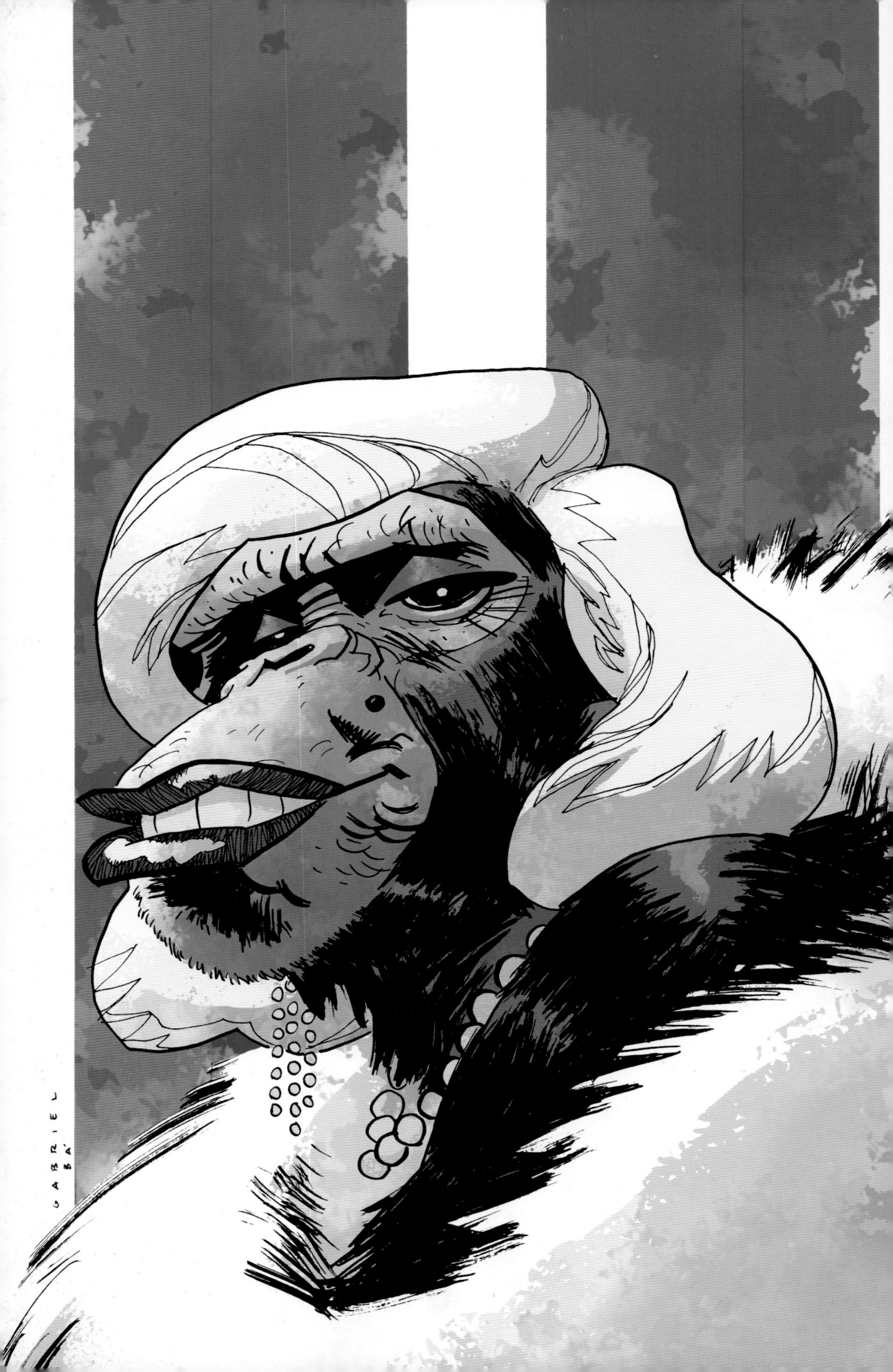
GABRIEL BÁ

DOWNTOWN.

ARE YOU *KIDDING* ME?! THIS PIE IS *INCREDIBLE--!*

YOU GOTTA TRY THIS--

I'M WATCHING MY FIGURE--

JUST *EAT* IT!

NOW, WE DON'T WANT NO TROUBLE--

WOW!

WHAT'S IN THAT PIE?

I *TOLD* YOU!

ONCE HAD A MAN COME ALL THE WAY FROM BARCELONA TRYNNA GET THE RECIPE...OFFERED ME FIVE THOUSAND DOLLARS FOR IT.

I TELLS HIM-- *"YOU'D HAVE TO CHOP OFF MY ARMS AND LEGS TO GET THAT OUTTA ME!"* Heh-heh...

Agnes

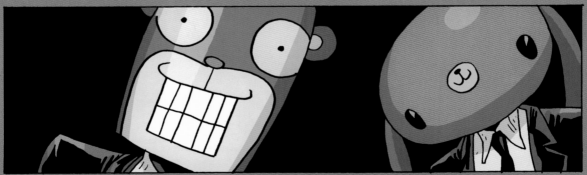

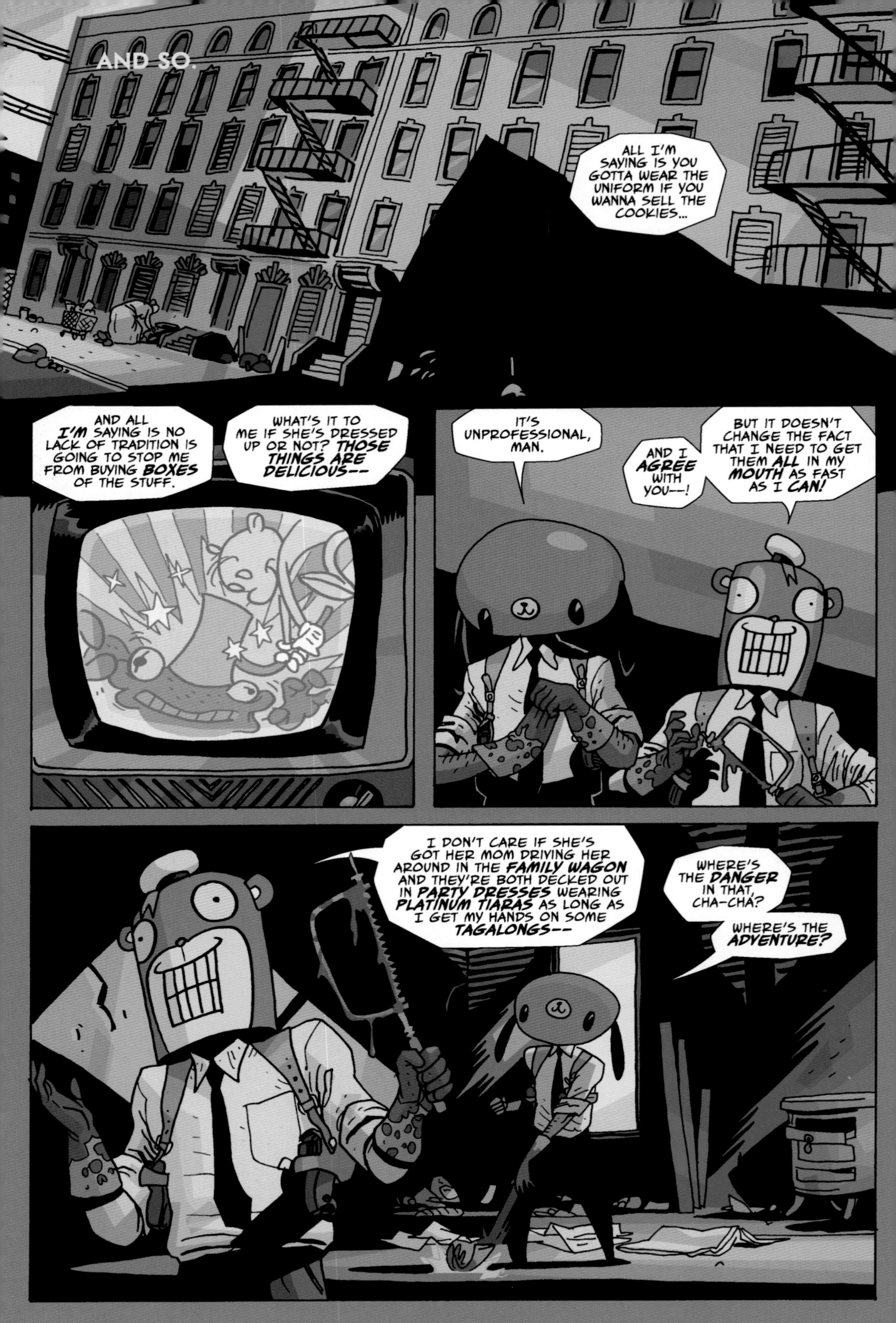

AND SO.
ALL I'M SAYING IS YOU GOTTA WEAR THE UNIFORM IF YOU WANNA SELL THE COOKIES...
AND ALL I'M SAYING IS NO LACK OF TRADITION IS GOING TO STOP ME FROM BUYING BOXES OF THE STUFF.
WHAT'S IT TO ME IF SHE'S DRESSED UP OR NOT? THOSE THINGS ARE DELICIOUS--
IT'S UNPROFESSIONAL, MAN.
AND I AGREE WITH YOU--!
BUT IT DOESN'T CHANGE THE FACT THAT I NEED TO GET THEM ALL IN MY MOUTH AS FAST AS I CAN!
I DON'T CARE IF SHE'S GOT HER MOM DRIVING HER AROUND IN THE FAMILY WAGON AND THEY'RE BOTH DECKED OUT IN PARTY DRESSES WEARING PLATINUM TIARAS AS LONG AS I GET MY HANDS ON SOME TAGALONGS--
WHERE'S THE DANGER IN THAT, CHA-CHA?
WHERE'S THE ADVENTURE?

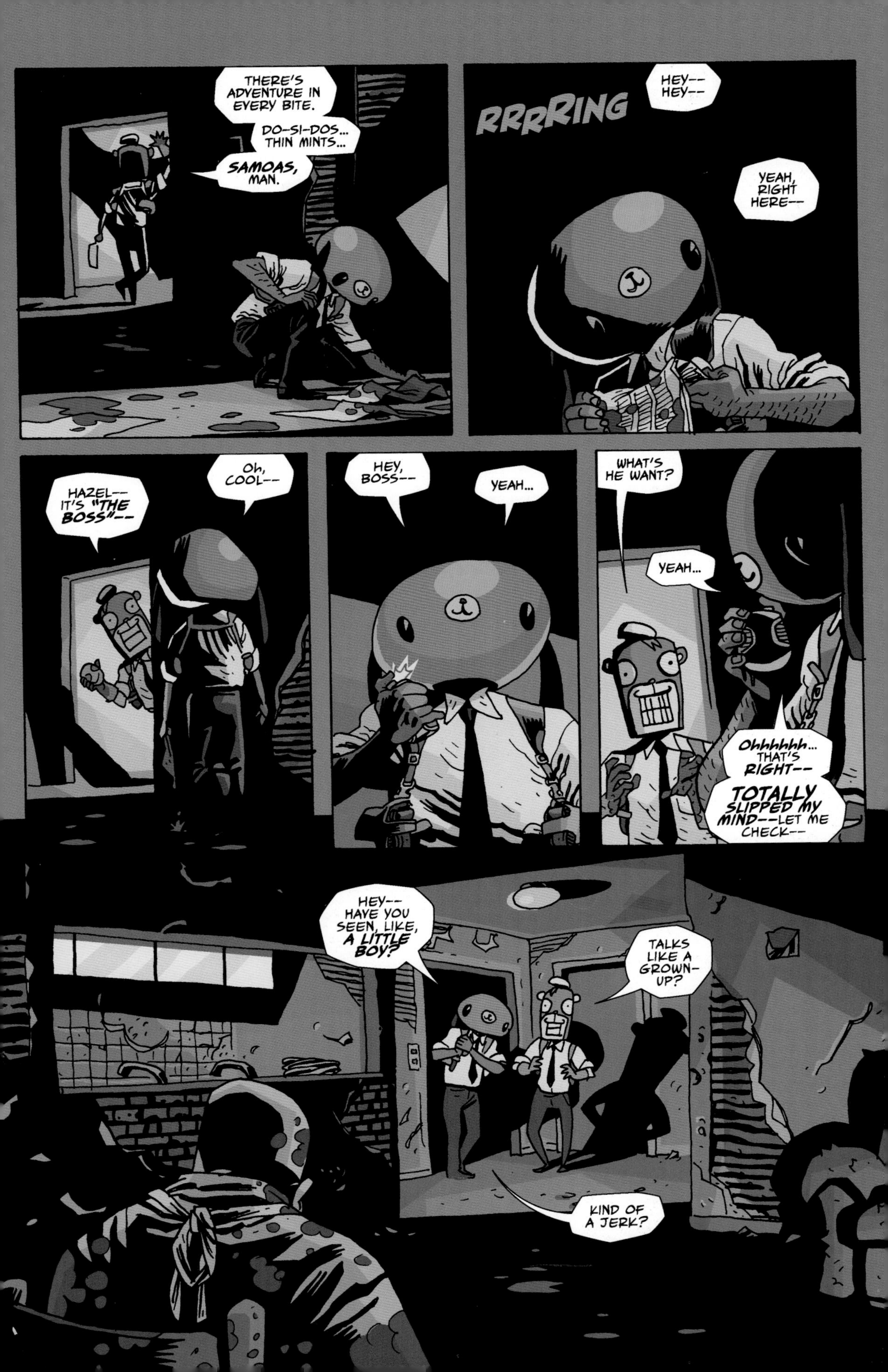
THERE'S ADVENTURE IN EVERY BITE.
DO-SI-DOS... THIN MINTS...
SAMOAS, MAN.
RRRRING
HEY-- HEY--
YEAH, RIGHT HERE--
HAZEL-- IT'S "THE BOSS"--
Oh, COOL--
HEY, BOSS--
YEAH...
WHAT'S HE WANT?
YEAH...
Ohhhhhh... THAT'S RIGHT--
TOTALLY SLIPPED MY MIND--LET ME CHECK--
HEY-- HAVE YOU SEEN, LIKE, A LITTLE BOY?
TALKS LIKE A GROWN-UP?
KIND OF A JERK?

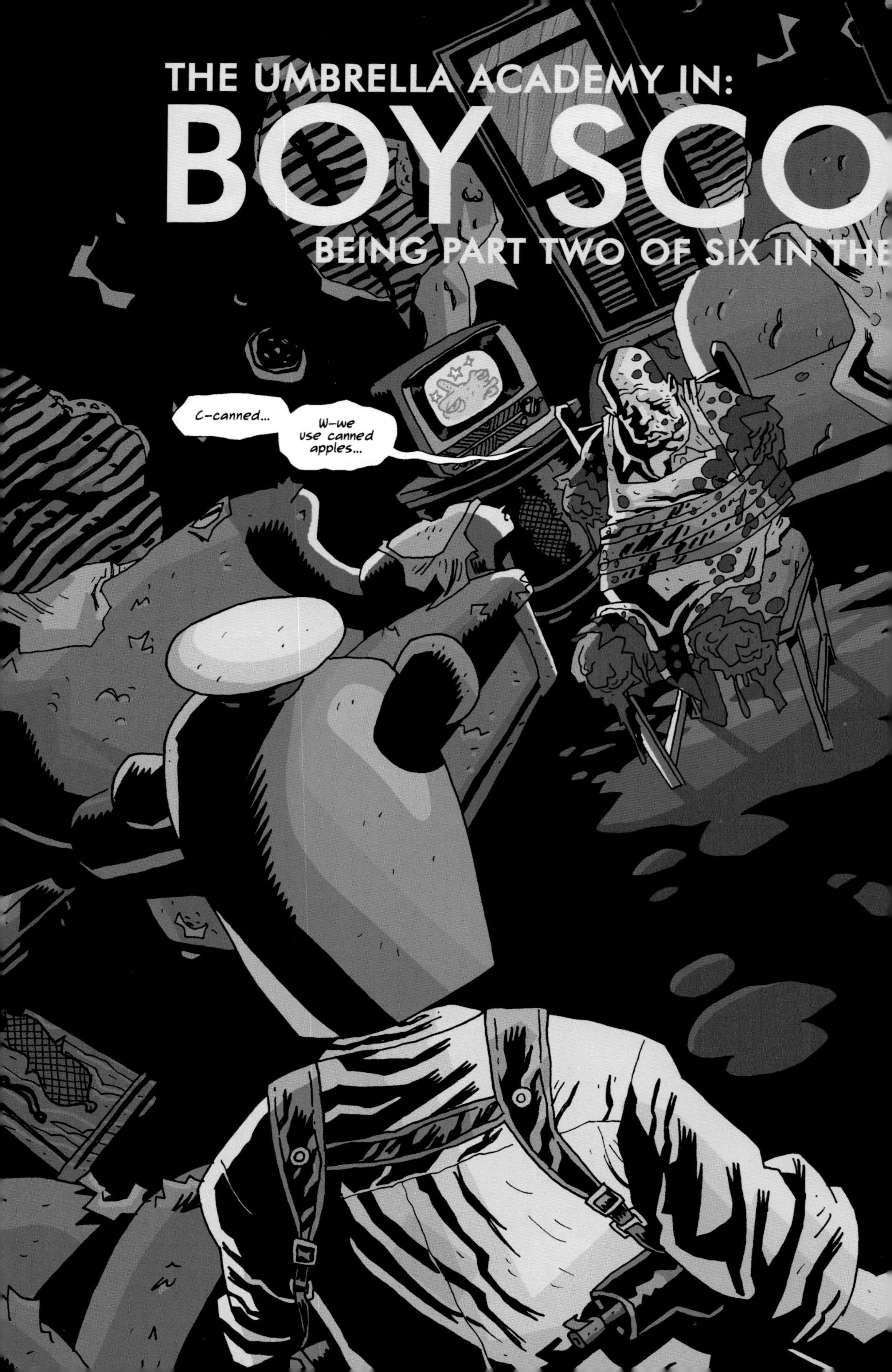
THE UMBRELLA ACADEMY IN:
BOY SCO
BEING PART TWO OF SIX IN THE
C-canned...
W-we use canned apples...

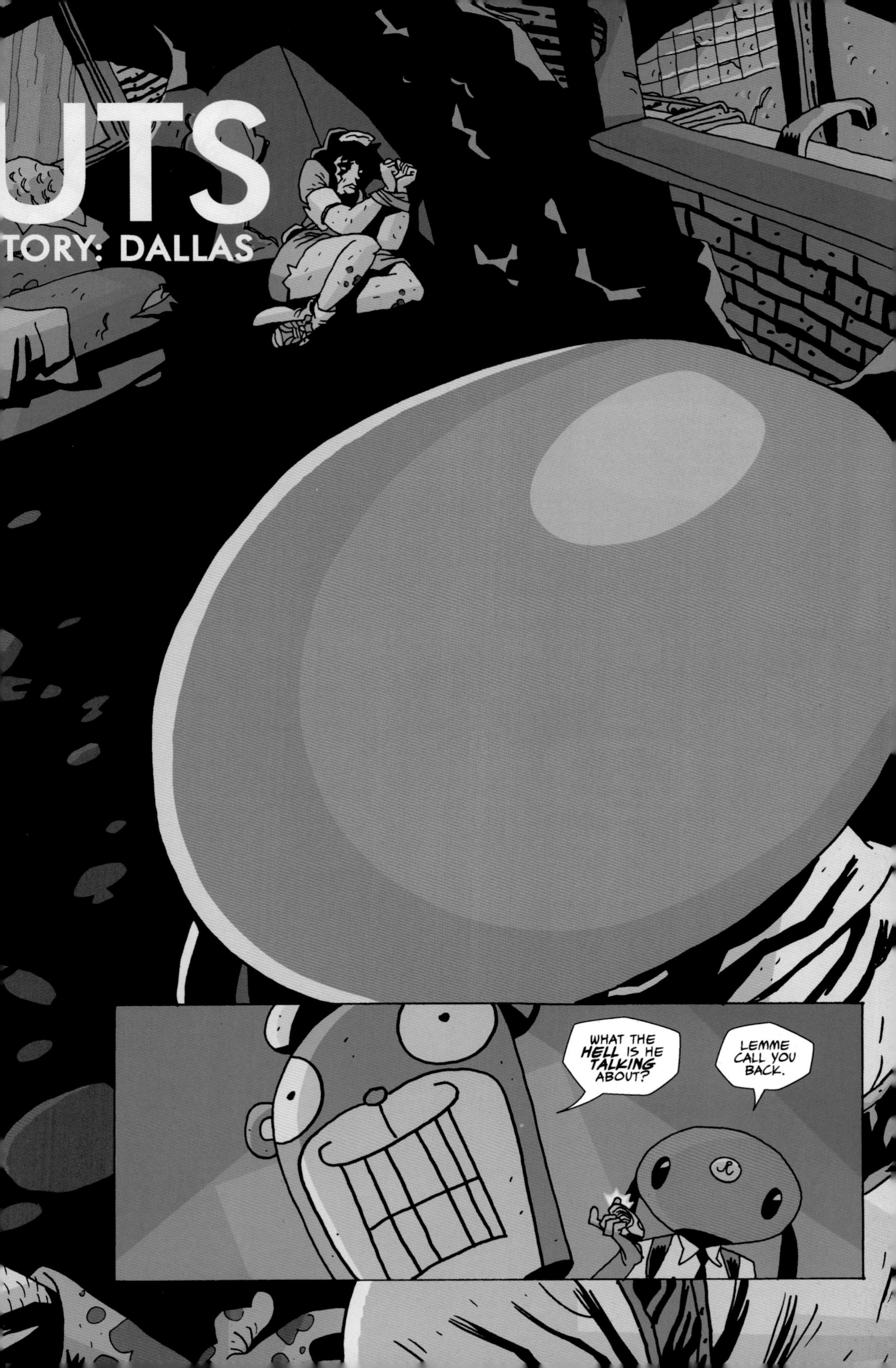
UTS
TORY: DALLAS
WHAT THE HELL IS HE TALKING ABOUT?
LEMME CALL YOU BACK.

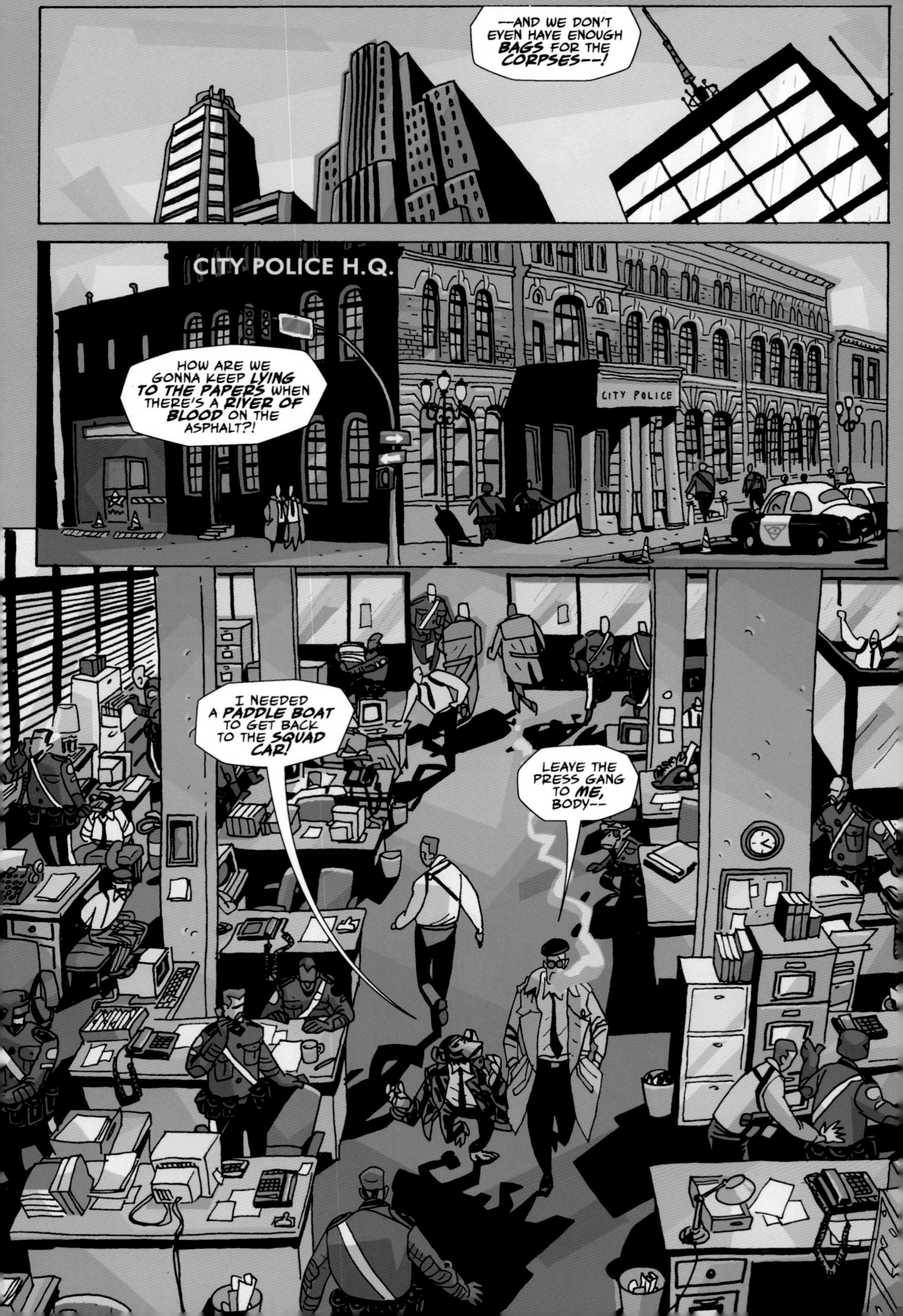
--AND WE DON'T EVEN HAVE ENOUGH BAGS FOR THE CORPSES--!
CITY POLICE H.Q.
HOW ARE WE GONNA KEEP LYING TO THE PAPERS WHEN THERE'S A RIVER OF BLOOD ON THE ASPHALT?!
CITY POLICE
I NEEDED A PADDLE BOAT TO GET BACK TO THE SQUAD CAR!
LEAVE THE PRESS GANG TO ME, BODY--

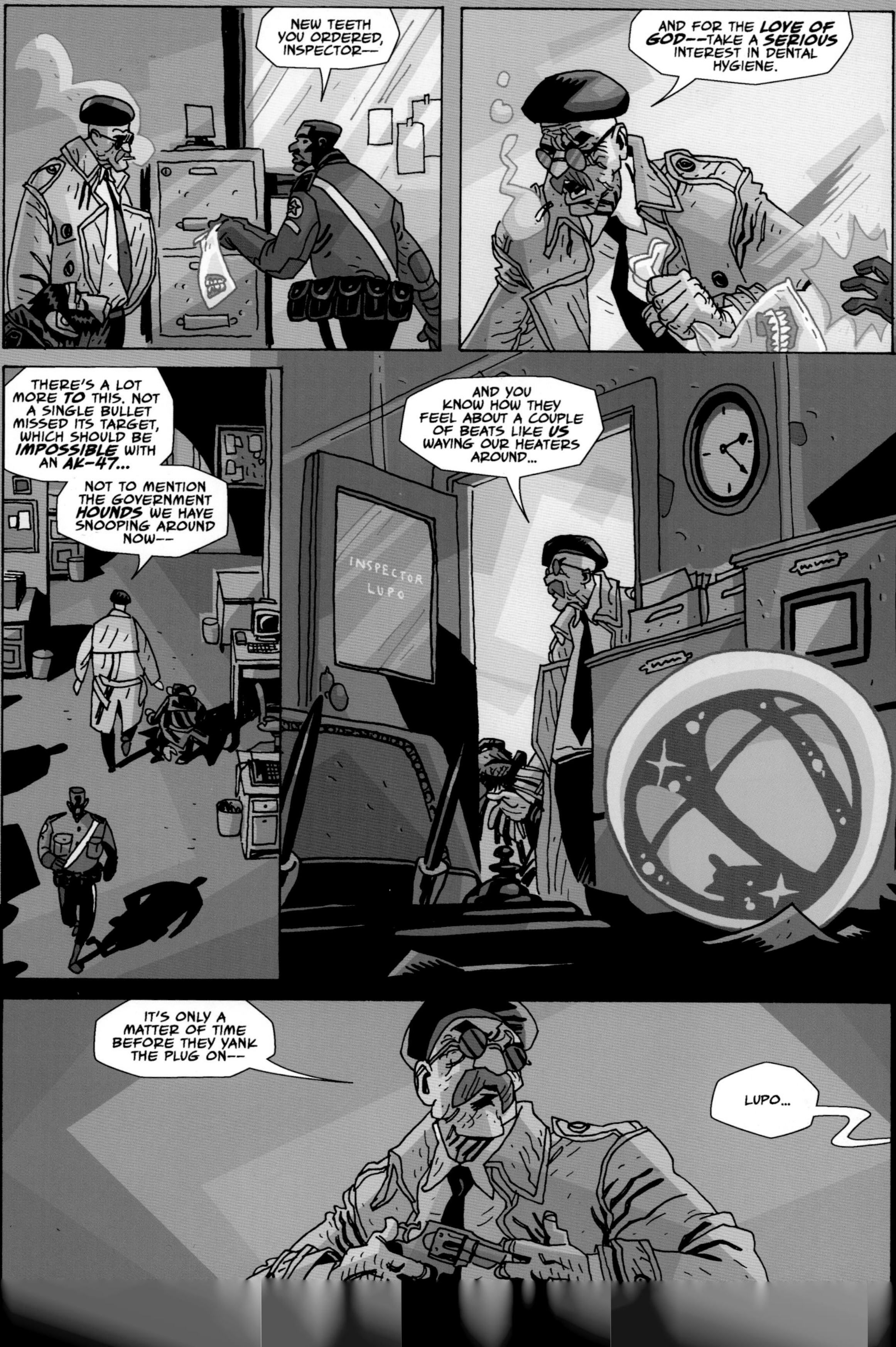
NEW TEETH YOU ORDERED, INSPECTOR--
AND FOR THE LOVE OF GOD--TAKE A SERIOUS INTEREST IN DENTAL HYGIENE.
THERE'S A LOT MORE TO THIS. NOT A SINGLE BULLET MISSED ITS TARGET, WHICH SHOULD BE IMPOSSIBLE WITH AN AK-47...
NOT TO MENTION THE GOVERNMENT HOUNDS WE HAVE SNOOPING AROUND NOW--
AND YOU KNOW HOW THEY FEEL ABOUT A COUPLE OF BEATS LIKE US WAVING OUR HEATERS AROUND...
INSPECTOR LUPO
IT'S ONLY A MATTER OF TIME BEFORE THEY YANK THE PLUG ON--
LUPO...

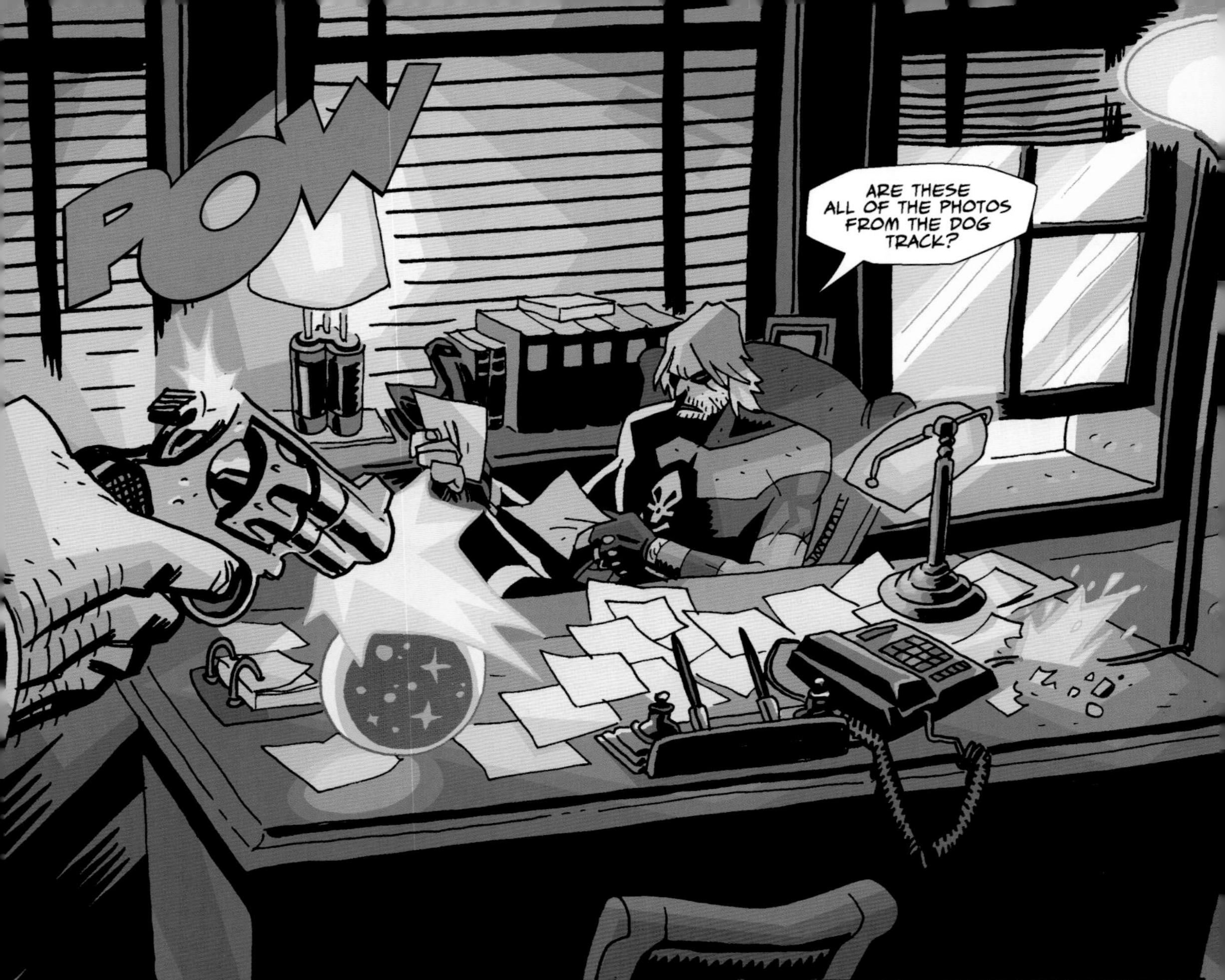
POW
ARE THESE ALL OF THE PHOTOS FROM THE DOG TRACK?

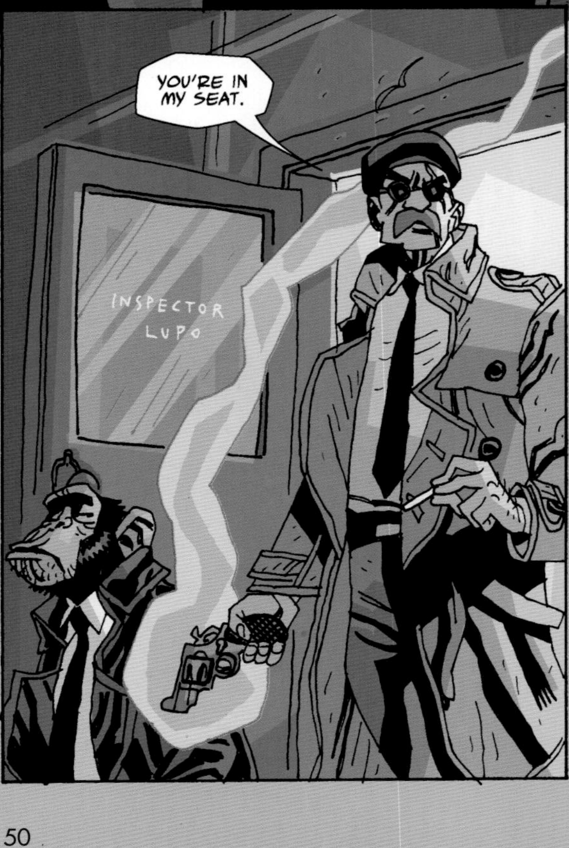
YOU'RE IN MY SEAT.
INSPECTOR LUPO

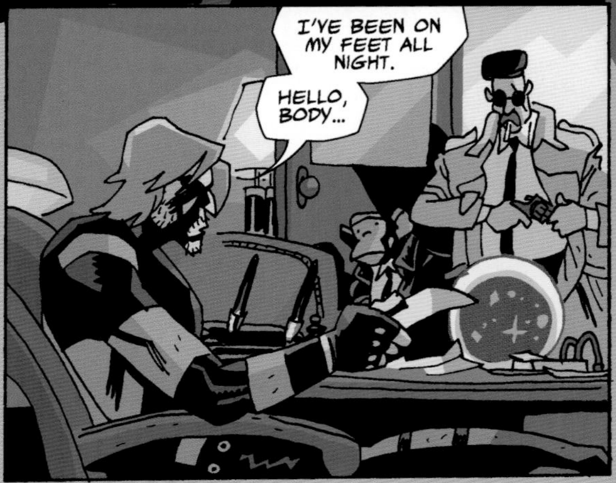
I'VE BEEN ON MY FEET ALL NIGHT.
HELLO, BODY...

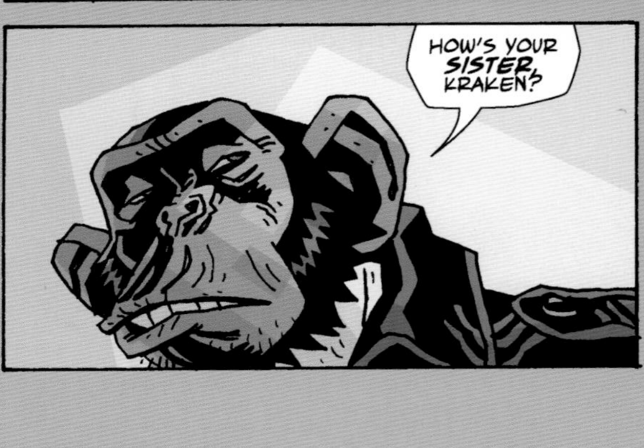
HOW'S YOUR SISTER, KRAKEN?

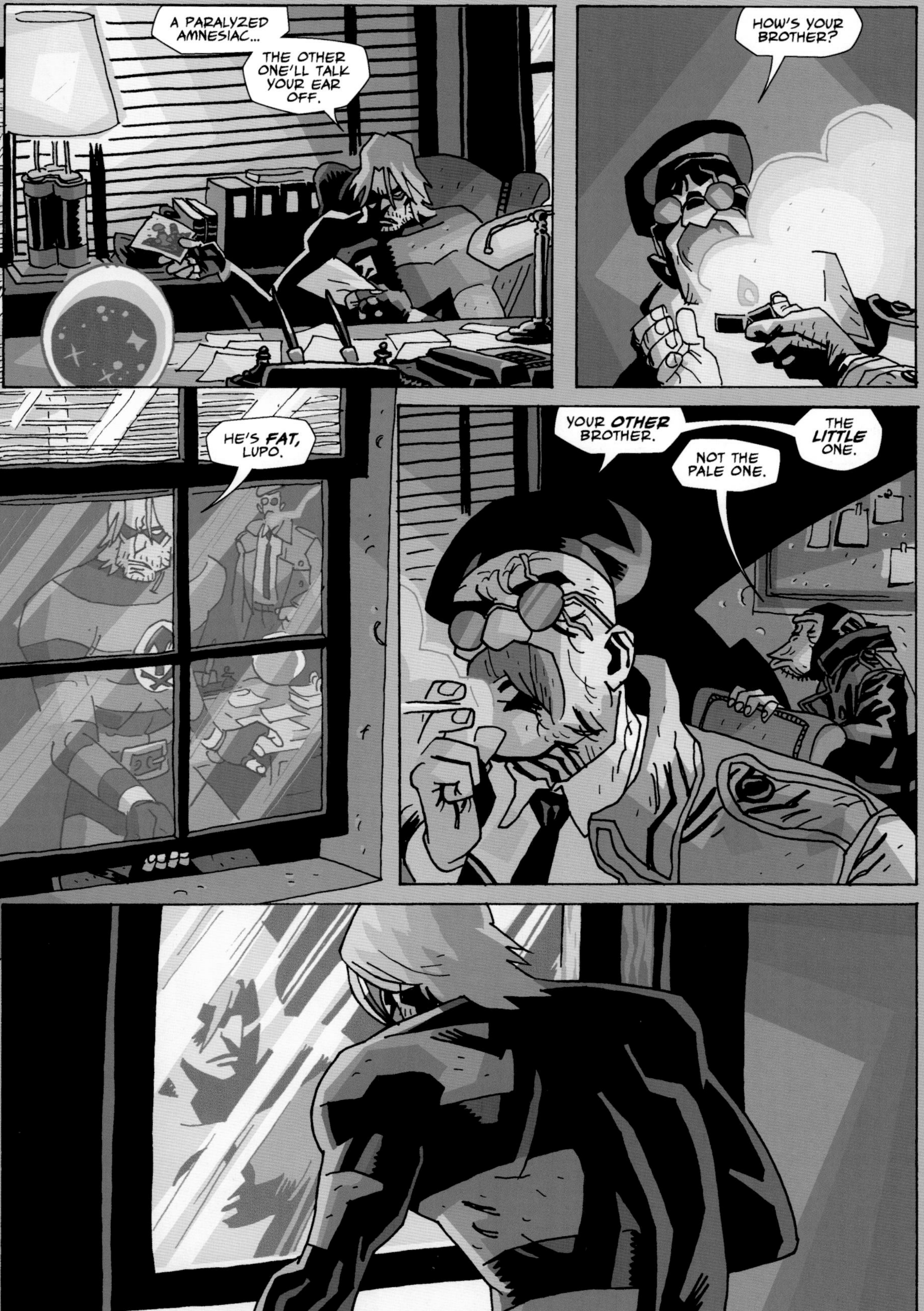
A PARALYZED AMNESIAC...
THE OTHER ONE'LL TALK YOUR EAR OFF.
HOW'S YOUR BROTHER?
HE'S FAT, LUPO.
YOUR OTHER BROTHER.
THE LITTLE ONE.
NOT THE PALE ONE.

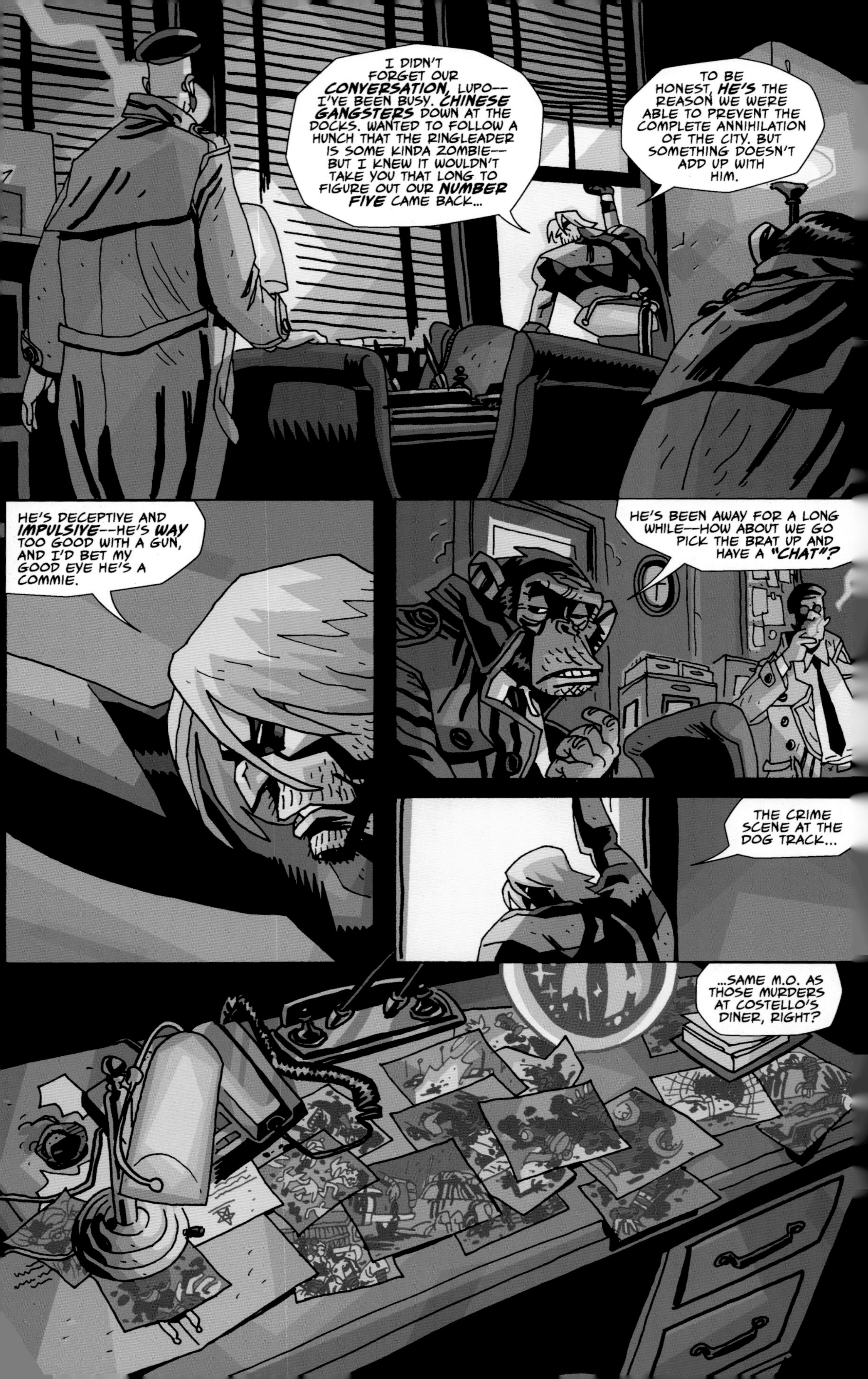
I DIDN'T FORGET OUR CONVERSATION, LUPO-- I'VE BEEN BUSY. CHINESE GANGSTERS DOWN AT THE DOCKS. WANTED TO FOLLOW A HUNCH THAT THE RINGLEADER IS SOME KINDA ZOMBIE-- BUT I KNEW IT WOULDN'T TAKE YOU THAT LONG TO FIGURE OUT OUR NUMBER FIVE CAME BACK...
TO BE HONEST, HE'S THE REASON WE WERE ABLE TO PREVENT THE COMPLETE ANNIHILATION OF THE CITY. BUT SOMETHING DOESN'T ADD UP WITH HIM.
HE'S DECEPTIVE AND IMPULSIVE--HE'S WAY TOO GOOD WITH A GUN, AND I'D BET MY GOOD EYE HE'S A COMMIE.
HE'S BEEN AWAY FOR A LONG WHILE--HOW ABOUT WE GO PICK THE BRAT UP AND HAVE A "CHAT"?
THE CRIME SCENE AT THE DOG TRACK...
...SAME M.O. AS THOSE MURDERS AT COSTELLO'S DINER, RIGHT?

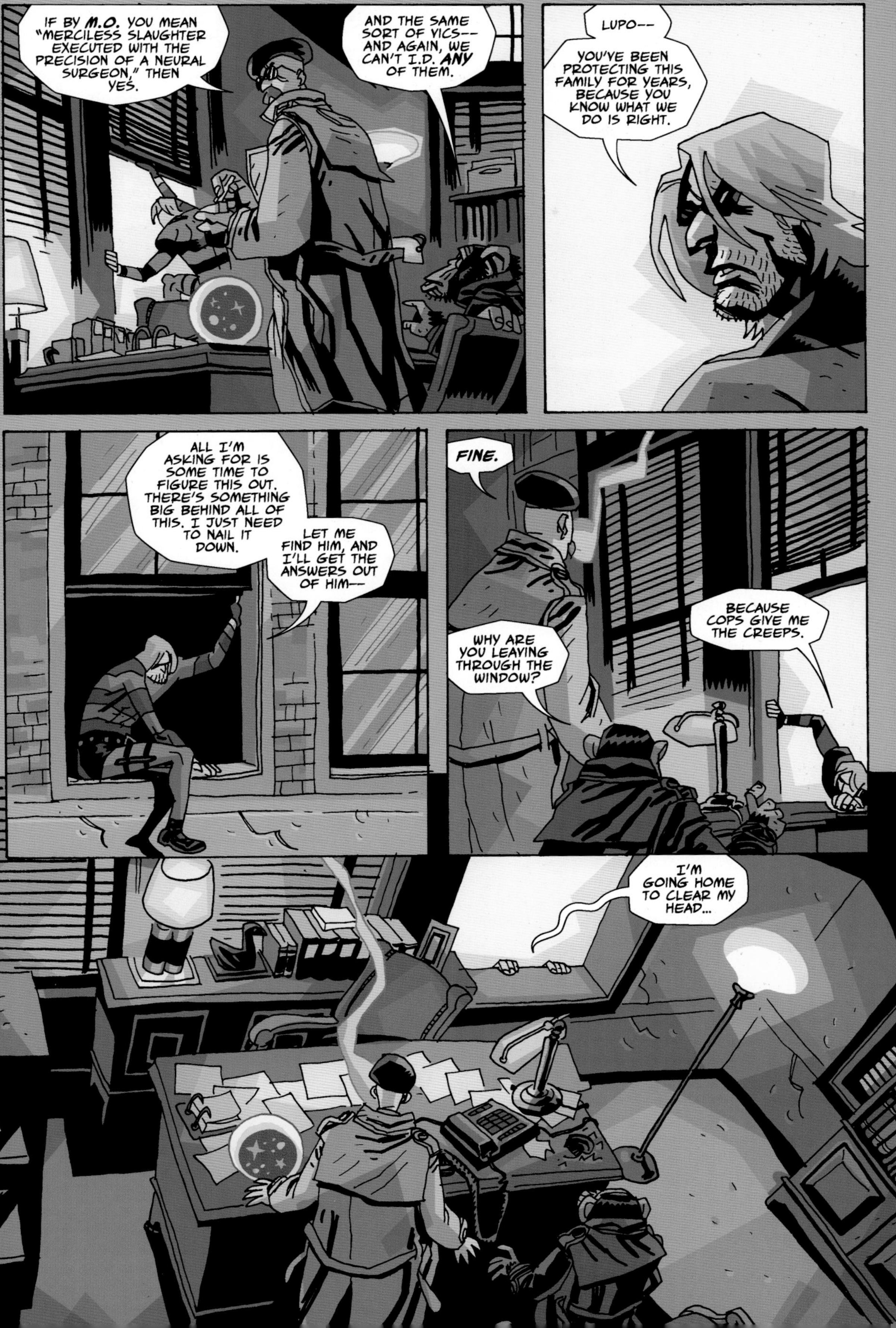
IF BY M.O. YOU MEAN "MERCILESS SLAUGHTER EXECUTED WITH THE PRECISION OF A NEURAL SURGEON," THEN YES.
AND THE SAME SORT OF VICS-- AND AGAIN, WE CAN'T I.D. ANY OF THEM.
LUPO--
YOU'VE BEEN PROTECTING THIS FAMILY FOR YEARS, BECAUSE YOU KNOW WHAT WE DO IS RIGHT.
ALL I'M ASKING FOR IS SOME TIME TO FIGURE THIS OUT. THERE'S SOMETHING BIG BEHIND ALL OF THIS. I JUST NEED TO NAIL IT DOWN.
LET ME FIND HIM, AND I'LL GET THE ANSWERS OUT OF HIM--
FINE.
WHY ARE YOU LEAVING THROUGH THE WINDOW?
BECAUSE COPS GIVE ME THE CREEPS.
I'M GOING HOME TO CLEAR MY HEAD...

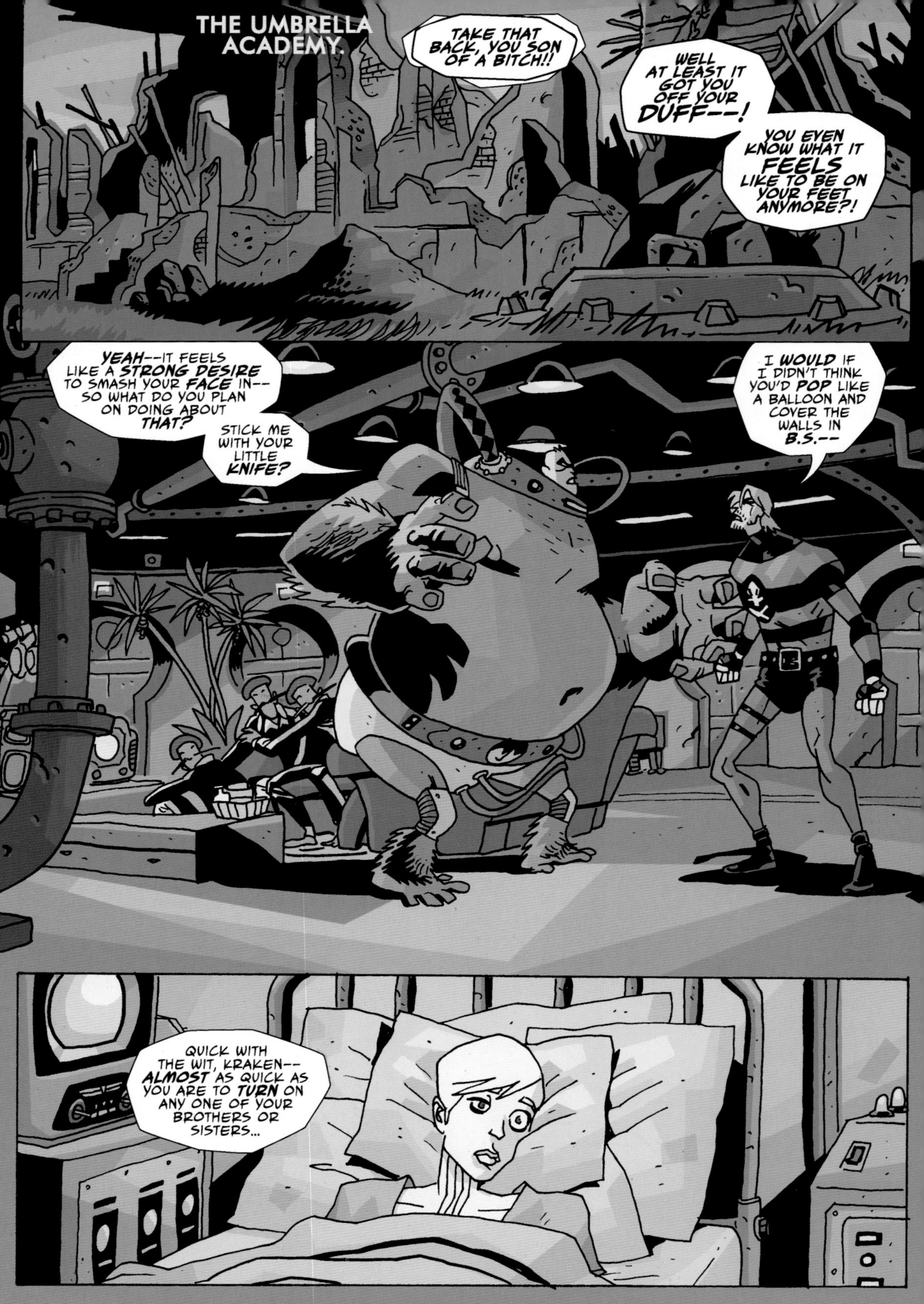
THE UMBRELLA ACADEMY.
TAKE THAT BACK, YOU SON OF A BITCH!!
WELL AT LEAST IT GOT YOU OFF YOUR DUFF--!
YOU EVEN KNOW WHAT IT FEELS LIKE TO BE ON YOUR FEET ANYMORE?!
YEAH--IT FEELS LIKE A STRONG DESIRE TO SMASH YOUR FACE IN--SO WHAT DO YOU PLAN ON DOING ABOUT THAT?
STICK ME WITH YOUR LITTLE KNIFE?
I WOULD IF I DIDN'T THINK YOU'D POP LIKE A BALLOON AND COVER THE WALLS IN B.S.--
QUICK WITH THE WIT, KRAKEN--ALMOST AS QUICK AS YOU ARE TO TURN ON ANY ONE OF YOUR BROTHERS OR SISTERS...

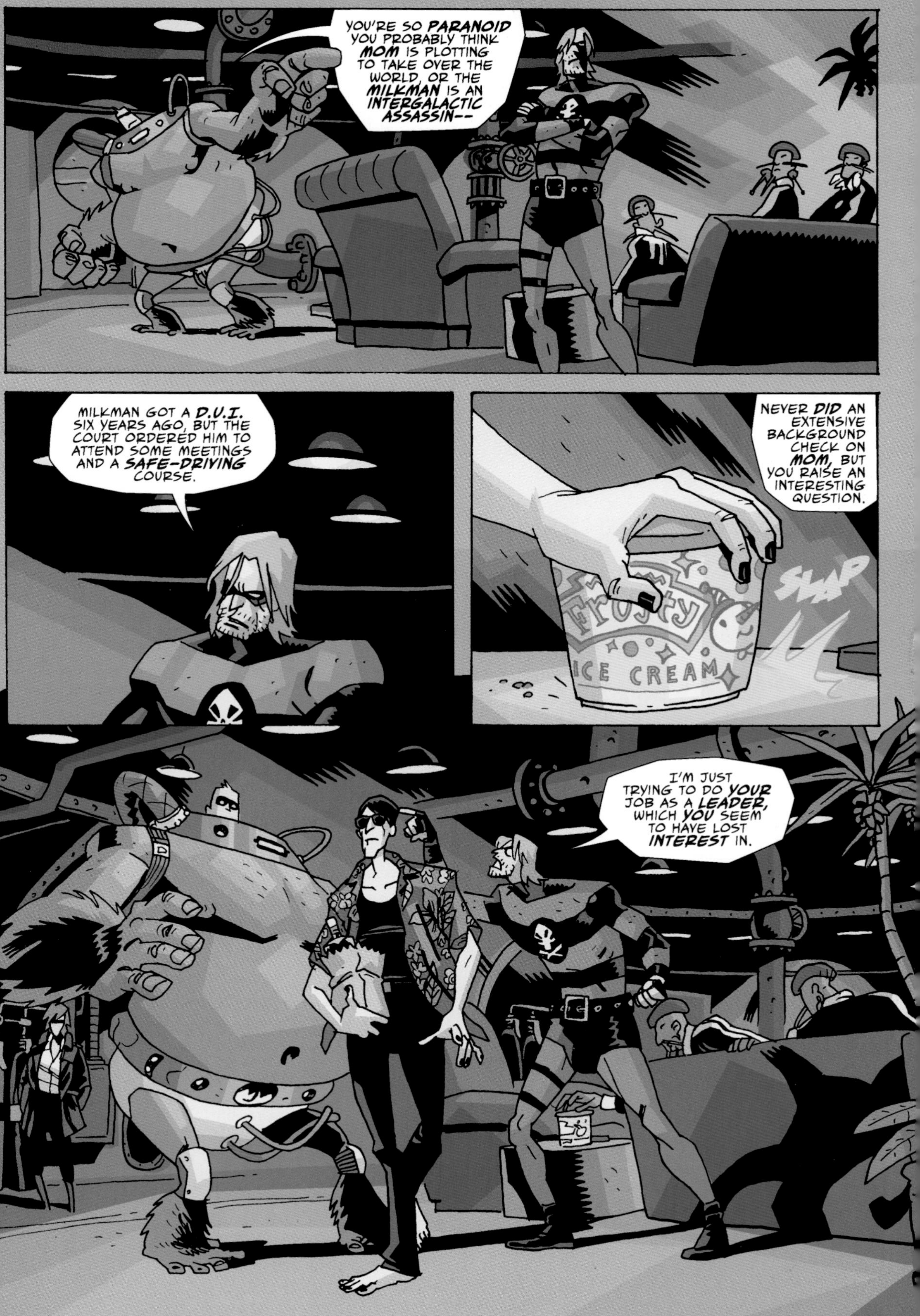
YOU'RE SO PARANOID YOU PROBABLY THINK MOM IS PLOTTING TO TAKE OVER THE WORLD, OR THE MILKMAN IS AN INTERGALACTIC ASSASSIN--
MILKMAN GOT A D.U.I. SIX YEARS AGO, BUT THE COURT ORDERED HIM TO ATTEND SOME MEETINGS AND A SAFE-DRIVING COURSE.
NEVER DID AN EXTENSIVE BACKGROUND CHECK ON MOM, BUT YOU RAISE AN INTERESTING QUESTION.
Frosty
ICE CREAM
SLAP
I'M JUST TRYING TO DO YOUR JOB AS A LEADER, WHICH YOU SEEM TO HAVE LOST INTEREST IN.

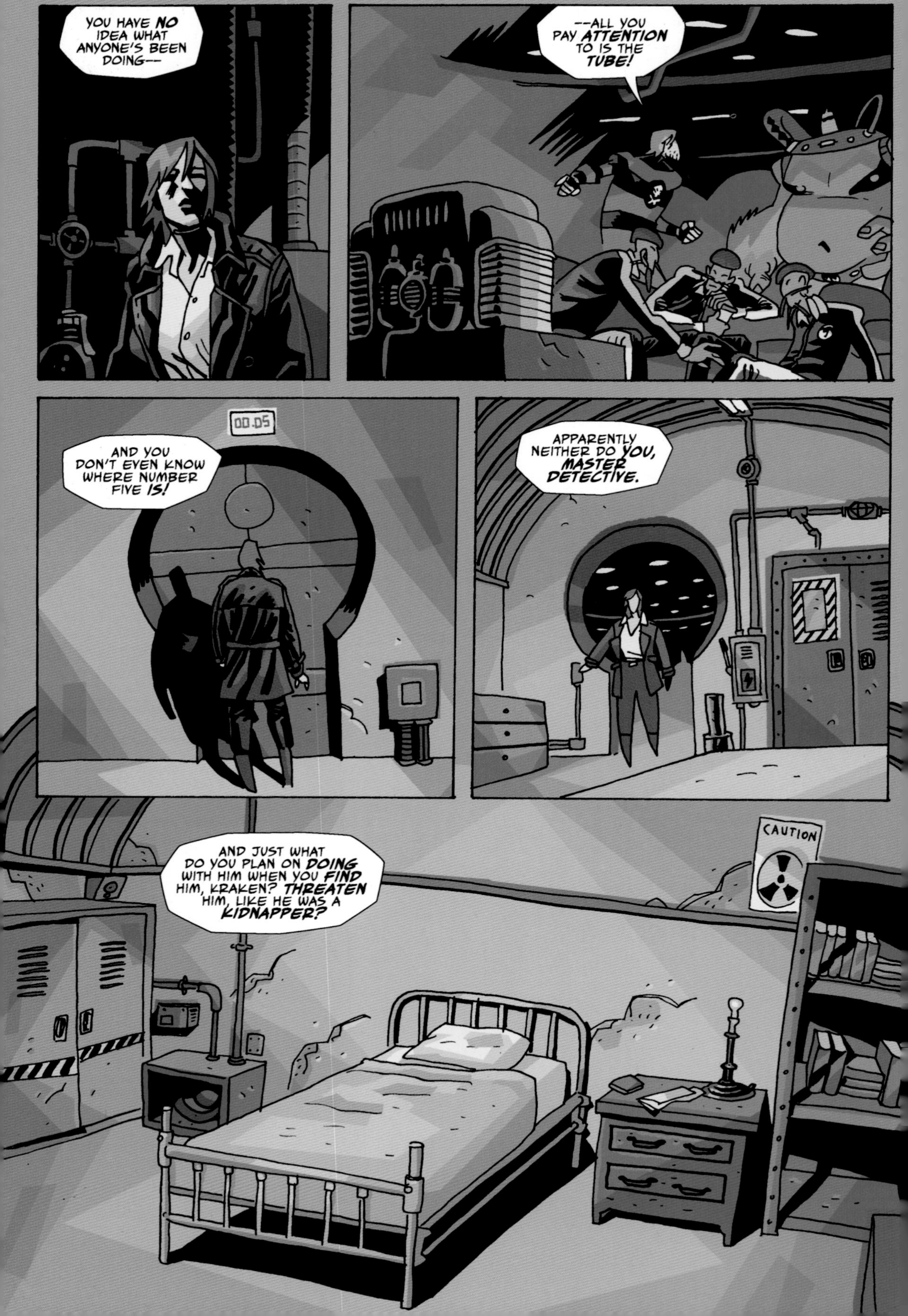
YOU HAVE NO IDEA WHAT ANYONE'S BEEN DOING--
--ALL YOU PAY ATTENTION TO IS THE TUBE!
00.05
AND YOU DON'T EVEN KNOW WHERE NUMBER FIVE IS!
APPARENTLY NEITHER DO YOU, MASTER DETECTIVE.
CAUTION
AND JUST WHAT DO YOU PLAN ON DOING WITH HIM WHEN YOU FIND HIM, KRAKEN? THREATEN HIM, LIKE HE WAS A KIDNAPPER?

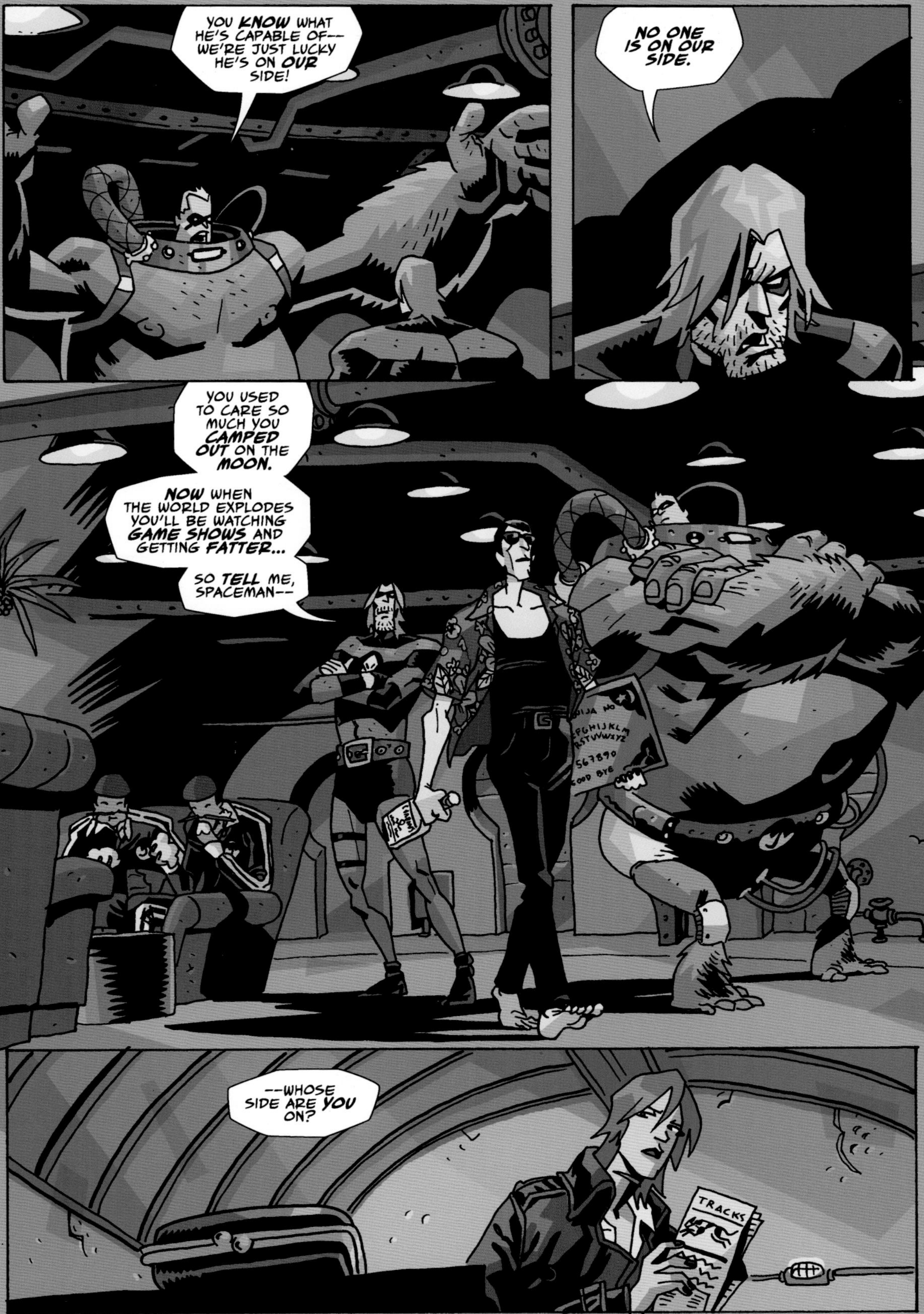
YOU KNOW WHAT HE'S CAPABLE OF-- WE'RE JUST LUCKY HE'S ON OUR SIDE!
NO ONE IS ON OUR SIDE.
YOU USED TO CARE SO MUCH YOU CAMPED OUT ON THE MOON.
NOW WHEN THE WORLD EXPLODES YOU'LL BE WATCHING GAME SHOWS AND GETTING FATTER...
SO TELL ME, SPACEMAN--
--WHOSE SIDE ARE YOU ON?
TRACKS

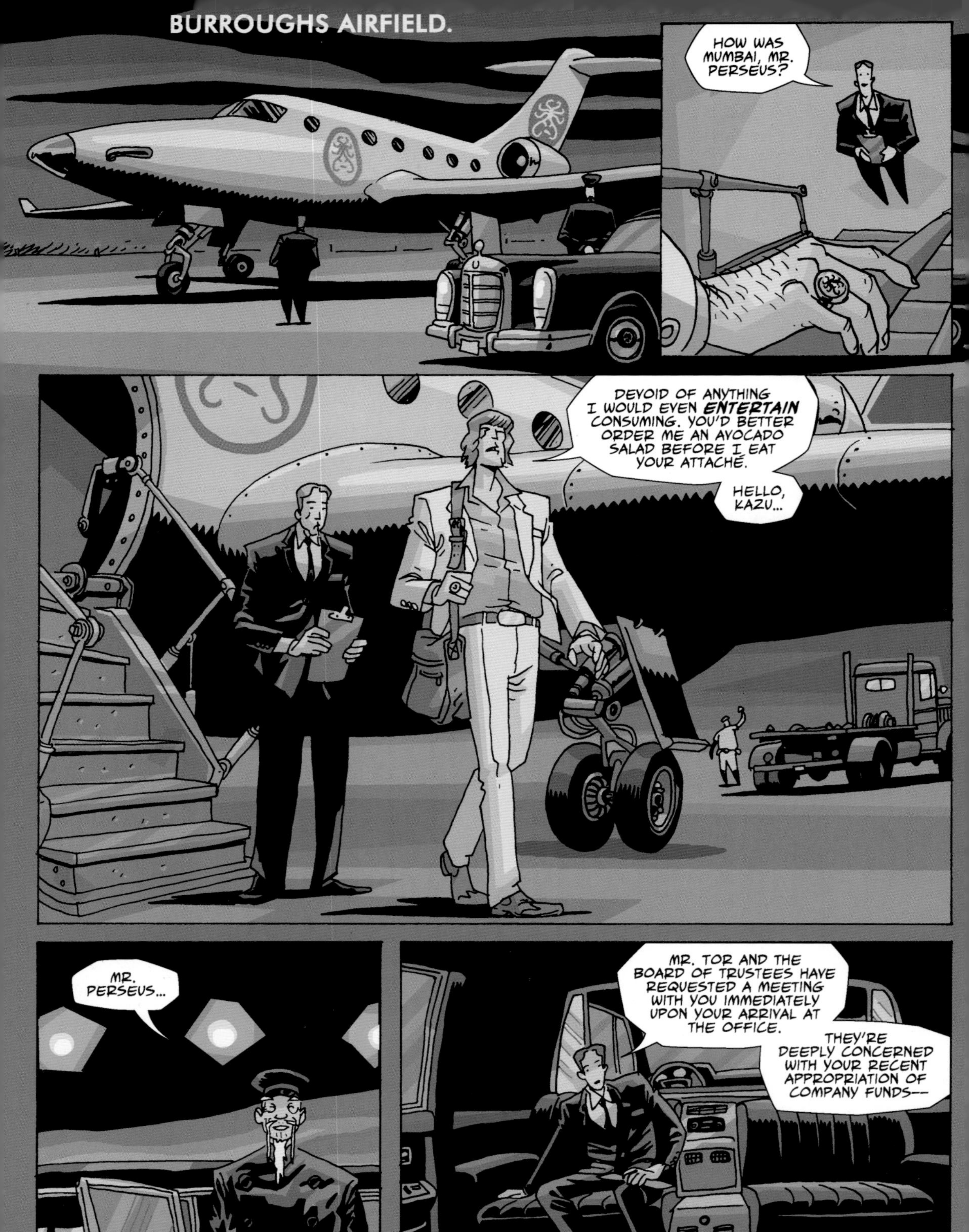
BURROUGHS AIRFIELD.
HOW WAS MUMBAI, MR. PERSEUS?
DEVOID OF ANYTHING I WOULD EVEN ENTERTAIN CONSUMING. YOU'D BETTER ORDER ME AN AVOCADO SALAD BEFORE I EAT YOUR ATTACHÉ.
HELLO, KAZU...
MR. PERSEUS...
MR. TOR AND THE BOARD OF TRUSTEES HAVE REQUESTED A MEETING WITH YOU IMMEDIATELY UPON YOUR ARRIVAL AT THE OFFICE.
THEY'RE DEEPLY CONCERNED WITH YOUR RECENT APPROPRIATION OF COMPANY FUNDS--

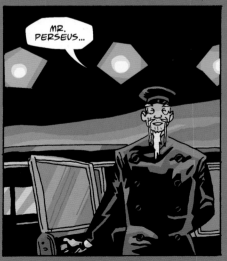

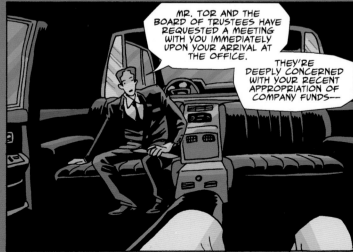

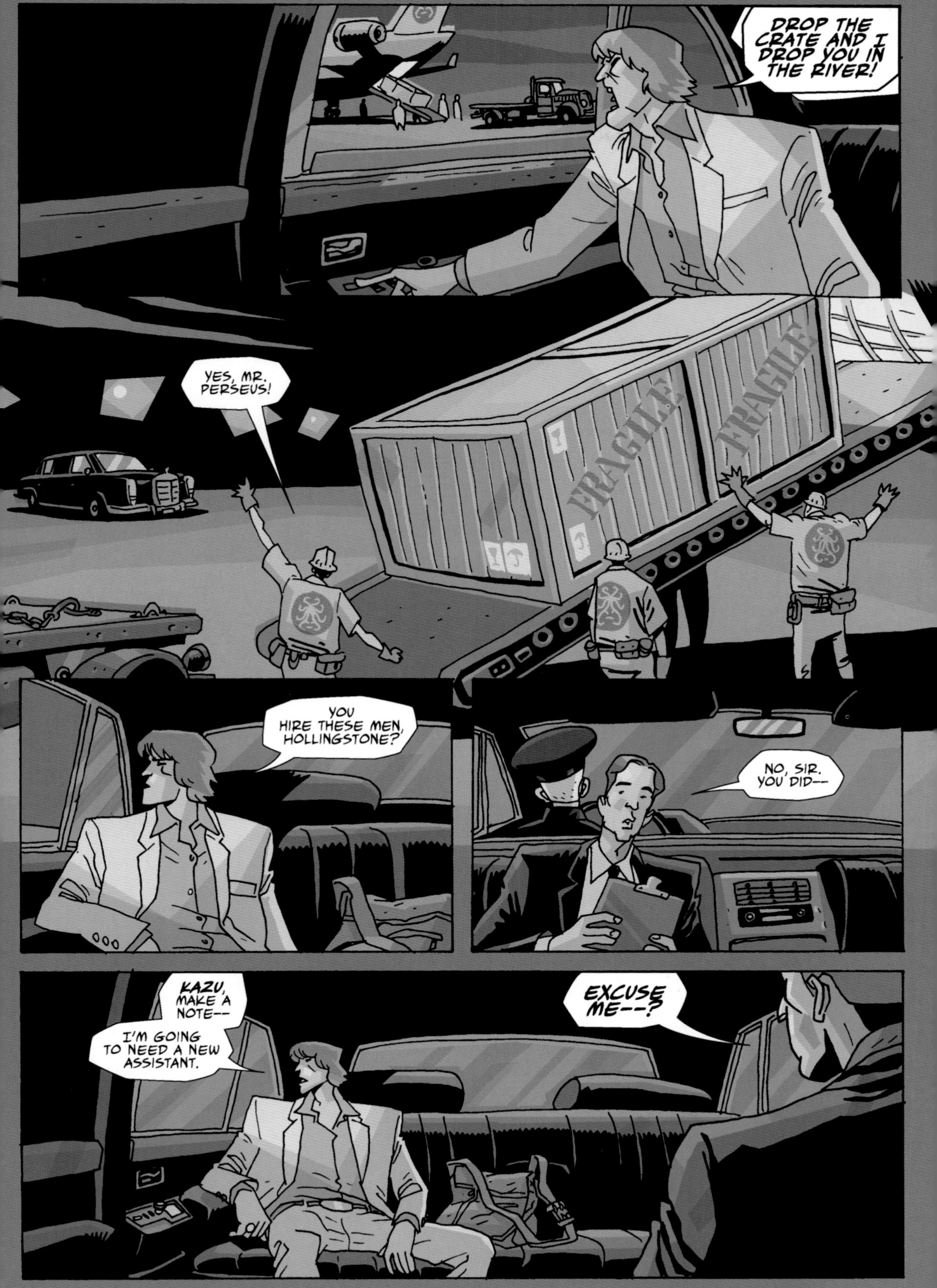
DROP THE CRATE AND I DROP YOU IN THE RIVER!
YES, MR. PERSEUS!
FRAGILE
FRAGILE
FRAGILE
YOU HIRE THESE MEN, HOLLINGSTONE?
NO, SIR. YOU DID--
KAZU, MAKE A NOTE--
I'M GOING TO NEED A NEW ASSISTANT.
EXCUSE ME--?

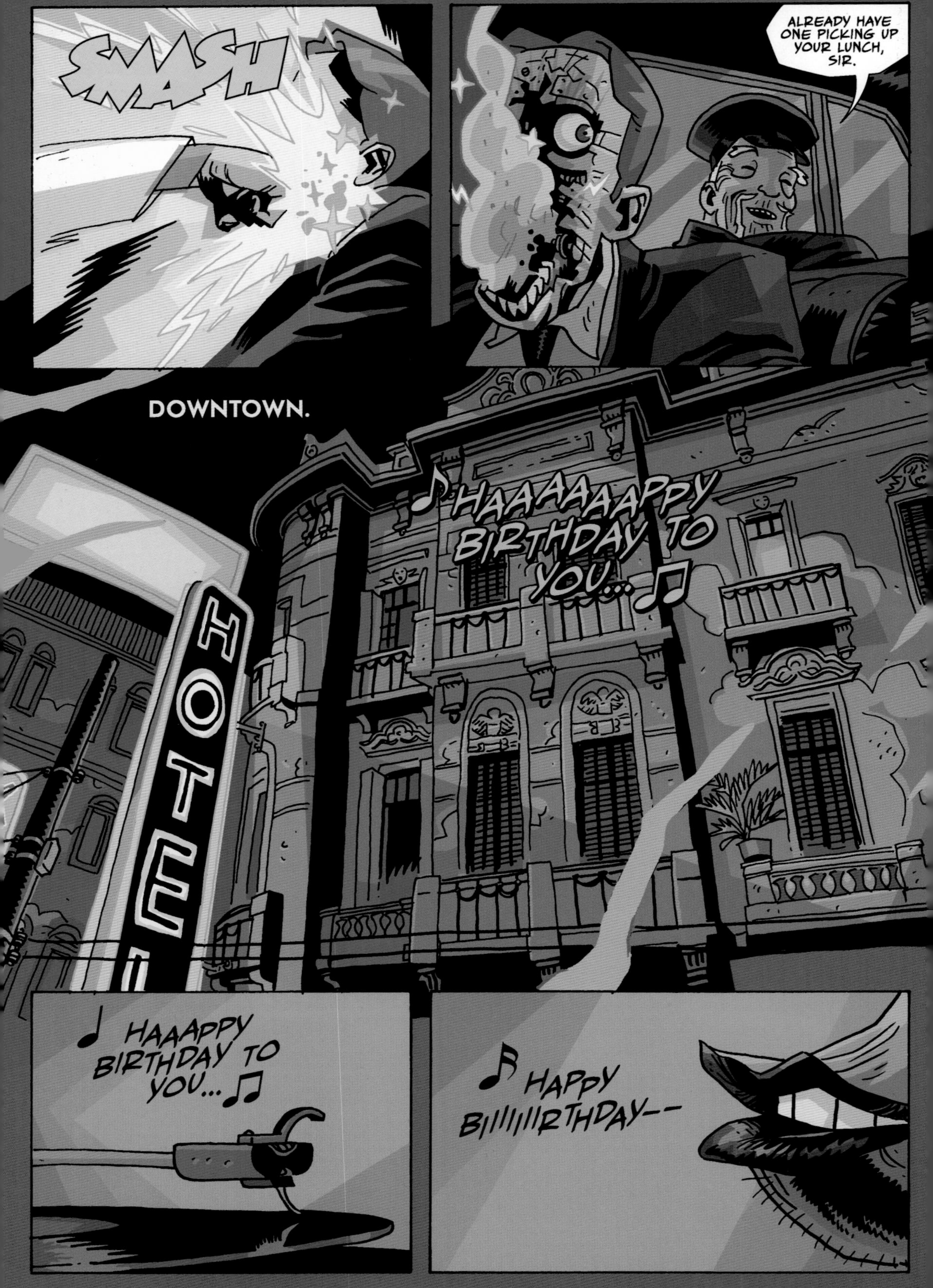
SMASH
ALREADY HAVE ONE PICKING UP YOUR LUNCH, SIR.
DOWNTOWN.
HAAAAAAPPY BIRTHDAY TO YOU...
HOTE
HAAAPPY BIRTHDAY TO YOU...
HAPPY BI////RTHDAY--

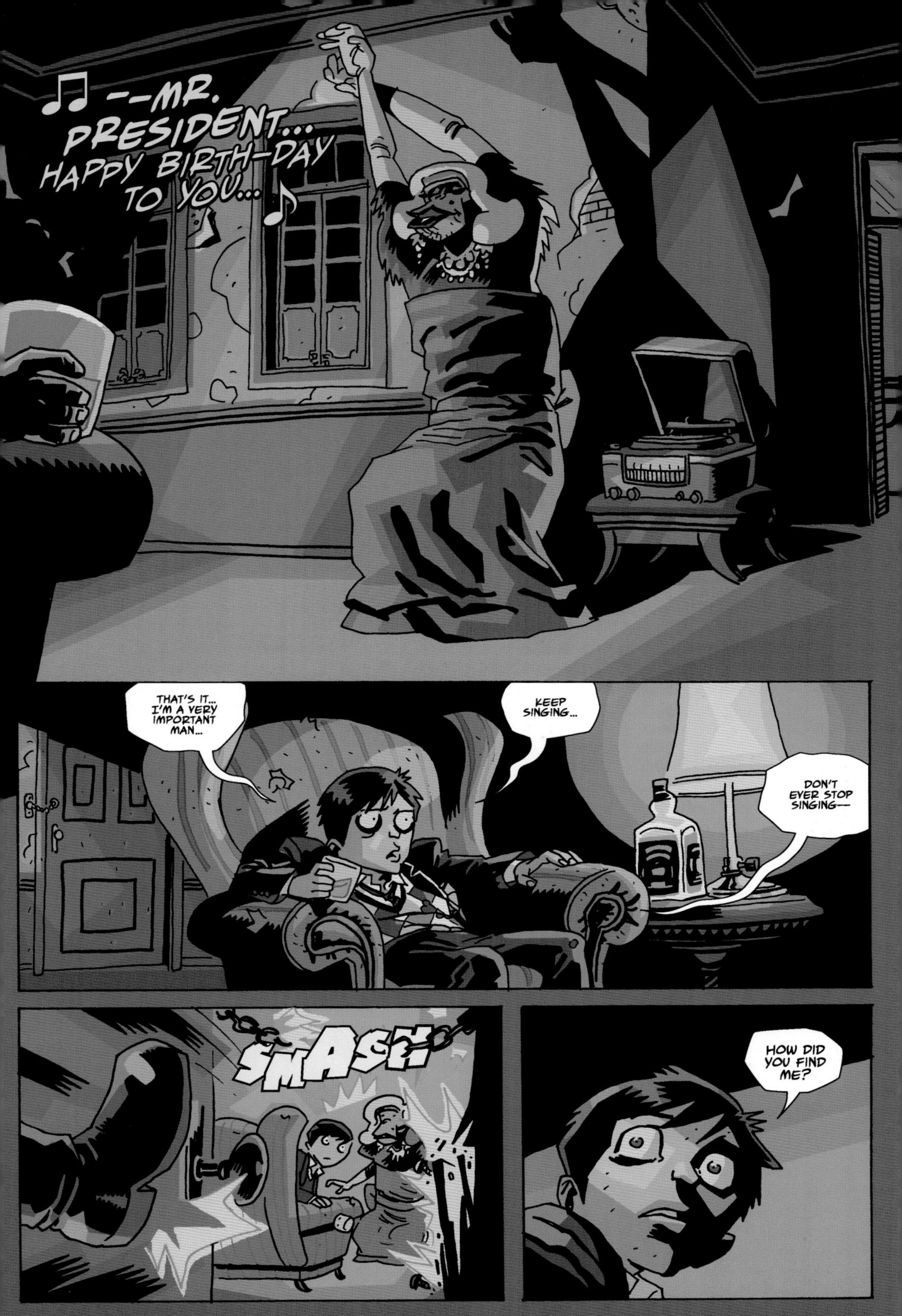
♫ --MR. PRESIDENT... HAPPY BIRTH-DAY TO YOU... ♪
THAT'S IT... I'M A VERY IMPORTANT MAN...
KEEP SINGING...
DON'T EVER STOP SINGING--
SMASH
HOW DID YOU FIND ME?

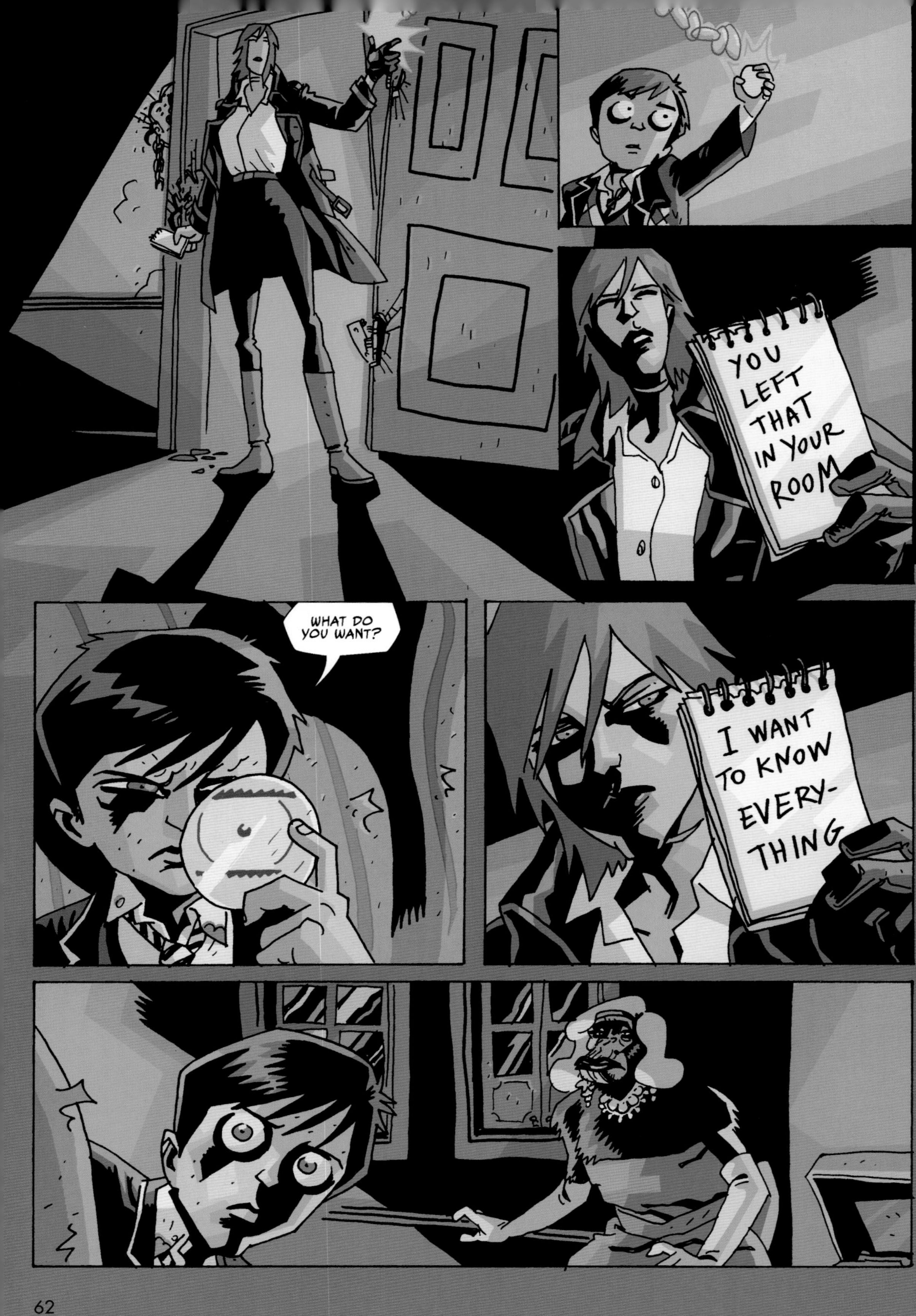
YOU LEFT THAT IN YOUR ROOM
WHAT DO YOU WANT?
I WANT TO KNOW EVERY-THING

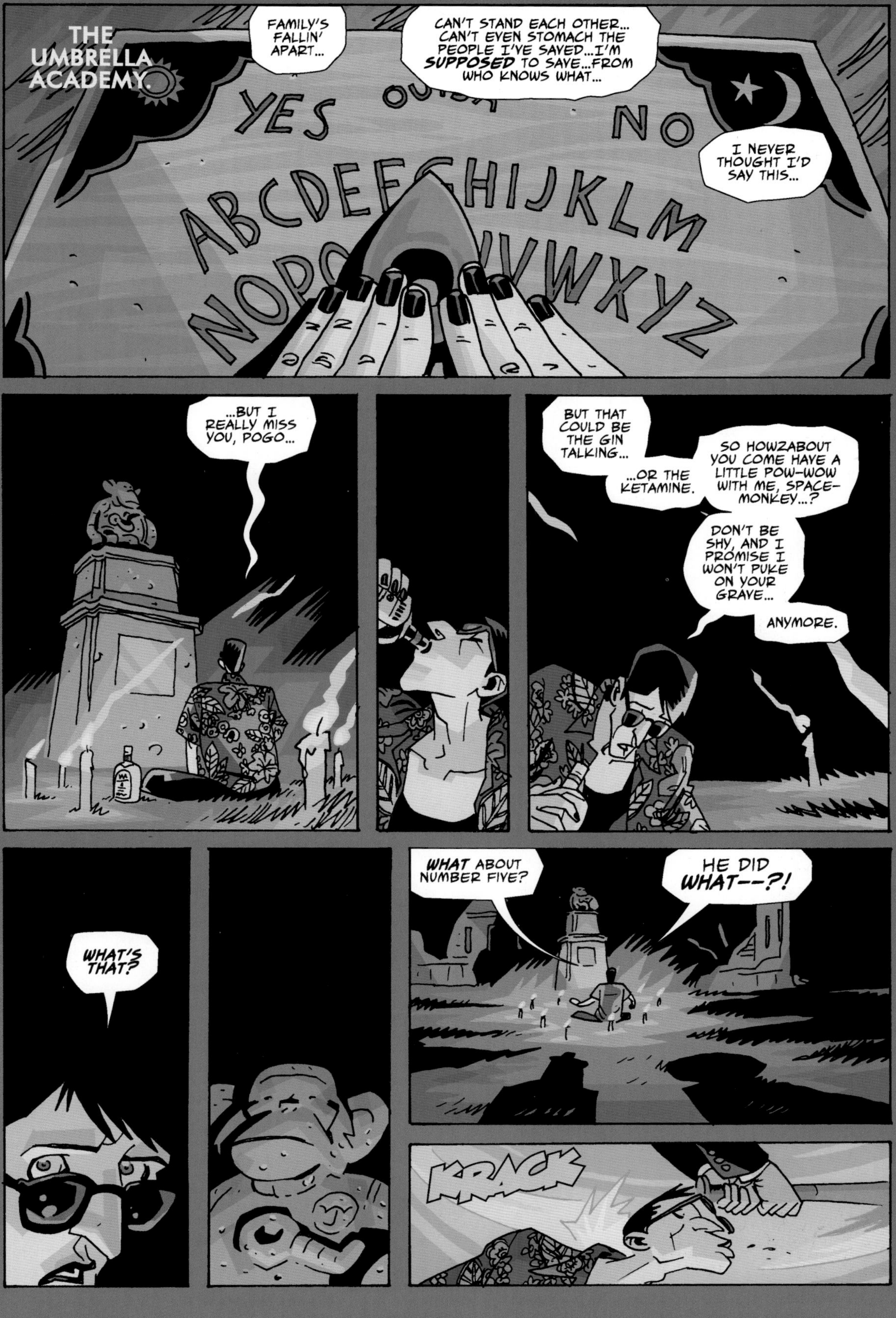
THE UMBRELLA ACADEMY
FAMILY'S FALLIN' APART...
CAN'T STAND EACH OTHER... CAN'T EVEN STOMACH THE PEOPLE I'VE SAVED...I'M SUPPOSED TO SAVE...FROM WHO KNOWS WHAT...
YES
NO
ABCDEFGHIJKLM
NOPQ
VWXYZ
I NEVER THOUGHT I'D SAY THIS...
...BUT I REALLY MISS YOU, POGO...
BUT THAT COULD BE THE GIN TALKING...
...OR THE KETAMINE.
SO HOWZABOUT YOU COME HAVE A LITTLE POW-WOW WITH ME, SPACE-MONKEY...?
DON'T BE SHY, AND I PROMISE I WON'T PUKE ON YOUR GRAVE...
ANYMORE.
WHAT'S THAT?
WHAT ABOUT NUMBER FIVE?
HE DID WHAT--?!
KRACK

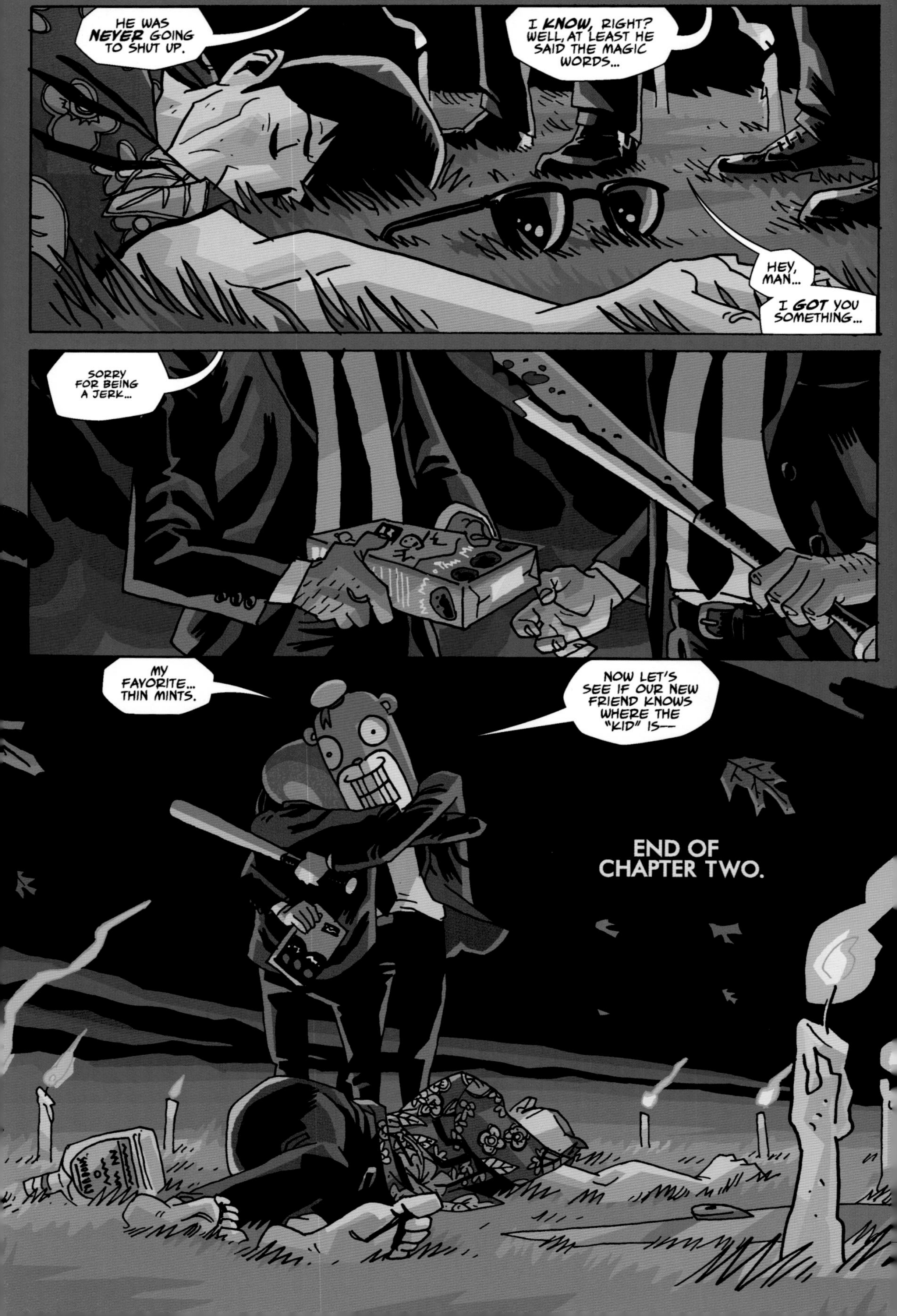
HE WAS NEVER GOING TO SHUT UP.
I KNOW, RIGHT? WELL, AT LEAST HE SAID THE MAGIC WORDS...
HEY, MAN...
I GOT YOU SOMETHING...
SORRY FOR BEING A JERK...
MY FAVORITE... THIN MINTS.
NOW LET'S SEE IF OUR NEW FRIEND KNOWS WHERE THE "KID" IS--
END OF CHAPTER TWO.

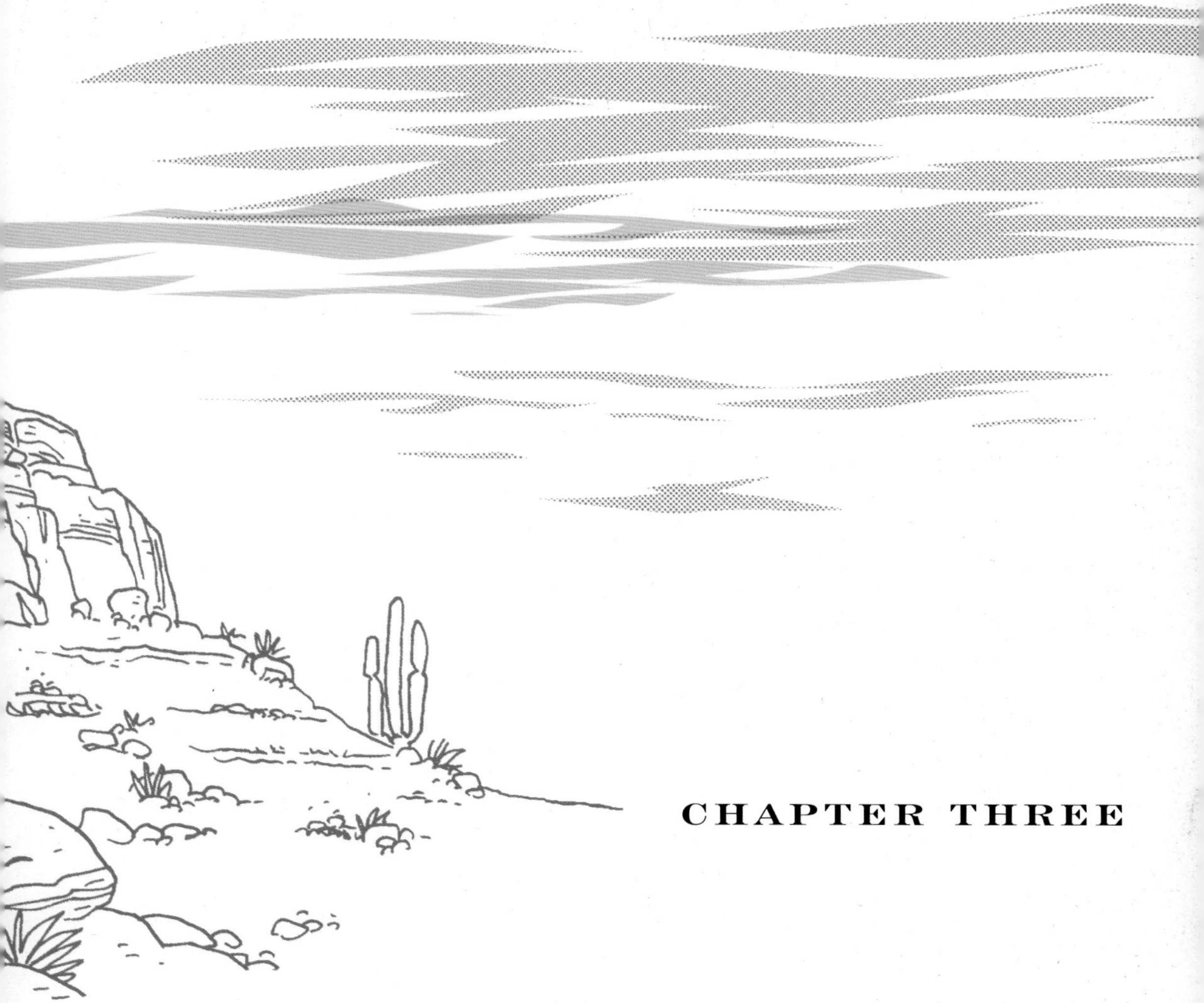

CHAPTER THREE

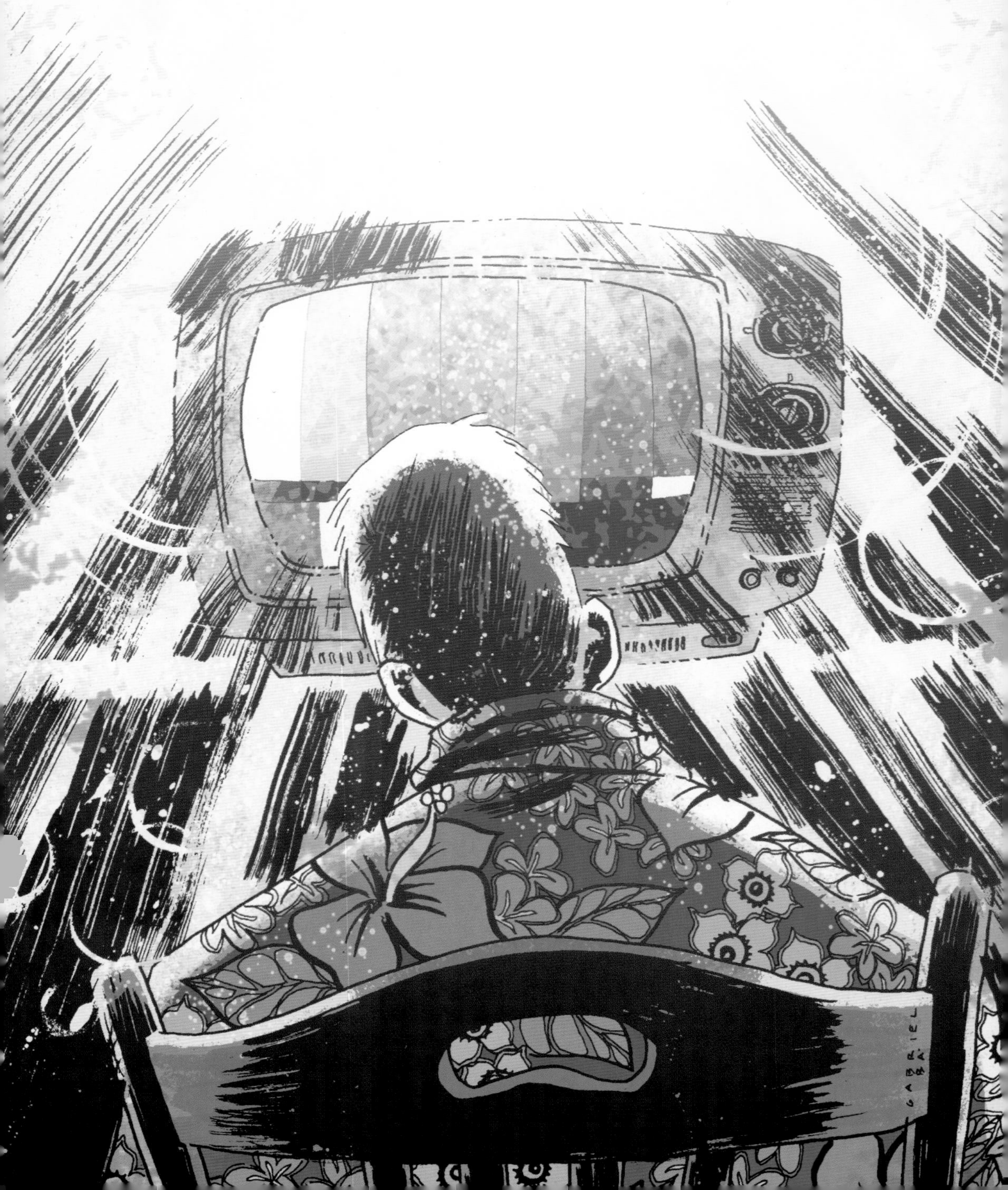
GABRIEL BÁ

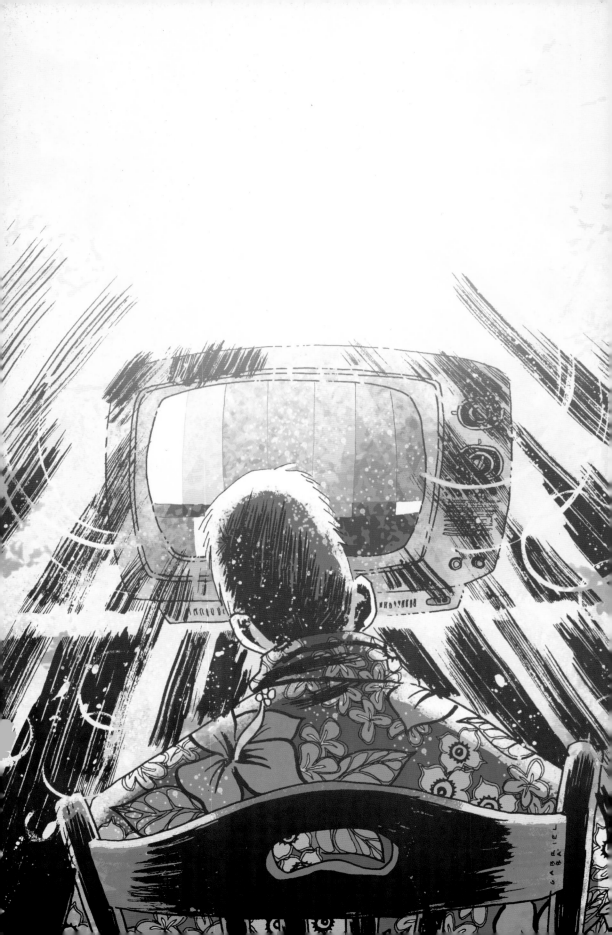

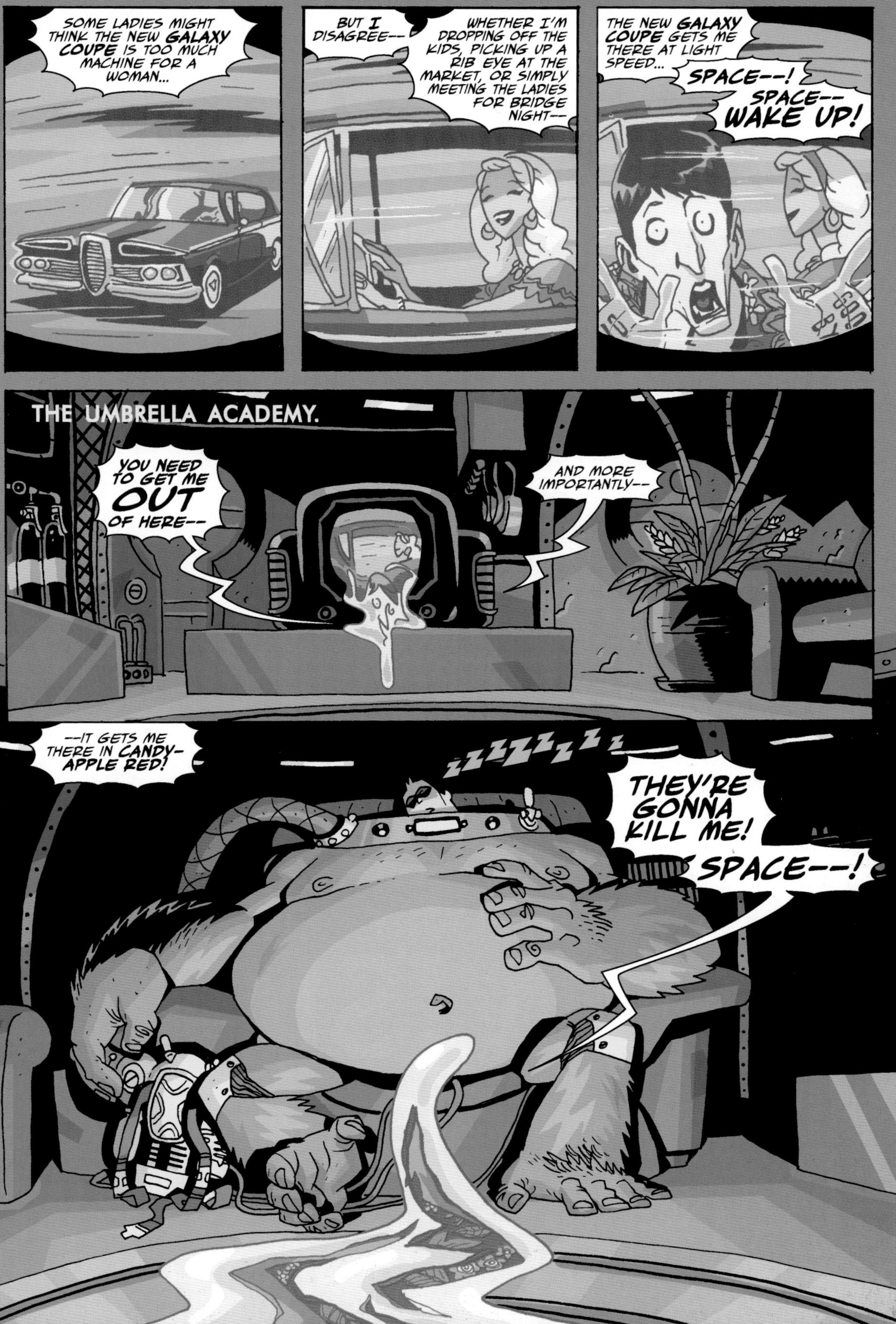
SOME LADIES MIGHT THINK THE NEW GALAXY COUPE IS TOO MUCH MACHINE FOR A WOMAN...
BUT I DISAGREE--
WHETHER I'M DROPPING OFF THE KIDS, PICKING UP A RIB EYE AT THE MARKET, OR SIMPLY MEETING THE LADIES FOR BRIDGE NIGHT--
THE NEW GALAXY COUPE GETS ME THERE AT LIGHT SPEED...
SPACE--!
SPACE-- WAKE UP!
THE UMBRELLA ACADEMY.
YOU NEED TO GET ME OUT OF HERE--
AND MORE IMPORTANTLY--
--IT GETS ME THERE IN CANDY-APPLE RED!
ZZZZZZZZZZ
THEY'RE GONNA KILL ME!
SPACE--!

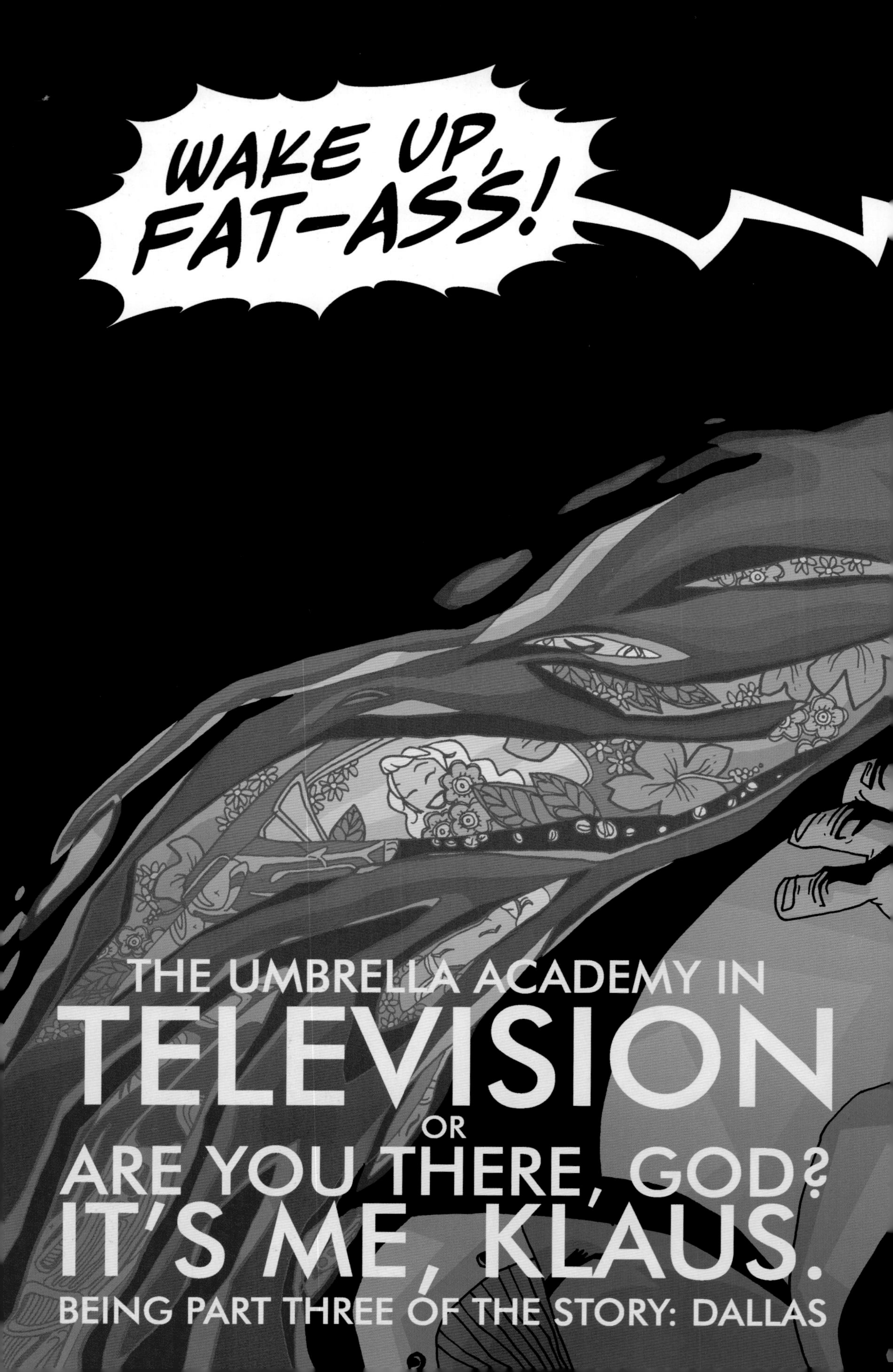
WAKE UP, FAT-ASS!
THE UMBRELLA ACADEMY IN
TELEVISION
OR
ARE YOU THERE, GOD? IT'S ME, KLAUS.
BEING PART THREE OF THE STORY: DALLAS

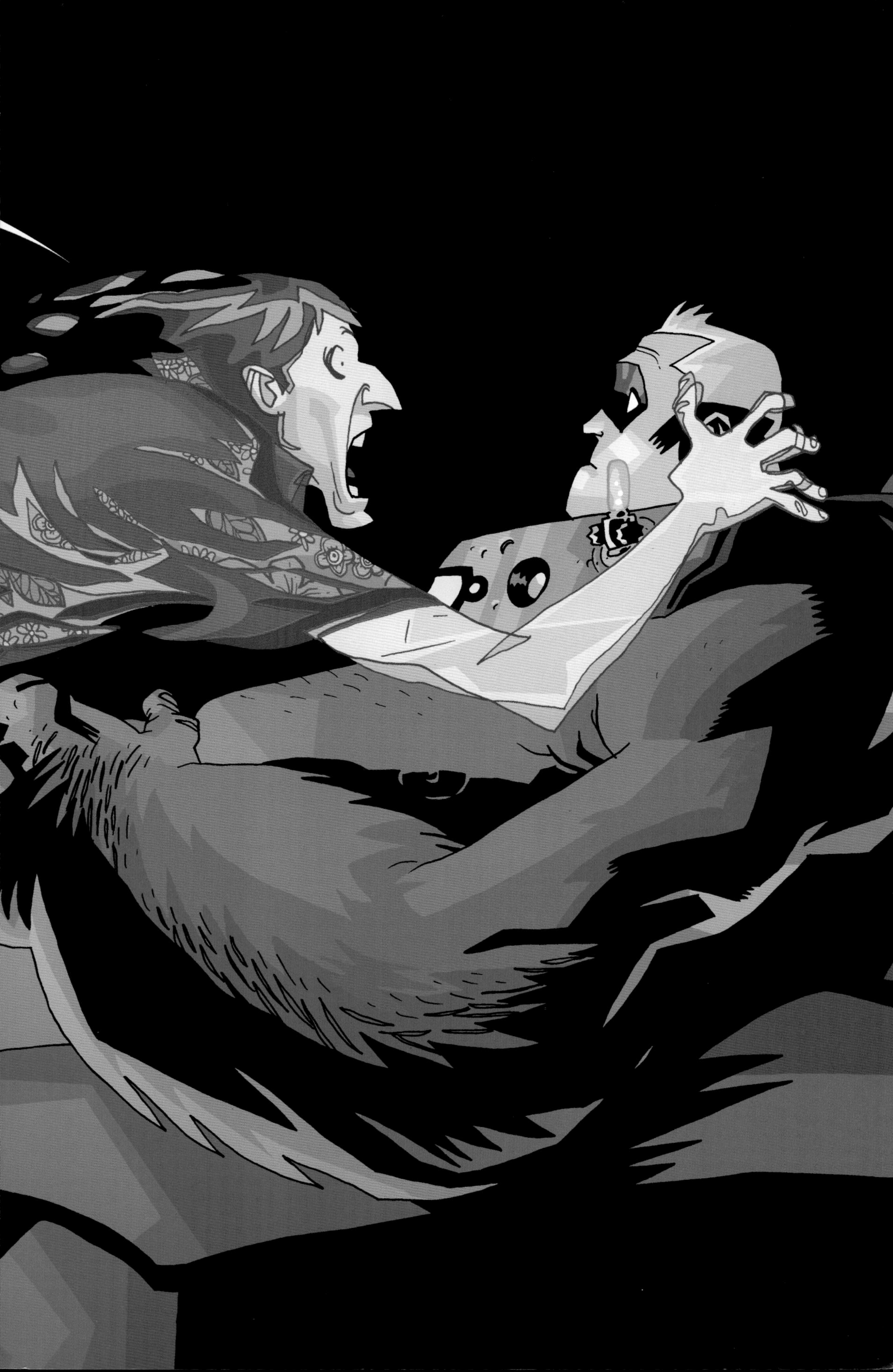

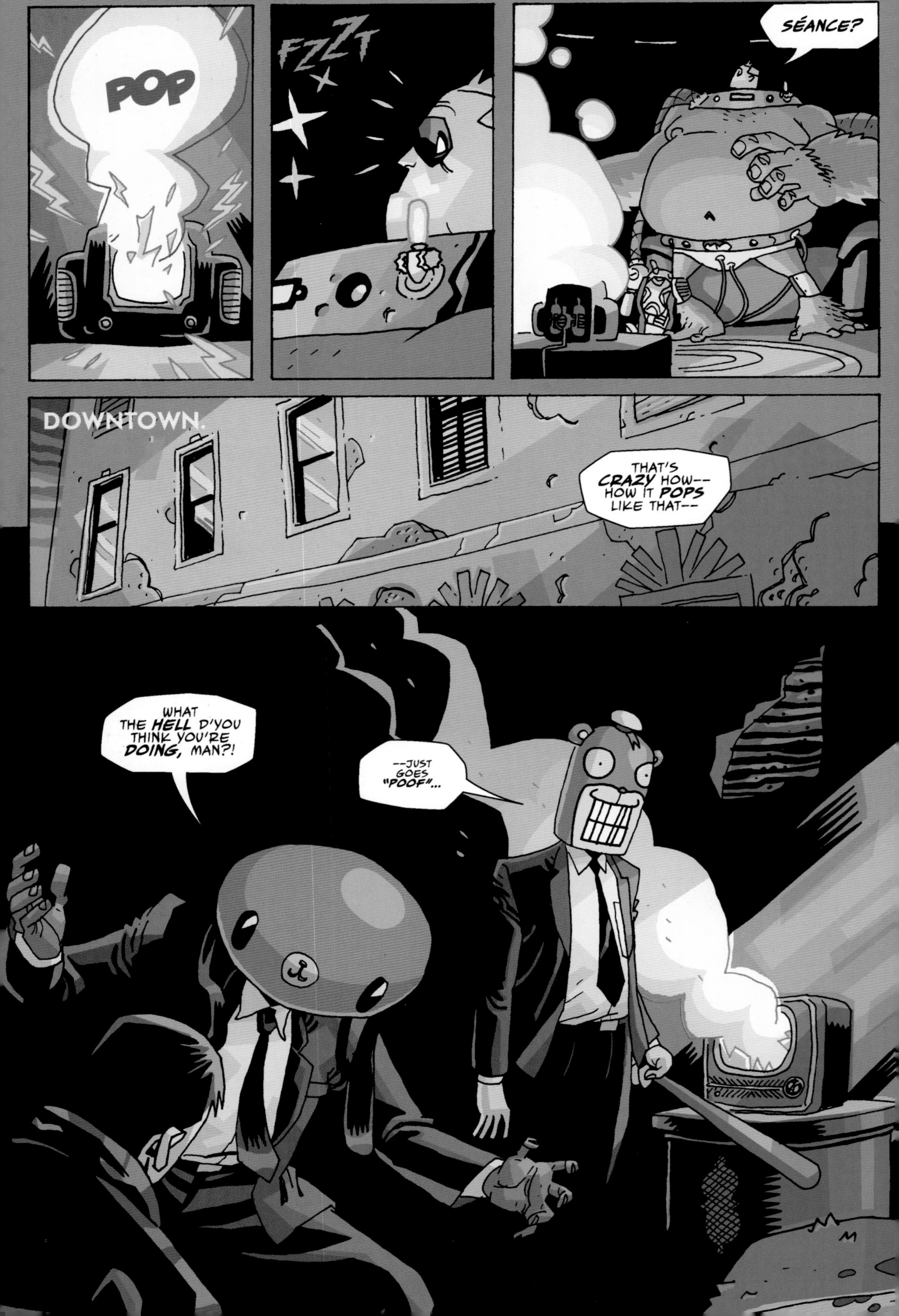
POP
FZZZT
SÉANCE?
DOWNTOWN.
THAT'S CRAZY HOW-- HOW IT POPS LIKE THAT--
WHAT THE HELL D'YOU THINK YOU'RE DOING, MAN?!
--JUST GOES "POOF"...

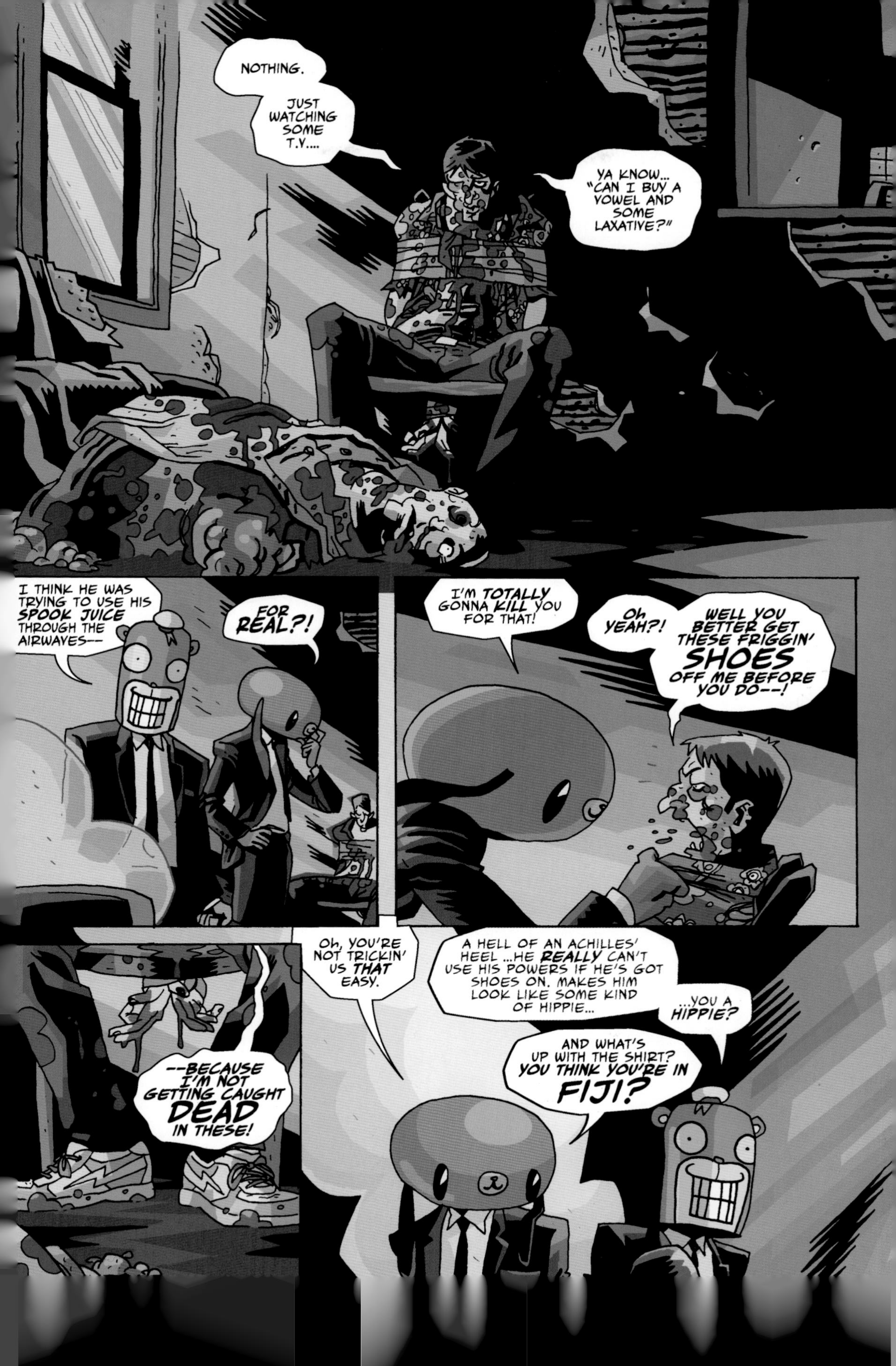
NOTHING.
JUST WATCHING SOME T.V....
YA KNOW... "CAN I BUY A VOWEL AND SOME LAXATIVE?"
I THINK HE WAS TRYING TO USE HIS SPOOK JUICE THROUGH THE AIRWAVES--
FOR REAL?!
I'M TOTALLY GONNA KILL YOU FOR THAT!
Oh YEAH?!
WELL YOU BETTER GET THESE FRIGGIN' SHOES OFF ME BEFORE YOU DO--!
--BECAUSE I'M NOT GETTING CAUGHT DEAD IN THESE!
Oh, YOU'RE NOT TRICKIN' US THAT EASY.
A HELL OF AN ACHILLES' HEEL ...HE REALLY CAN'T USE HIS POWERS IF HE'S GOT SHOES ON. MAKES HIM LOOK LIKE SOME KIND OF HIPPIE...
...YOU A HIPPIE?
AND WHAT'S UP WITH THE SHIRT? YOU THINK YOU'RE IN FIJI?

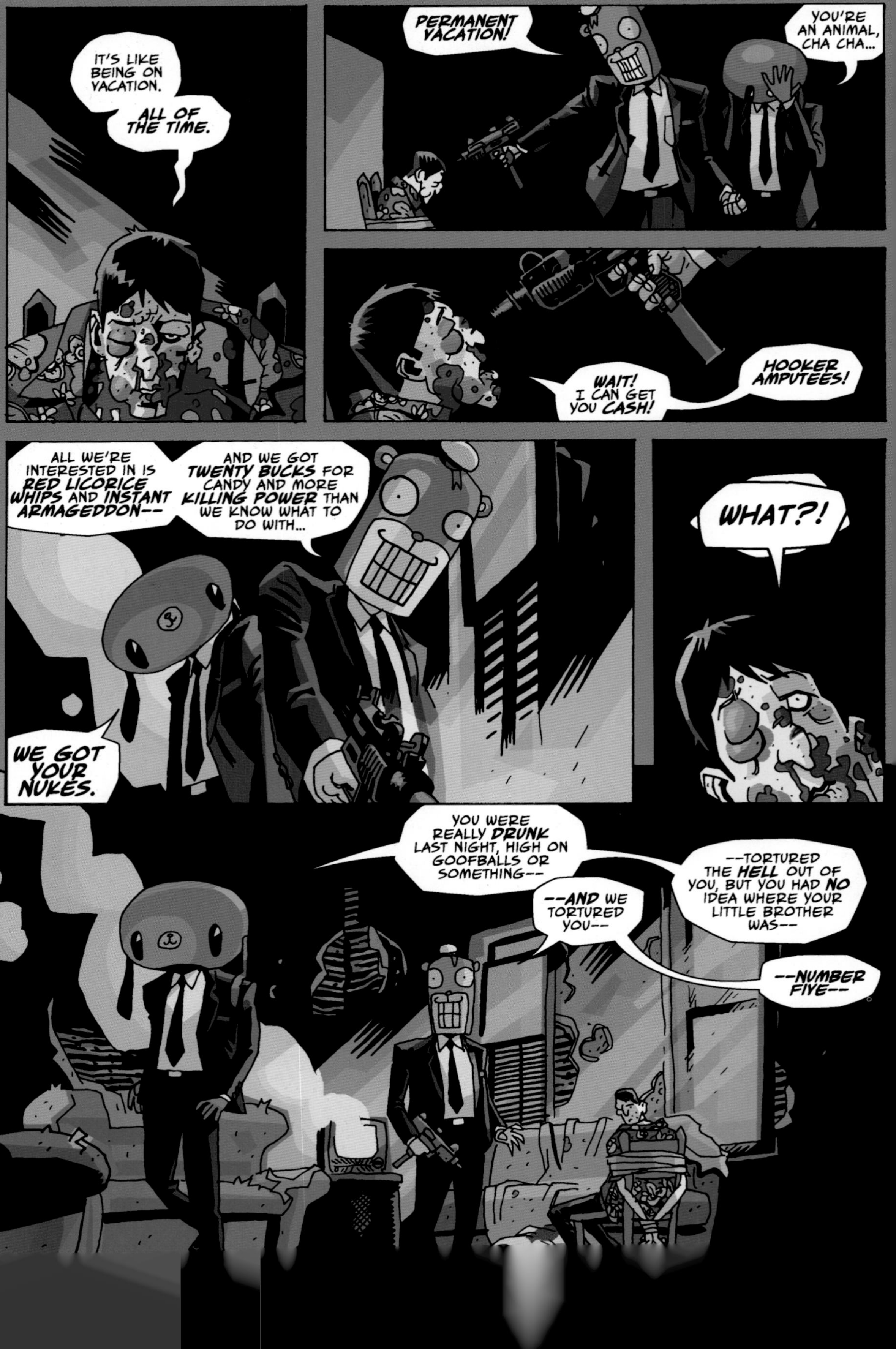
IT'S LIKE BEING ON VACATION.
ALL OF THE TIME.
PERMANENT VACATION!
YOU'RE AN ANIMAL, CHA CHA...
WAIT! I CAN GET YOU CASH!
HOOKER AMPUTEES!
ALL WE'RE INTERESTED IN IS RED LICORICE WHIPS AND INSTANT ARMAGEDDON--
AND WE GOT TWENTY BUCKS FOR CANDY AND MORE KILLING POWER THAN WE KNOW WHAT TO DO WITH...
WE GOT YOUR NUKES.
WHAT?!
YOU WERE REALLY DRUNK LAST NIGHT, HIGH ON GOOFBALLS OR SOMETHING--
--AND WE TORTURED YOU--
--TORTURED THE HELL OUT OF YOU, BUT YOU HAD NO IDEA WHERE YOUR LITTLE BROTHER WAS--
--NUMBER FIVE--

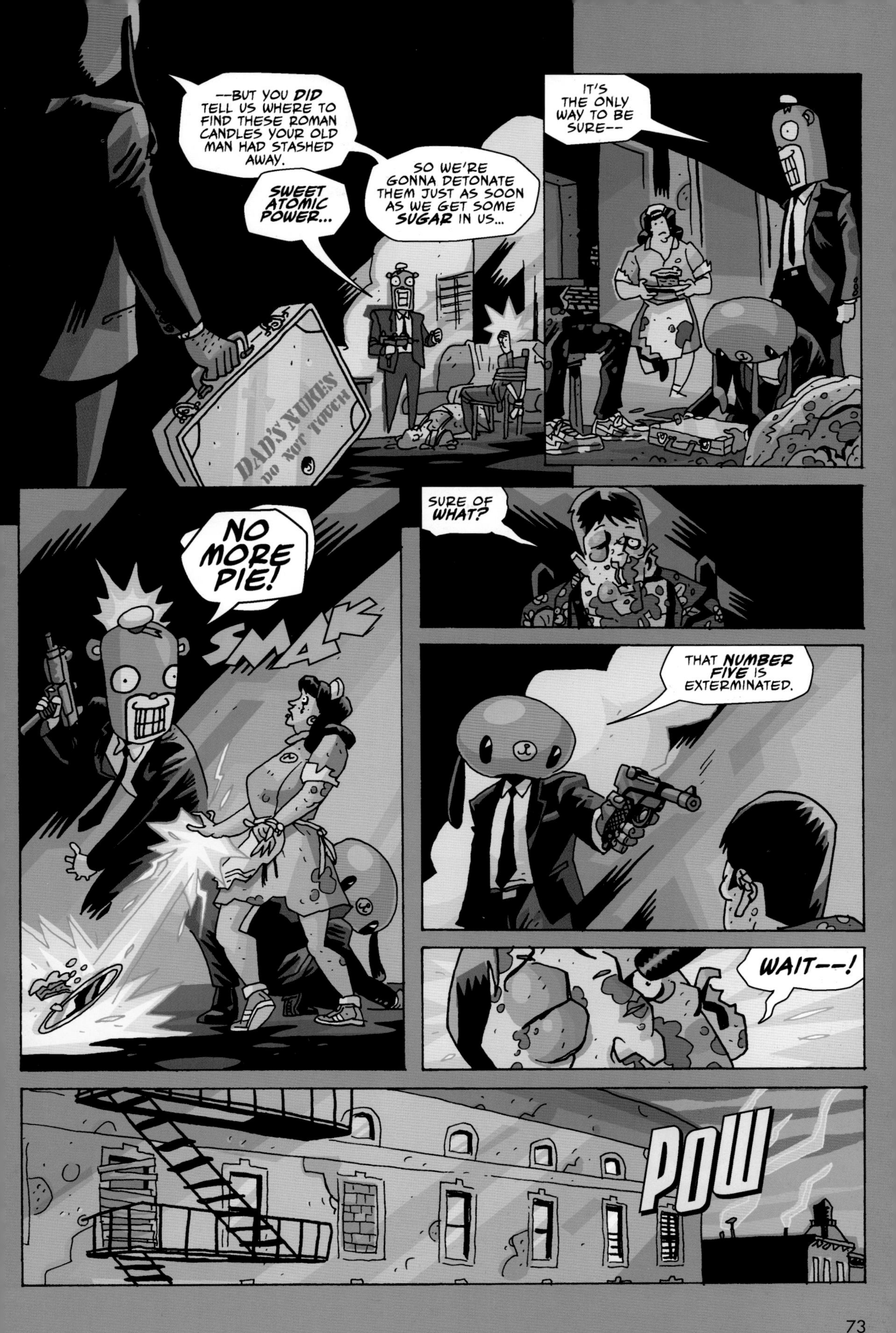
--BUT YOU DID TELL US WHERE TO FIND THESE ROMAN CANDLES YOUR OLD MAN HAD STASHED AWAY.
SO WE'RE GONNA DETONATE THEM JUST AS SOON AS WE GET SOME SUGAR IN US...
SWEET ATOMIC POWER...
DAD'S NUKES DO NOT TOUCH
IT'S THE ONLY WAY TO BE SURE--
NO MORE PIE!
SMAK
SURE OF WHAT?
THAT NUMBER FIVE IS EXTERMINATED.
WAIT--!
POW

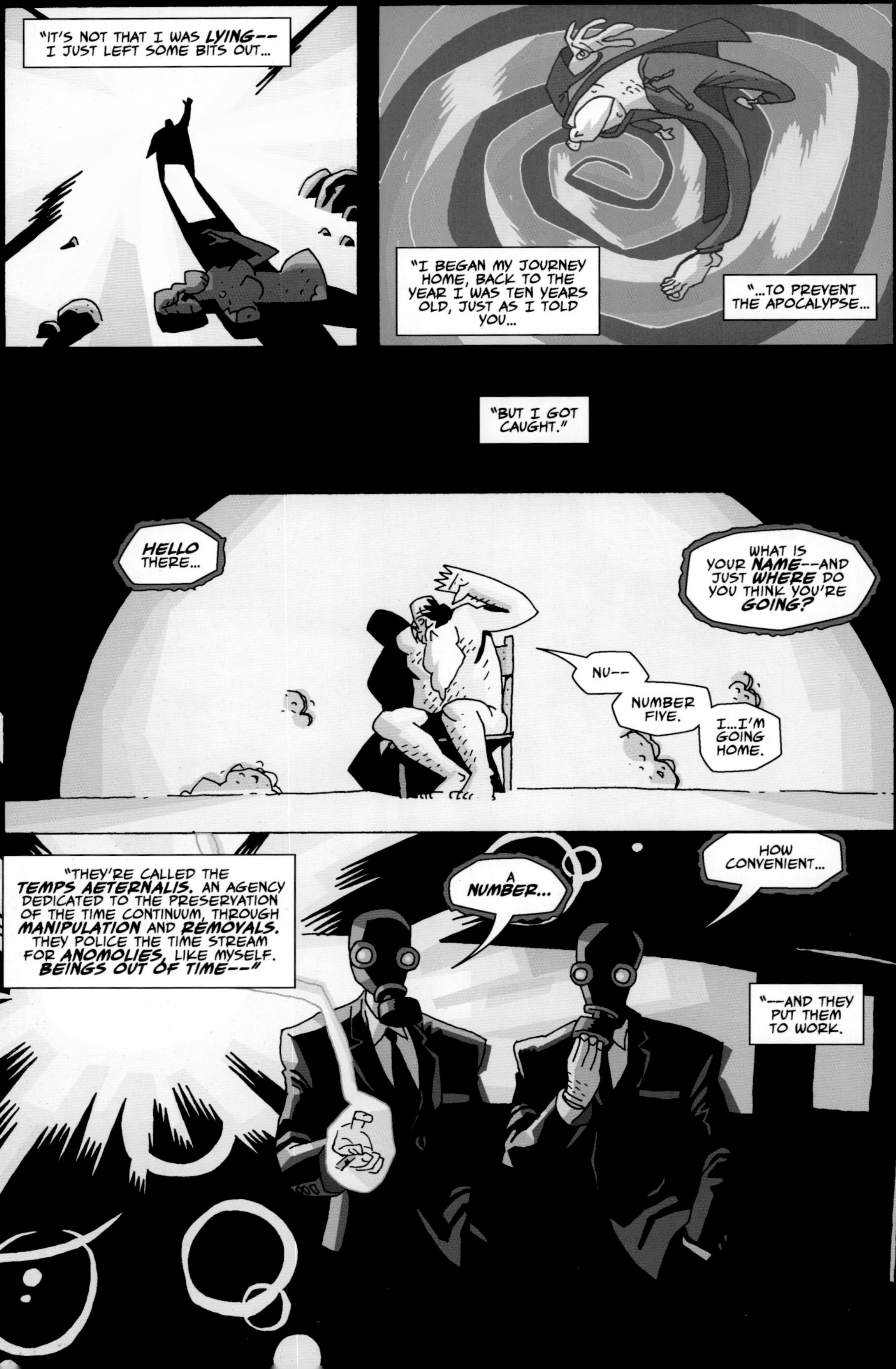
"IT'S NOT THAT I WAS LYING-- I JUST LEFT SOME BITS OUT...
"I BEGAN MY JOURNEY HOME, BACK TO THE YEAR I WAS TEN YEARS OLD, JUST AS I TOLD YOU...
"...TO PREVENT THE APOCALYPSE...
"BUT I GOT CAUGHT."
HELLO THERE...
WHAT IS YOUR NAME--AND JUST WHERE DO YOU THINK YOU'RE GOING?
NU--
NUMBER FIVE.
I...I'M GOING HOME.
"THEY'RE CALLED THE TEMPS AETERNALIS. AN AGENCY DEDICATED TO THE PRESERVATION OF THE TIME CONTINUUM, THROUGH MANIPULATION AND REMOVALS. THEY POLICE THE TIME STREAM FOR ANOMOLIES, LIKE MYSELF. BEINGS OUT OF TIME--"
A NUMBER...
HOW CONVENIENT...
"--AND THEY PUT THEM TO WORK.

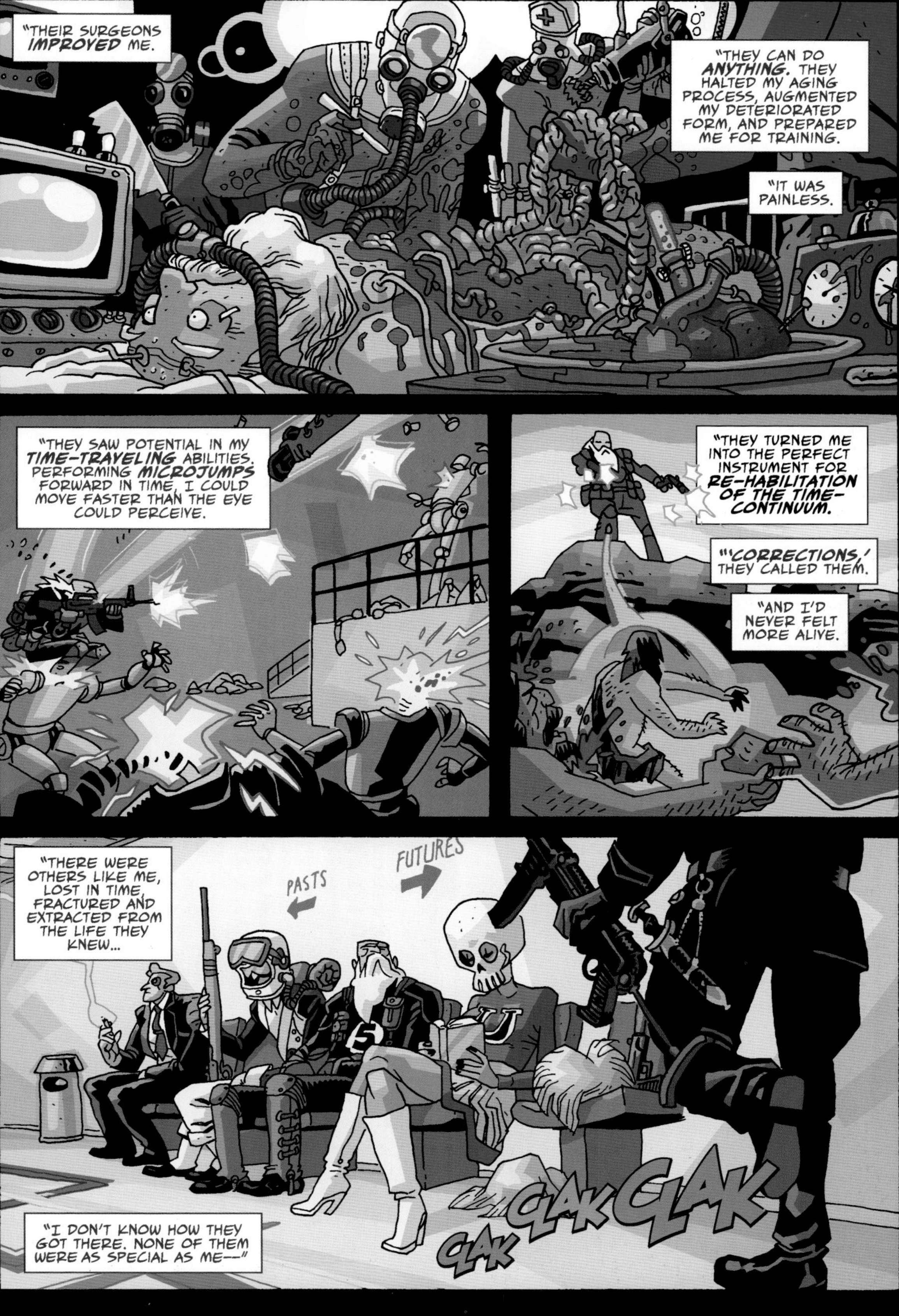
"THEIR SURGEONS IMPROVED ME.
"THEY CAN DO ANYTHING. THEY HALTED MY AGING PROCESS, AUGMENTED MY DETERIORATED FORM, AND PREPARED ME FOR TRAINING.
"IT WAS PAINLESS.
"THEY SAW POTENTIAL IN MY TIME-TRAVELING ABILITIES. PERFORMING MICROJUMPS FORWARD IN TIME, I COULD MOVE FASTER THAN THE EYE COULD PERCEIVE.
"THEY TURNED ME INTO THE PERFECT INSTRUMENT FOR RE-HABILITATION OF THE TIME-CONTINUUM.
"'CORRECTIONS,' THEY CALLED THEM.
"AND I'D NEVER FELT MORE ALIVE.
"THERE WERE OTHERS LIKE ME, LOST IN TIME, FRACTURED AND EXTRACTED FROM THE LIFE THEY KNEW...
FUTURES
PASTS
"I DON'T KNOW HOW THEY GOT THERE. NONE OF THEM WERE AS SPECIAL AS ME--"
CLAK CLAK CLAK

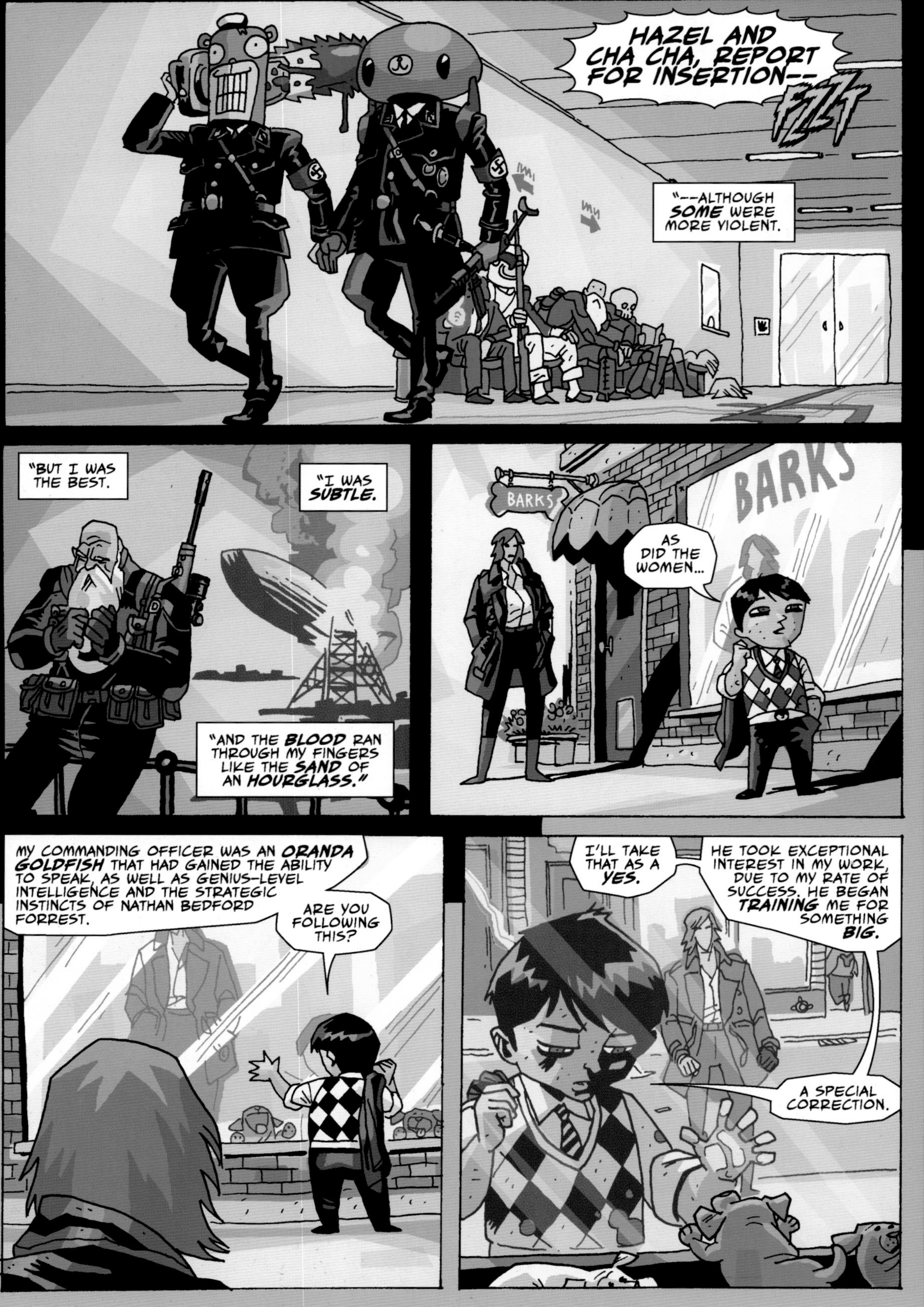
HAZEL AND CHA CHA, REPORT FOR INSERTION--
FZZT
"--ALTHOUGH SOME WERE MORE VIOLENT.
"BUT I WAS THE BEST.
"I WAS SUBTLE.
"AND THE BLOOD RAN THROUGH MY FINGERS LIKE THE SAND OF AN HOURGLASS."
BARKS
BARKS
AS DID THE WOMEN...
MY COMMANDING OFFICER WAS AN ORANDA GOLDFISH THAT HAD GAINED THE ABILITY TO SPEAK, AS WELL AS GENIUS-LEVEL INTELLIGENCE AND THE STRATEGIC INSTINCTS OF NATHAN BEDFORD FORREST.
ARE YOU FOLLOWING THIS?
I'LL TAKE THAT AS A YES.
HE TOOK EXCEPTIONAL INTEREST IN MY WORK, DUE TO MY RATE OF SUCCESS. HE BEGAN TRAINING ME FOR SOMETHING BIG.
A SPECIAL CORRECTION.

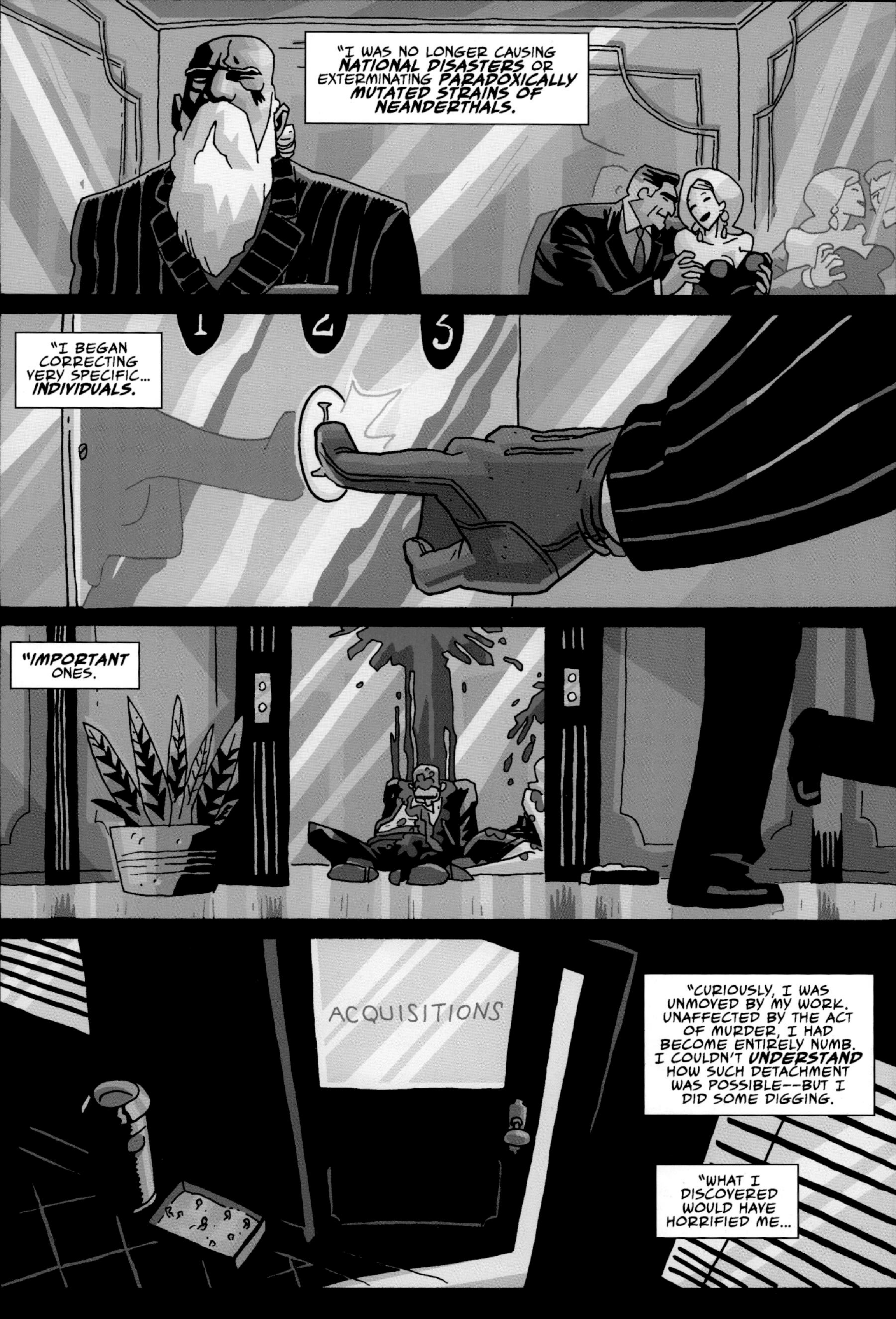
"I WAS NO LONGER CAUSING NATIONAL DISASTERS OR EXTERMINATING PARADOXICALLY MUTATED STRAINS OF NEANDERTHALS.
1 2 3
"I BEGAN CORRECTING VERY SPECIFIC... INDIVIDUALS.
"IMPORTANT ONES.
ACQUISITIONS
"CURIOUSLY, I WAS UNMOVED BY MY WORK. UNAFFECTED BY THE ACT OF MURDER, I HAD BECOME ENTIRELY NUMB. I COULDN'T UNDERSTAND HOW SUCH DETACHMENT WAS POSSIBLE--BUT I DID SOME DIGGING.
"WHAT I DISCOVERED WOULD HAVE HORRIFIED ME...

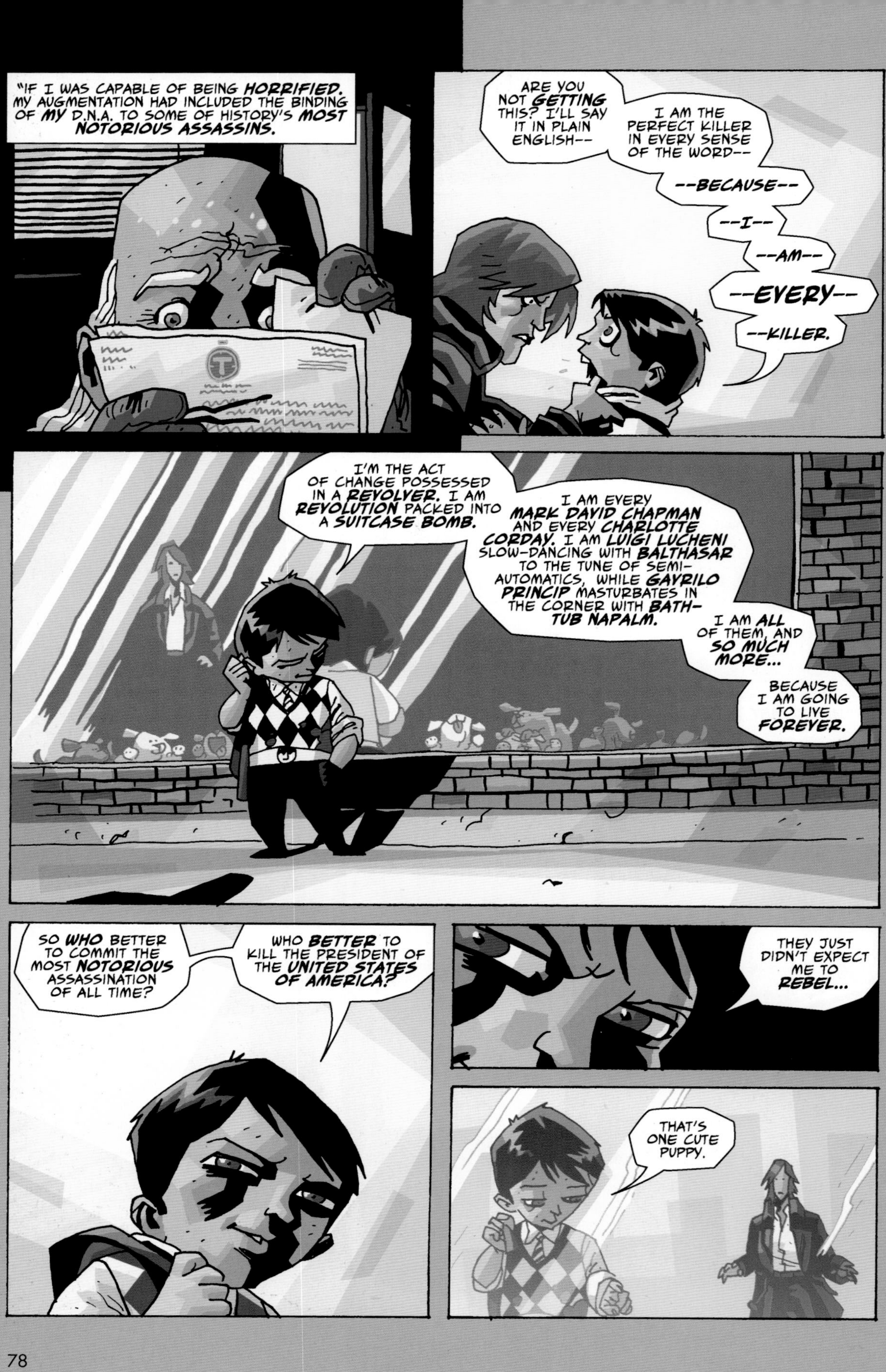
"IF I WAS CAPABLE OF BEING HORRIFIED. MY AUGMENTATION HAD INCLUDED THE BINDING OF MY D.N.A. TO SOME OF HISTORY'S MOST NOTORIOUS ASSASSINS.
ARE YOU NOT GETTING THIS? I'LL SAY IT IN PLAIN ENGLISH--
I AM THE PERFECT KILLER IN EVERY SENSE OF THE WORD--
--BECAUSE--
--I--
--AM--
--EVERY--
--KILLER.
I'M THE ACT OF CHANGE POSSESSED IN A REVOLVER. I AM REVOLUTION PACKED INTO A SUITCASE BOMB.
I AM EVERY MARK DAVID CHAPMAN AND EVERY CHARLOTTE CORDAY. I AM LUIGI LUCHENI SLOW-DANCING WITH BALTHASAR TO THE TUNE OF SEMI-AUTOMATICS, WHILE GAVRILO PRINCIP MASTURBATES IN THE CORNER WITH BATH-TUB NAPALM.
I AM ALL OF THEM, AND SO MUCH MORE...
BECAUSE I AM GOING TO LIVE FOREVER.
SO WHO BETTER TO COMMIT THE MOST NOTORIOUS ASSASSINATION OF ALL TIME?
WHO BETTER TO KILL THE PRESIDENT OF THE UNITED STATES OF AMERICA?
THEY JUST DIDN'T EXPECT ME TO REBEL...
THAT'S ONE CUTE PUPPY.

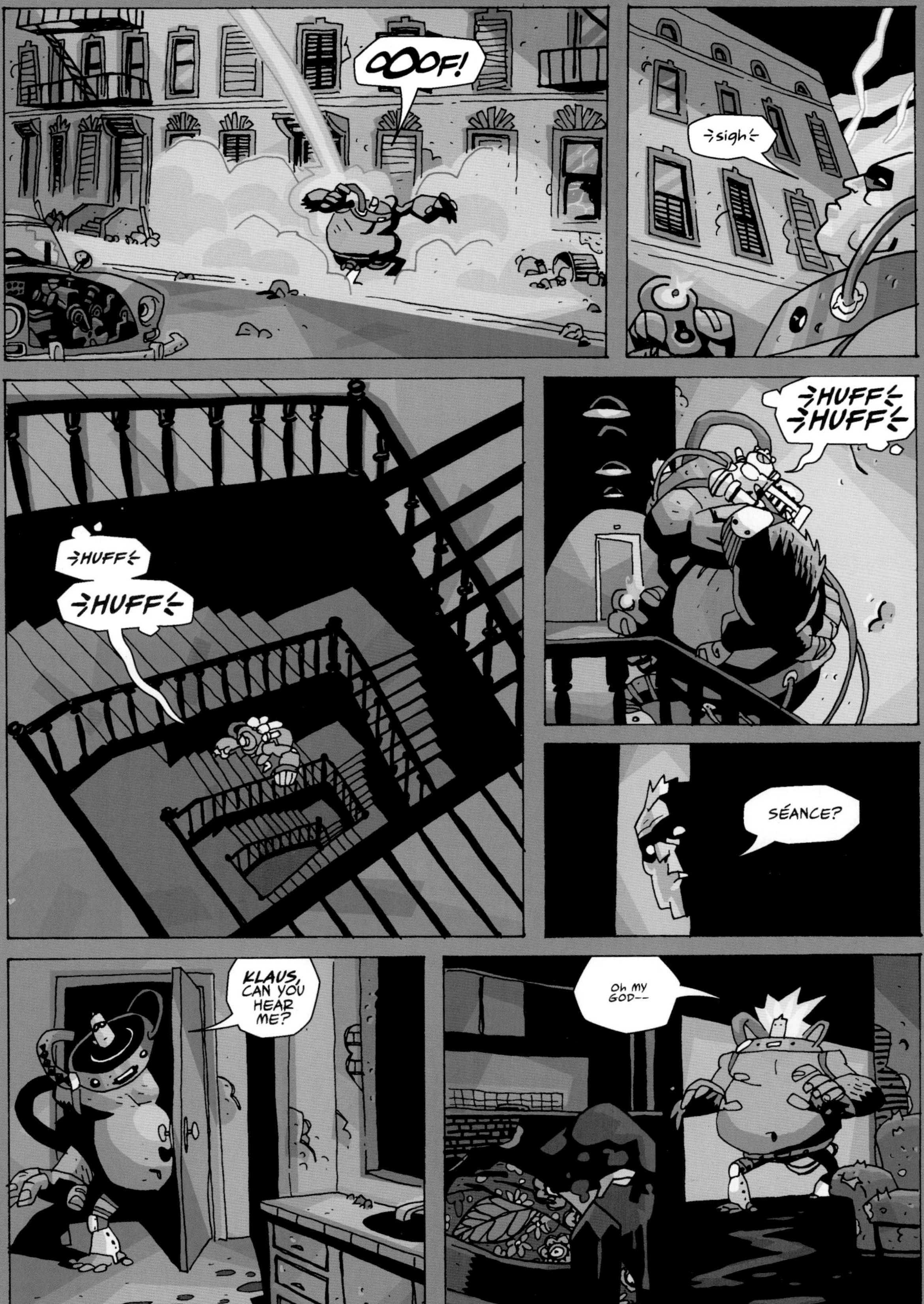
OOOF!
sigh
HUFF
HUFF
HUFF
HUFF
SÉANCE?
KLAUS, CAN YOU HEAR ME?
Oh MY GOD--

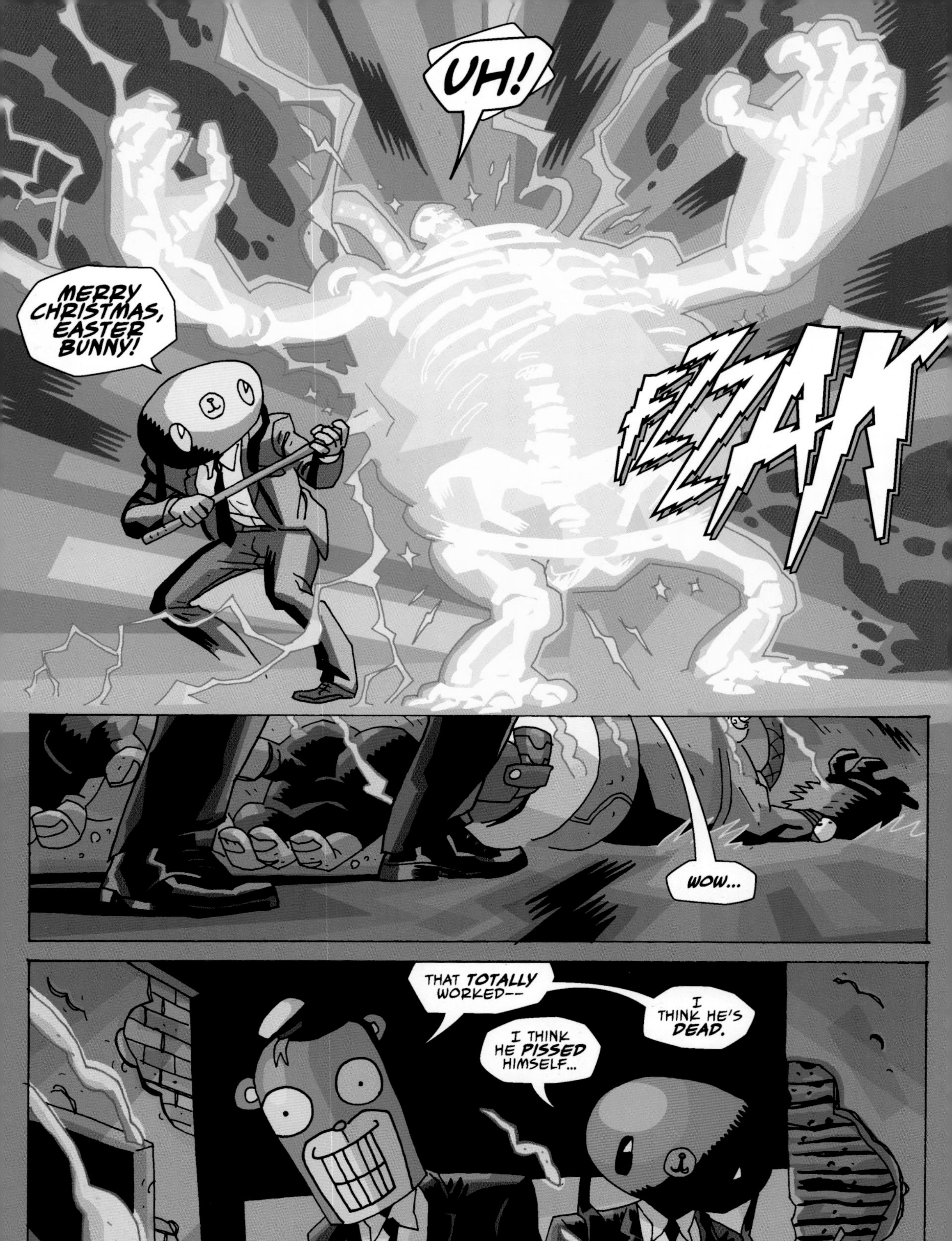
UH!
MERRY CHRISTMAS, EASTER BUNNY!
FZZAK
WOW...
THAT TOTALLY WORKED--
I THINK HE'S DEAD.
I THINK HE PISSED HIMSELF...

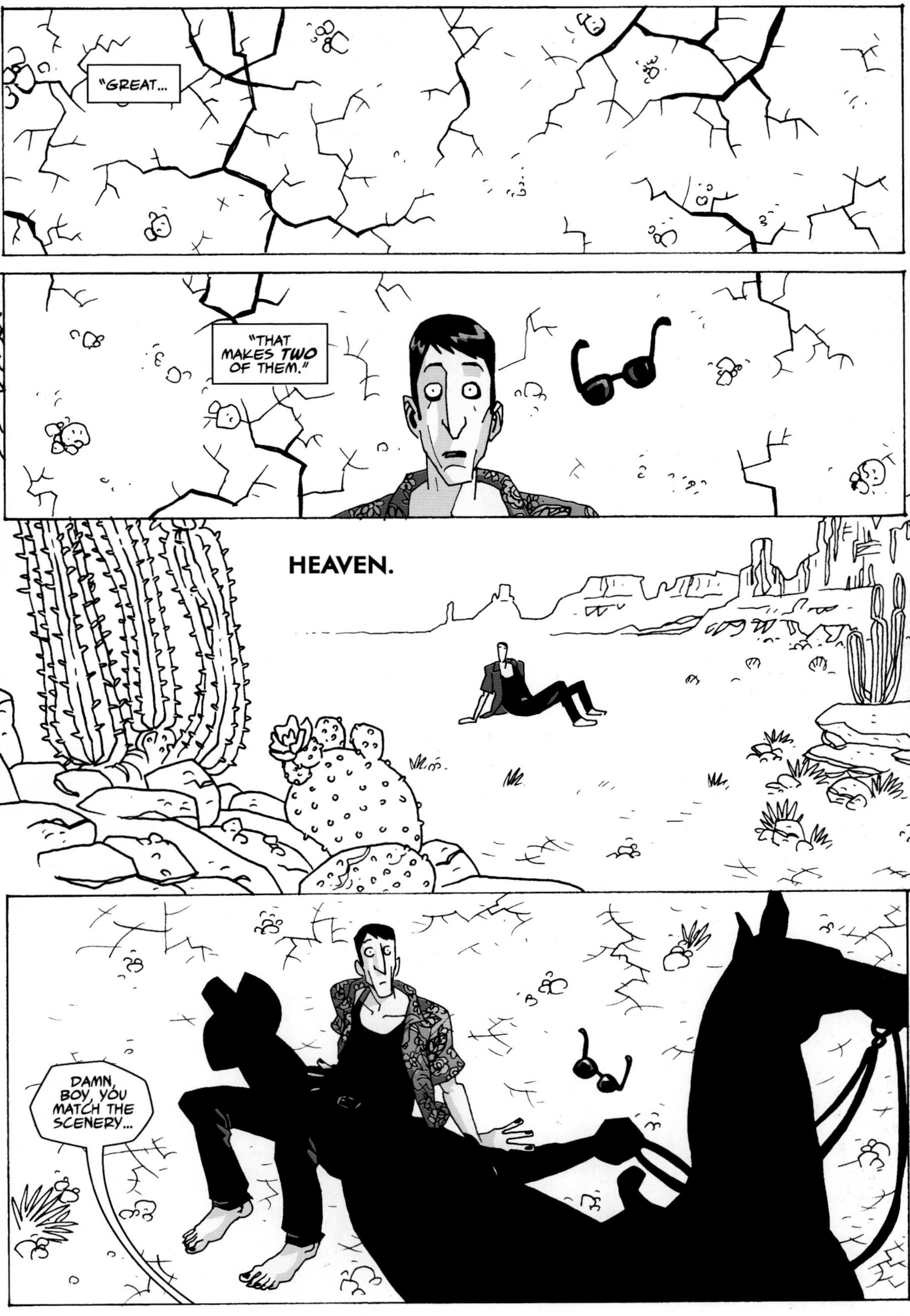
"GREAT...
"THAT MAKES TWO OF THEM."
HEAVEN.
DAMN, BOY, YOU MATCH THE SCENERY...

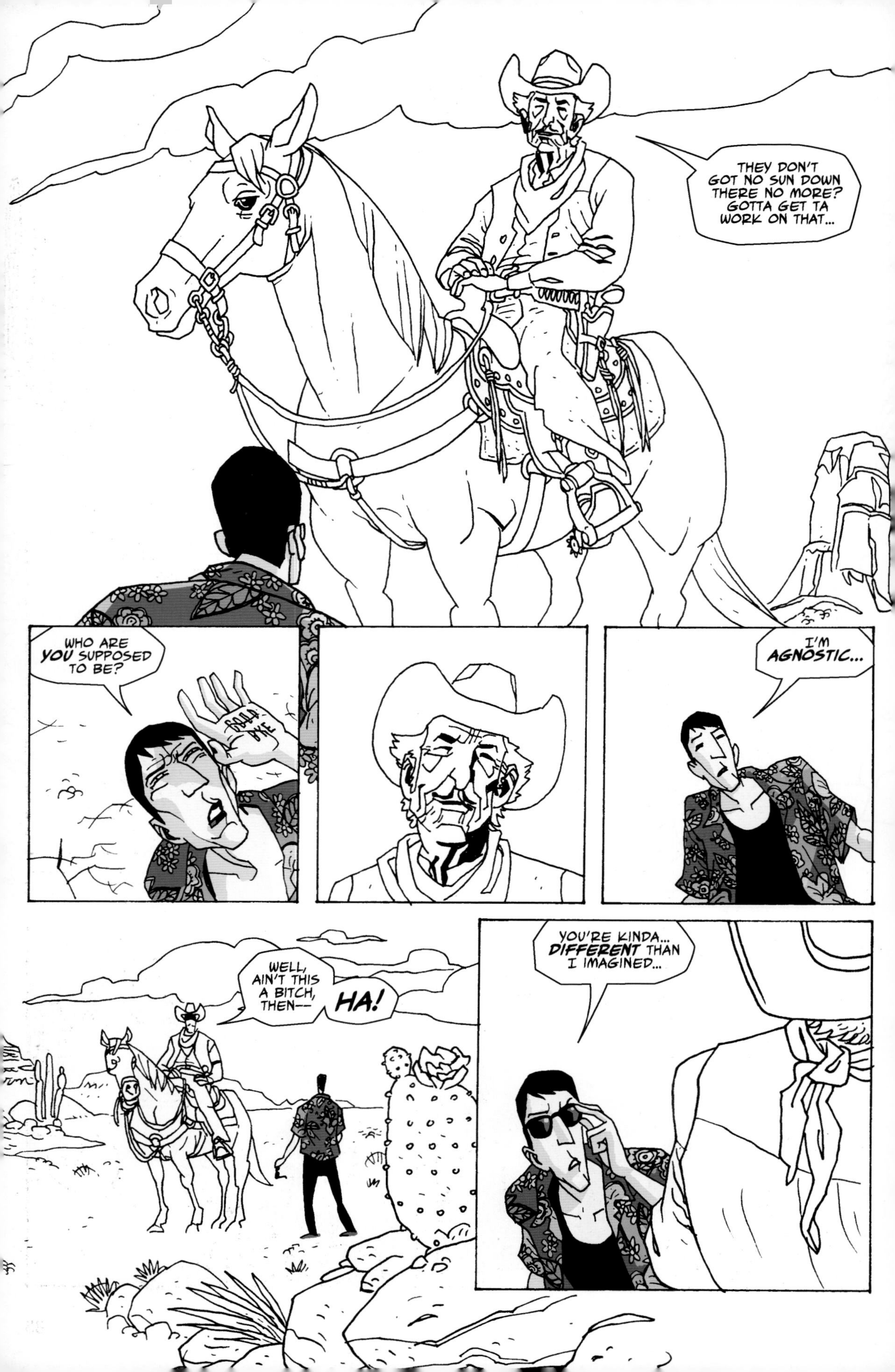
THEY DON'T GOT NO SUN DOWN THERE NO MORE? GOTTA GET TA WORK ON THAT...
WHO ARE YOU SUPPOSED TO BE?
I'M AGNOSTIC...
WELL, AIN'T THIS A BITCH, THEN--
HA!
YOU'RE KINDA... DIFFERENT THAN I IMAGINED...

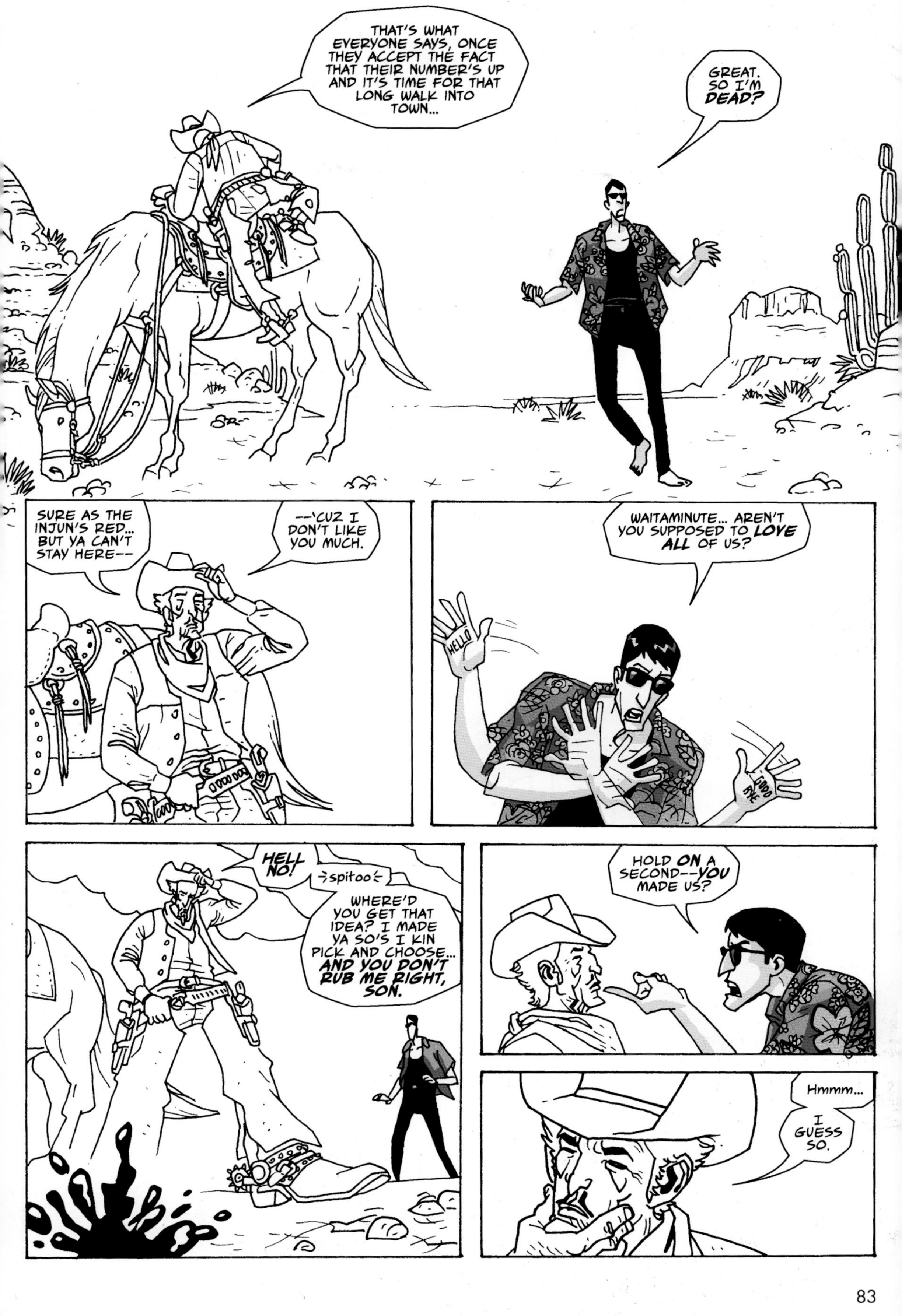
THAT'S WHAT EVERYONE SAYS, ONCE THEY ACCEPT THE FACT THAT THEIR NUMBER'S UP AND IT'S TIME FOR THAT LONG WALK INTO TOWN...
GREAT. SO I'M DEAD?
SURE AS THE INJUN'S RED... BUT YA CAN'T STAY HERE--
--'CUZ I DON'T LIKE YOU MUCH.
WAITAMINUTE... AREN'T YOU SUPPOSED TO LOVE ALL OF US?
HELLO
GOOD BYE
HELL NO!
spitoo
WHERE'D YOU GET THAT IDEA? I MADE YA SO'S I KIN PICK AND CHOOSE... AND YOU DON'T RUB ME RIGHT, SON.
HOLD ON A SECOND--YOU MADE US?
Hmmm...
I GUESS SO.

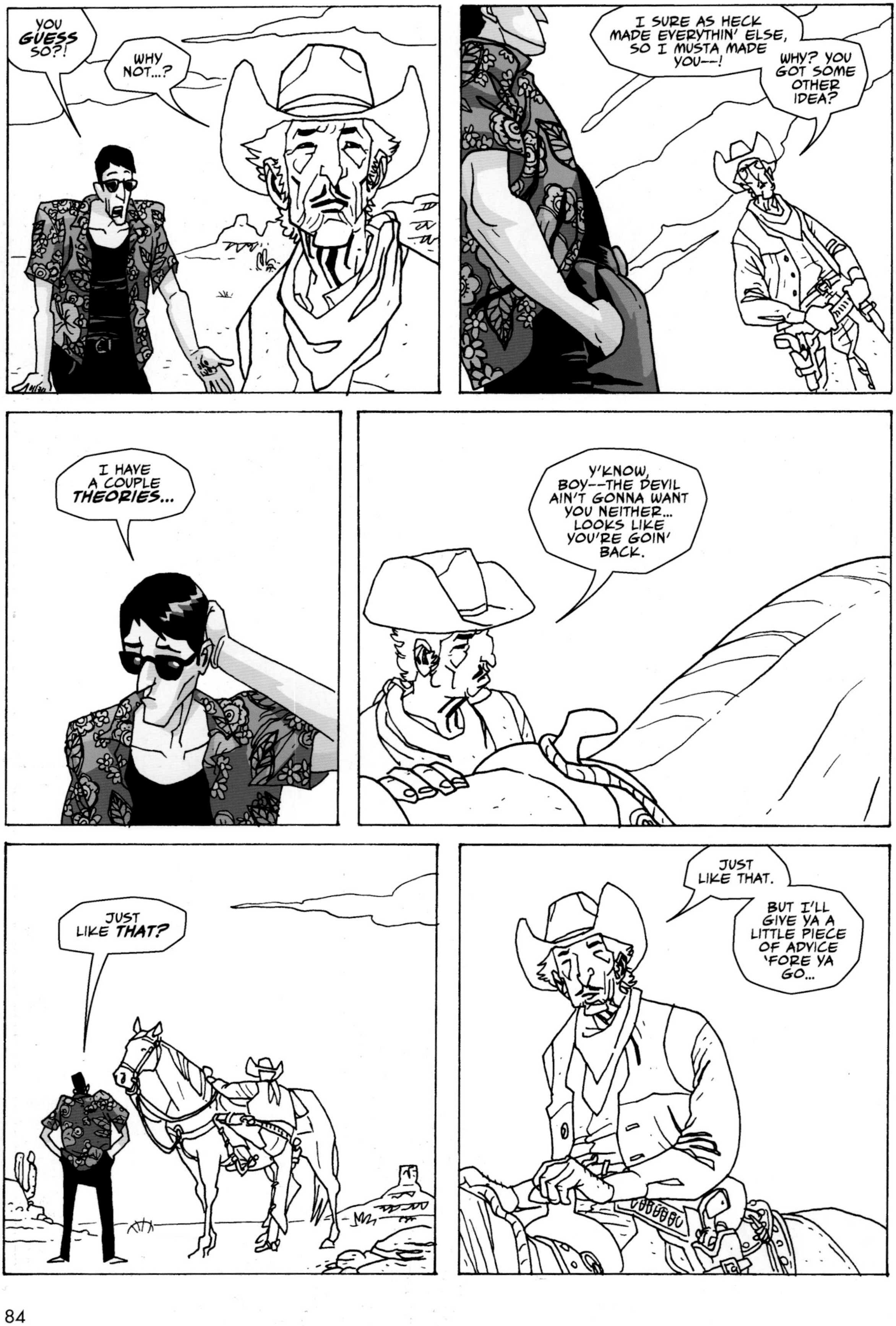

YOU GUESS SO?!
WHY NOT...?
I SURE AS HECK MADE EVERYTHIN' ELSE, SO I MUSTA MADE YOU--!
WHY? YOU GOT SOME OTHER IDEA?
I HAVE A COUPLE THEORIES...
Y'KNOW, BOY--THE DEVIL AIN'T GONNA WANT YOU NEITHER... LOOKS LIKE YOU'RE GOIN' BACK.
JUST LIKE THAT?
JUST LIKE THAT.
BUT I'LL GIVE YA A LITTLE PIECE OF ADVICE 'FORE YA GO...

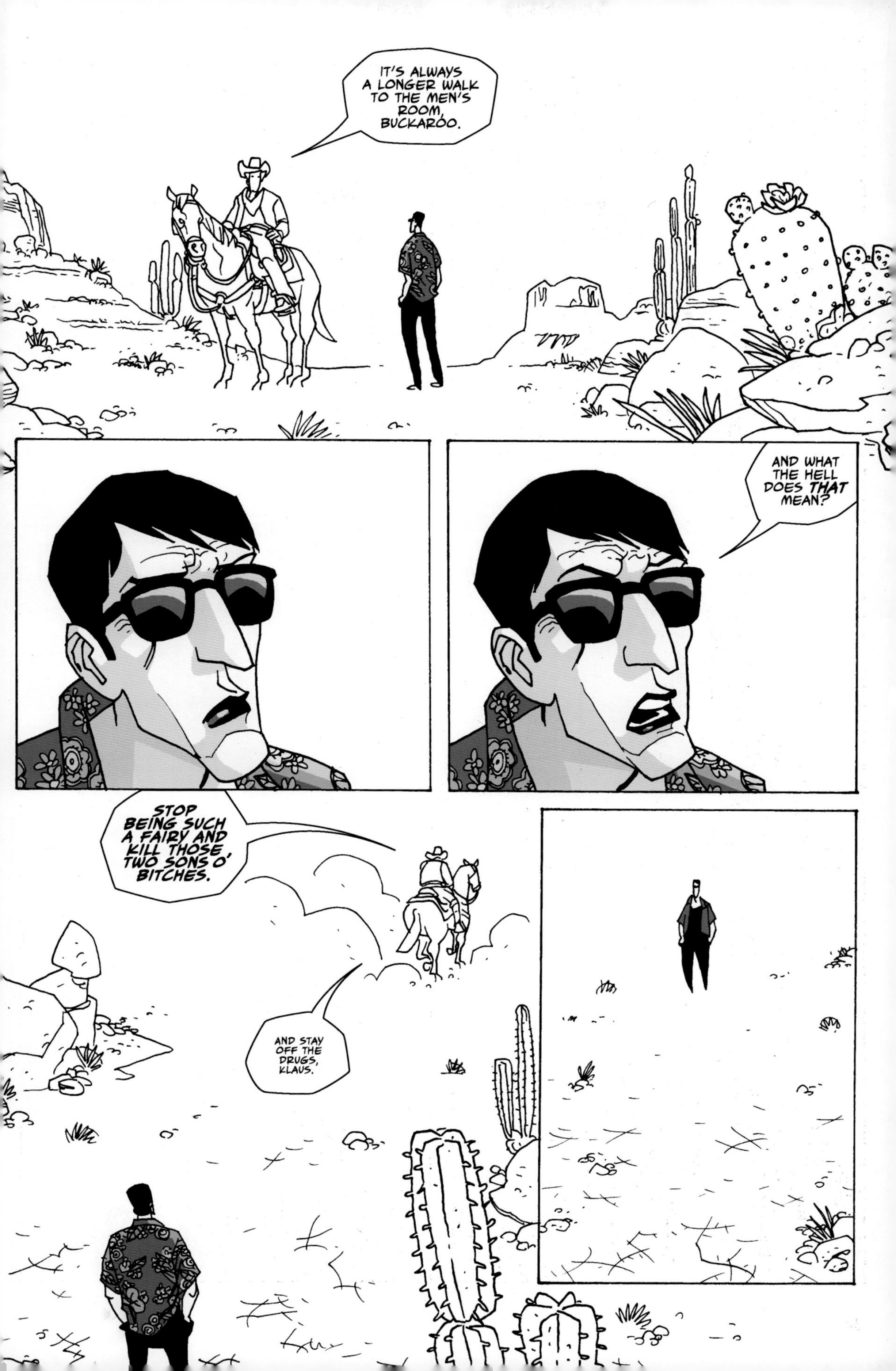
IT'S ALWAYS A LONGER WALK TO THE MEN'S ROOM, BUCKAROO.
AND WHAT THE HELL DOES THAT MEAN?
STOP BEING SUCH A FAIRY AND KILL THOSE TWO SONS O' BITCHES.
AND STAY OFF THE DRUGS, KLAUS.

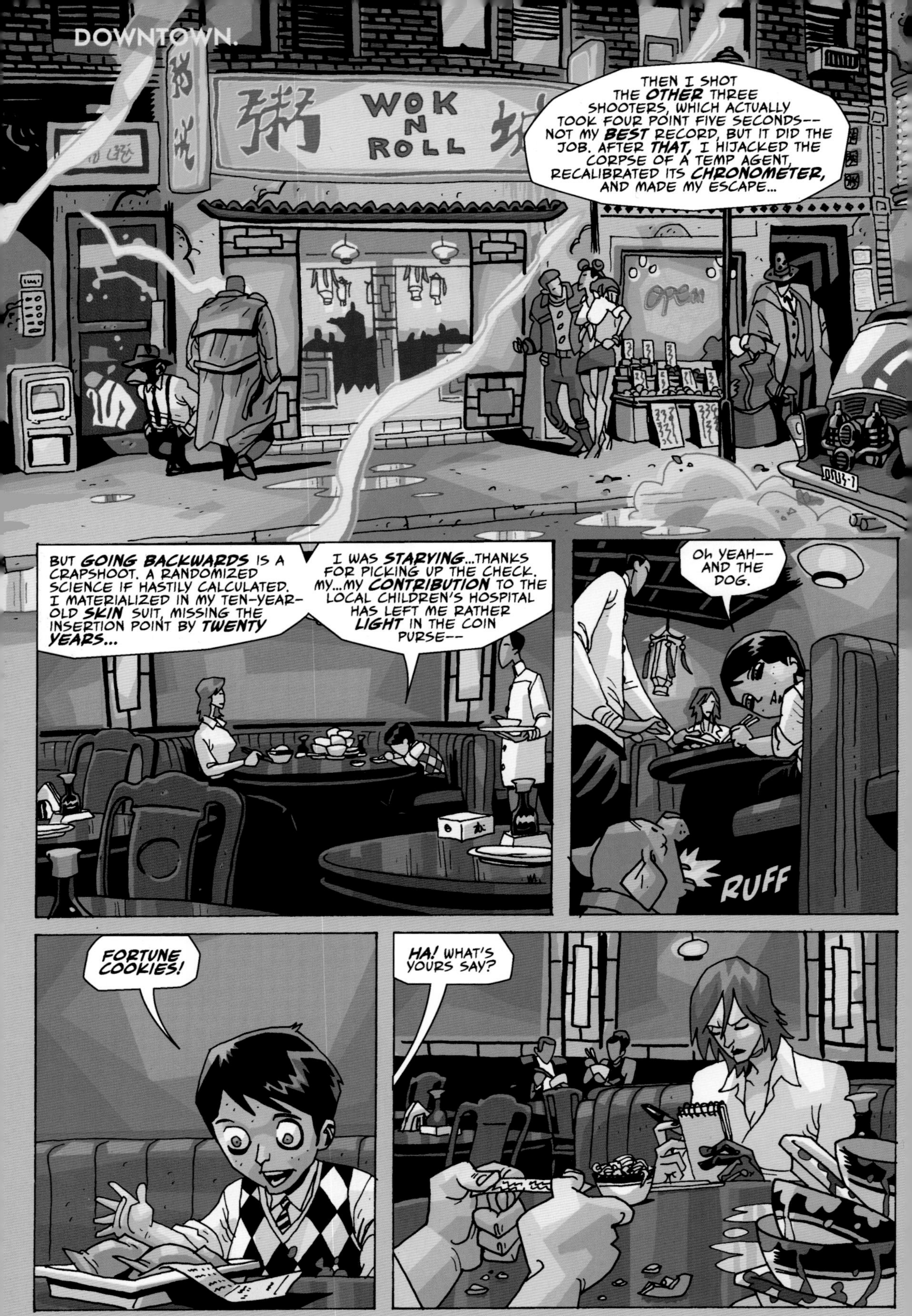
DOWNTOWN.
WOK N ROLL
THEN I SHOT THE OTHER THREE SHOOTERS, WHICH ACTUALLY TOOK FOUR POINT FIVE SECONDS-- NOT MY BEST RECORD, BUT IT DID THE JOB. AFTER THAT, I HIJACKED THE CORPSE OF A TEMP AGENT, RECALIBRATED ITS CHRONOMETER, AND MADE MY ESCAPE...
OPEN
BUT GOING BACKWARDS IS A CRAPSHOOT. A RANDOMIZED SCIENCE IF HASTILY CALCULATED. I MATERIALIZED IN MY TEN-YEAR-OLD SKIN SUIT, MISSING THE INSERTION POINT BY TWENTY YEARS...
I WAS STARVING...THANKS FOR PICKING UP THE CHECK. MY...MY CONTRIBUTION TO THE LOCAL CHILDREN'S HOSPITAL HAS LEFT ME RATHER LIGHT IN THE COIN PURSE--
Oh YEAH-- AND THE DOG.
RUFF
FORTUNE COOKIES!
HA! WHAT'S YOURS SAY?

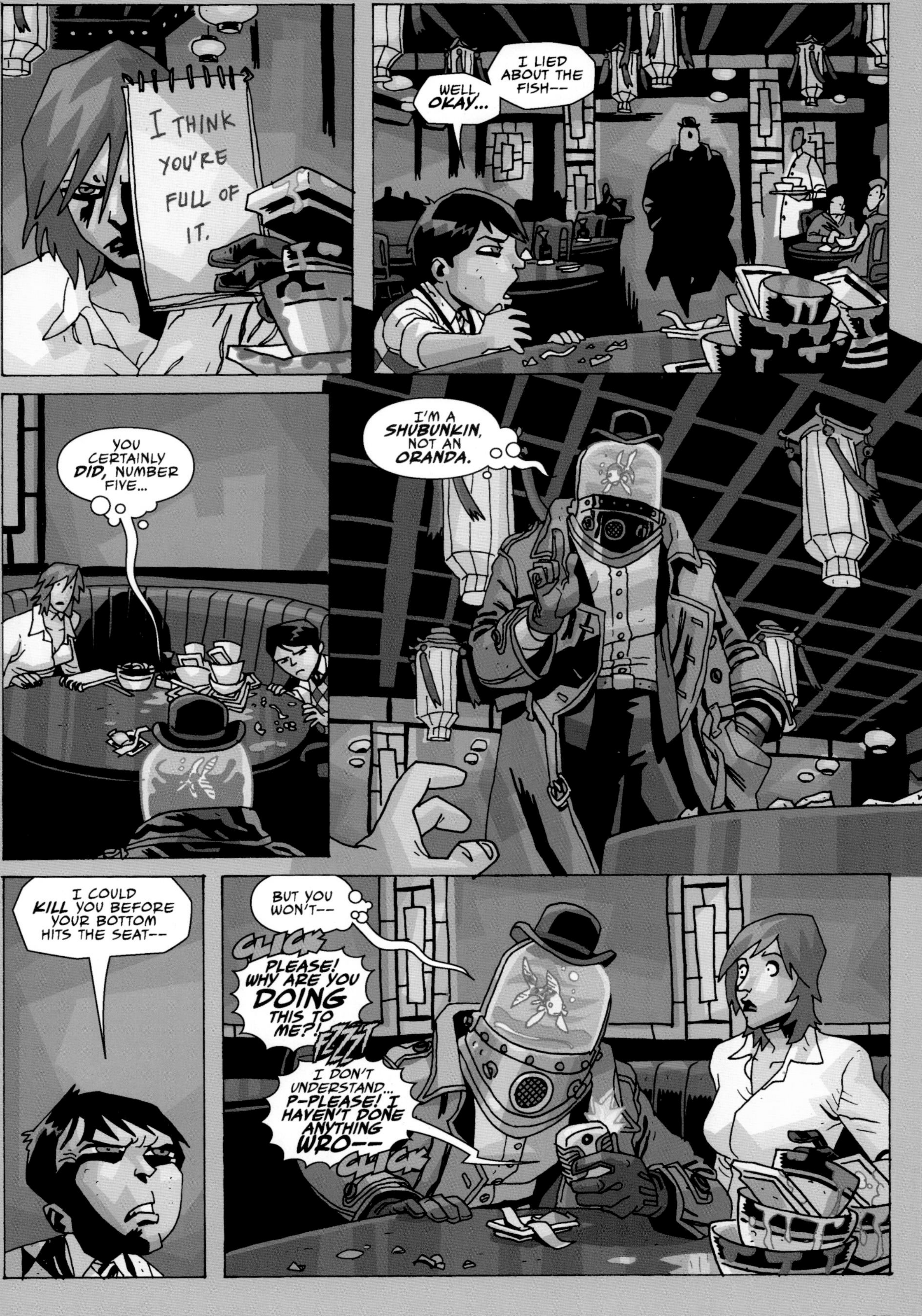
I THINK YOU'RE FULL OF IT.
I LIED ABOUT THE FISH--
WELL OKAY...
YOU CERTAINLY DID, NUMBER FIVE...
I'M A SHUBUNKIN, NOT AN ORANDA.
I COULD KILL YOU BEFORE YOUR BOTTOM HITS THE SEAT--
BUT YOU WON'T--
CLICK
PLEASE! WHY ARE YOU DOING THIS TO ME?!
EZZZT
I DON'T UNDERSTAND... P-PLEASE! I HAVEN'T DONE ANYTHING WRO--
CLICK

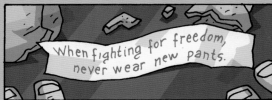

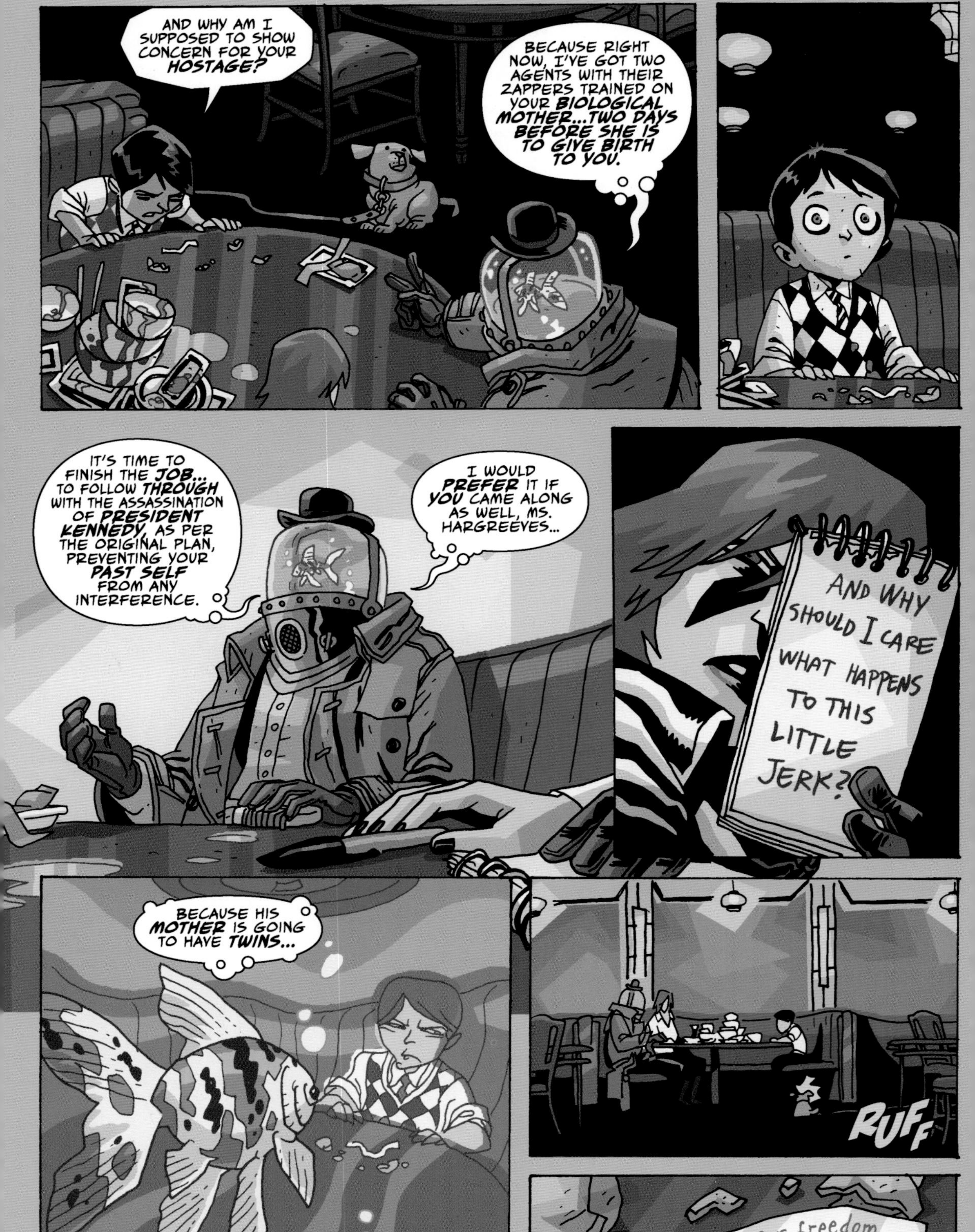
AND WHY AM I SUPPOSED TO SHOW CONCERN FOR YOUR HOSTAGE?
BECAUSE RIGHT NOW, I'VE GOT TWO AGENTS WITH THEIR ZAPPERS TRAINED ON YOUR BIOLOGICAL MOTHER...TWO DAYS BEFORE SHE IS TO GIVE BIRTH TO YOU.
IT'S TIME TO FINISH THE JOB... TO FOLLOW THROUGH WITH THE ASSASSINATION OF PRESIDENT KENNEDY, AS PER THE ORIGINAL PLAN, PREVENTING YOUR PAST SELF FROM ANY INTERFERENCE.
I WOULD PREFER IT IF YOU CAME ALONG AS WELL, MS. HARGREEVES...
AND WHY SHOULD I CARE WHAT HAPPENS TO THIS LITTLE JERK?
BECAUSE HIS MOTHER IS GOING TO HAVE TWINS...
RUFF
When fighting for freedom, never wear new pants.

END OF PART THREE.

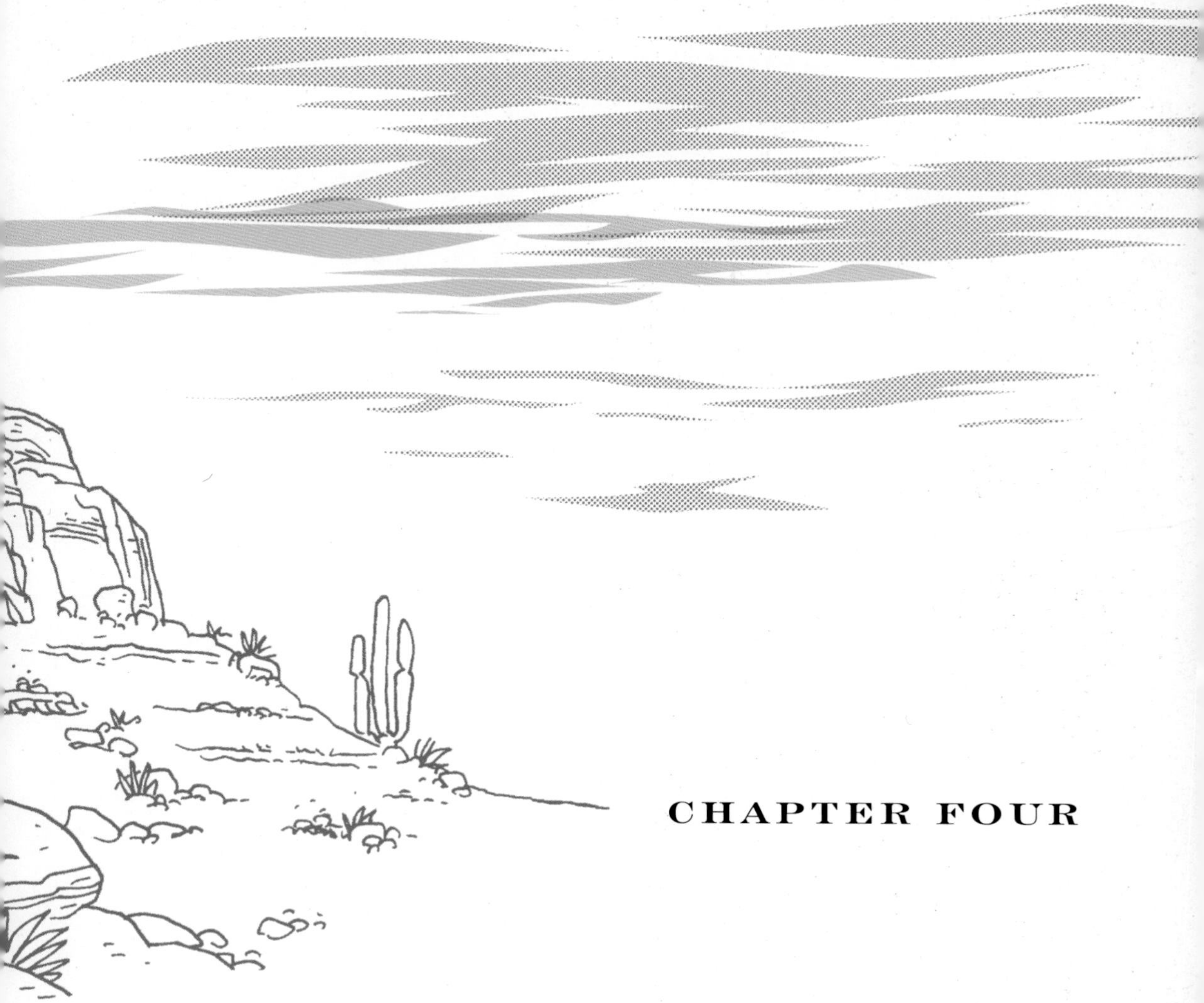

CHAPTER FOUR

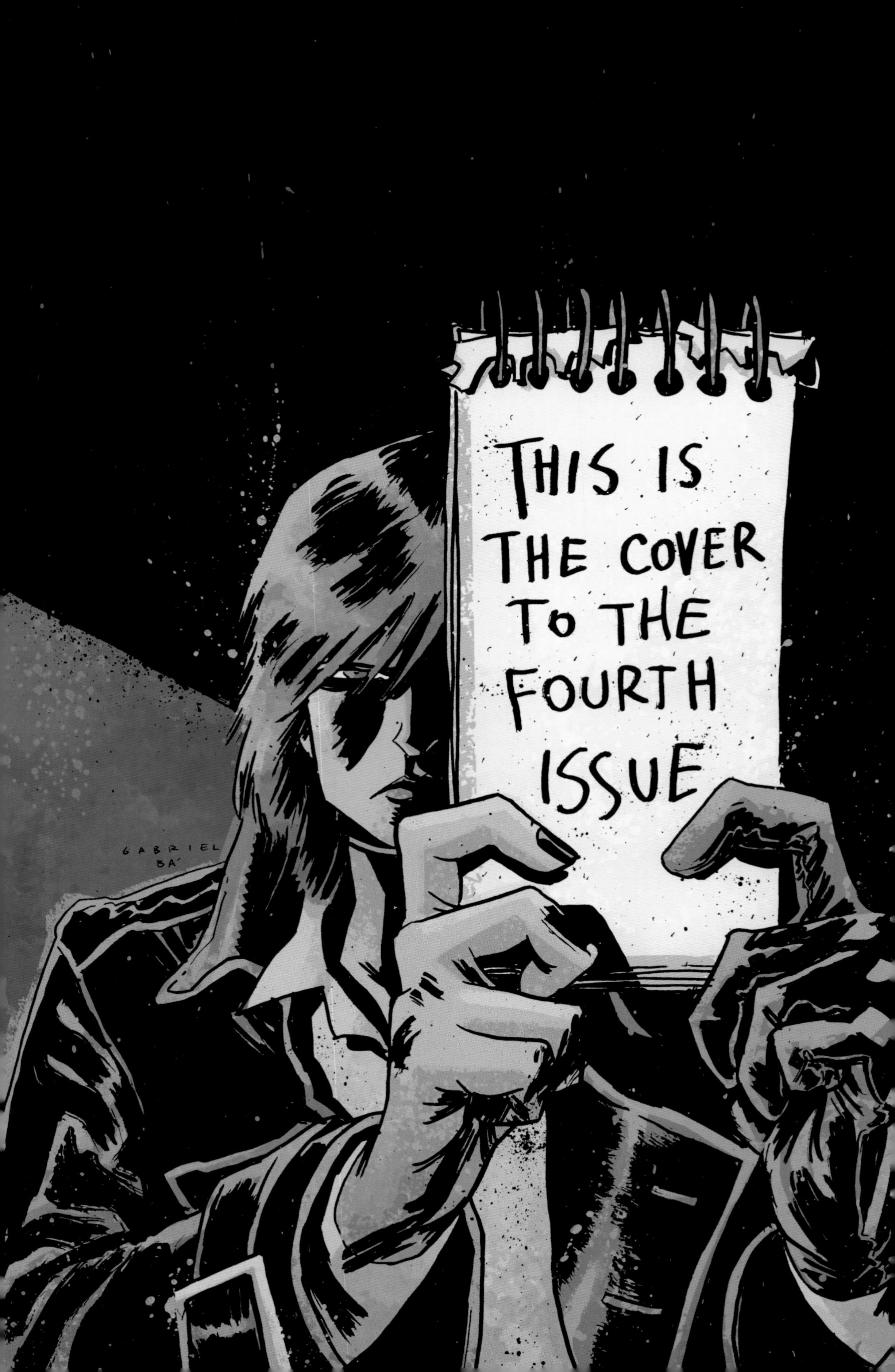
THIS IS THE COVER TO THE FOURTH ISSUE
GABRIEL BÁ

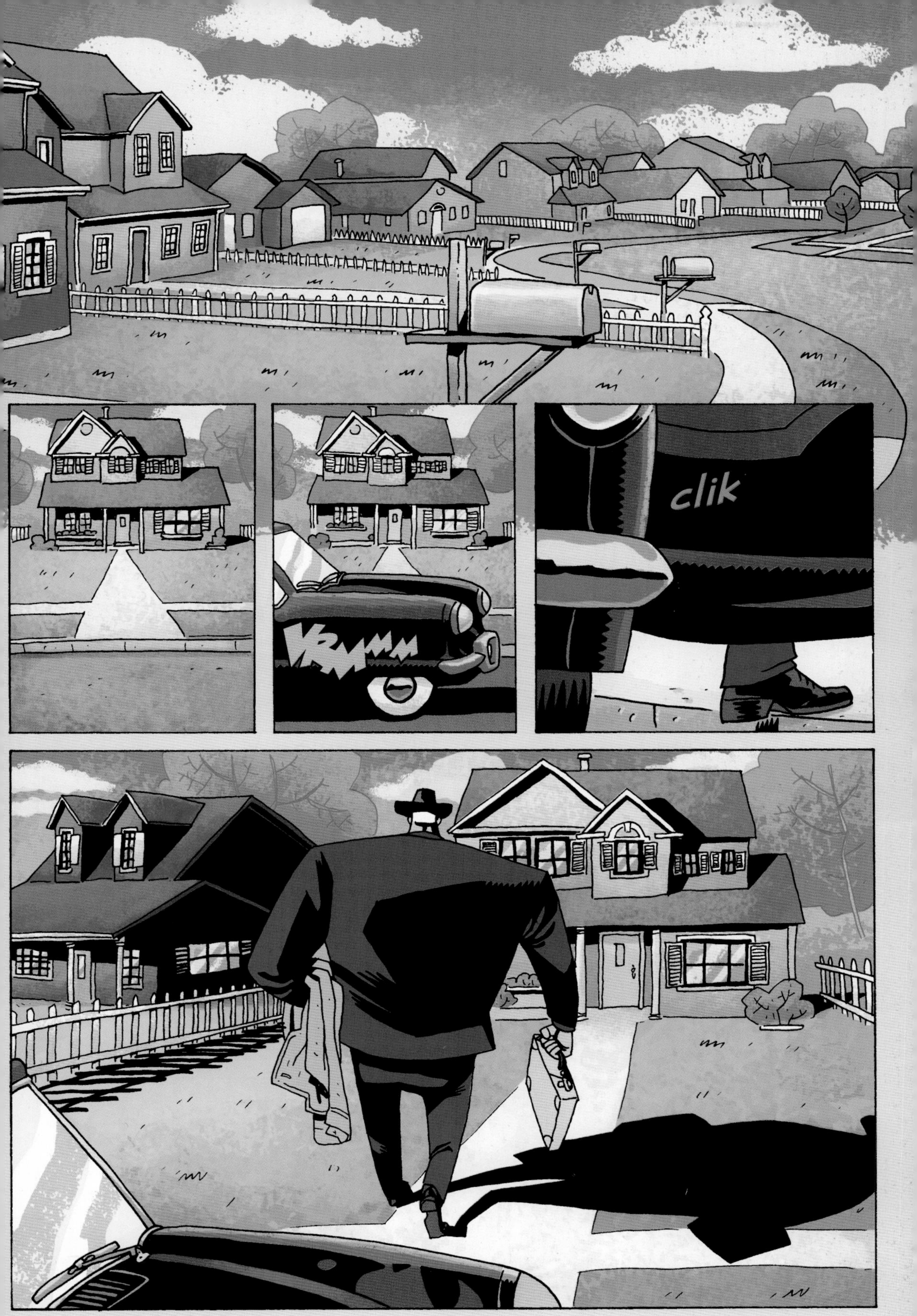
clik

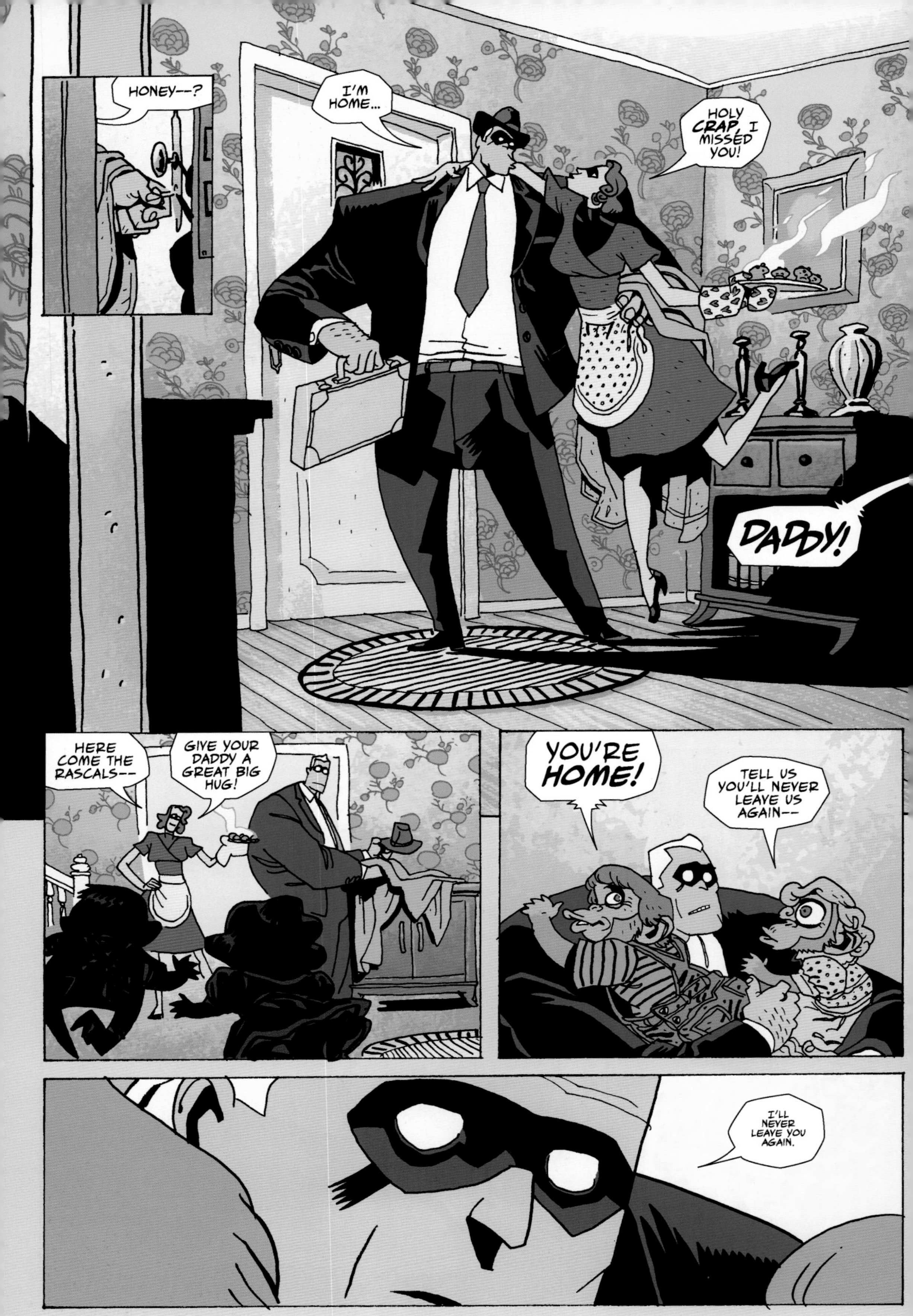
HONEY--?
I'M HOME...
HOLY CRAP, I MISSED YOU!
DADDY!
HERE COME THE RASCALS--
GIVE YOUR DADDY A GREAT BIG HUG!
YOU'RE HOME!
TELL US YOU'LL NEVER LEAVE US AGAIN--
I'LL NEVER LEAVE YOU AGAIN.

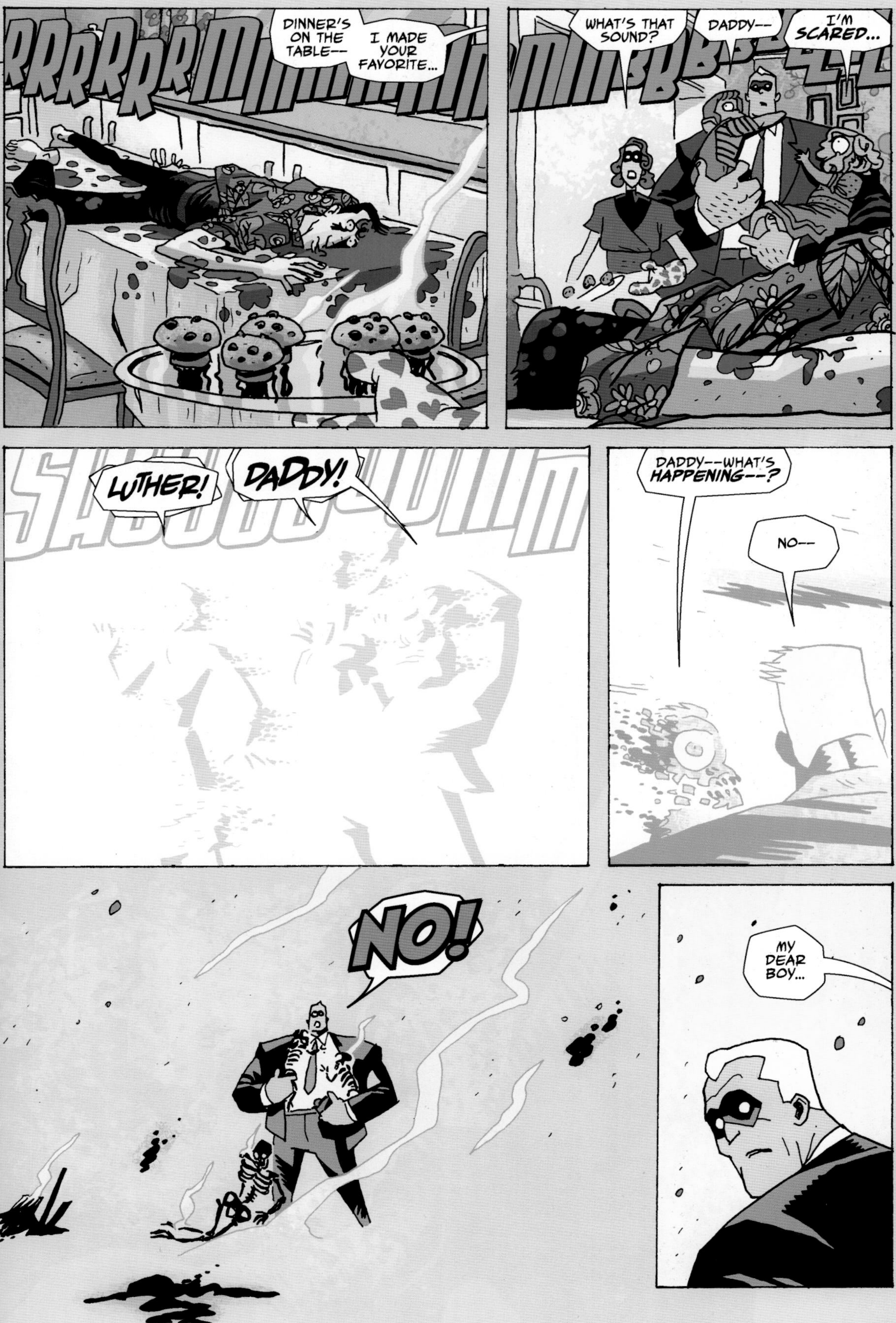

DINNER'S ON THE TABLE--
I MADE YOUR FAVORITE...
WHAT'S THAT SOUND?
DADDY--
I'M SCARED...
LUTHER!
DADDY!
DADDY--WHAT'S HAPPENING--?
NO--
NO!
MY DEAR BOY...

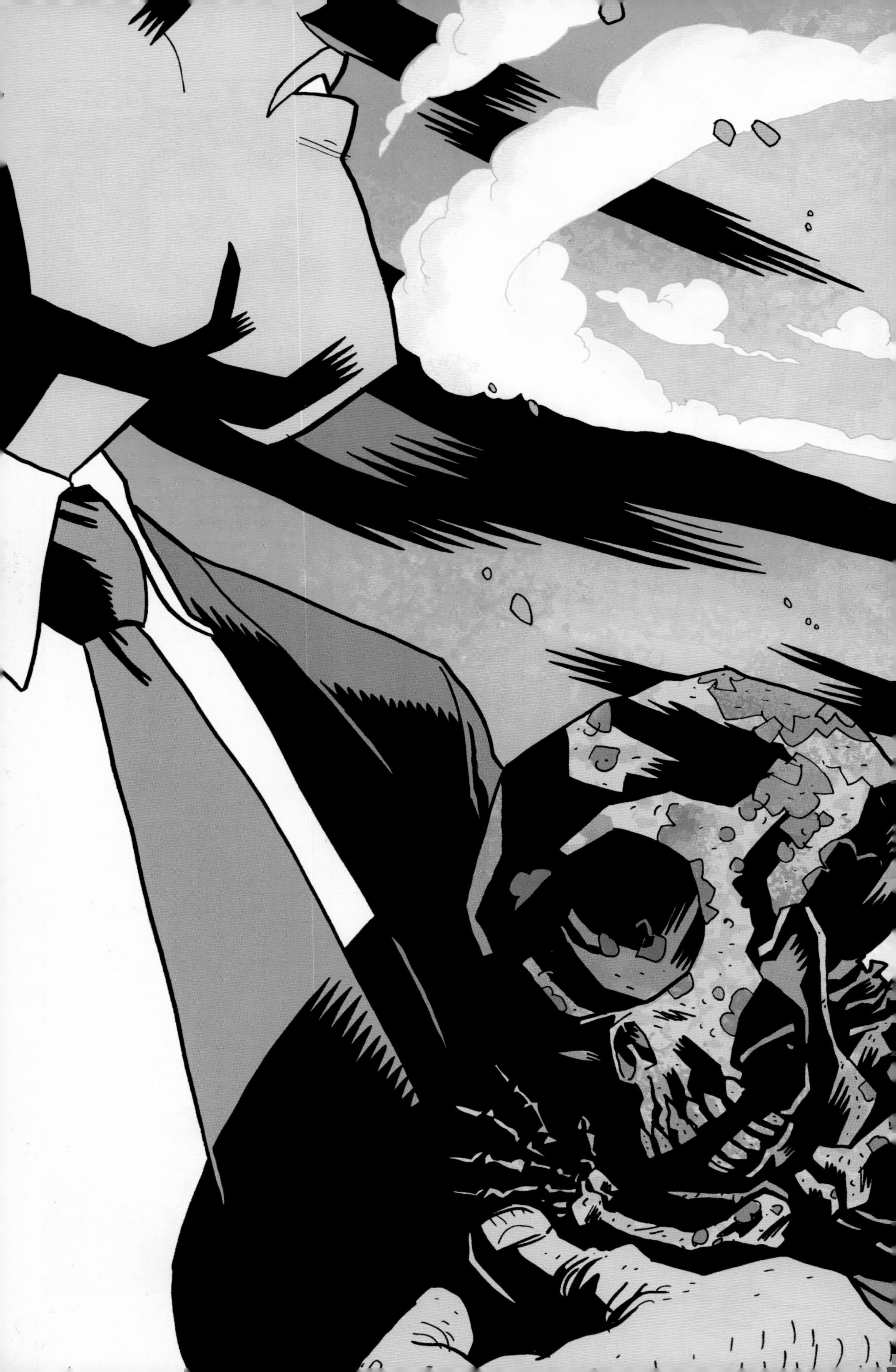

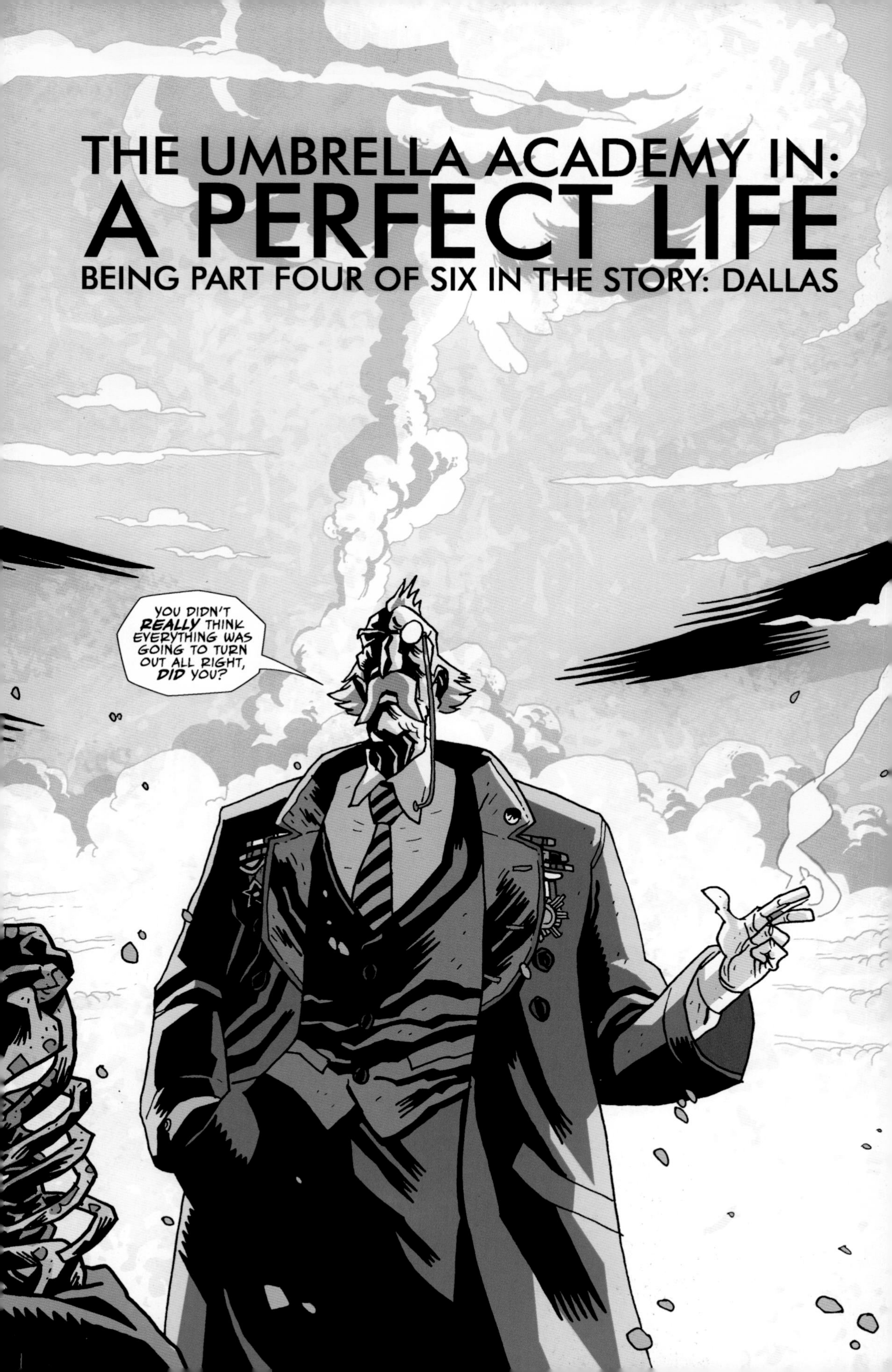
THE UMBRELLA ACADEMY IN:
A PERFECT LIFE
BEING PART FOUR OF SIX IN THE STORY: DALLAS
YOU DIDN'T REALLY THINK EVERYTHING WAS GOING TO TURN OUT ALL RIGHT, DID YOU?

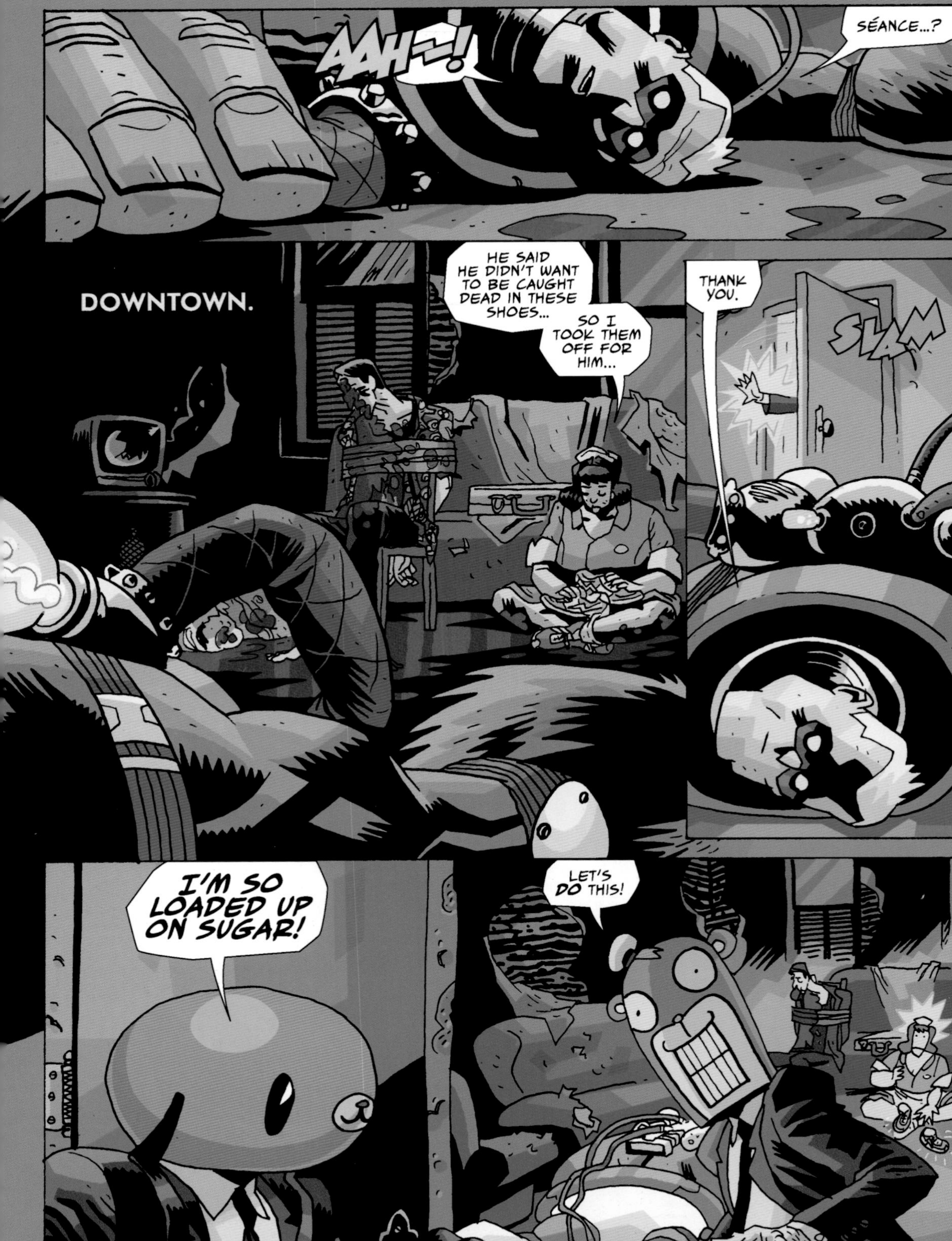
AAHH!
SÉANCE...?
DOWNTOWN.
HE SAID HE DIDN'T WANT TO BE CAUGHT DEAD IN THESE SHOES...
SO I TOOK THEM OFF FOR HIM...
THANK YOU.
SLAM
I'M SO LOADED UP ON SUGAR!
LET'S DO THIS!

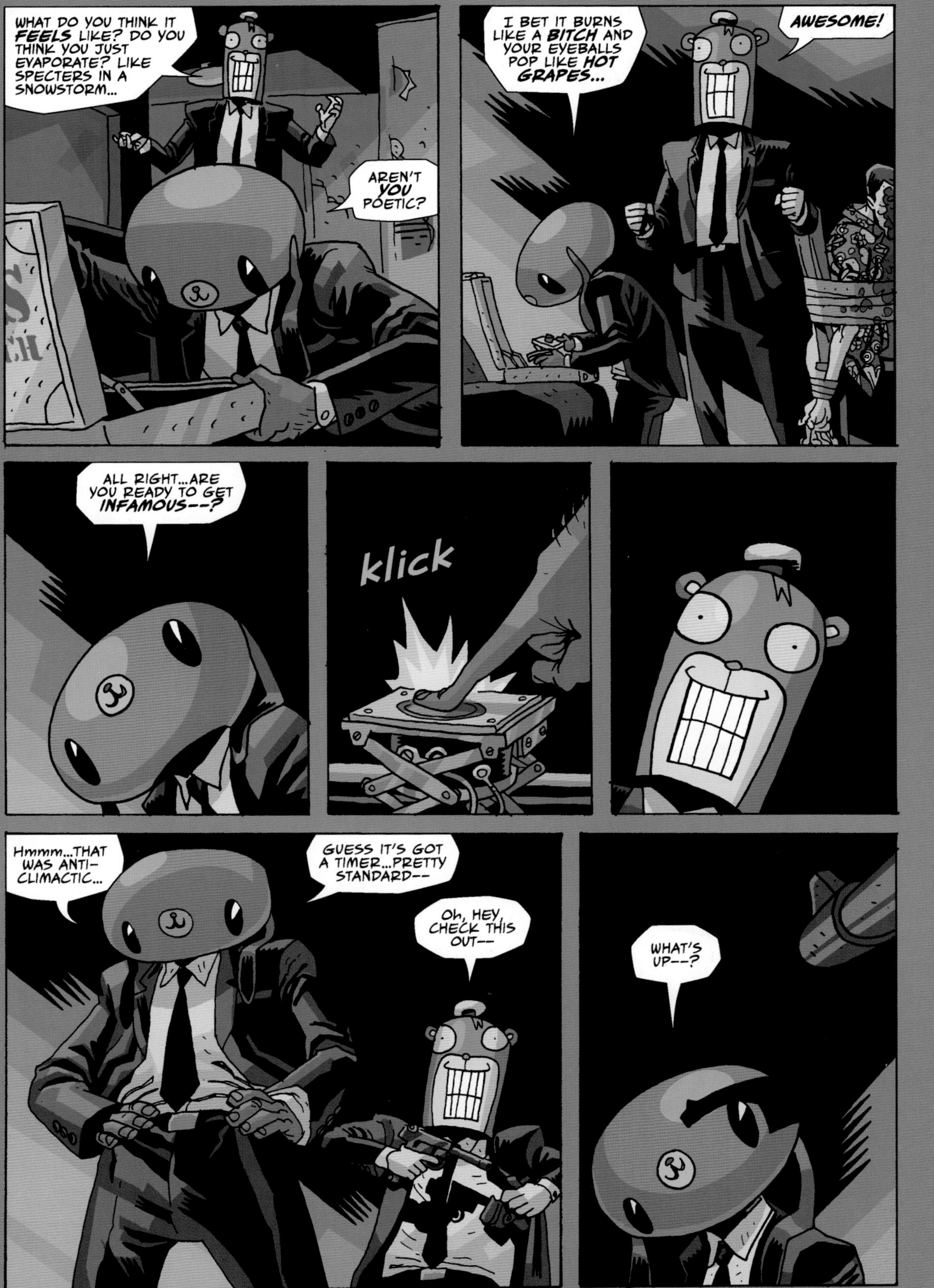
WHAT DO YOU THINK IT FEELS LIKE? DO YOU THINK YOU JUST EVAPORATE? LIKE SPECTERS IN A SNOWSTORM...
AREN'T YOU POETIC?
I BET IT BURNS LIKE A BITCH AND YOUR EYEBALLS POP LIKE HOT GRAPES...
AWESOME!
ALL RIGHT...ARE YOU READY TO GET INFAMOUS--?
klick
Hmmm...THAT WAS ANTI-CLIMACTIC...
GUESS IT'S GOT A TIMER...PRETTY STANDARD--
Oh, HEY, CHECK THIS OUT--
WHAT'S UP--?

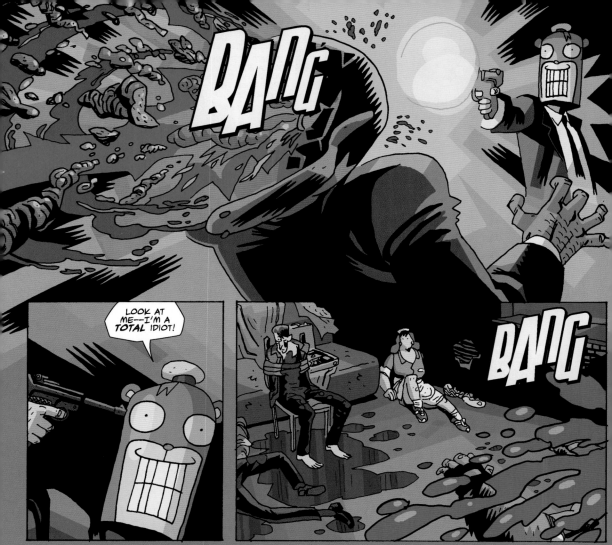

BANG

LOOK AT ME--I'M A **TOTAL** IDIOT!

BANG

HOW WAS **THAT?!**

MAN ENOUGH FOR YOU, COWBOY?

SÉANCE!

WE HAVE TO DISARM THAT **DETONATOR**--

ALREADY DONE... I'VE LOST A LOT OF BLOOD, BUT APPARENTLY WHEN A MEMBER OF THIS FAMILY GETS SHOT IN THE HEAD IT'S NO BIG DEAL...

WHAT **HAPPENED?!**

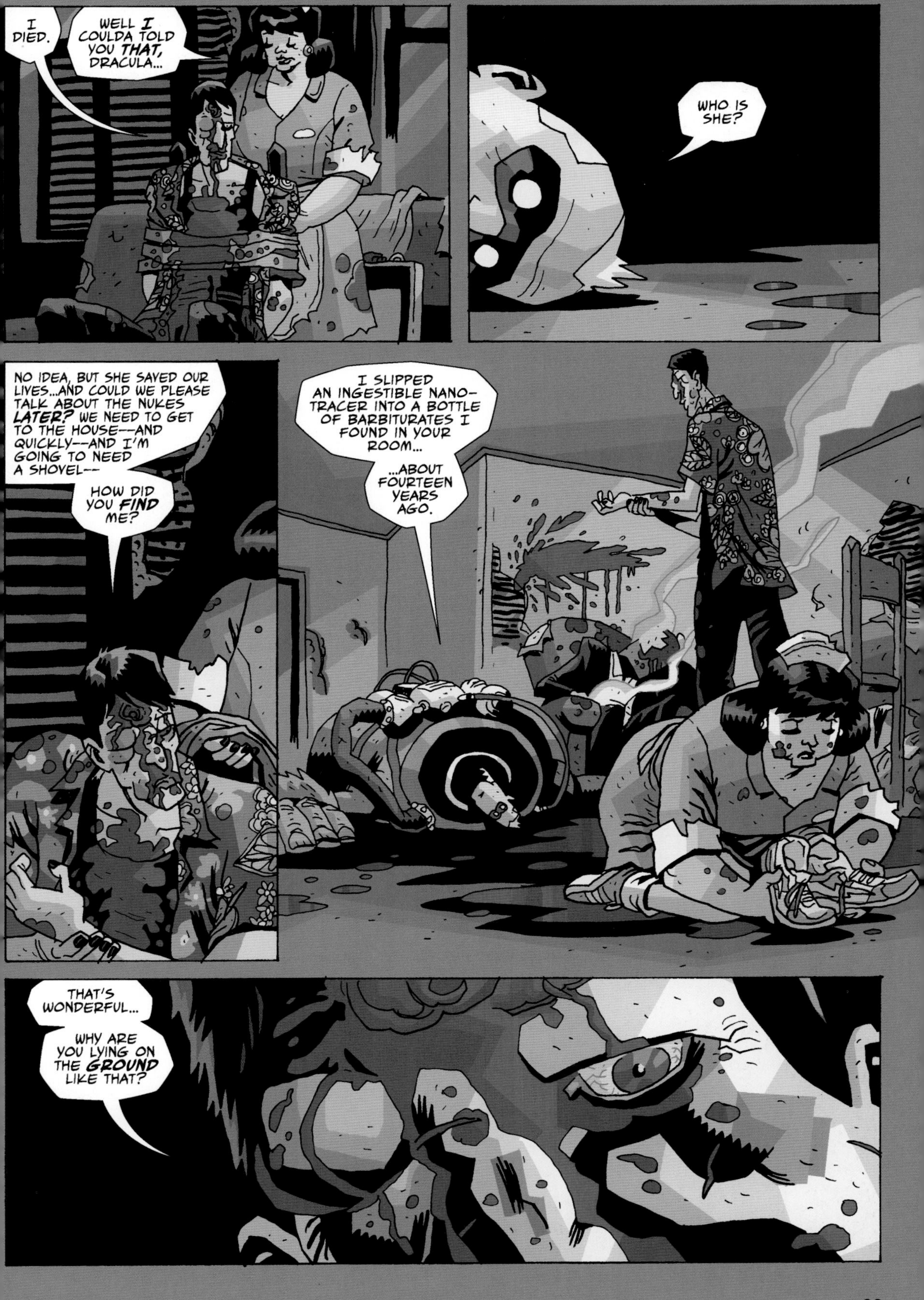
I DIED.
WELL I COULDA TOLD YOU THAT, DRACULA...
WHO IS SHE?
NO IDEA, BUT SHE SAVED OUR LIVES...AND COULD WE PLEASE TALK ABOUT THE NUKES LATER? WE NEED TO GET TO THE HOUSE--AND QUICKLY--AND I'M GOING TO NEED A SHOVEL--
HOW DID YOU FIND ME?
I SLIPPED AN INGESTIBLE NANO-TRACER INTO A BOTTLE OF BARBITURATES I FOUND IN YOUR ROOM...
...ABOUT FOURTEEN YEARS AGO.
THAT'S WONDERFUL...
WHY ARE YOU LYING ON THE GROUND LIKE THAT?

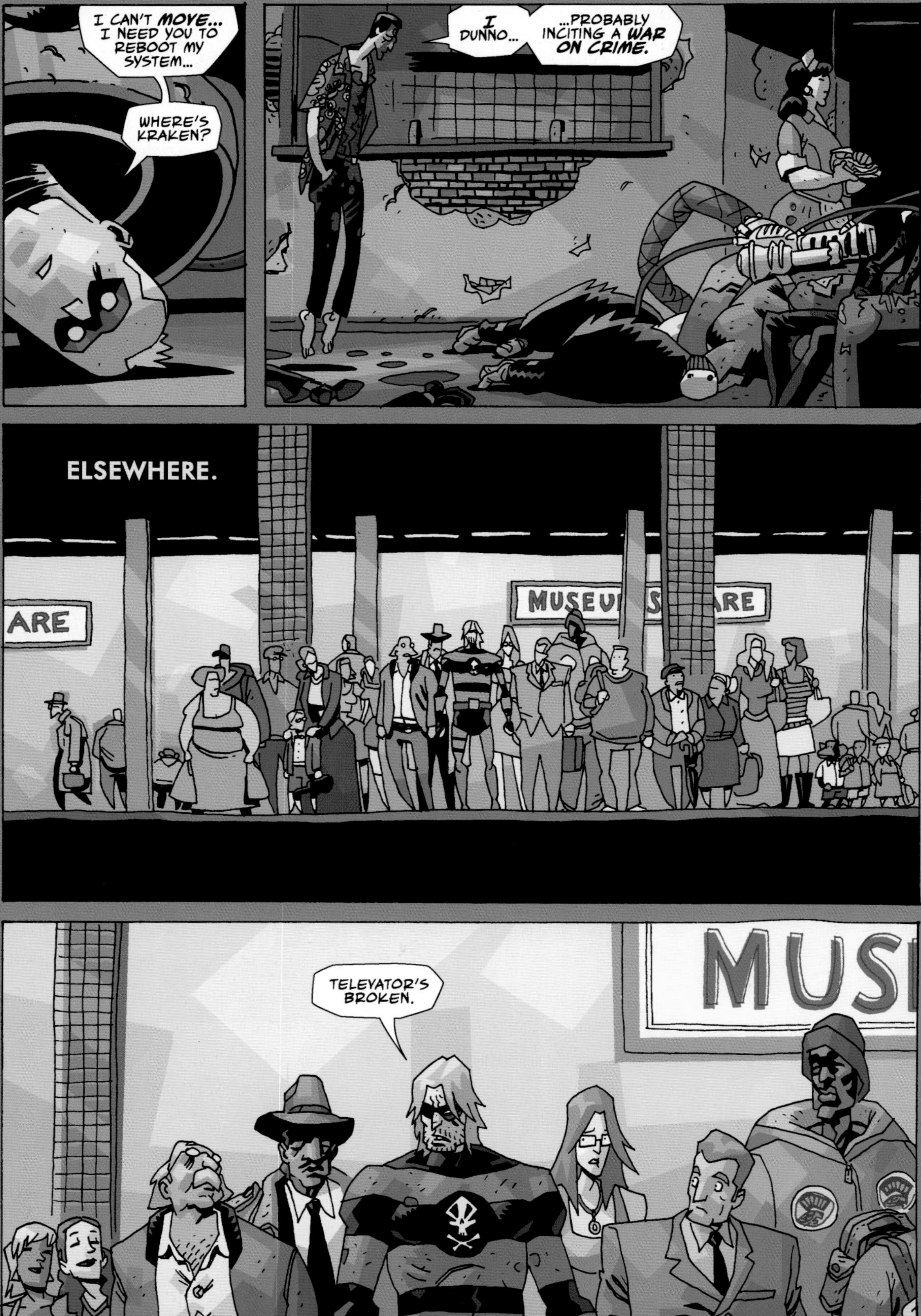
I CAN'T MOVE... I NEED YOU TO REBOOT MY SYSTEM...
WHERE'S KRAKEN?
I DUNNO...
...PROBABLY INCITING A WAR ON CRIME.
ELSEWHERE.
ARE
MUSEU S ARE
TELEVATOR'S BROKEN.
MUS

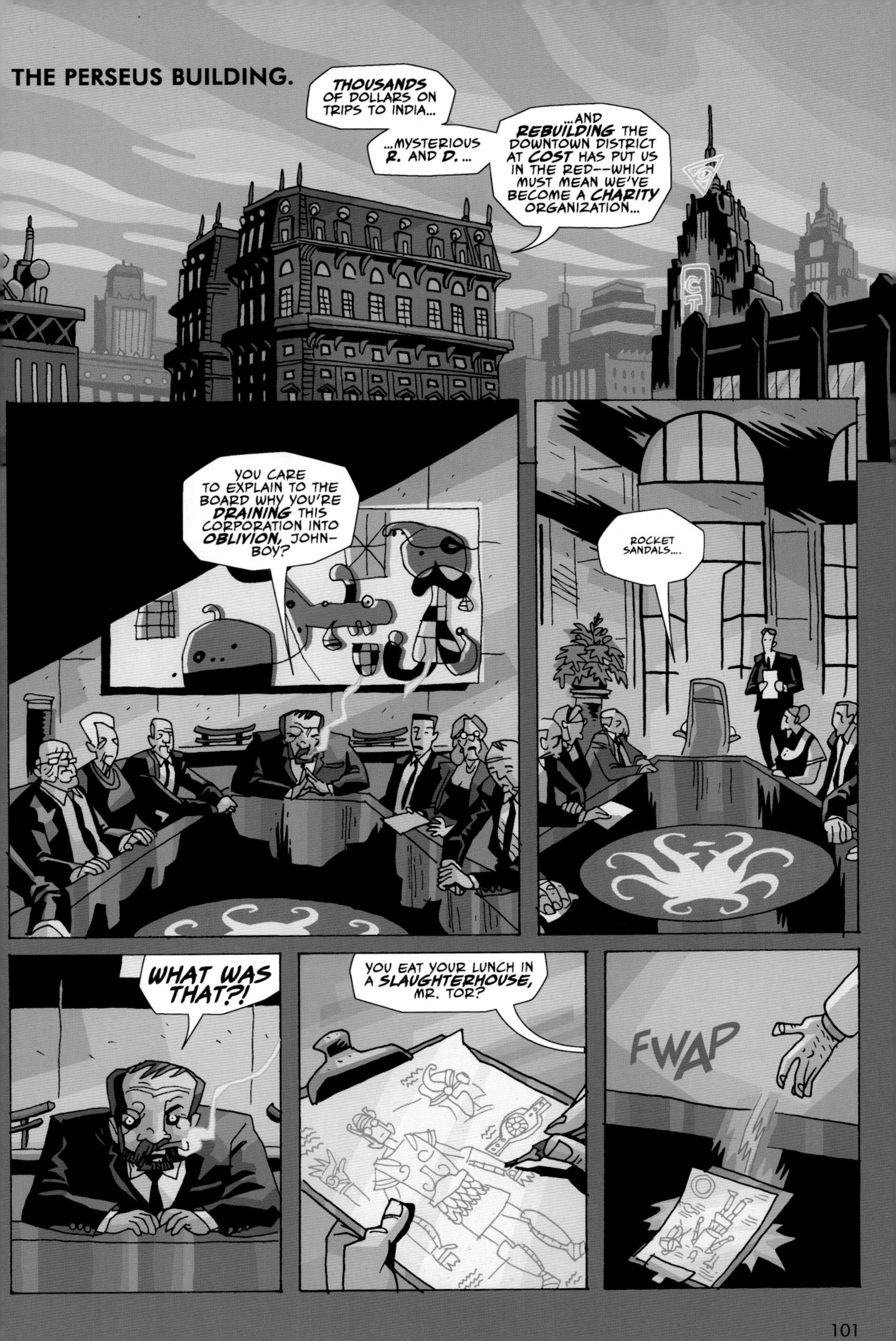

THE PERSEUS BUILDING.
THOUSANDS OF DOLLARS ON TRIPS TO INDIA...
...MYSTERIOUS R. AND D. ...
...AND REBUILDING THE DOWNTOWN DISTRICT AT COST HAS PUT US IN THE RED--WHICH MUST MEAN WE'VE BECOME A CHARITY ORGANIZATION...
YOU CARE TO EXPLAIN TO THE BOARD WHY YOU'RE DRAINING THIS CORPORATION INTO OBLIVION, JOHN-BOY?
ROCKET SANDALS....
WHAT WAS THAT?!
YOU EAT YOUR LUNCH IN A SLAUGHTERHOUSE, MR. TOR?
FWAP

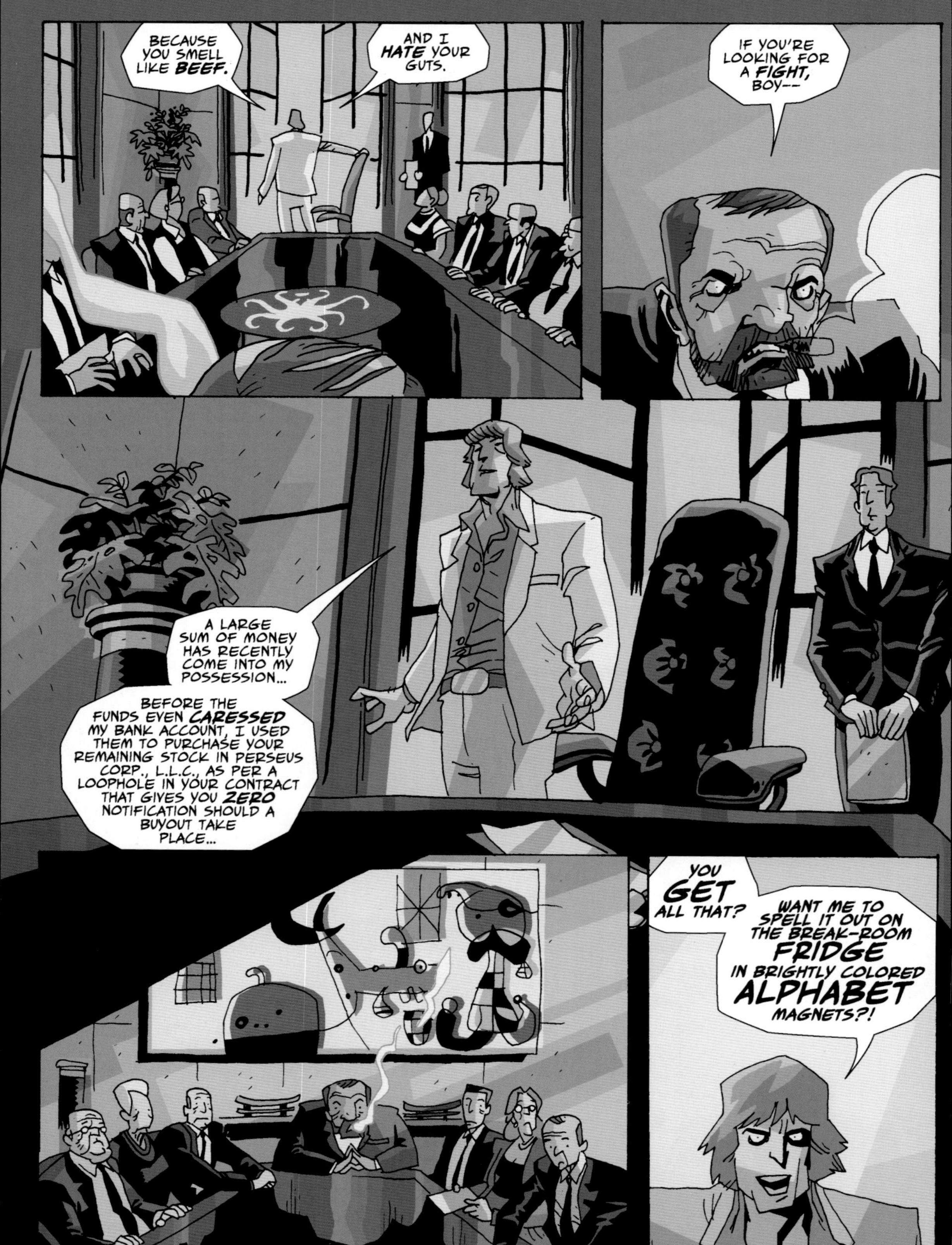
BECAUSE YOU SMELL LIKE BEEF.
AND I HATE YOUR GUTS.
IF YOU'RE LOOKING FOR A FIGHT, BOY--
A LARGE SUM OF MONEY HAS RECENTLY COME INTO MY POSSESSION...
BEFORE THE FUNDS EVEN CARESSED MY BANK ACCOUNT, I USED THEM TO PURCHASE YOUR REMAINING STOCK IN PERSEUS CORP., L.L.C., AS PER A LOOPHOLE IN YOUR CONTRACT THAT GIVES YOU ZERO NOTIFICATION SHOULD A BUYOUT TAKE PLACE...
YOU GET ALL THAT?
WANT ME TO SPELL IT OUT ON THE BREAK-ROOM FRIDGE IN BRIGHTLY COLORED ALPHABET MAGNETS?!

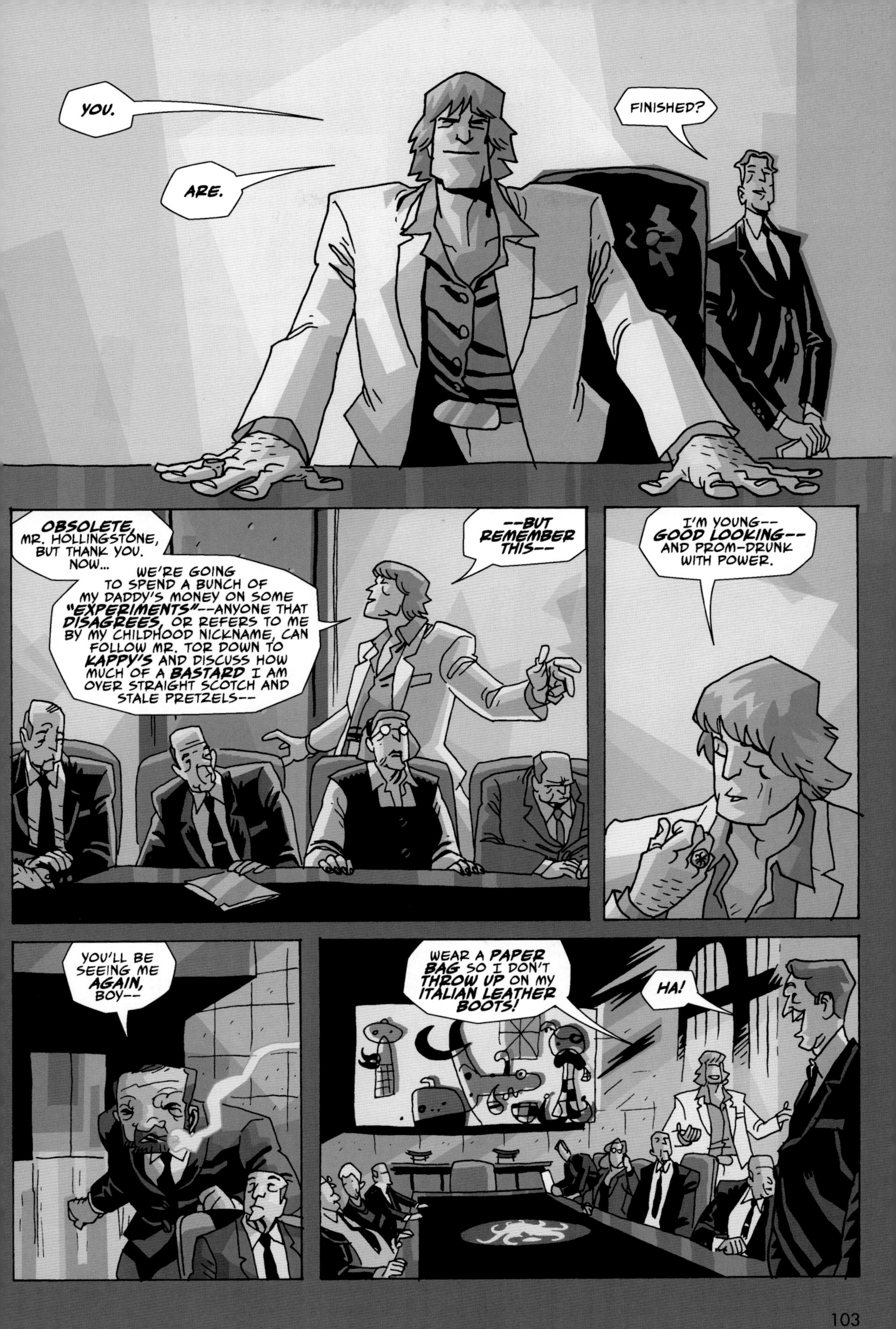
YOU.
ARE.
FINISHED?
OBSOLETE, MR. HOLLINGSTONE, BUT THANK YOU. NOW...
WE'RE GOING TO SPEND A BUNCH OF MY DADDY'S MONEY ON SOME "EXPERIMENTS"--ANYONE THAT DISAGREES, OR REFERS TO ME BY MY CHILDHOOD NICKNAME, CAN FOLLOW MR. TOR DOWN TO KAPPY'S AND DISCUSS HOW MUCH OF A BASTARD I AM OVER STRAIGHT SCOTCH AND STALE PRETZELS--
--BUT REMEMBER THIS--
I'M YOUNG-- GOOD LOOKING-- AND PROM-DRUNK WITH POWER.
YOU'LL BE SEEING ME AGAIN, BOY--
WEAR A PAPER BAG SO I DON'T THROW UP ON MY ITALIAN LEATHER BOOTS!
HA!

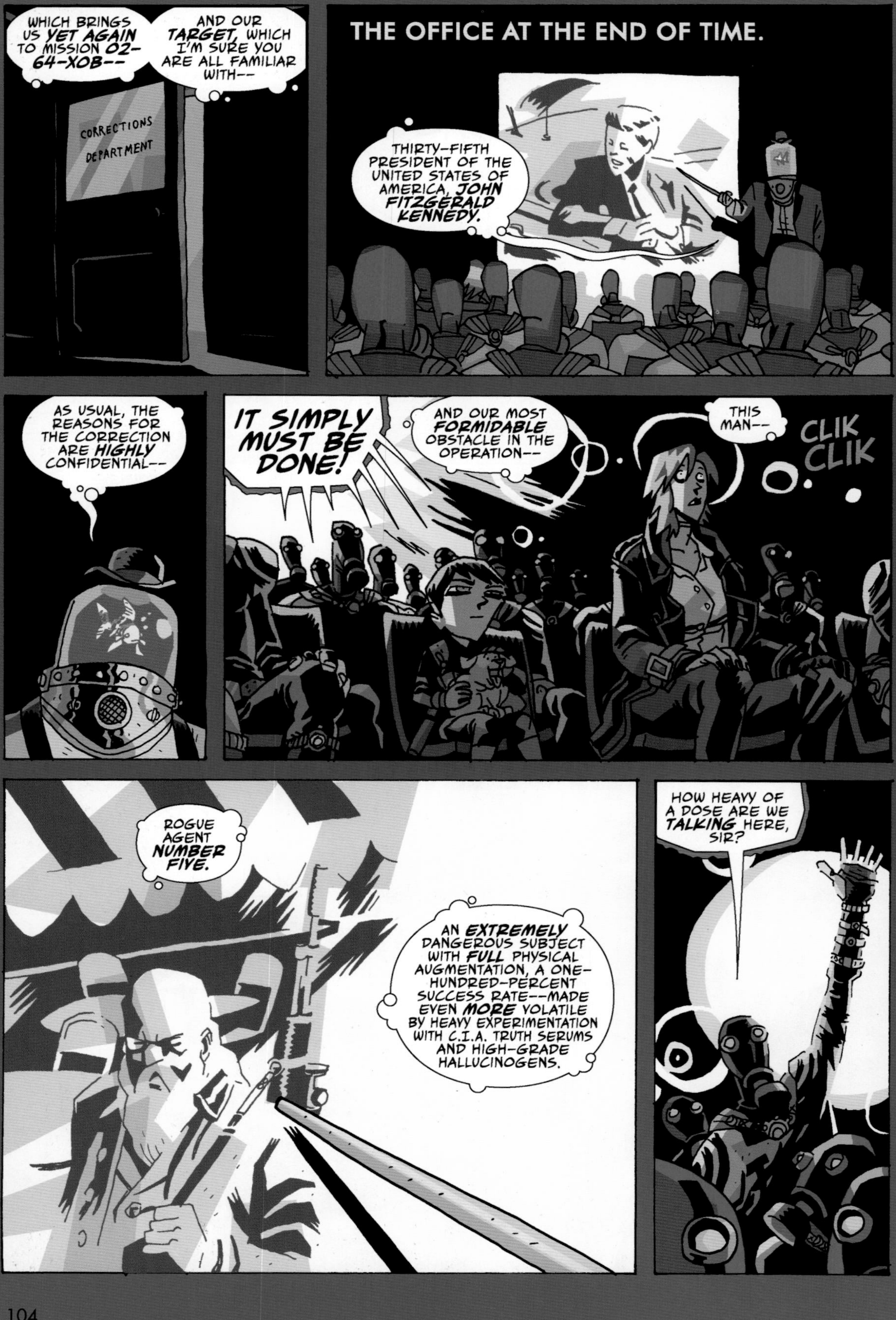
WHICH BRINGS US YET AGAIN TO MISSION 02-64-XOB--
AND OUR TARGET, WHICH I'M SURE YOU ARE ALL FAMILIAR WITH--
CORRECTIONS DEPARTMENT
THE OFFICE AT THE END OF TIME.
THIRTY-FIFTH PRESIDENT OF THE UNITED STATES OF AMERICA, JOHN FITZGERALD KENNEDY.
AS USUAL, THE REASONS FOR THE CORRECTION ARE HIGHLY CONFIDENTIAL--
IT SIMPLY MUST BE DONE!
AND OUR MOST FORMIDABLE OBSTACLE IN THE OPERATION--
THIS MAN--
CLIK CLIK
ROGUE AGENT NUMBER FIVE.
AN EXTREMELY DANGEROUS SUBJECT WITH FULL PHYSICAL AUGMENTATION, A ONE-HUNDRED-PERCENT SUCCESS RATE--MADE EVEN MORE VOLATILE BY HEAVY EXPERIMENTATION WITH C.I.A. TRUTH SERUMS AND HIGH-GRADE HALLUCINOGENS.
HOW HEAVY OF A DOSE ARE WE TALKING HERE, SIR?

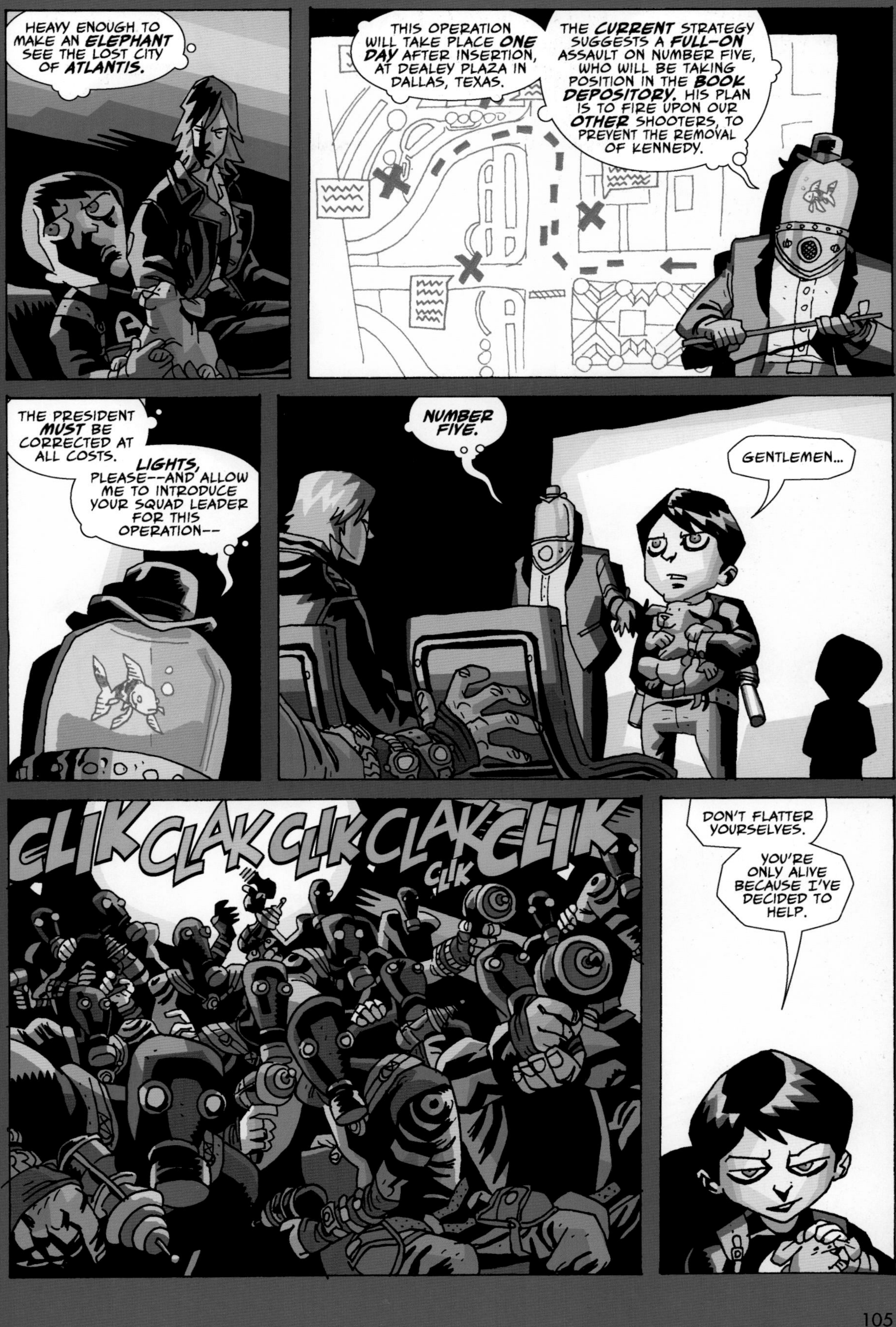
HEAVY ENOUGH TO MAKE AN ELEPHANT SEE THE LOST CITY OF ATLANTIS.
THIS OPERATION WILL TAKE PLACE ONE DAY AFTER INSERTION, AT DEALEY PLAZA IN DALLAS, TEXAS.
THE CURRENT STRATEGY SUGGESTS A FULL-ON ASSAULT ON NUMBER FIVE, WHO WILL BE TAKING POSITION IN THE BOOK DEPOSITORY. HIS PLAN IS TO FIRE UPON OUR OTHER SHOOTERS, TO PREVENT THE REMOVAL OF KENNEDY.
THE PRESIDENT MUST BE CORRECTED AT ALL COSTS.
LIGHTS, PLEASE--AND ALLOW ME TO INTRODUCE YOUR SQUAD LEADER FOR THIS OPERATION--
NUMBER FIVE.
GENTLEMEN...
CLIK CLAK CLIK CLAK CLIK
CLIK
DON'T FLATTER YOURSELVES.
YOU'RE ONLY ALIVE BECAUSE I'VE DECIDED TO HELP.

EXACTLY, NUMBER FIVE-- TEN YEARS OLD OR SIXTY YEARS OLD, YOU ARE STILL THE MOST DANGEROUS AGENT WE HAVE.

HOW EXACTLY DO YOU PLAN ON STOPPING YOURSELF?

I PITY YOU ALL...

MOST OF YOU WILL DIE--

--SCRATCH THAT--

ALL OF YOU.

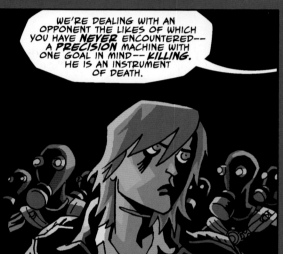

WE'RE DEALING WITH AN OPPONENT THE LIKES OF WHICH YOU HAVE NEVER ENCOUNTERED-- A PRECISION MACHINE WITH ONE GOAL IN MIND-- KILLING. HE IS AN INSTRUMENT OF DEATH.

BUT I HAVE A PLAN.

CARMICHAEL--

--I'M GOING TO NEED YOUR SURGEONS.

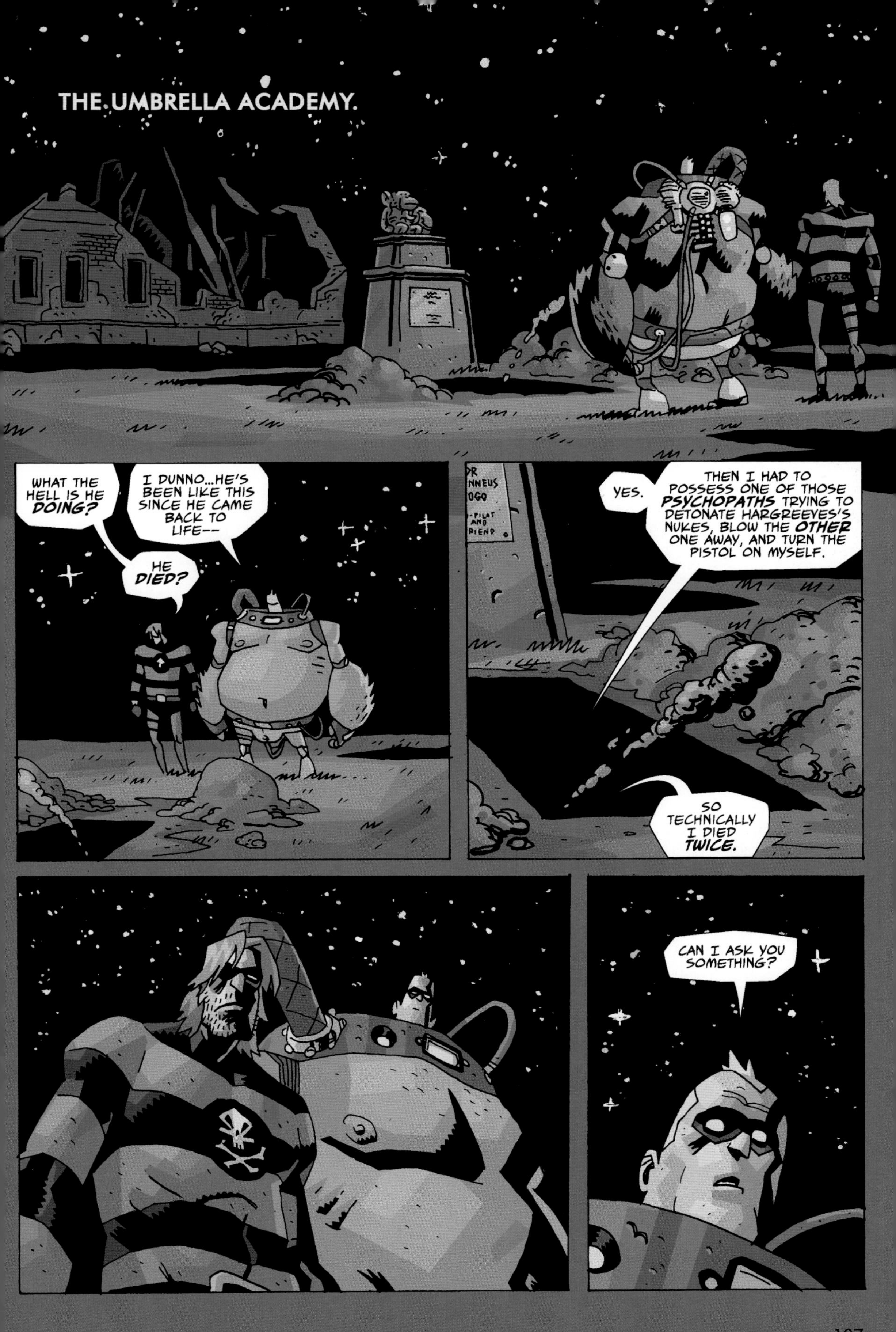
WHAT THE HELL IS HE *DOING?*
I DUNNO...HE'S BEEN LIKE THIS SINCE HE CAME BACK TO LIFE--
HE *DIED?*
YES.
THEN I HAD TO POSSESS ONE OF THOSE *PSYCHOPATHS* TRYING TO DETONATE HARGREEVES'S NUKES, BLOW THE *OTHER* ONE AWAY, AND TURN THE PISTOL ON MYSELF.
SO TECHNICALLY I DIED *TWICE.*
CAN I ASK YOU SOMETHING?

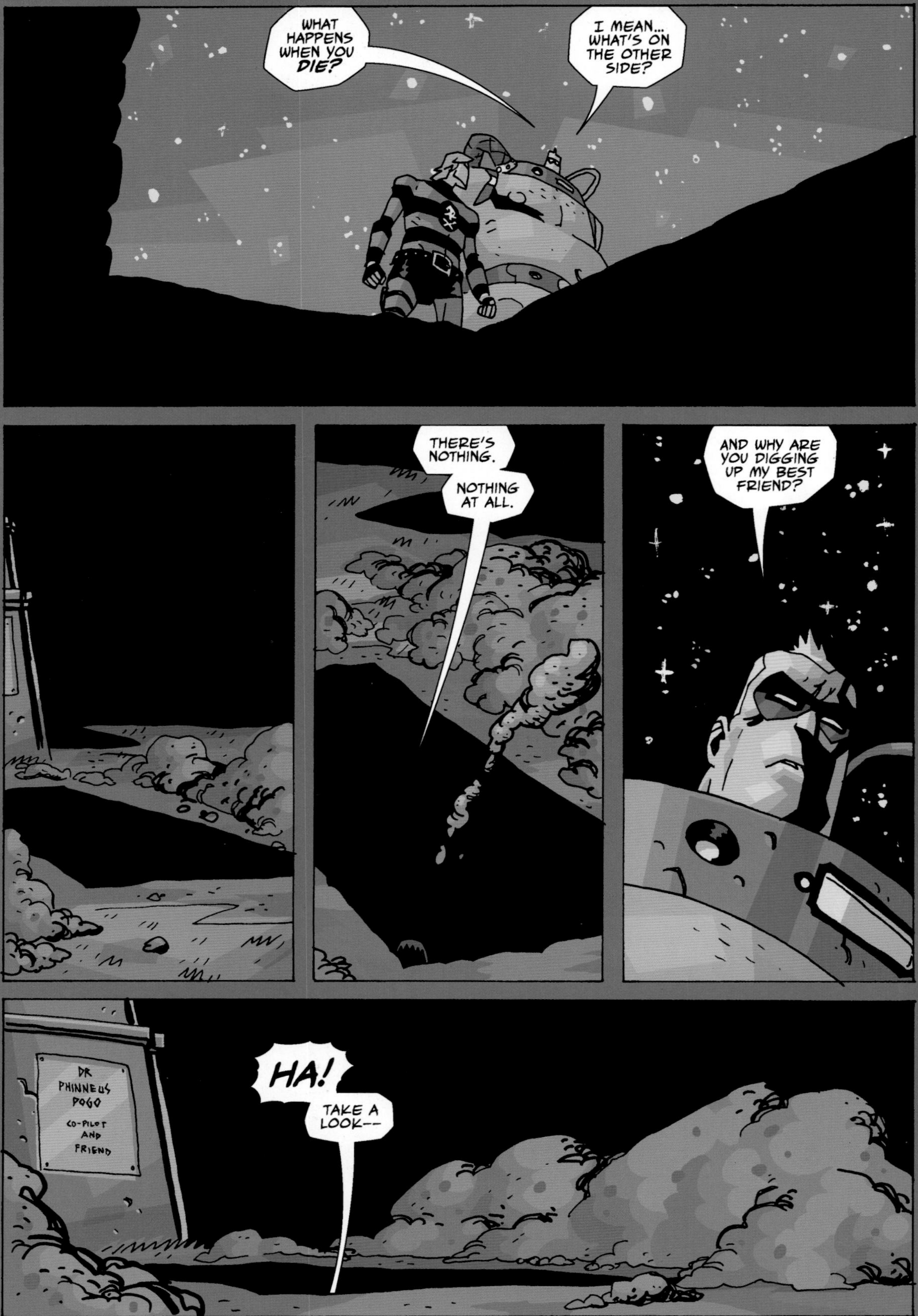
WHAT HAPPENS WHEN YOU *DIE?*
I MEAN... WHAT'S ON THE OTHER SIDE?
THERE'S NOTHING.
NOTHING AT ALL.
AND WHY ARE YOU DIGGING UP MY BEST FRIEND?
DR PHINNEUS POGO CO-PILOT AND FRIEND
HA!
TAKE A LOOK--

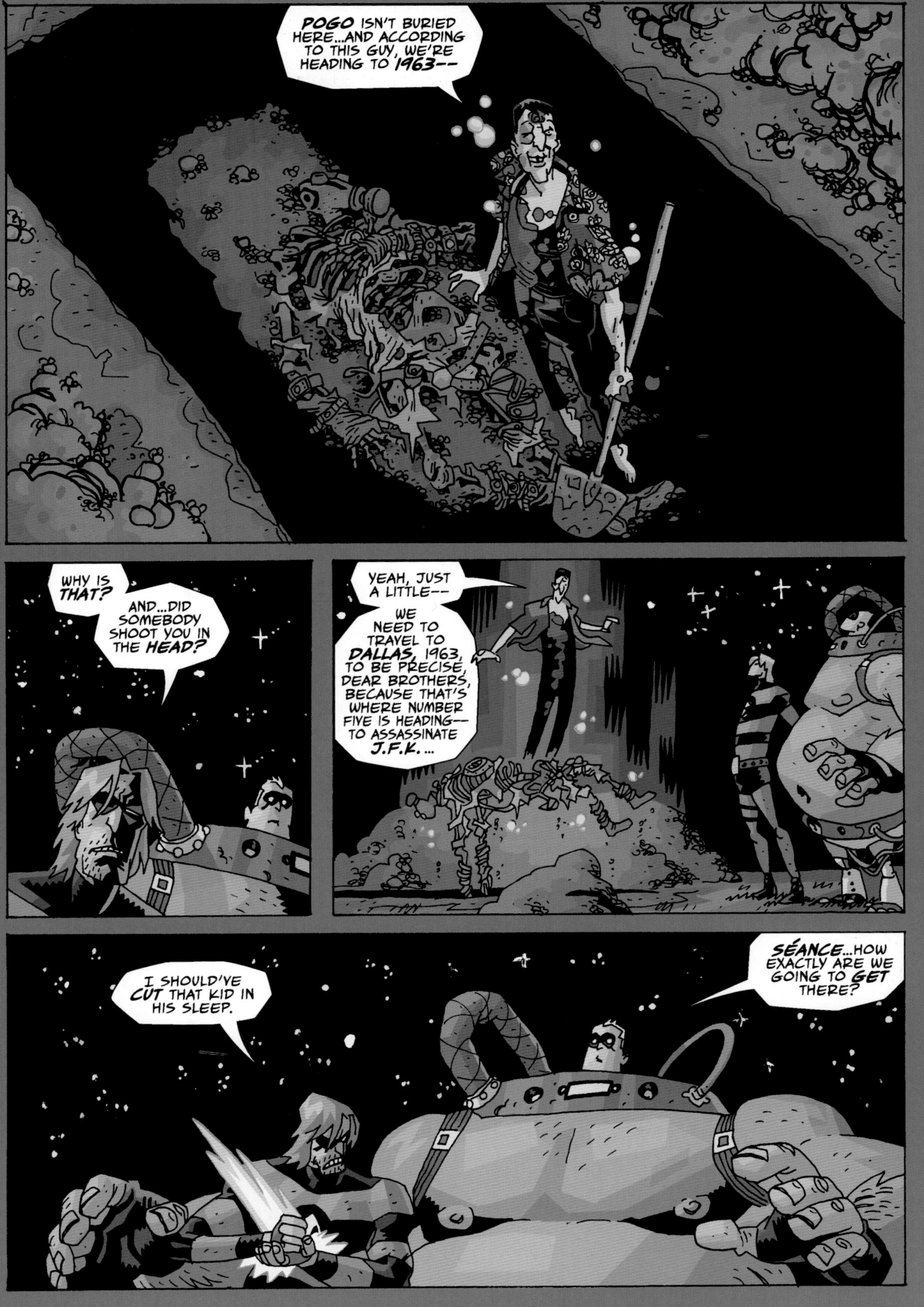
POGO ISN'T BURIED HERE...AND ACCORDING TO THIS GUY, WE'RE HEADING TO 1963--
WHY IS THAT?
AND...DID SOMEBODY SHOOT YOU IN THE HEAD?
YEAH, JUST A LITTLE--
WE NEED TO TRAVEL TO DALLAS, 1963, TO BE PRECISE, DEAR BROTHERS, BECAUSE THAT'S WHERE NUMBER FIVE IS HEADING-- TO ASSASSINATE J.F.K. ...
I SHOULD'VE CUT THAT KID IN HIS SLEEP.
SÉANCE...HOW EXACTLY ARE WE GOING TO GET THERE?

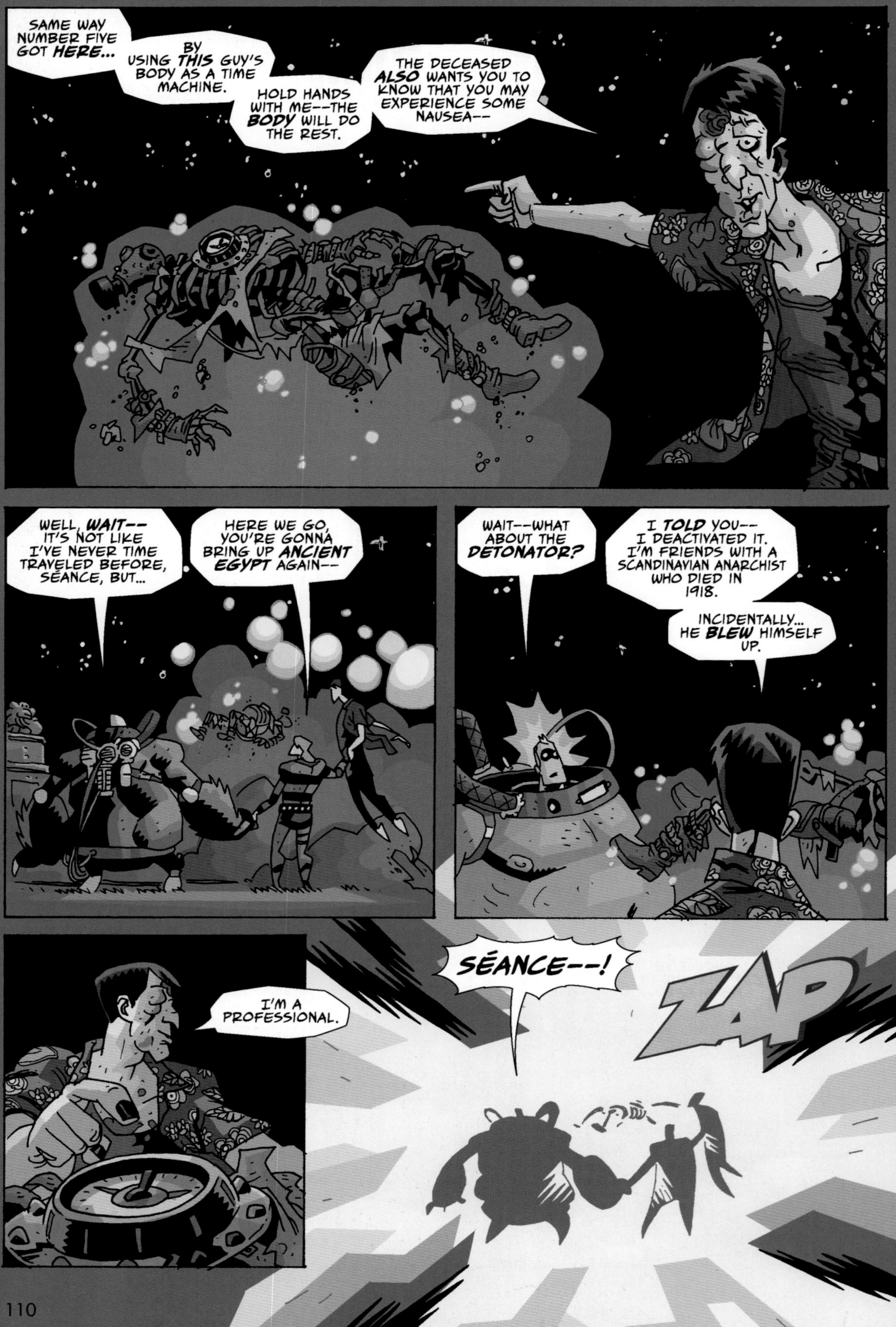
SAME WAY NUMBER FIVE GOT HERE...
BY USING THIS GUY'S BODY AS A TIME MACHINE.
HOLD HANDS WITH ME--THE BODY WILL DO THE REST.
THE DECEASED ALSO WANTS YOU TO KNOW THAT YOU MAY EXPERIENCE SOME NAUSEA--
WELL, WAIT-- IT'S NOT LIKE I'VE NEVER TIME TRAVELED BEFORE, SÉANCE, BUT...
HERE WE GO, YOU'RE GONNA BRING UP ANCIENT EGYPT AGAIN--
WAIT--WHAT ABOUT THE DETONATOR?
I TOLD YOU-- I DEACTIVATED IT. I'M FRIENDS WITH A SCANDINAVIAN ANARCHIST WHO DIED IN 1918.
INCIDENTALLY... HE BLEW HIMSELF UP.
I'M A PROFESSIONAL.
SÉANCE--!
ZAP

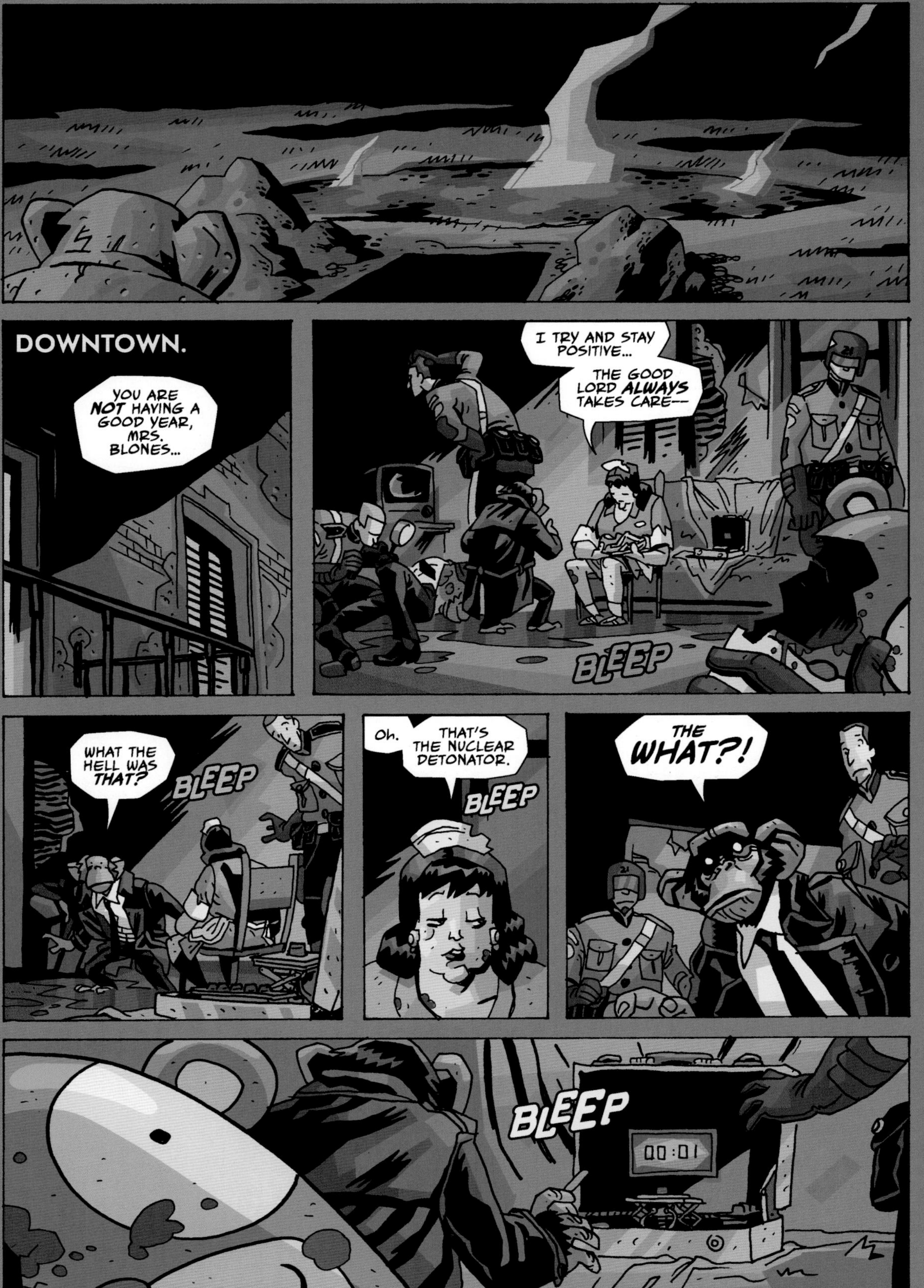
DOWNTOWN.
YOU ARE NOT HAVING A GOOD YEAR, MRS. BLONES...
I TRY AND STAY POSITIVE...
THE GOOD LORD ALWAYS TAKES CARE--
BLEEP
WHAT THE HELL WAS THAT?
BLEEP
Oh.
THAT'S THE NUCLEAR DETONATOR.
BLEEP
THE WHAT?!
BLEEP
00:01

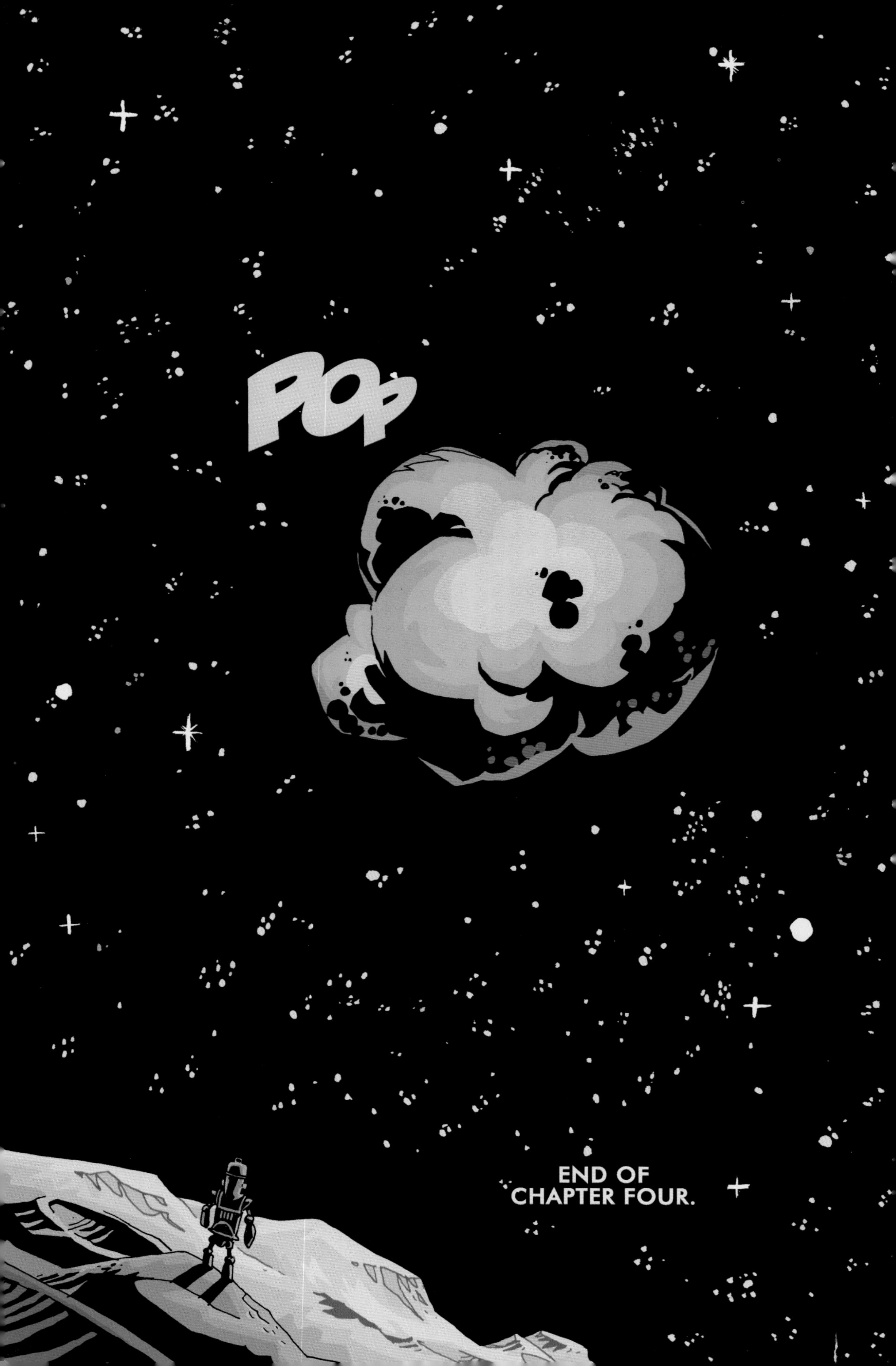
POP
END OF CHAPTER FOUR.

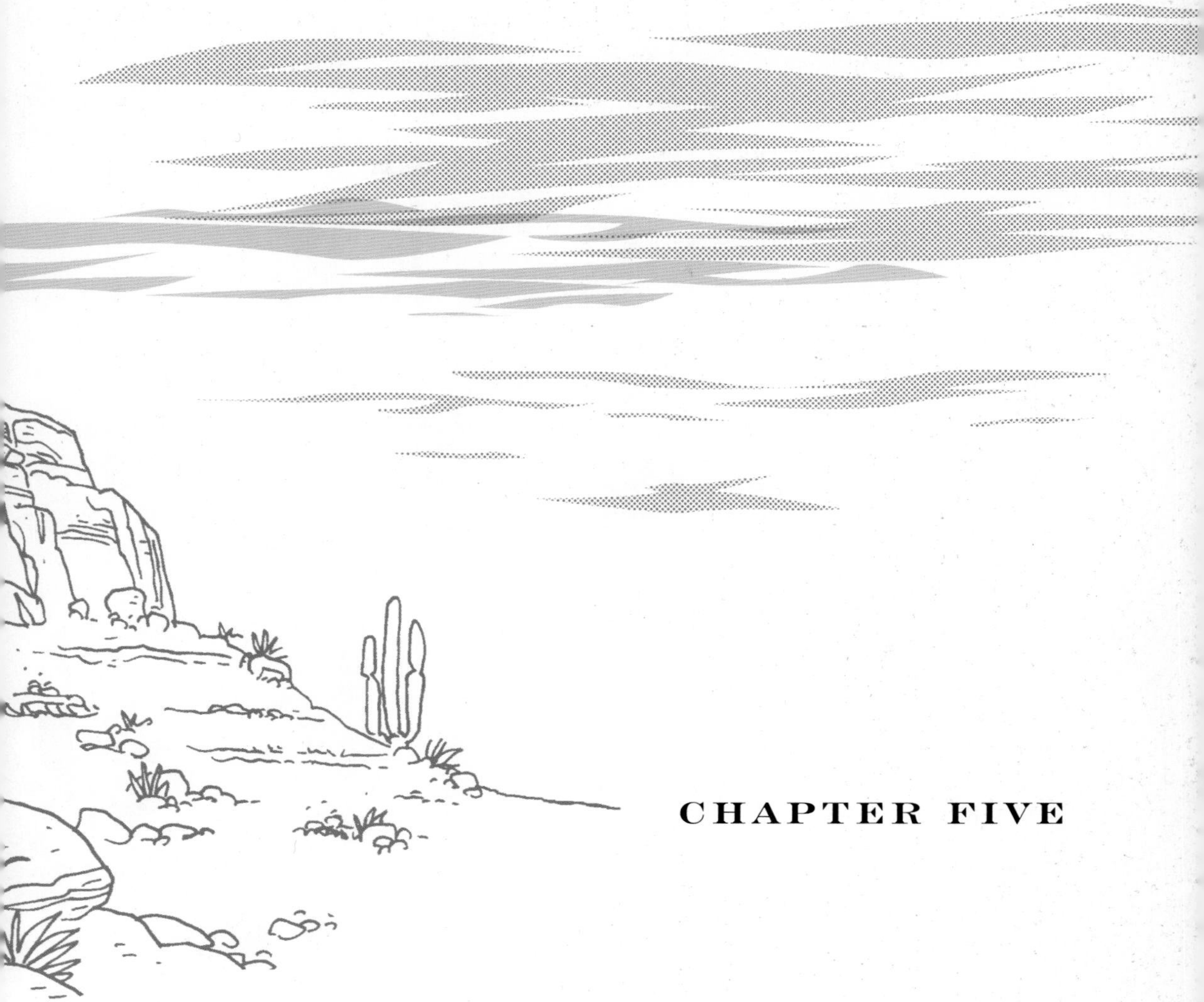

CHAPTER FIVE

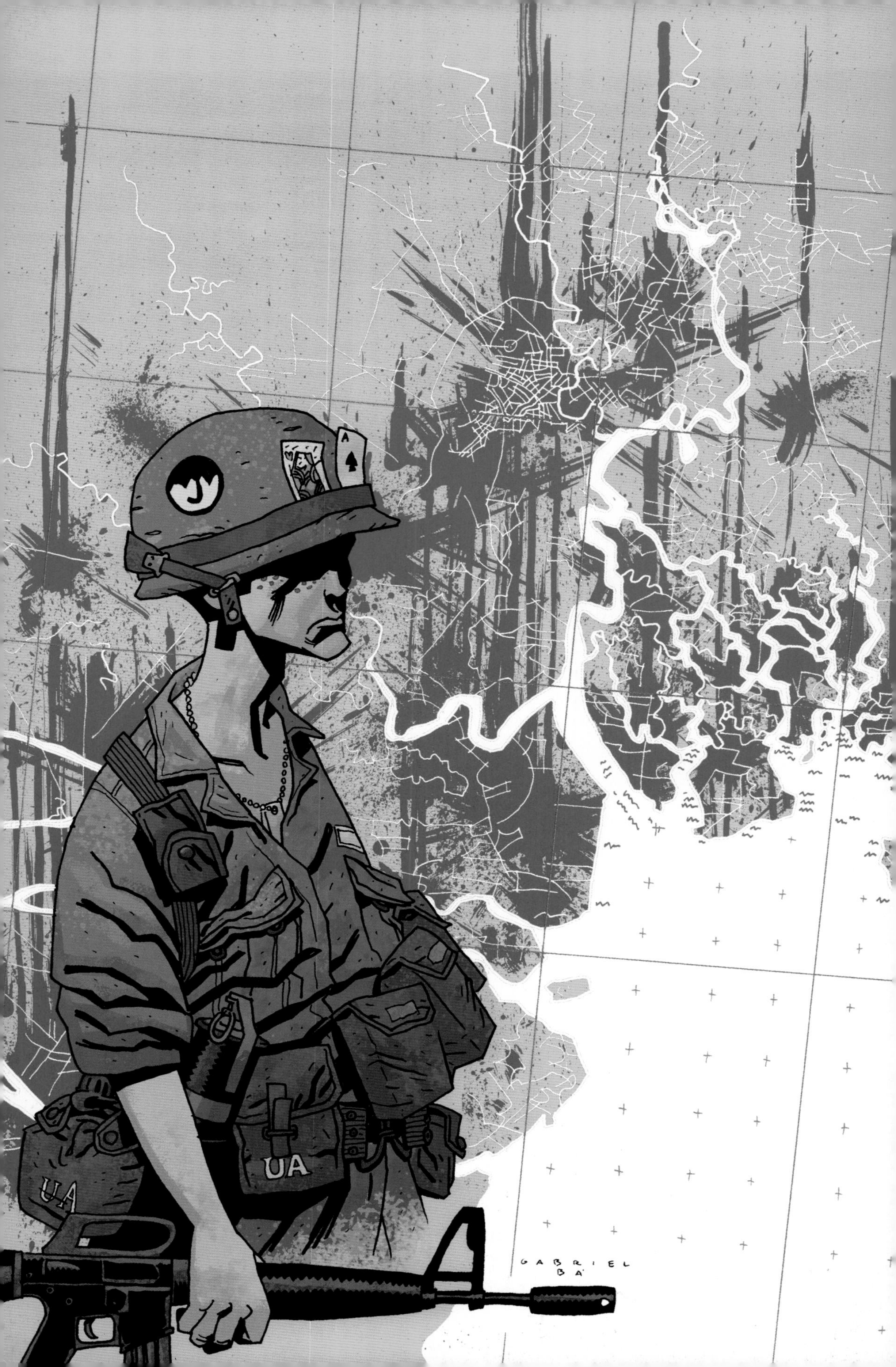
UA
UA
GABRIEL BÁ

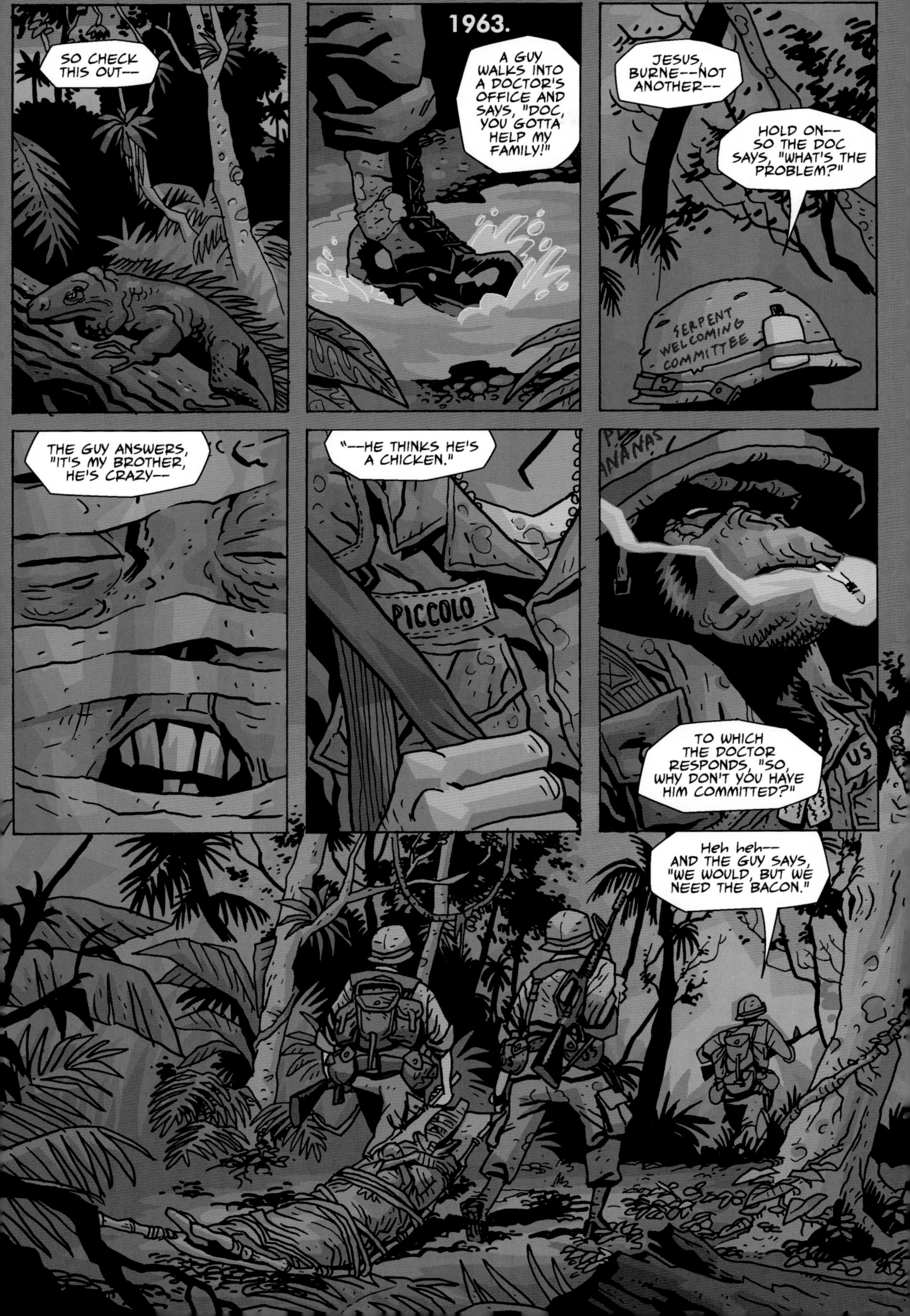
SO CHECK THIS OUT--
1963.
A GUY WALKS INTO A DOCTOR'S OFFICE AND SAYS, "DOC, YOU GOTTA HELP MY FAMILY!"
JESUS, BURNE--NOT ANOTHER--
HOLD ON-- SO THE DOC SAYS, "WHAT'S THE PROBLEM?"
SERPENT WELCOMING COMMITTEE
THE GUY ANSWERS, "IT'S MY BROTHER, HE'S CRAZY--
"--HE THINKS HE'S A CHICKEN."
PICCOLO
TO WHICH THE DOCTOR RESPONDS, "SO, WHY DON'T YOU HAVE HIM COMMITTED?"
US
Heh heh-- AND THE GUY SAYS, "WE WOULD, BUT WE NEED THE BACON."

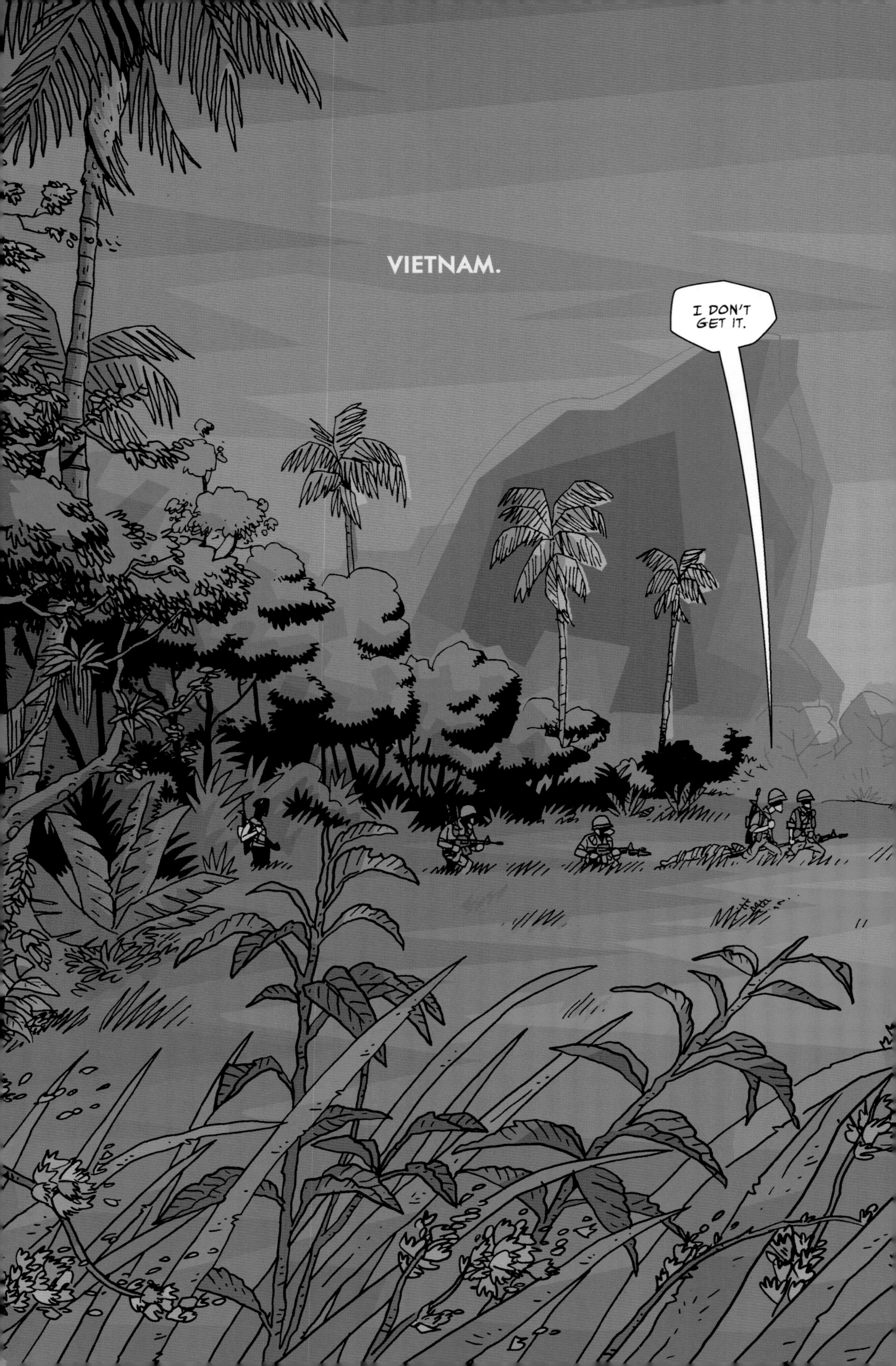
VIETNAM.
I DON'T GET IT.

THE UMBRELLA ACADEMY IN:
ALL THE ANIMALS IN THE ZOO
BEING PART FIVE OF SIX IN THE STORY: DALLAS

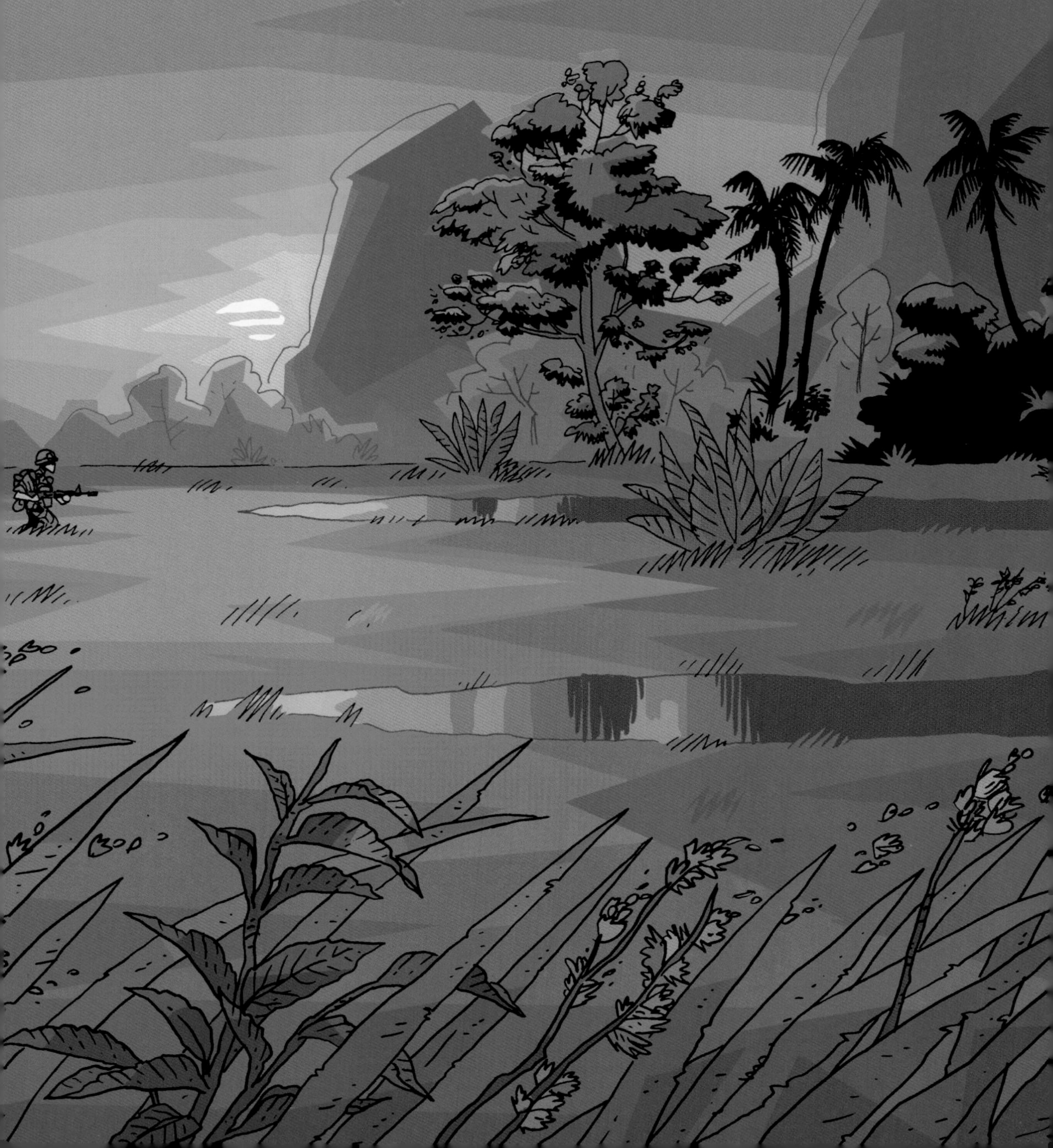

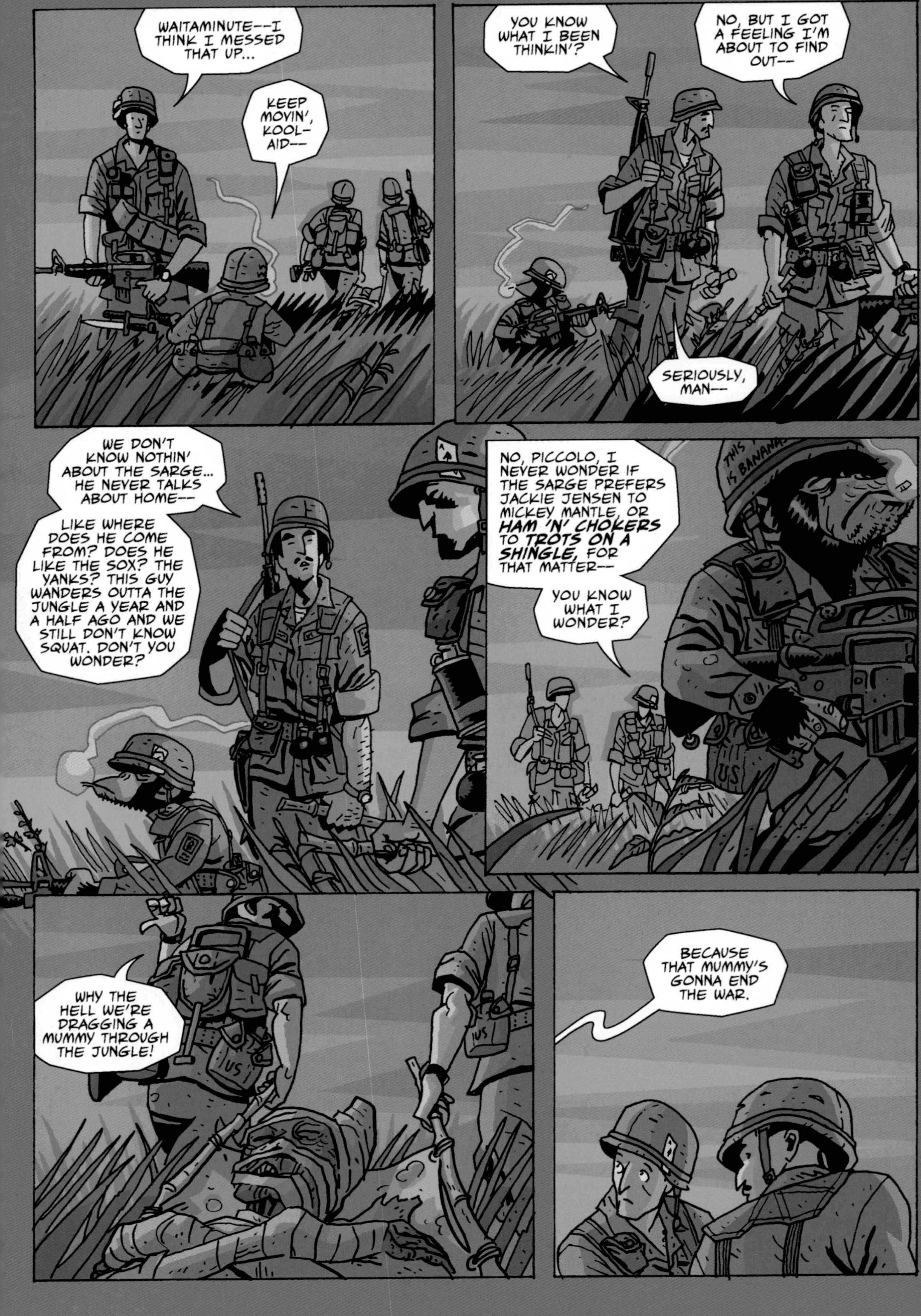
WAITAMINUTE--I THINK I MESSED THAT UP...
KEEP MOVIN', KOOL-AID--
YOU KNOW WHAT I BEEN THINKIN'?
NO, BUT I GOT A FEELING I'M ABOUT TO FIND OUT--
SERIOUSLY, MAN--
WE DON'T KNOW NOTHIN' ABOUT THE SARGE... HE NEVER TALKS ABOUT HOME--
LIKE WHERE DOES HE COME FROM? DOES HE LIKE THE SOX? THE YANKS? THIS GUY WANDERS OUTTA THE JUNGLE A YEAR AND A HALF AGO AND WE STILL DON'T KNOW SQUAT. DON'T YOU WONDER?
NO, PICCOLO, I NEVER WONDER IF THE SARGE PREFERS JACKIE JENSEN TO MICKEY MANTLE, OR ***HAM 'N' CHOKERS*** TO ***TROTS ON A SHINGLE,*** FOR THAT MATTER--
YOU KNOW WHAT I WONDER?
WHY THE HELL WE'RE DRAGGING A MUMMY THROUGH THE JUNGLE!
BECAUSE THAT MUMMY'S GONNA END THE WAR.

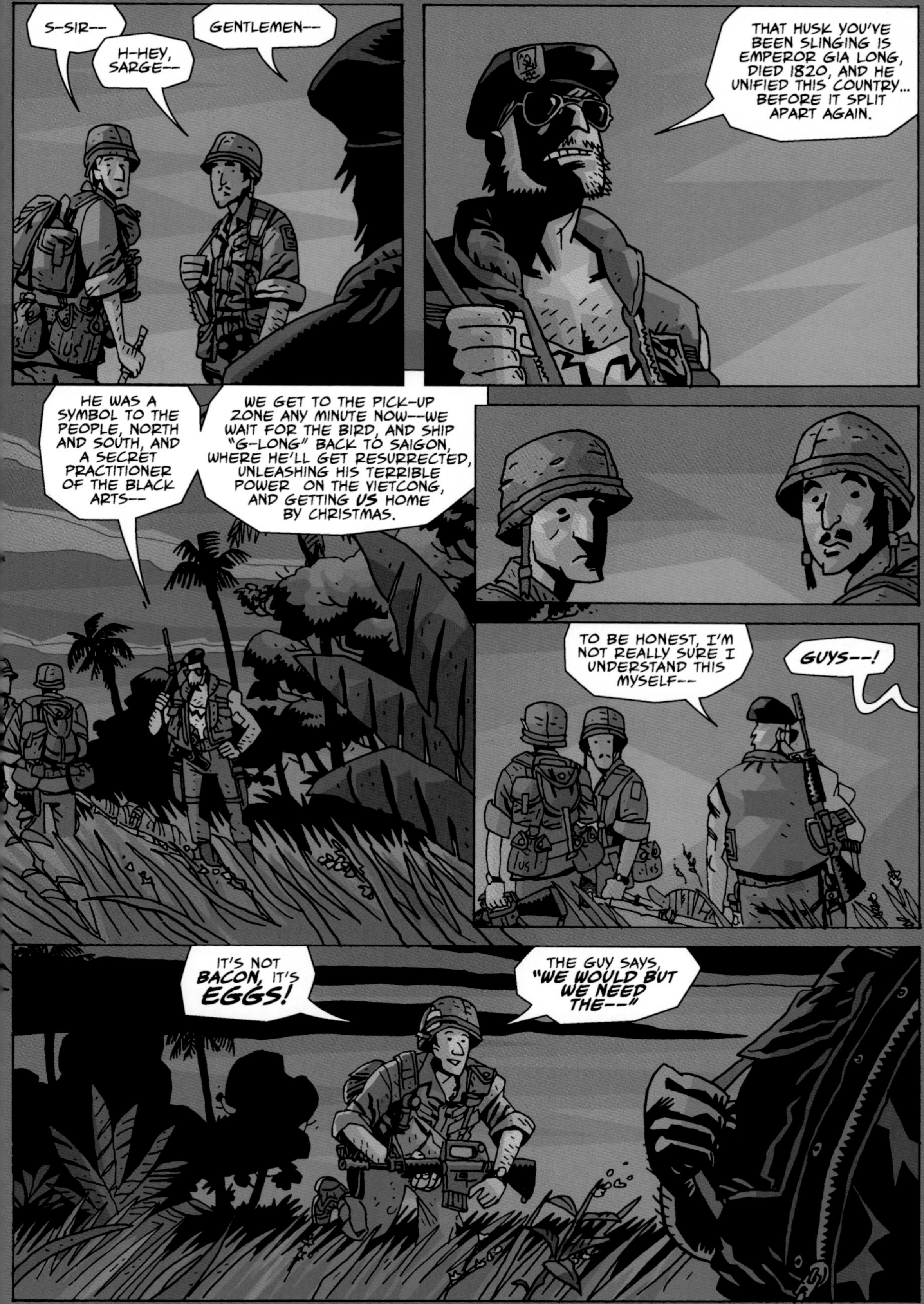
S-SIR--
H-HEY, SARGE--
GENTLEMEN--
THAT HUSK YOU'VE BEEN SLINGING IS EMPEROR GIA LONG, DIED 1820, AND HE UNIFIED THIS COUNTRY... BEFORE IT SPLIT APART AGAIN.
HE WAS A SYMBOL TO THE PEOPLE, NORTH AND SOUTH, AND A SECRET PRACTITIONER OF THE BLACK ARTS--
WE GET TO THE PICK-UP ZONE ANY MINUTE NOW--WE WAIT FOR THE BIRD, AND SHIP "G-LONG" BACK TO SAIGON, WHERE HE'LL GET RESURRECTED, UNLEASHING HIS TERRIBLE POWER ON THE VIETCONG, AND GETTING US HOME BY CHRISTMAS.
TO BE HONEST, I'M NOT REALLY SURE I UNDERSTAND THIS MYSELF--
GUYS--!
IT'S NOT BACON, IT'S EGGS!
THE GUY SAYS, "WE WOULD BUT WE NEED THE--"

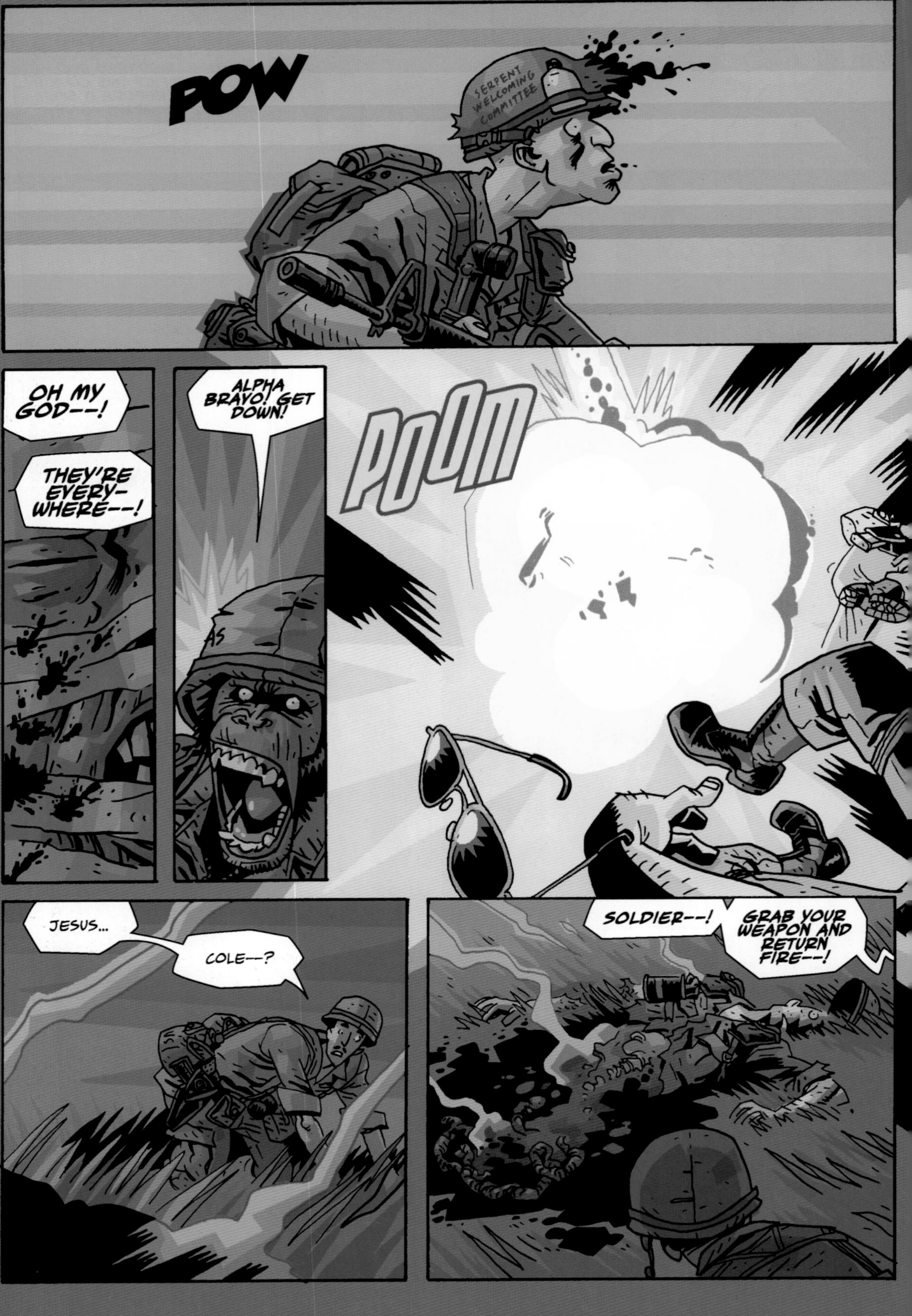
POW
SERPENT WELCOMING COMMITTEE
OH MY GOD--!
THEY'RE EVERY-WHERE--!
ALPHA BRAVO! GET DOWN!
POOM
AS
JESUS...
COLE--?
SOLDIER--!
GRAB YOUR WEAPON AND RETURN FIRE--!

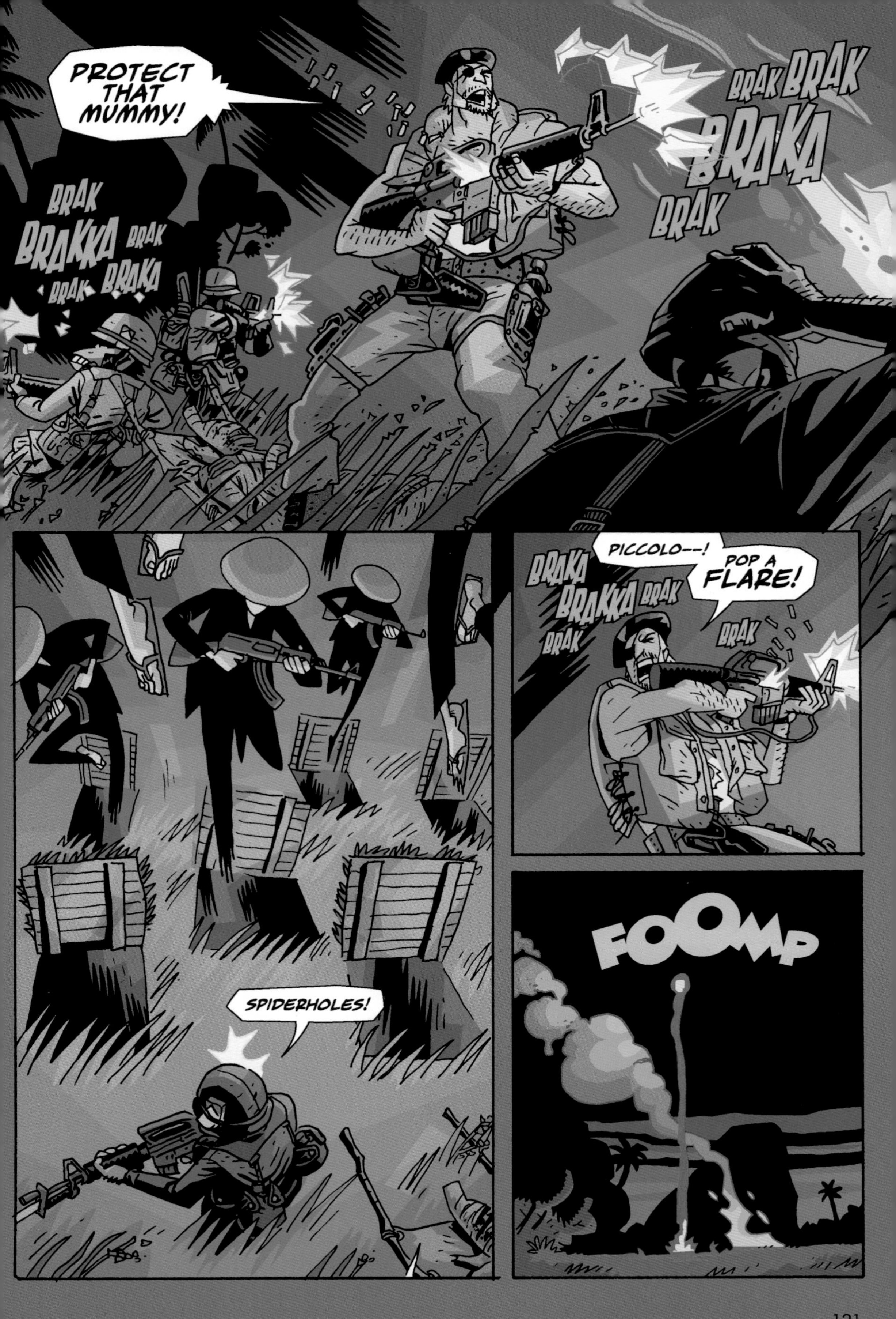
PROTECT THAT MUMMY!
BRAK BRAK BRAKA BRAK
BRAK BRAKKA BRAK BRAK BRAKA
BRAKA BRAKKA BRAK BRAK
PICCOLO--!
POP A FLARE!
BRAK
SPIDERHOLES!
FOOMP

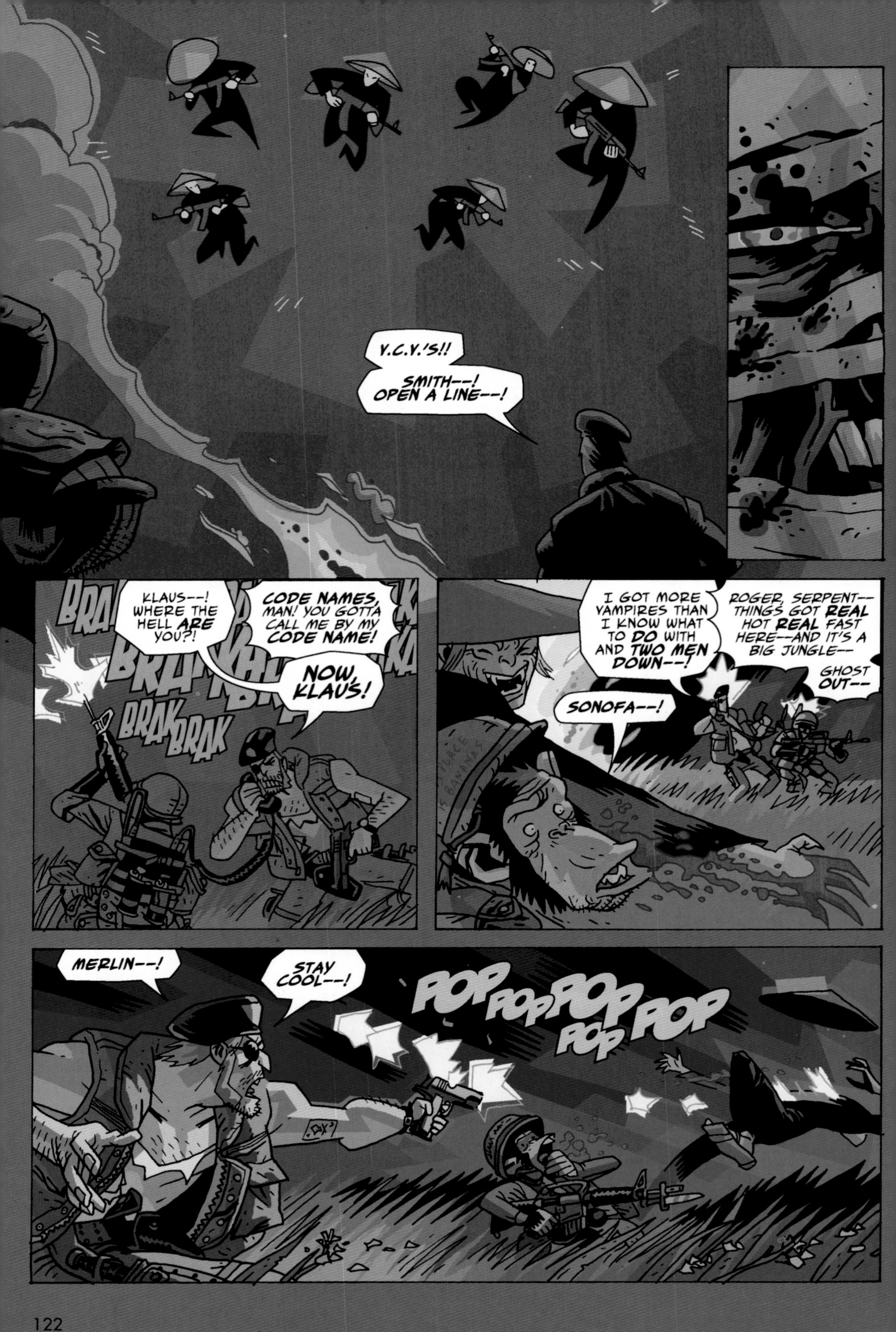
V.C.V.'S!!
SMITH--! OPEN A LINE--!
KLAUS--! WHERE THE HELL ARE YOU?!
CODE NAMES, MAN! YOU GOTTA CALL ME BY MY CODE NAME!
NOW, KLAUS!
BRAK BRAK
I GOT MORE VAMPIRES THAN I KNOW WHAT TO DO WITH AND TWO MEN DOWN--!
ROGER, SERPENT-- THINGS GOT REAL HOT REAL FAST HERE--AND IT'S A BIG JUNGLE--
GHOST OUT--
SONOFA--!
MERLIN--!
STAY COOL--!
POP POP POP POP POP POP

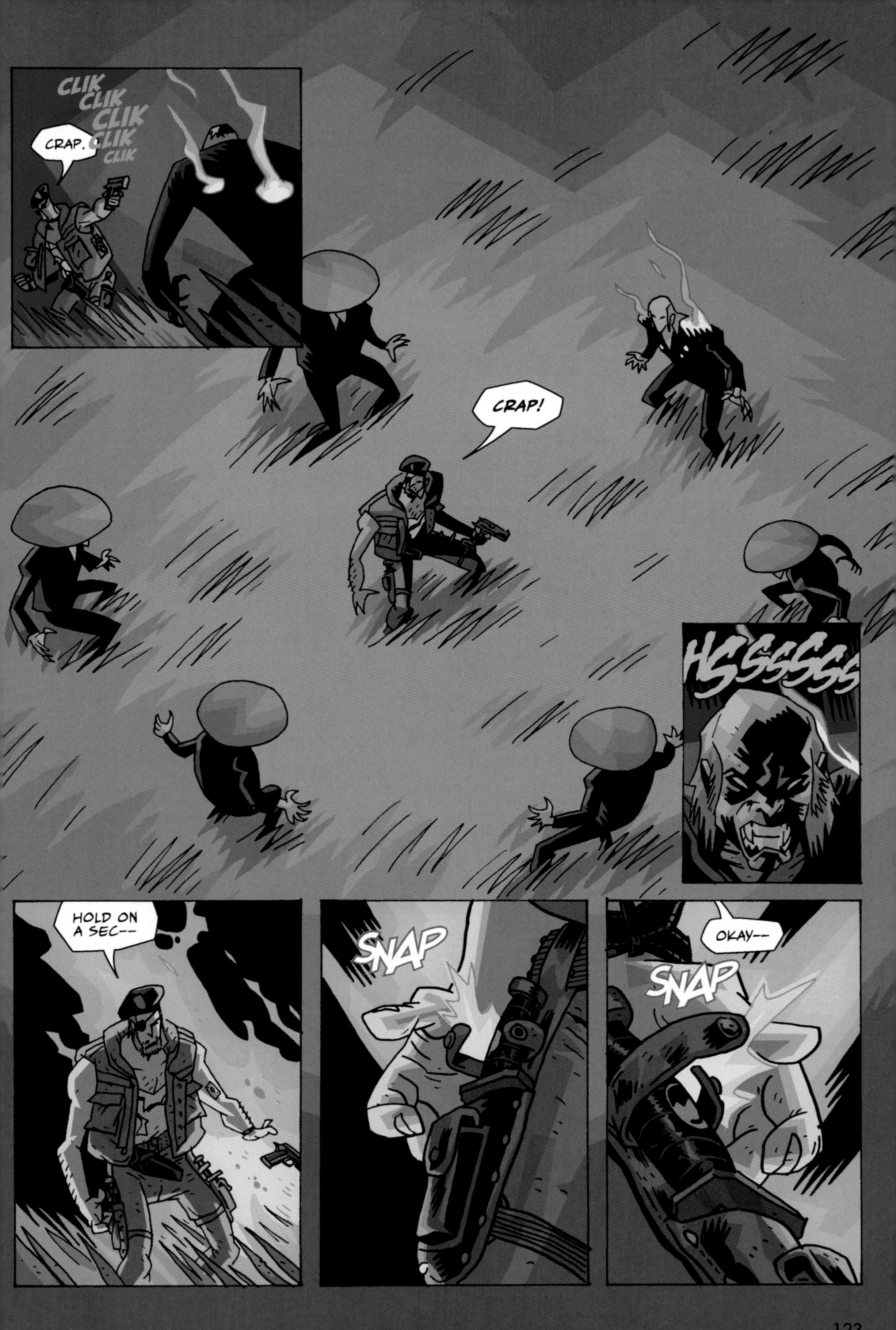
CLIK CLIK CLIK CLIK CLIK
CRAP.
CRAP!
HSSSSSS
HOLD ON A SEC--
SNAP
OKAY--
SNAP

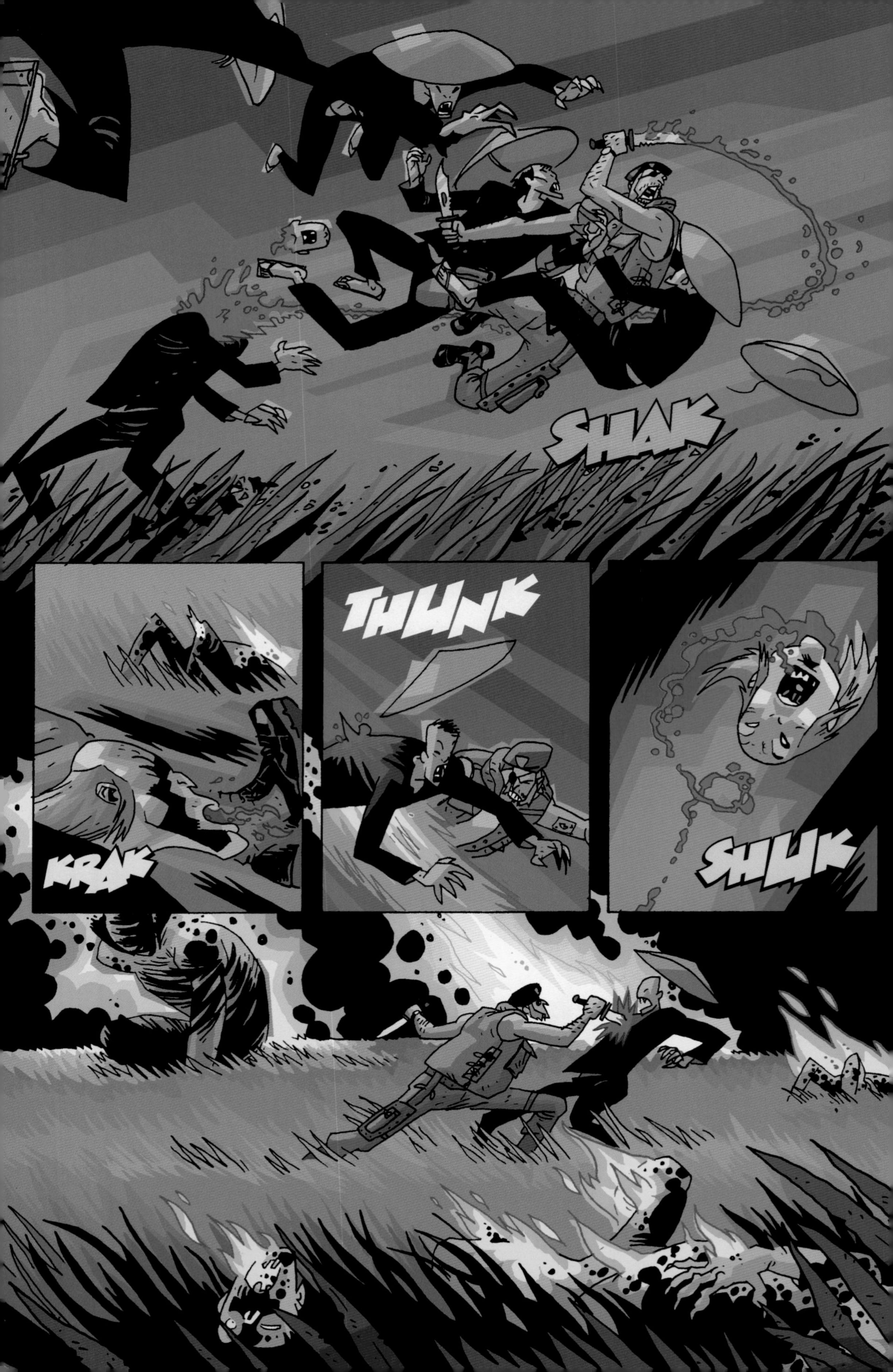
SHAK
KRAK
THUNK
SHUK

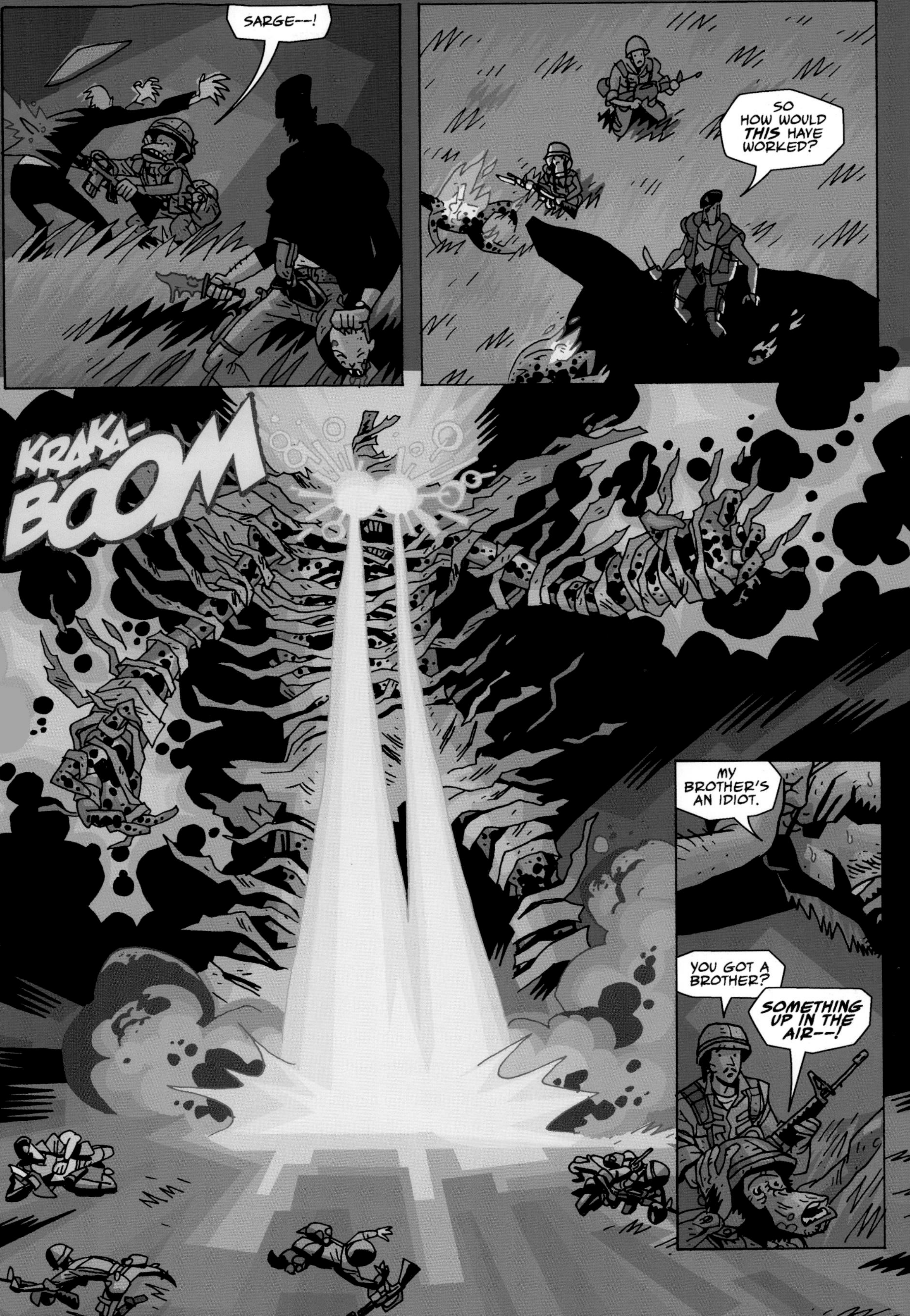
SARGE--!
SO HOW WOULD THIS HAVE WORKED?
KRAKA-BOOM
MY BROTHER'S AN IDIOT.
YOU GOT A BROTHER?
SOMETHING UP IN THE AIR--!

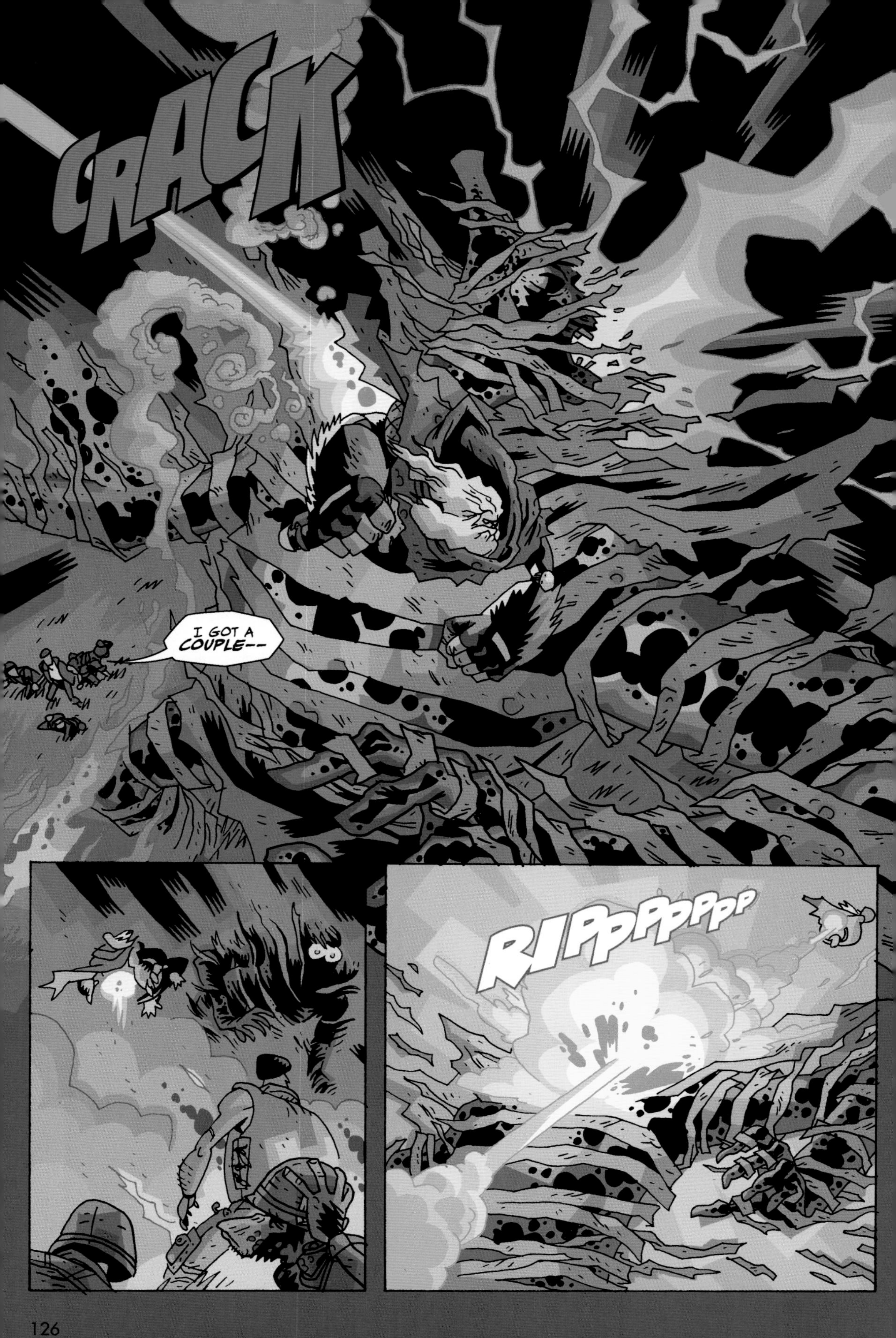
CRACK
I GOT A COUPLE--
RIPPPPPPP

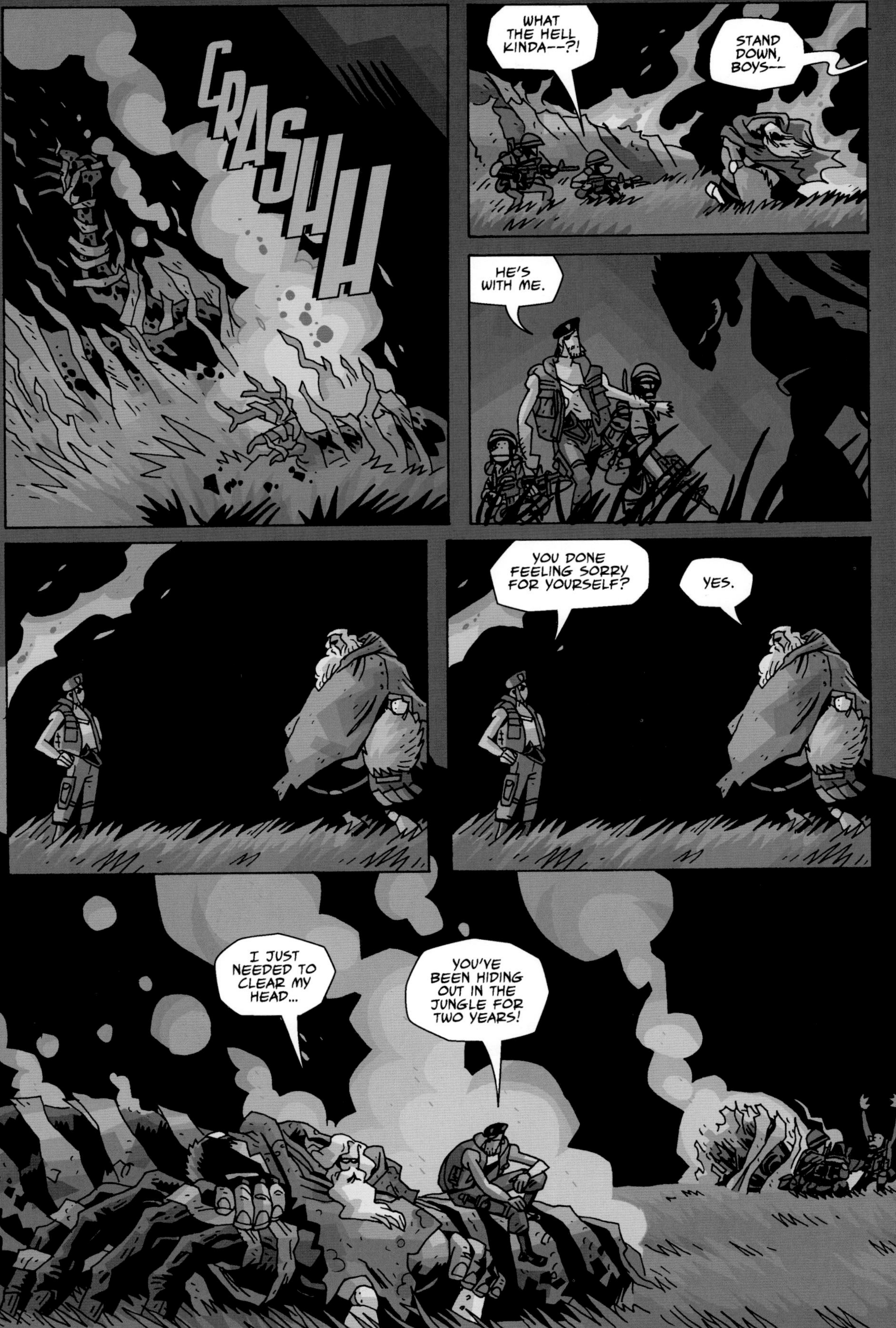
CRASHH
WHAT THE HELL KINDA--?!
STAND DOWN, BOYS--
HE'S WITH ME.
YOU DONE FEELING SORRY FOR YOURSELF?
YES.
I JUST NEEDED TO CLEAR MY HEAD...
YOU'VE BEEN HIDING OUT IN THE JUNGLE FOR TWO YEARS!

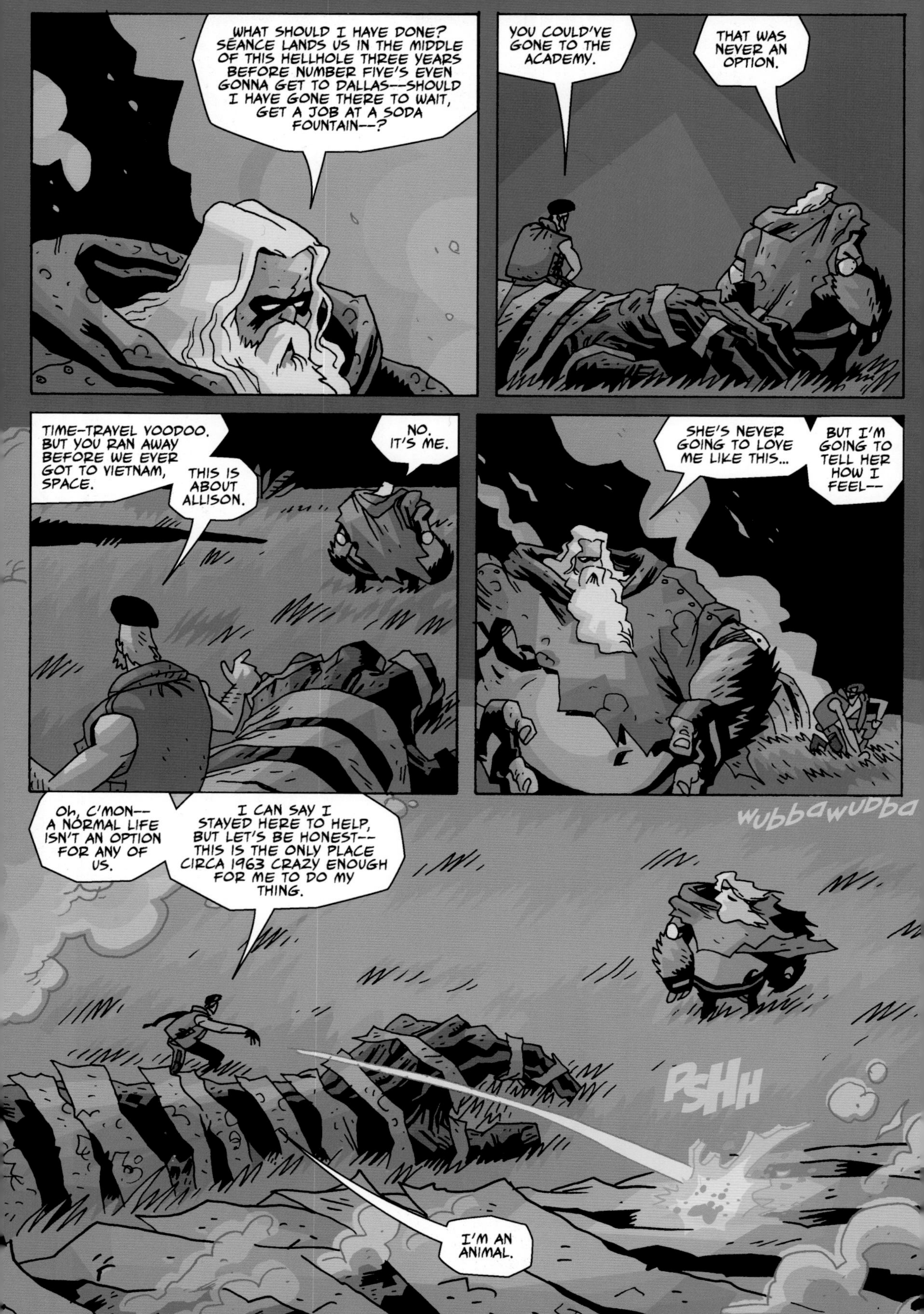
WHAT SHOULD I HAVE DONE? SÉANCE LANDS US IN THE MIDDLE OF THIS HELLHOLE THREE YEARS BEFORE NUMBER FIVE'S EVEN GONNA GET TO DALLAS--SHOULD I HAVE GONE THERE TO WAIT, GET A JOB AT A SODA FOUNTAIN--?
YOU COULD'VE GONE TO THE ACADEMY.
THAT WAS NEVER AN OPTION.
TIME-TRAVEL VOODOO. BUT YOU RAN AWAY BEFORE WE EVER GOT TO VIETNAM, SPACE.
THIS IS ABOUT ALLISON.
NO. IT'S ME.
SHE'S NEVER GOING TO LOVE ME LIKE THIS...
BUT I'M GOING TO TELL HER HOW I FEEL--
Oh, C'MON-- A NORMAL LIFE ISN'T AN OPTION FOR ANY OF US.
I CAN SAY I STAYED HERE TO HELP, BUT LET'S BE HONEST-- THIS IS THE ONLY PLACE CIRCA 1963 CRAZY ENOUGH FOR ME TO DO MY THING.
WUBBAWUBBA
PSHH
I'M AN ANIMAL.

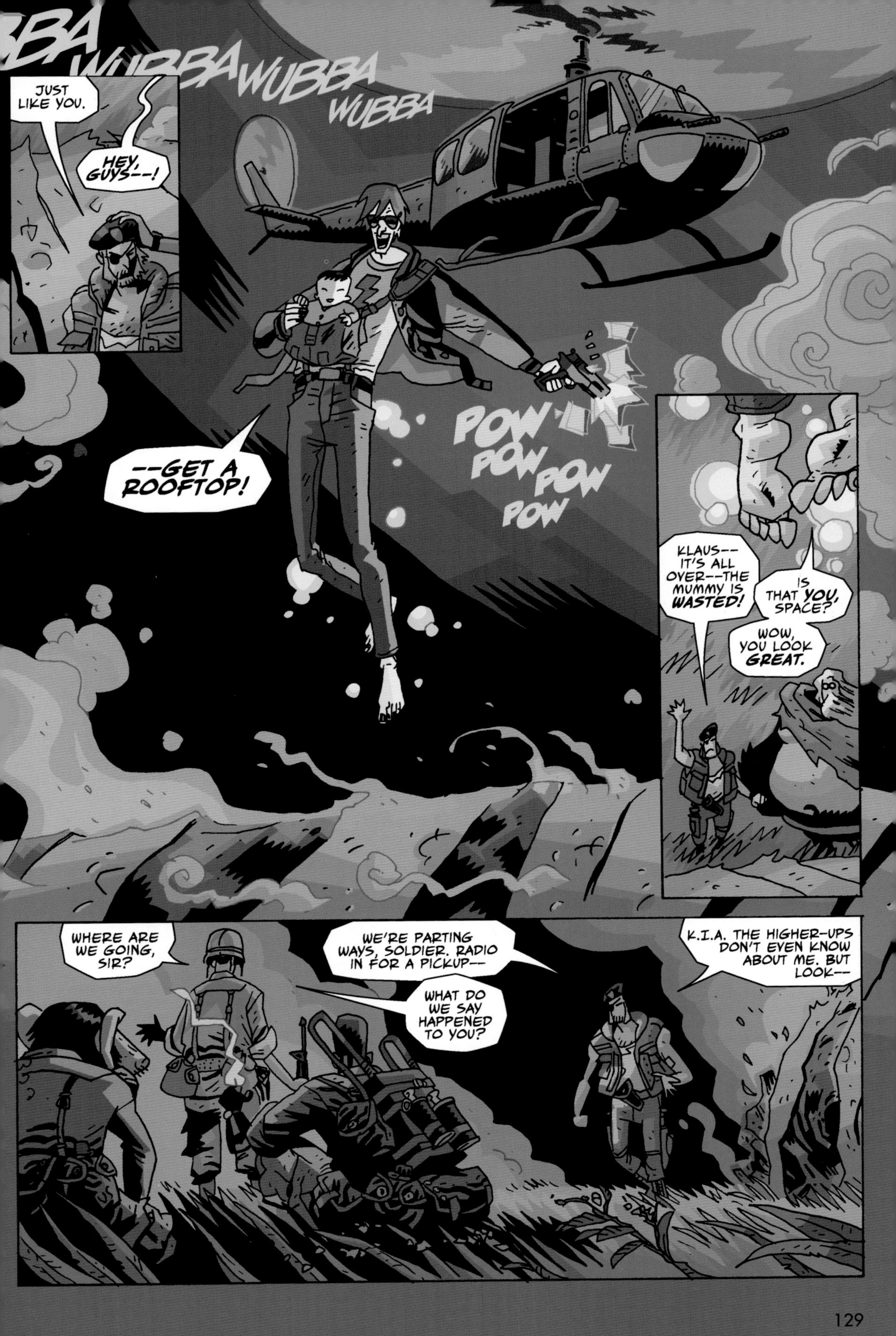
BBA WUBBA WUBBA WUBBA
JUST LIKE YOU.
HEY, GUYS--!
--GET A ROOFTOP!
POW POW POW POW POW
KLAUS-- IT'S ALL OVER--THE MUMMY IS WASTED!
IS THAT YOU, SPACE?
WOW, YOU LOOK GREAT.
WHERE ARE WE GOING, SIR?
WE'RE PARTING WAYS, SOLDIER. RADIO IN FOR A PICKUP--
WHAT DO WE SAY HAPPENED TO YOU?
K.I.A. THE HIGHER-UPS DON'T EVEN KNOW ABOUT ME. BUT LOOK--

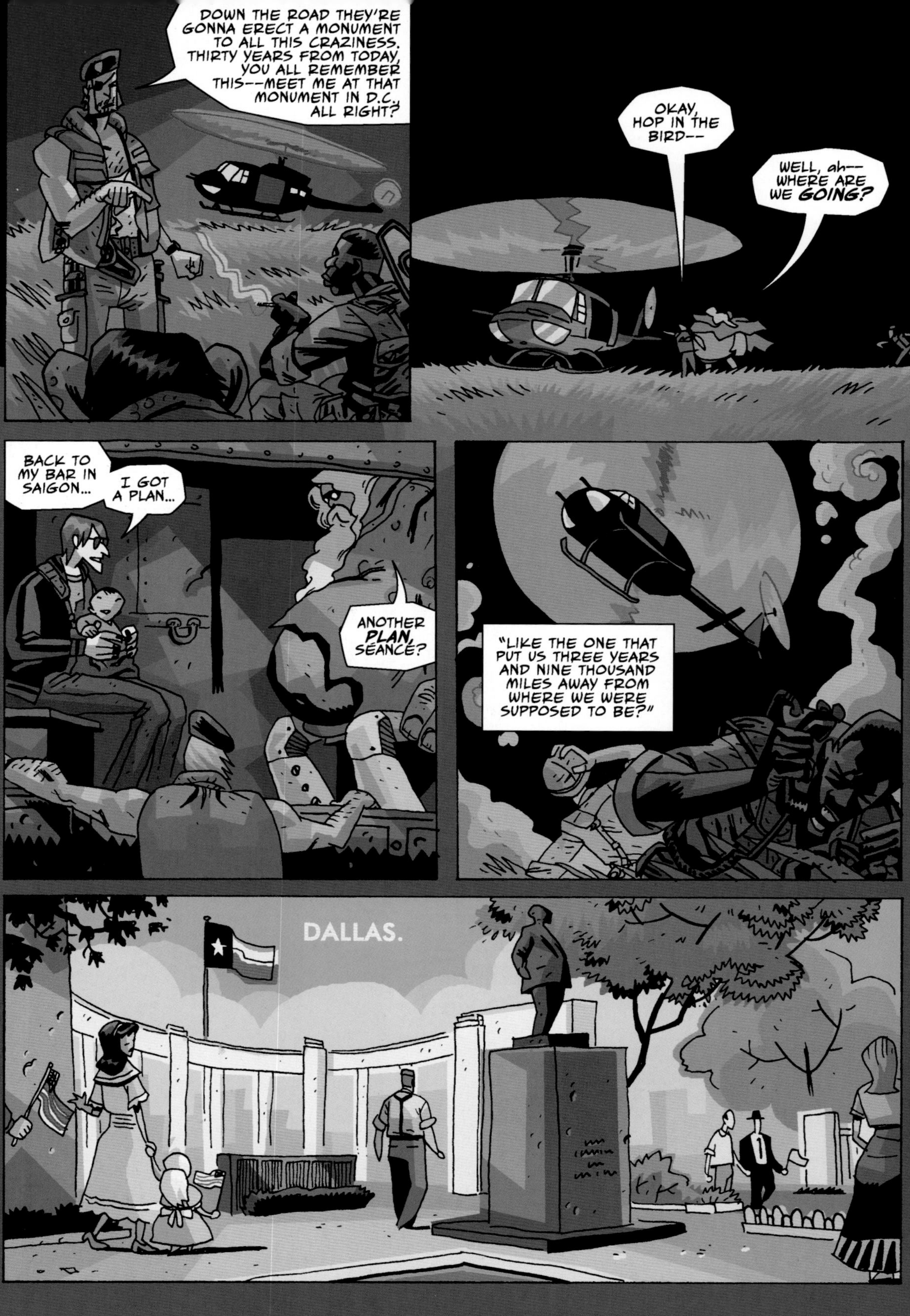
DOWN THE ROAD THEY'RE GONNA ERECT A MONUMENT TO ALL THIS CRAZINESS. THIRTY YEARS FROM TODAY, YOU ALL REMEMBER THIS--MEET ME AT THAT MONUMENT IN D.C., ALL RIGHT?
OKAY, HOP IN THE BIRD--
WELL, ah-- WHERE ARE WE GOING?
BACK TO MY BAR IN SAIGON...
I GOT A PLAN...
ANOTHER PLAN, SEANCE?
"LIKE THE ONE THAT PUT US THREE YEARS AND NINE THOUSAND MILES AWAY FROM WHERE WE WERE SUPPOSED TO BE?"
DALLAS.

BOOK DEPOSITORY COMING UP--

KILL THE LIGHTS AND DROP YOUR SPEED--!

AMBULANCE

EARS ON ME, PEOPLE--!

RIGHT NOW, MY OLD SELF IS HOLED UP ON THE SIXTH FLOOR OF THE BOOK DEPOSITORY, LISTENING TO FREEFORM JAZZ ON AN EYEDROPPER FULL OF PURE L.S.D.

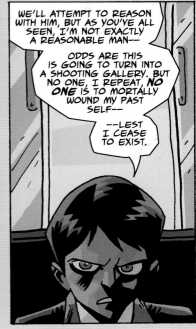

WE'LL ATTEMPT TO REASON WITH HIM, BUT AS YOU'VE ALL SEEN, I'M NOT EXACTLY A REASONABLE MAN--

ODDS ARE THIS IS GOING TO TURN INTO A SHOOTING GALLERY. BUT NO ONE, I REPEAT, **NO ONE** IS TO MORTALLY WOUND MY PAST SELF--

--LEST I CEASE TO EXIST.

RED TEAM ON ME--YOU KNOW THE DRILL--

RUN IN AND GET KILLED--

BLUE TEAM, YOU HAVE YOUR ORDERS--

STICK TO THE PLAN AND AVOID EXPOSURE AT ALL COST--

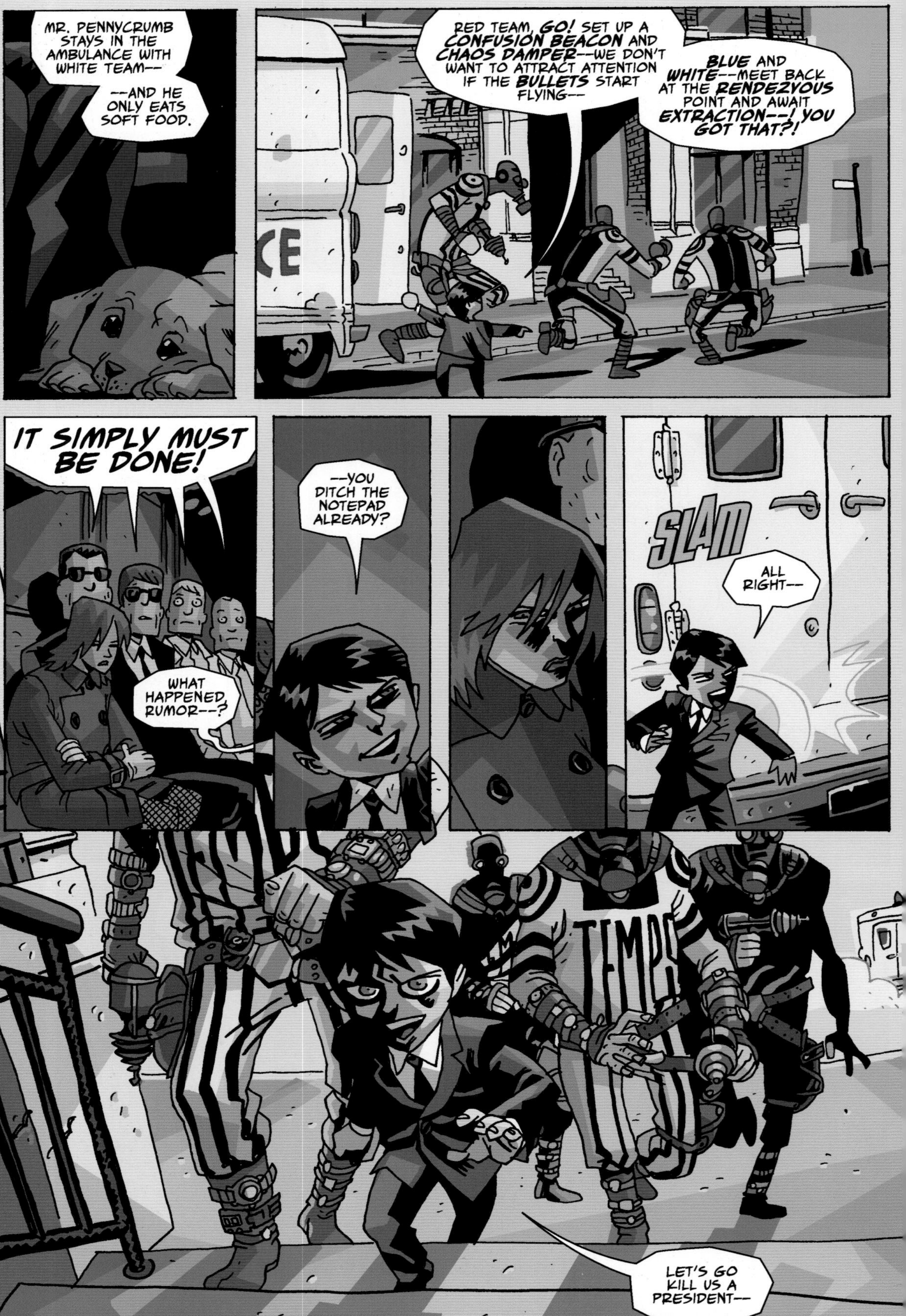

MR. PENNYCRUMB STAYS IN THE AMBULANCE WITH WHITE TEAM--
--AND HE ONLY EATS SOFT FOOD.
RED TEAM, GO! SET UP A CONFUSION BEACON AND CHAOS DAMPER--WE DON'T WANT TO ATTRACT ATTENTION IF THE BULLETS START FLYING--
BLUE AND WHITE--MEET BACK AT THE RENDEZVOUS POINT AND AWAIT EXTRACTION--! YOU GOT THAT?!
CE
IT SIMPLY MUST BE DONE!
WHAT HAPPENED, RUMOR--?
--YOU DITCH THE NOTEPAD ALREADY?
SLAM
ALL RIGHT--
TEMPS
LET'S GO KILL US A PRESIDENT--

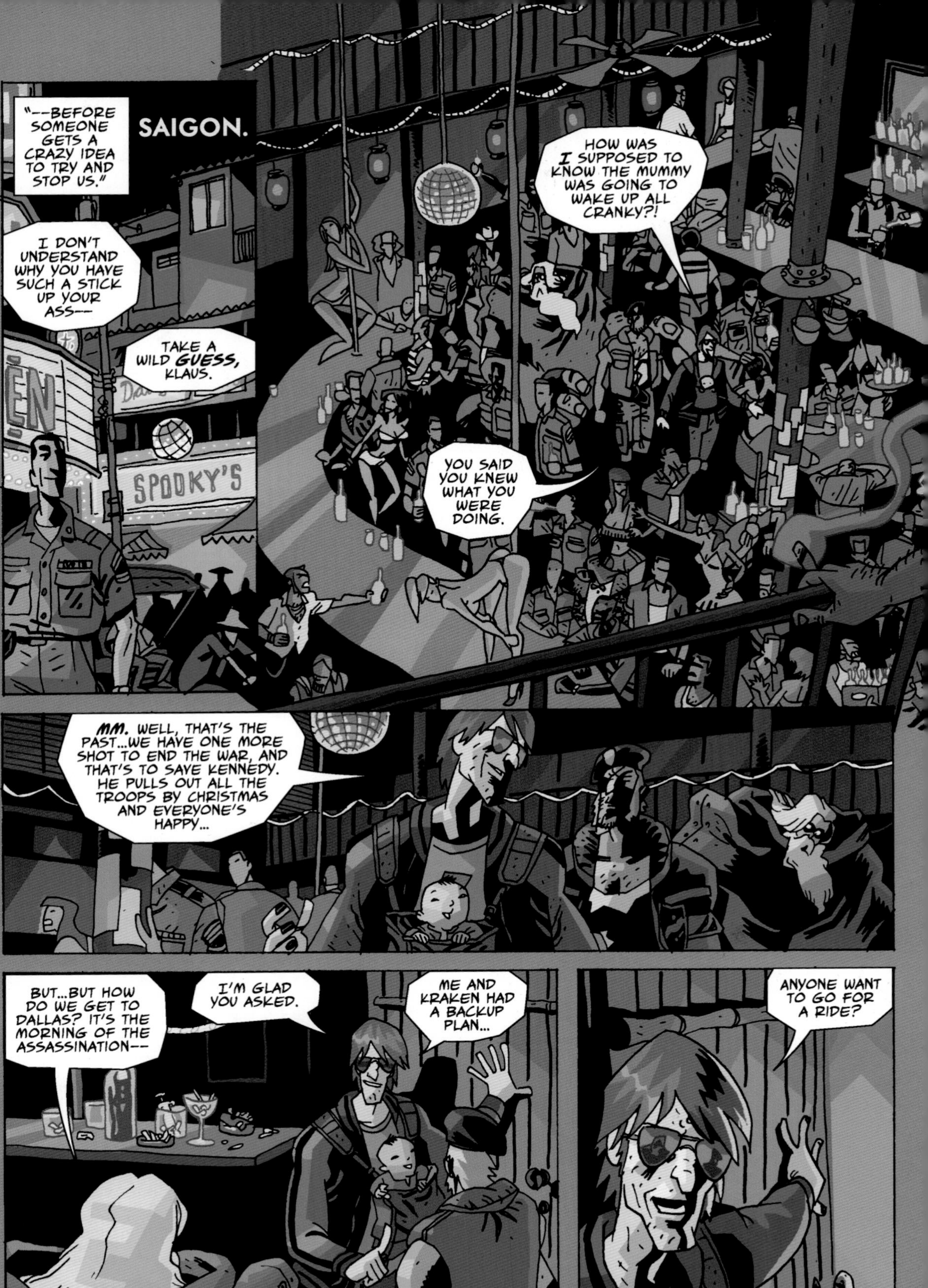
"--BEFORE SOMEONE GETS A CRAZY IDEA TO TRY AND STOP US."
SAIGON.
I DON'T UNDERSTAND WHY YOU HAVE SUCH A STICK UP YOUR ASS--
TAKE A WILD GUESS, KLAUS.
SPOOKY'S
HOW WAS I SUPPOSED TO KNOW THE MUMMY WAS GOING TO WAKE UP ALL CRANKY?!
YOU SAID YOU KNEW WHAT YOU WERE DOING.
MM. WELL, THAT'S THE PAST...WE HAVE ONE MORE SHOT TO END THE WAR, AND THAT'S TO SAVE KENNEDY. HE PULLS OUT ALL THE TROOPS BY CHRISTMAS AND EVERYONE'S HAPPY...
BUT...BUT HOW DO WE GET TO DALLAS? IT'S THE MORNING OF THE ASSASSINATION--
I'M GLAD YOU ASKED.
ME AND KRAKEN HAD A BACKUP PLAN...
ANYONE WANT TO GO FOR A RIDE?

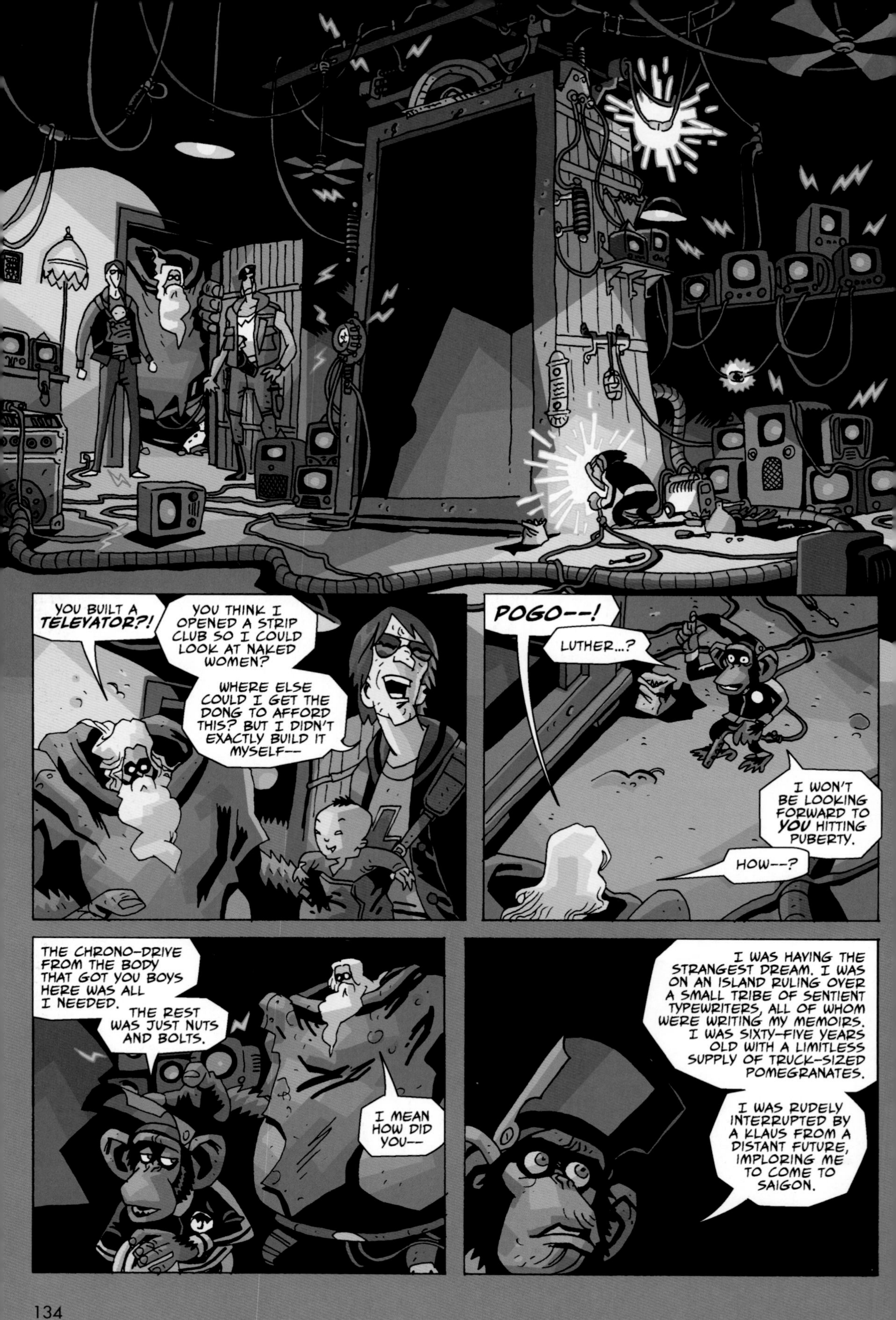
YOU BUILT A TELEVATOR?!
YOU THINK I OPENED A STRIP CLUB SO I COULD LOOK AT NAKED WOMEN?
WHERE ELSE COULD I GET THE DONG TO AFFORD THIS? BUT I DIDN'T EXACTLY BUILD IT MYSELF--
POGO--!
LUTHER...?
I WON'T BE LOOKING FORWARD TO YOU HITTING PUBERTY.
HOW--?
THE CHRONO-DRIVE FROM THE BODY THAT GOT YOU BOYS HERE WAS ALL I NEEDED.
THE REST WAS JUST NUTS AND BOLTS.
I MEAN HOW DID YOU--
I WAS HAVING THE STRANGEST DREAM. I WAS ON AN ISLAND RULING OVER A SMALL TRIBE OF SENTIENT TYPEWRITERS, ALL OF WHOM WERE WRITING MY MEMOIRS. I WAS SIXTY-FIVE YEARS OLD WITH A LIMITLESS SUPPLY OF TRUCK-SIZED POMEGRANATES.
I WAS RUDELY INTERRUPTED BY A KLAUS FROM A DISTANT FUTURE, IMPLORING ME TO COME TO SAIGON.

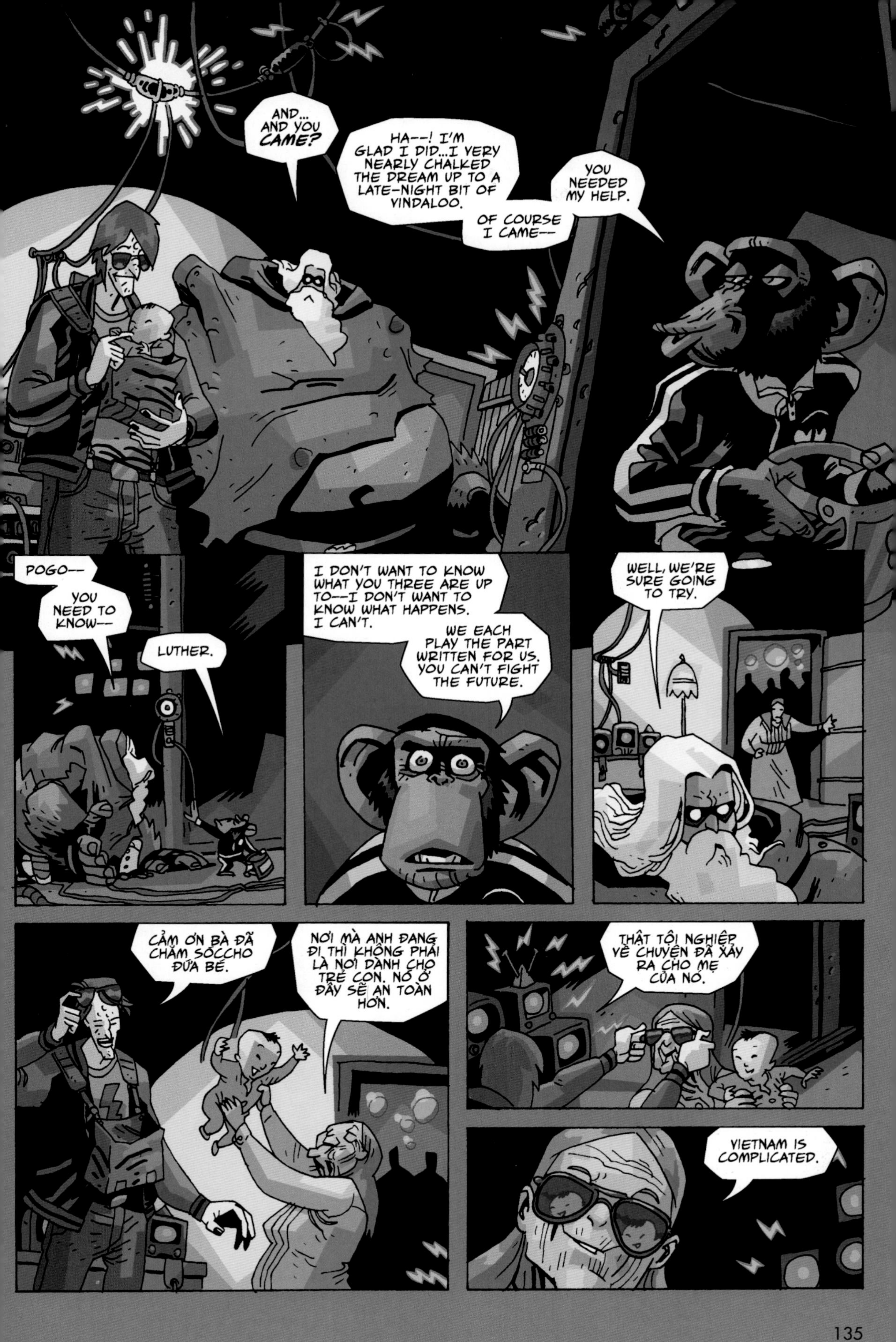

AND... AND YOU *CAME?*
HA--! I'M GLAD I DID...I VERY NEARLY CHALKED THE DREAM UP TO A LATE-NIGHT BIT OF VINDALOO.
OF COURSE I CAME--
YOU NEEDED MY HELP.
POGO--
YOU NEED TO KNOW--
LUTHER.
I DON'T WANT TO KNOW WHAT YOU THREE ARE UP TO--I DON'T WANT TO KNOW WHAT HAPPENS. I CAN'T.
WE EACH PLAY THE PART WRITTEN FOR US. YOU CAN'T FIGHT THE FUTURE.
WELL, WE'RE SURE GOING TO TRY.
CẢM ƠN BÀ ĐÃ CHĂM SÓCCHO ĐỨA BÉ.
NƠI MÀ ANH ĐANG ĐI THÌ KHÔNG PHẢI LÀ NƠI DÀNH CHO TRẺ CON. NÓ Ở ĐÂY SẼ AN TOÀN HƠN.
THẬT TỘI NGHIỆP VỀ CHUYỆN ĐÃ XẢY RA CHO MẸ CỦA NÓ.
VIETNAM IS COMPLICATED.

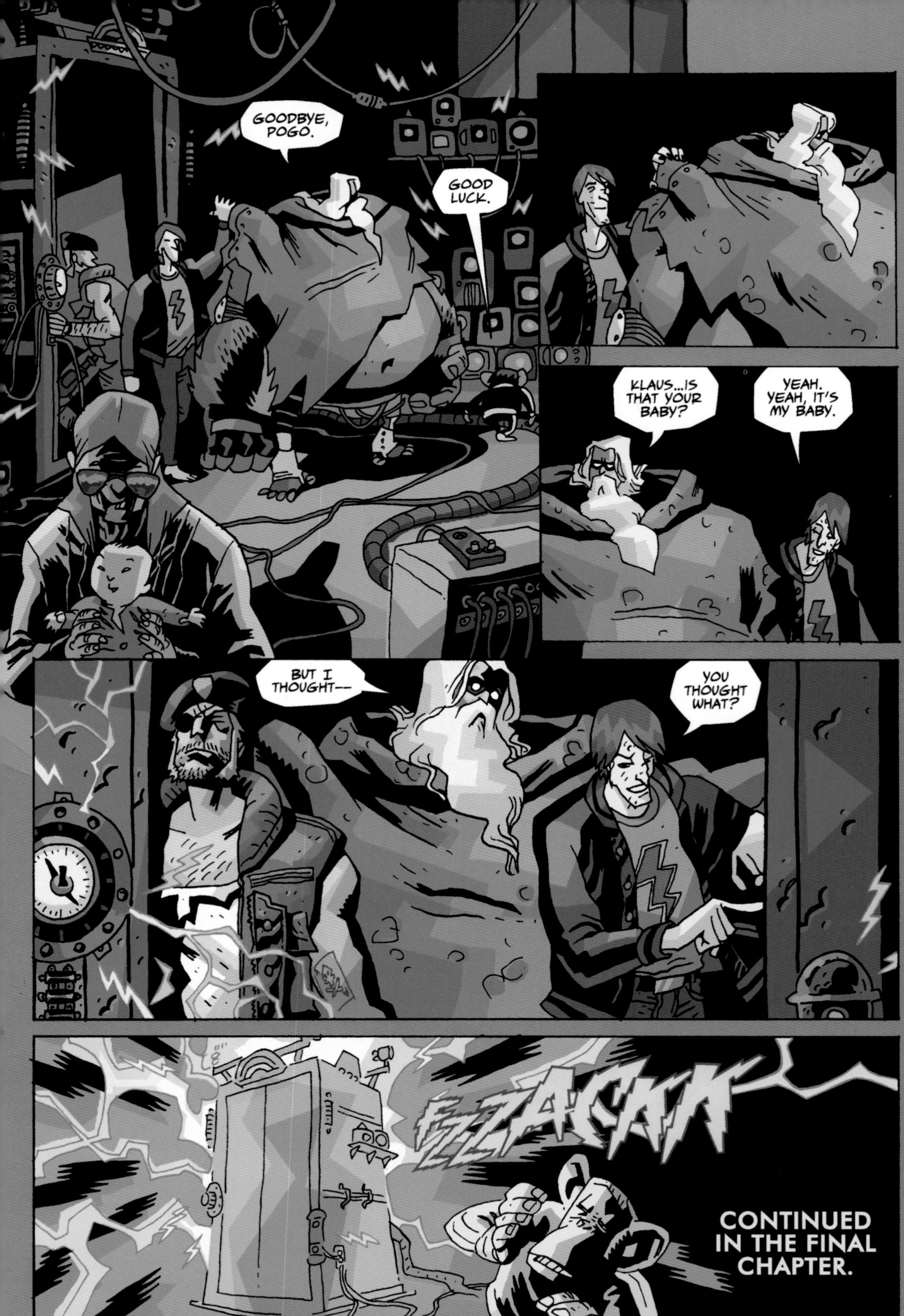
GOODBYE, POGO.
GOOD LUCK.
KLAUS...IS THAT YOUR BABY?
YEAH. YEAH, IT'S MY BABY.
BUT I THOUGHT--
YOU THOUGHT WHAT?
FZZACKK
CONTINUED IN THE FINAL CHAPTER.

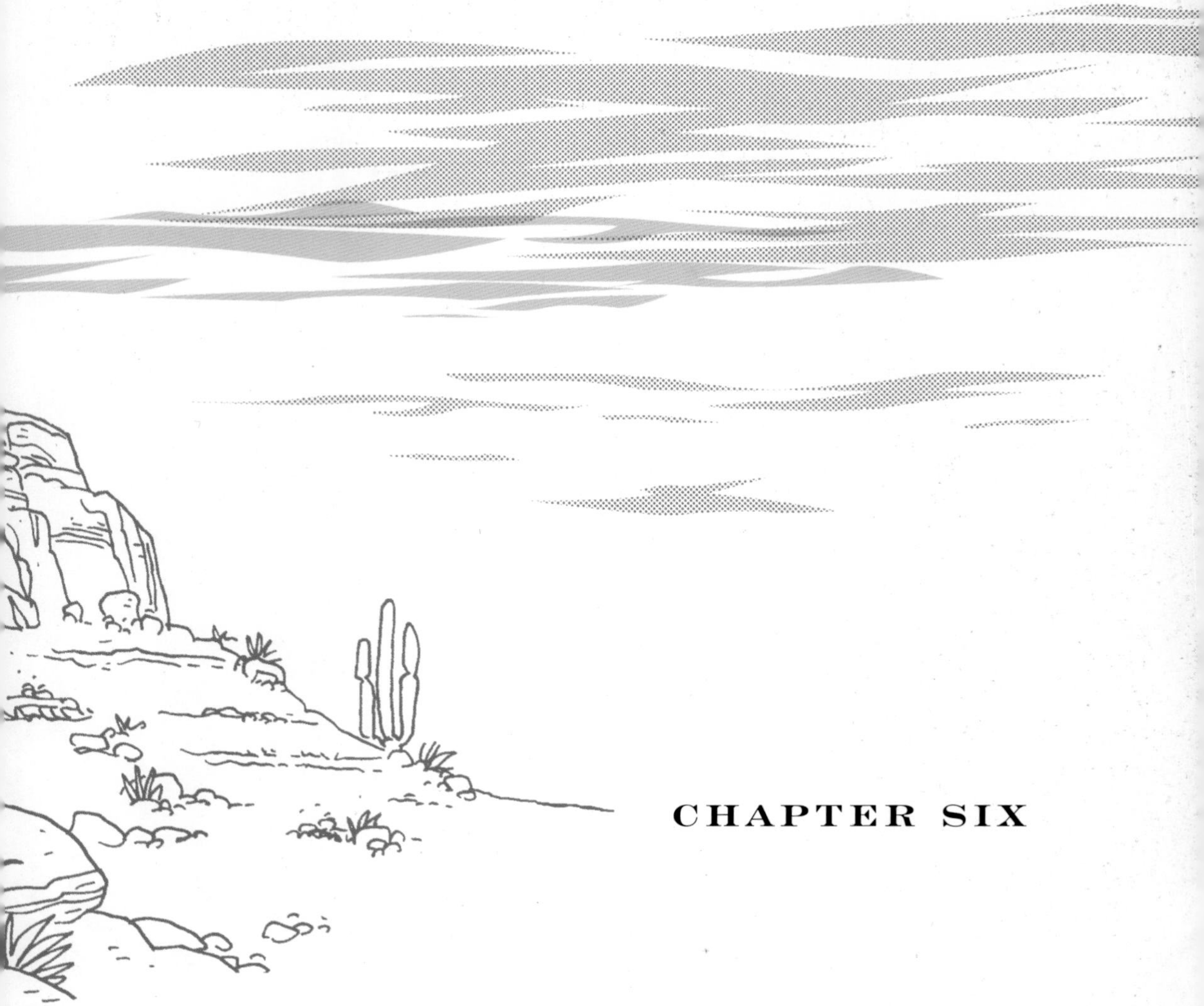

CHAPTER SIX

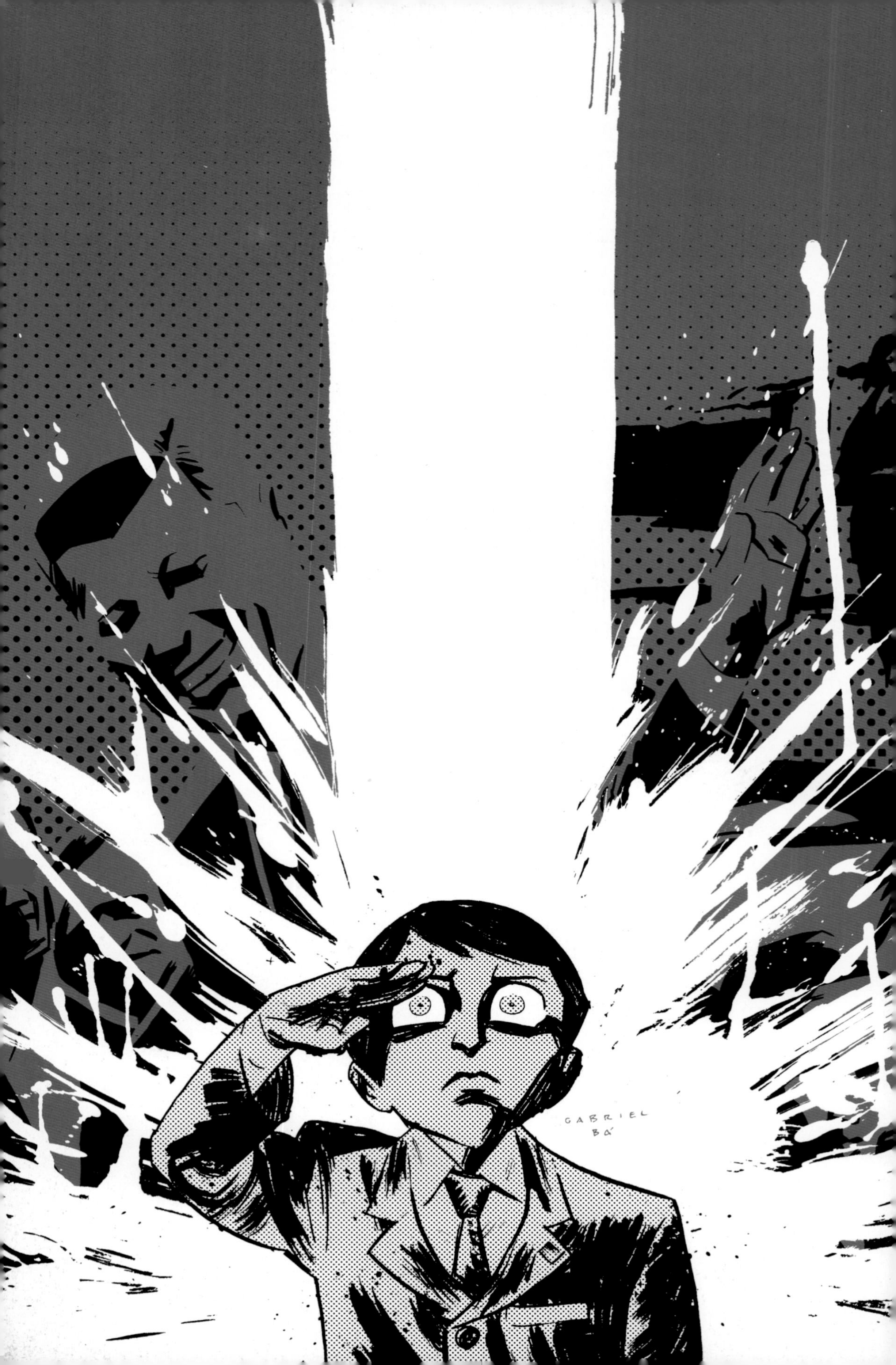
GABRIEL
BÁ

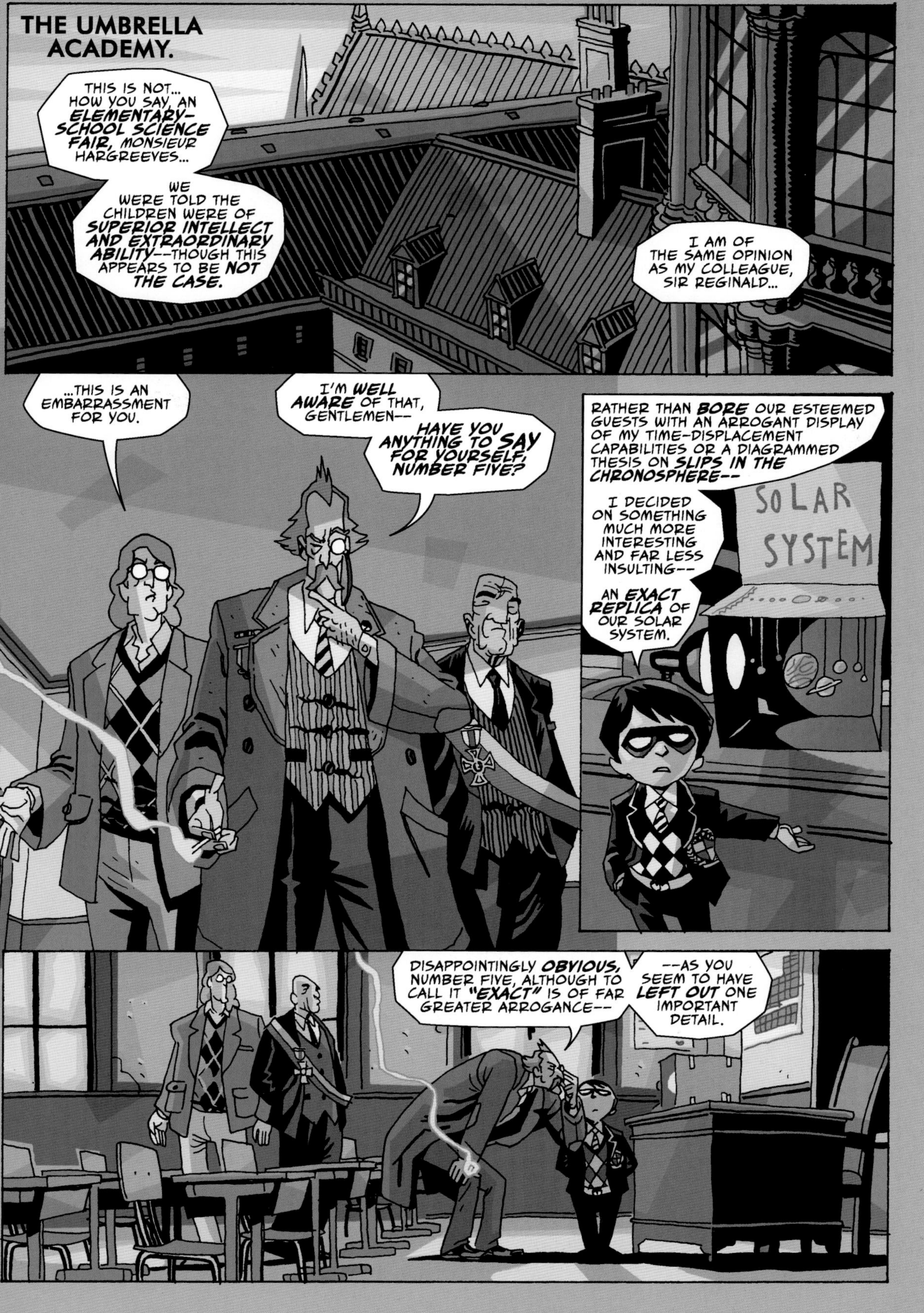
THE UMBRELLA ACADEMY.
THIS IS NOT... HOW YOU SAY, AN ELEMENTARY-SCHOOL SCIENCE FAIR, MONSIEUR HARGREEVES...
WE WERE TOLD THE CHILDREN WERE OF SUPERIOR INTELLECT AND EXTRAORDINARY ABILITY--THOUGH THIS APPEARS TO BE NOT THE CASE.
I AM OF THE SAME OPINION AS MY COLLEAGUE, SIR REGINALD...
...THIS IS AN EMBARRASSMENT FOR YOU.
I'M WELL AWARE OF THAT, GENTLEMEN--
HAVE YOU ANYTHING TO SAY FOR YOURSELF, NUMBER FIVE?
RATHER THAN BORE OUR ESTEEMED GUESTS WITH AN ARROGANT DISPLAY OF MY TIME-DISPLACEMENT CAPABILITIES OR A DIAGRAMMED THESIS ON SLIPS IN THE CHRONOSPHERE--
I DECIDED ON SOMETHING MUCH MORE INTERESTING AND FAR LESS INSULTING--
AN EXACT REPLICA OF OUR SOLAR SYSTEM.
SOLAR SYSTEM
DISAPPOINTINGLY OBVIOUS, NUMBER FIVE, ALTHOUGH TO CALL IT "EXACT" IS OF FAR GREATER ARROGANCE--
--AS YOU SEEM TO HAVE LEFT OUT ONE IMPORTANT DETAIL.

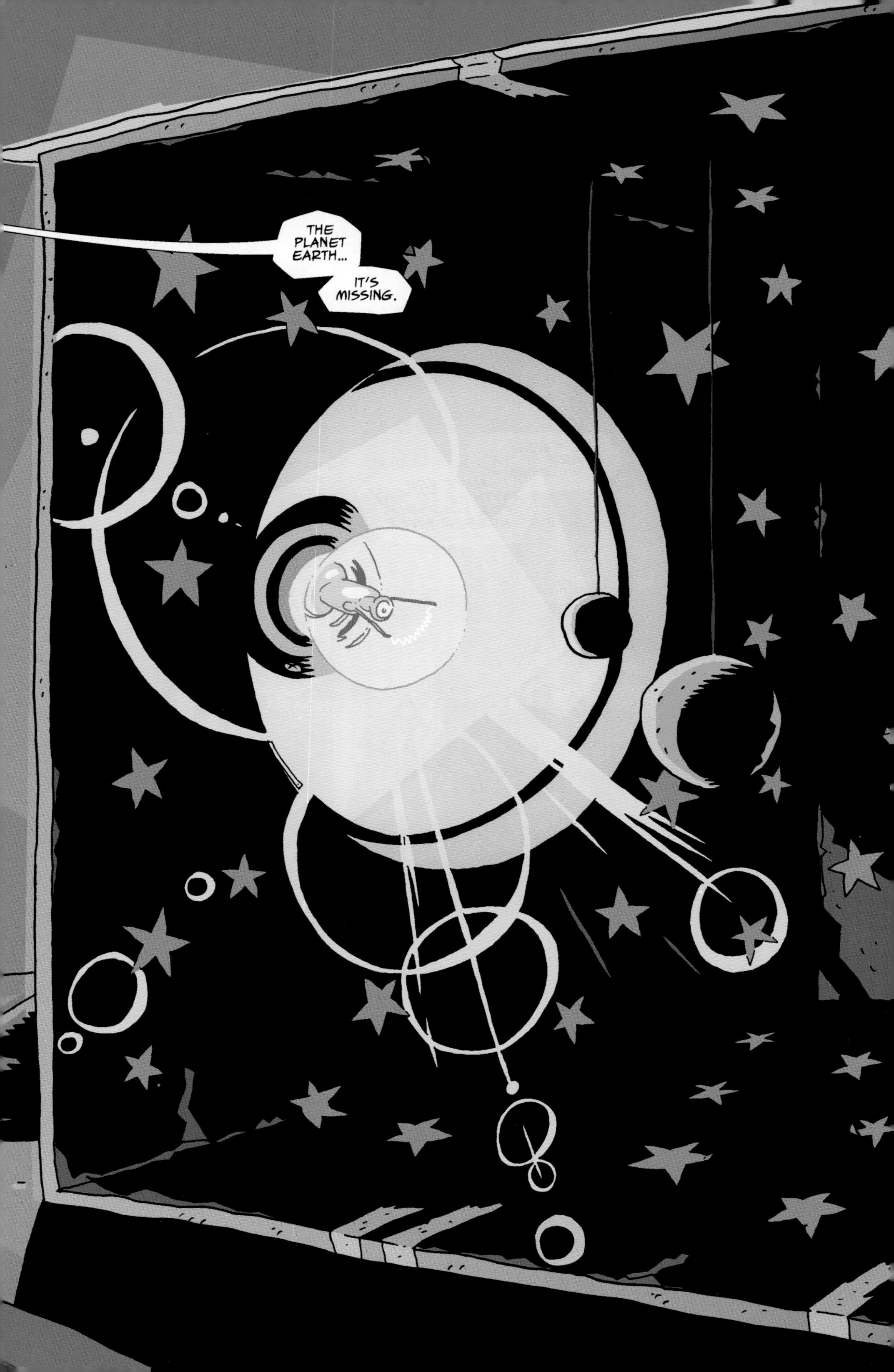
THE PLANET EARTH...
IT'S MISSING.

THE UMBRELLA ACADEMY IN:

THE WORLD IS BIG ENOUGH WITHOUT YOU

BEING THE FINAL PART IN THE STORY: DALLAS

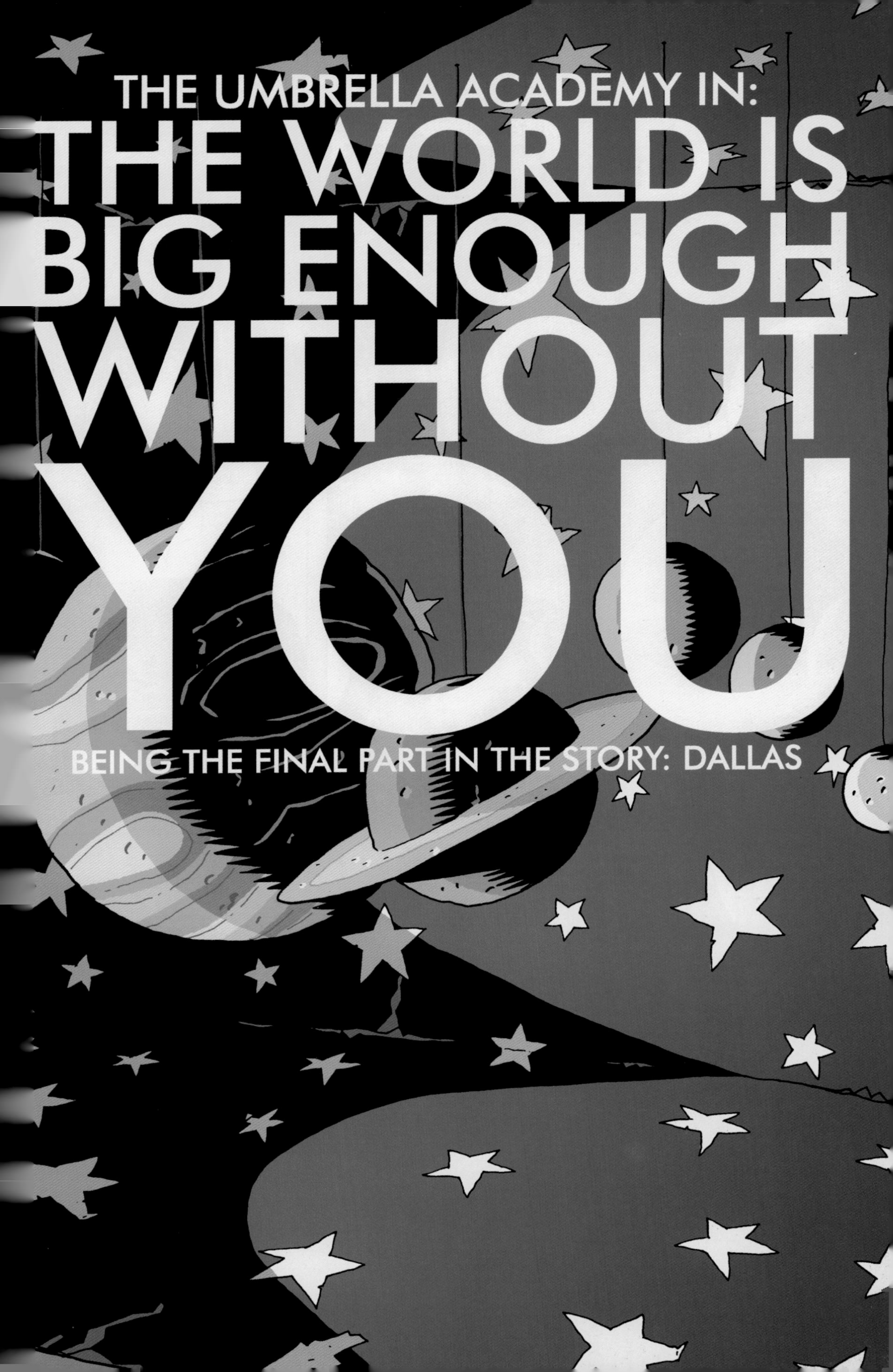

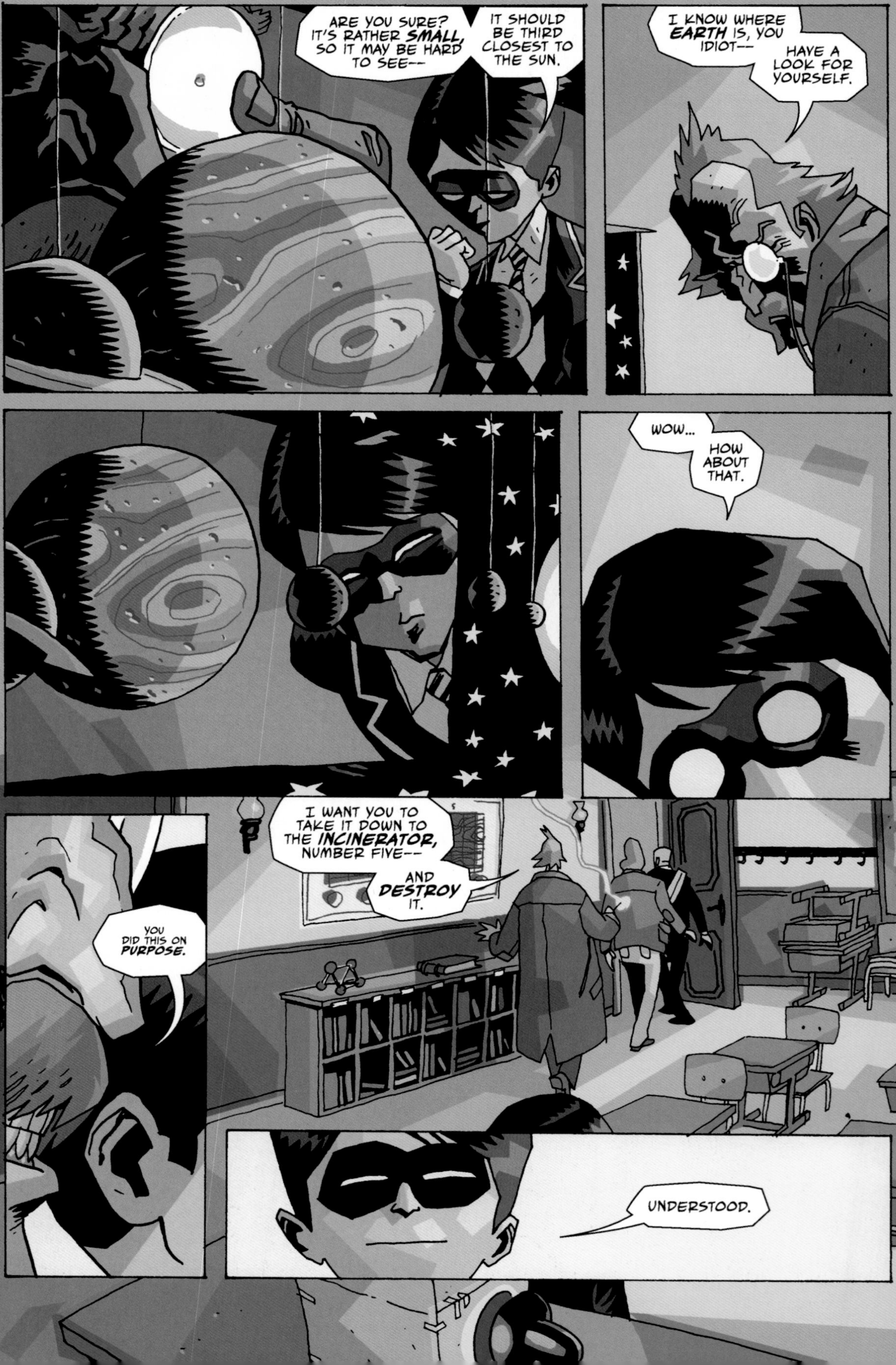
ARE YOU SURE? IT'S RATHER **SMALL**, SO IT MAY BE HARD TO SEE--
IT SHOULD BE THIRD CLOSEST TO THE SUN.
I KNOW WHERE **EARTH** IS, YOU IDIOT--
HAVE A LOOK FOR YOURSELF.
WOW...
HOW ABOUT THAT.
YOU DID THIS ON **PURPOSE**.
I WANT YOU TO TAKE IT DOWN TO THE **INCINERATOR**, NUMBER FIVE--
AND **DESTROY** IT.
UNDERSTOOD.

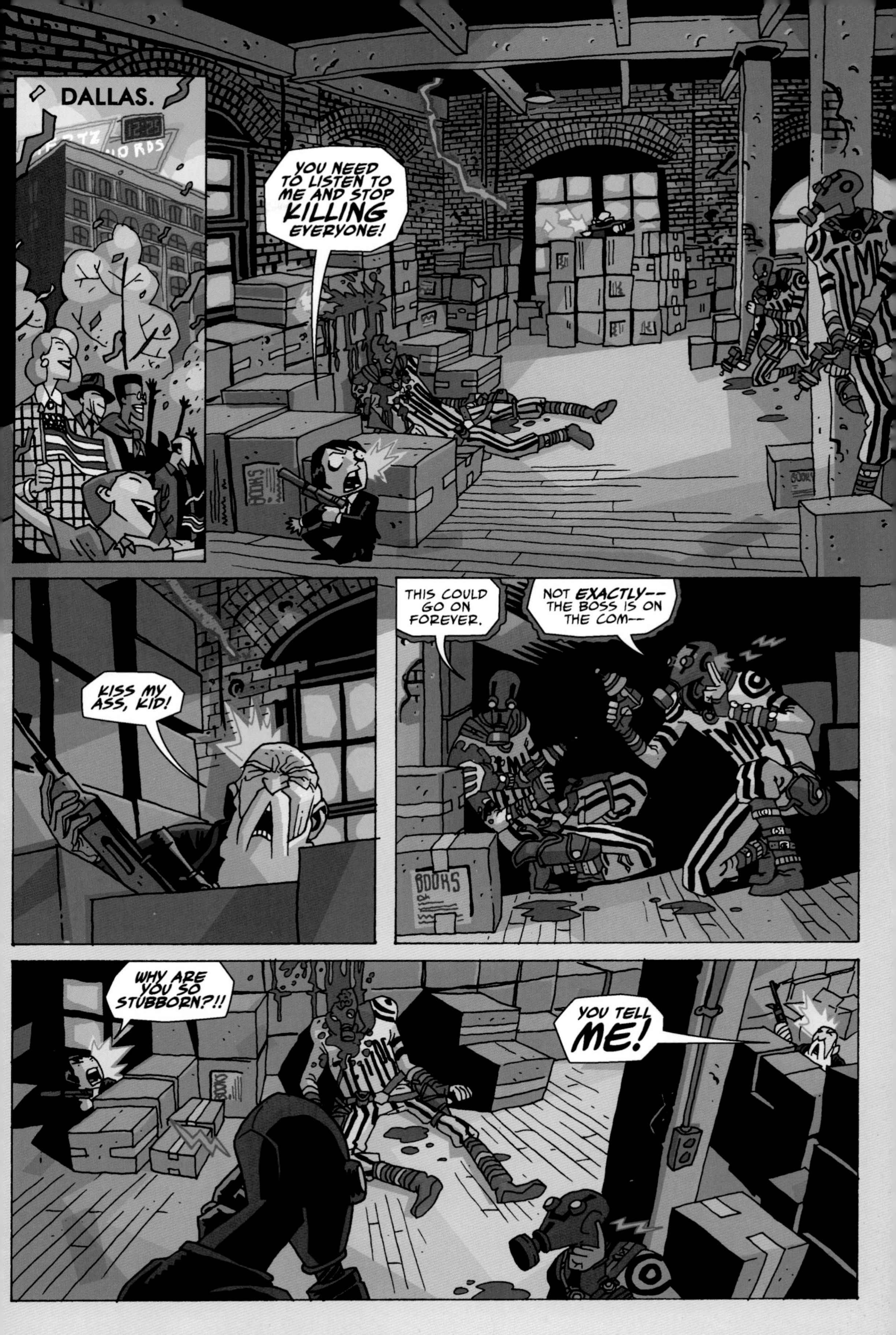
DALLAS.
YOU NEED TO LISTEN TO ME AND STOP KILLING EVERYONE!
KISS MY ASS, KID!
THIS COULD GO ON FOREVER.
NOT EXACTLY-- THE BOSS IS ON THE COM--
WHY ARE YOU SO STUBBORN?!!
YOU TELL ME!

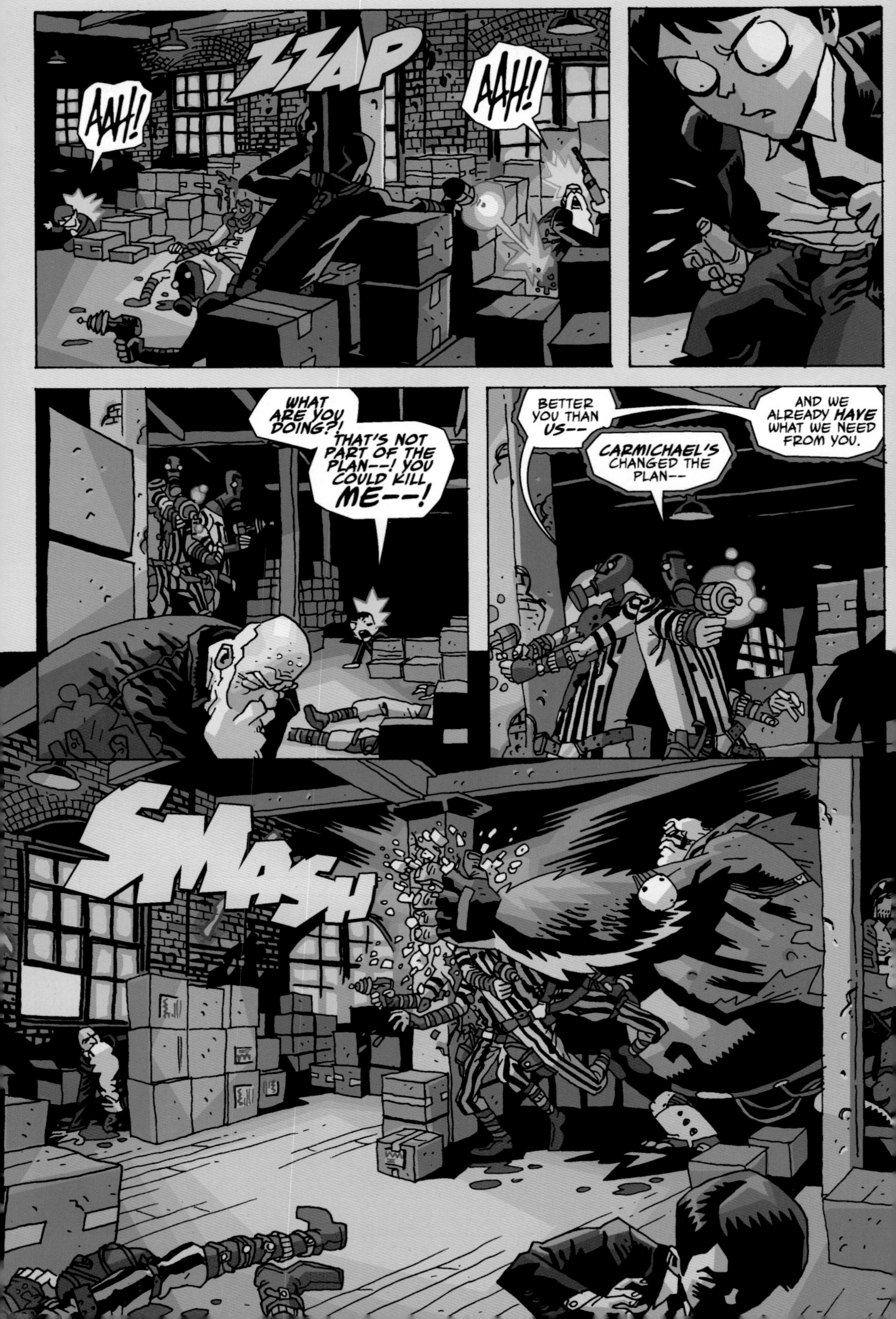
AAH!
ZZAP
AAH!
WHAT ARE YOU DOING?!
THAT'S NOT PART OF THE PLAN--! YOU COULD KILL ME--!
BETTER YOU THAN US--
CARMICHAEL'S CHANGED THE PLAN--
AND WE ALREADY HAVE WHAT WE NEED FROM YOU.
SMASH

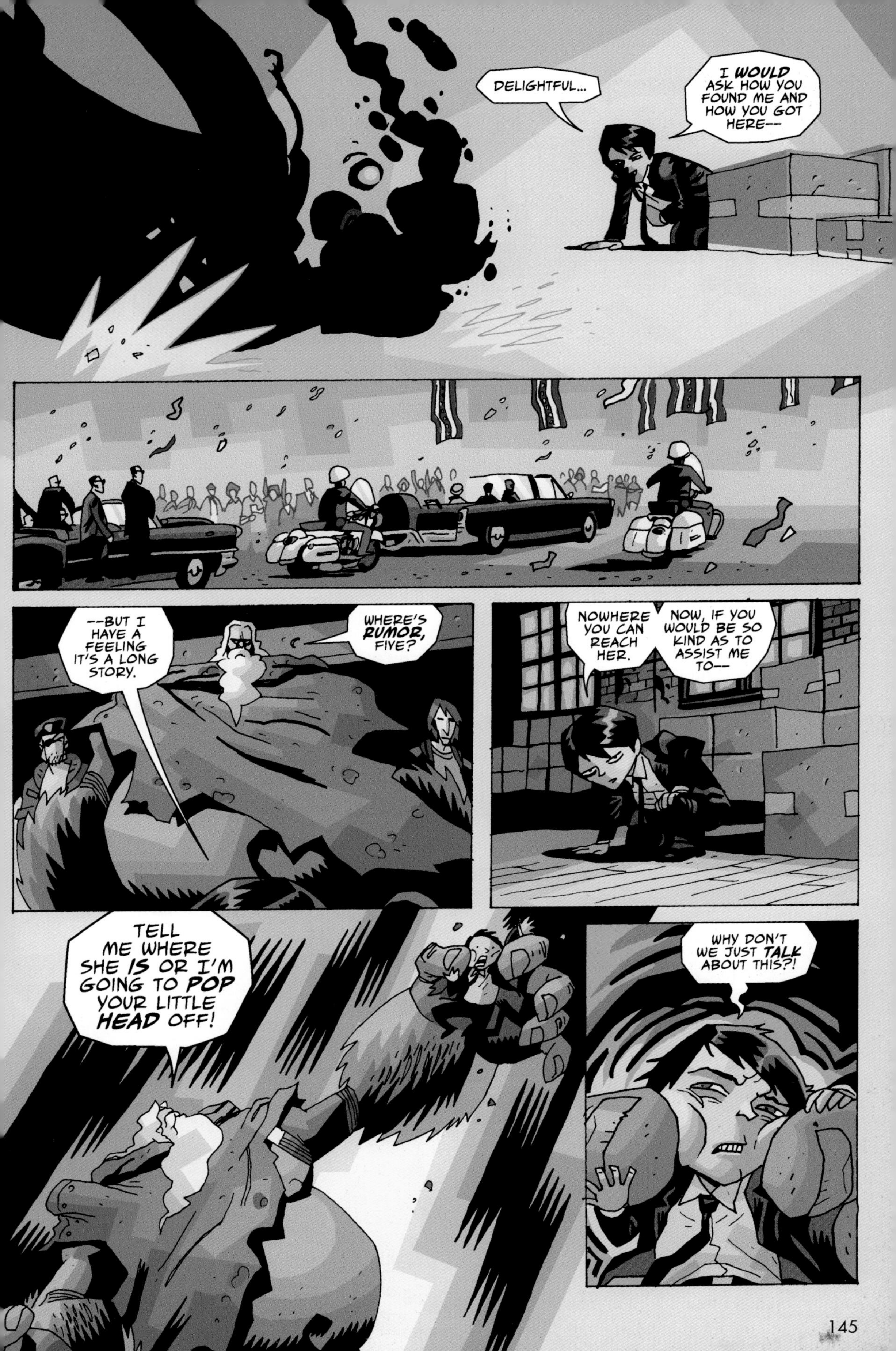

DELIGHTFUL...
I WOULD ASK HOW YOU FOUND ME AND HOW YOU GOT HERE--
--BUT I HAVE A FEELING IT'S A LONG STORY.
WHERE'S RUMOR, FIVE?
NOWHERE YOU CAN REACH HER.
NOW, IF YOU WOULD BE SO KIND AS TO ASSIST ME TO--
TELL ME WHERE SHE IS OR I'M GOING TO POP YOUR LITTLE HEAD OFF!
WHY DON'T WE JUST TALK ABOUT THIS?!

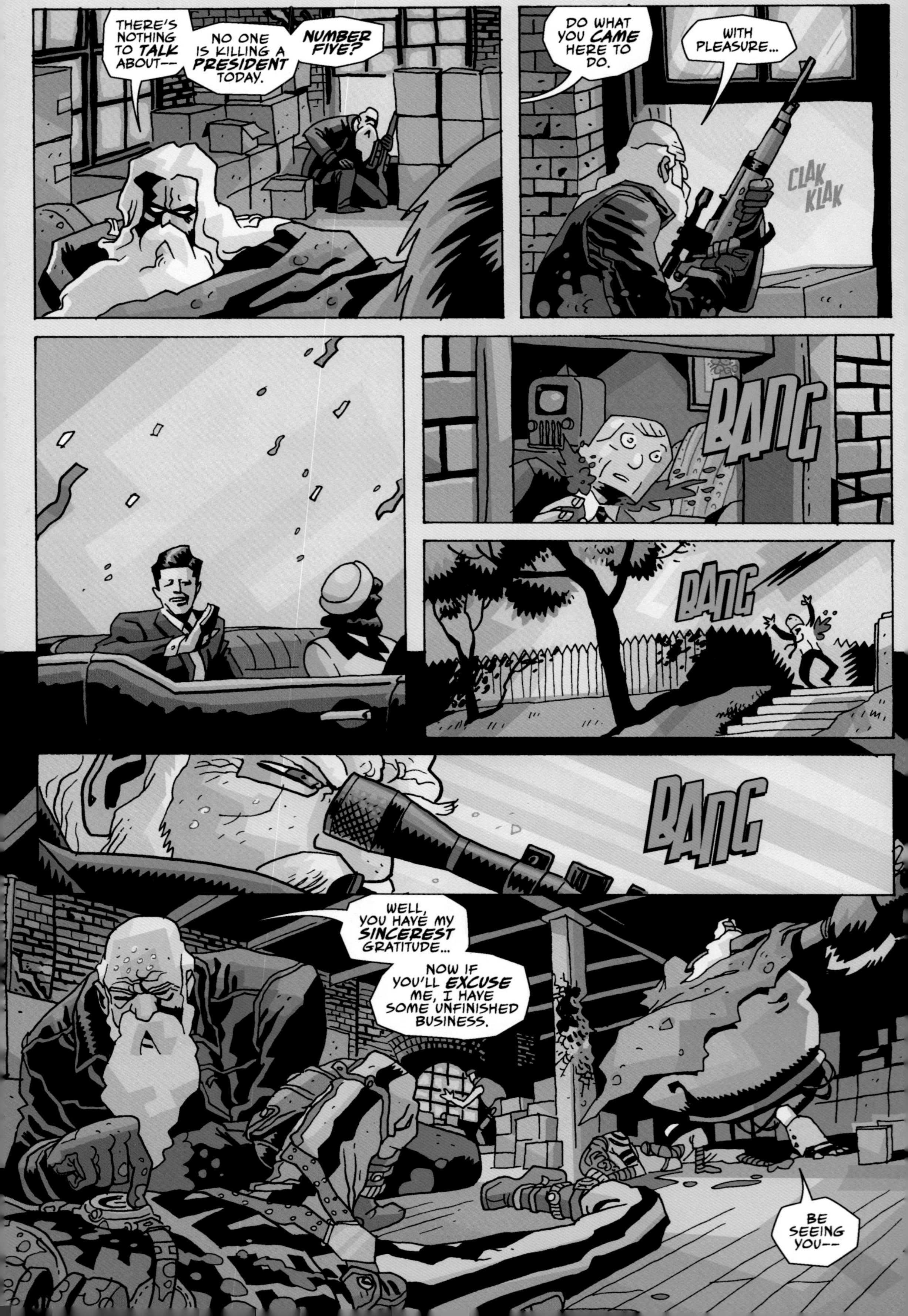

THERE'S NOTHING TO TALK ABOUT--
NO ONE IS KILLING A PRESIDENT TODAY.
NUMBER FIVE?
DO WHAT YOU CAME HERE TO DO.
WITH PLEASURE...
CLAK KLAK
BANG
BANG
BANG
WELL, YOU HAVE MY SINCEREST GRATITUDE...
NOW IF YOU'LL EXCUSE ME, I HAVE SOME UNFINISHED BUSINESS.
BE SEEING YOU--

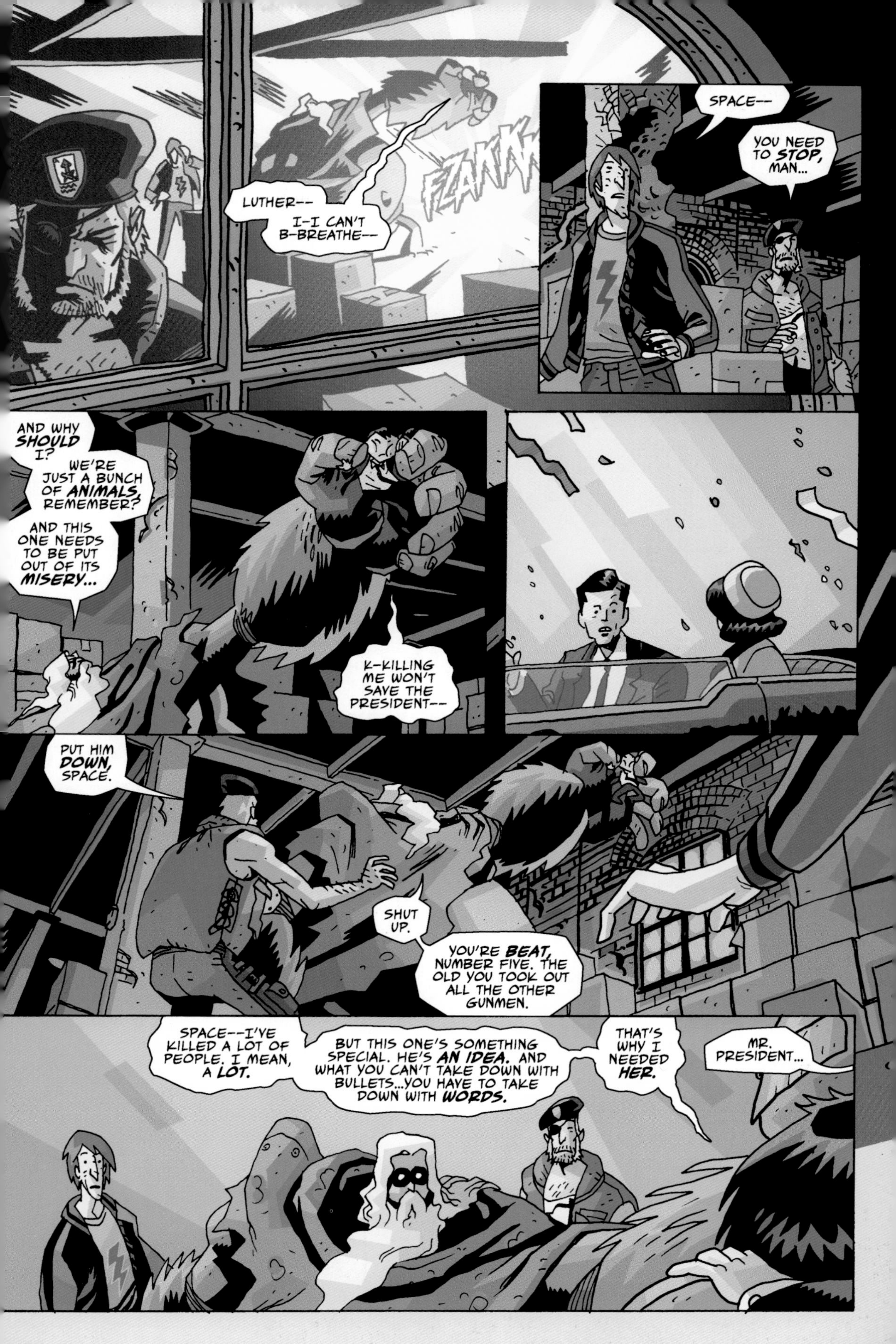
LUTHER--
I-I CAN'T B-BREATHE--
FZAKK
SPACE--
YOU NEED TO STOP, MAN...
AND WHY SHOULD I?
WE'RE JUST A BUNCH OF ANIMALS, REMEMBER?
AND THIS ONE NEEDS TO BE PUT OUT OF ITS MISERY...
K-KILLING ME WON'T SAVE THE PRESIDENT--
PUT HIM DOWN, SPACE.
SHUT UP.
YOU'RE BEAT, NUMBER FIVE. THE OLD YOU TOOK OUT ALL THE OTHER GUNMEN.
SPACE--I'VE KILLED A LOT OF PEOPLE. I MEAN, A LOT.
BUT THIS ONE'S SOMETHING SPECIAL. HE'S AN IDEA. AND WHAT YOU CAN'T TAKE DOWN WITH BULLETS...YOU HAVE TO TAKE DOWN WITH WORDS.
THAT'S WHY I NEEDED HER.
MR. PRESIDENT...

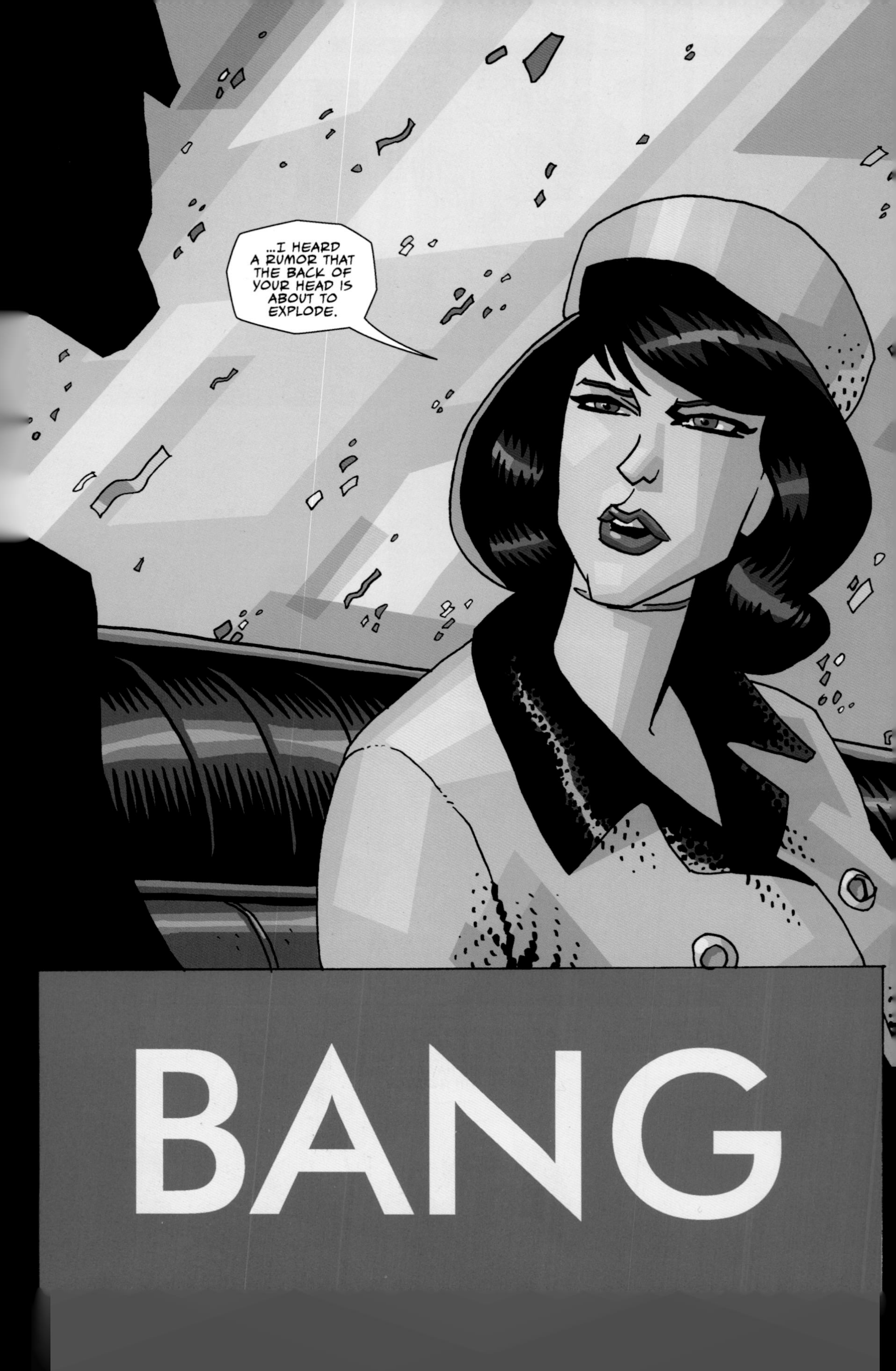
...I HEARD A RUMOR THAT THE BACK OF YOUR HEAD IS ABOUT TO EXPLODE.
BANG

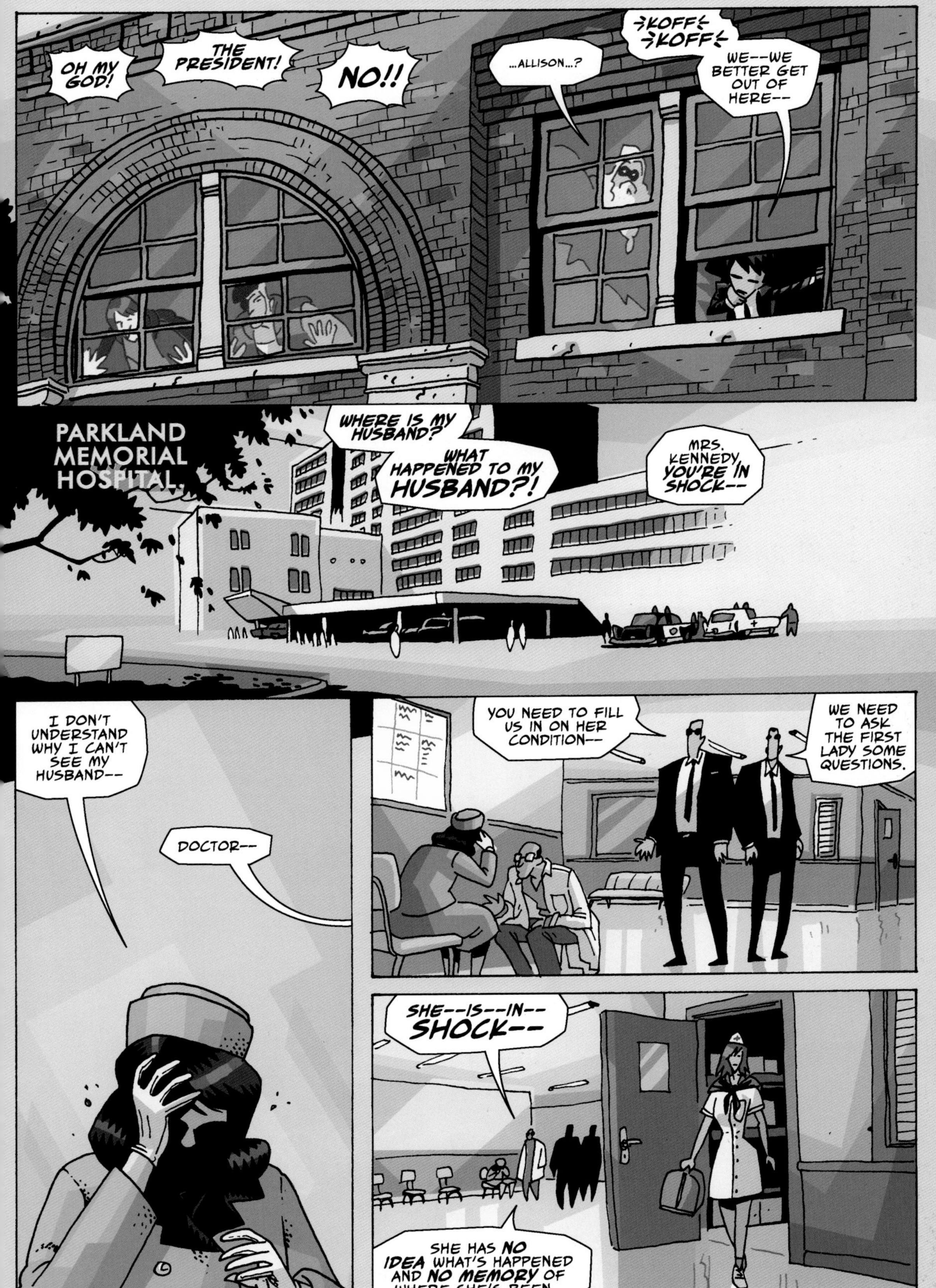

OH MY GOD!
THE PRESIDENT!
NO!!
...ALLISON...?
KOFF KOFF
WE--WE BETTER GET OUT OF HERE--
PARKLAND MEMORIAL HOSPITAL.
WHERE IS MY HUSBAND?
WHAT HAPPENED TO MY HUSBAND?!
MRS. KENNEDY, YOU'RE IN SHOCK--
I DON'T UNDERSTAND WHY I CAN'T SEE MY HUSBAND--
DOCTOR--
YOU NEED TO FILL US IN ON HER CONDITION--
WE NEED TO ASK THE FIRST LADY SOME QUESTIONS.
SHE--IS--IN-- SHOCK--
SHE HAS NO IDEA WHAT'S HAPPENED AND NO MEMORY OF WHERE SHE'S BEEN...

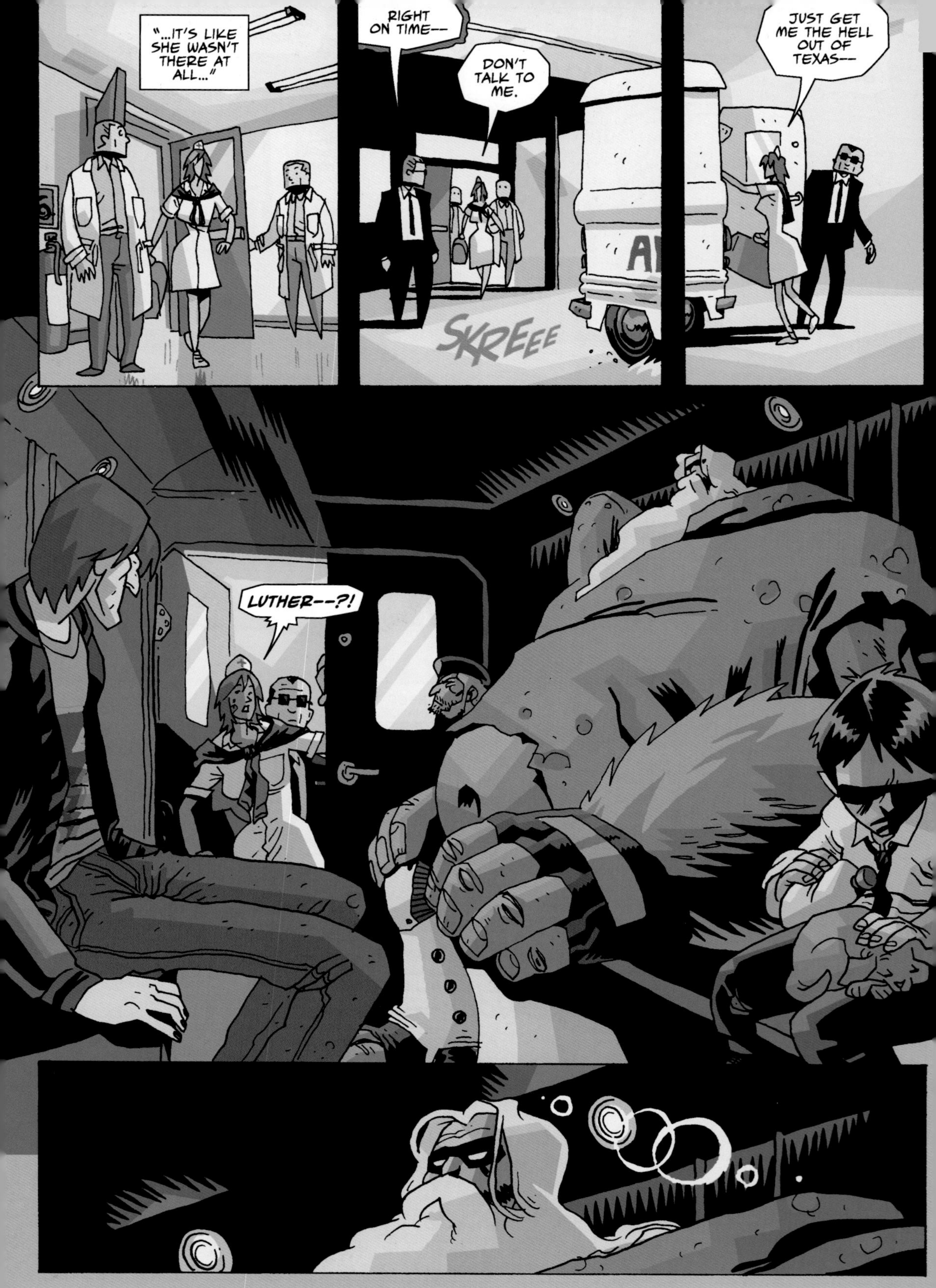
"...IT'S LIKE SHE WASN'T THERE AT ALL..."
RIGHT ON TIME--
DON'T TALK TO ME.
SKREEEE
JUST GET ME THE HELL OUT OF TEXAS--
LUTHER--?!

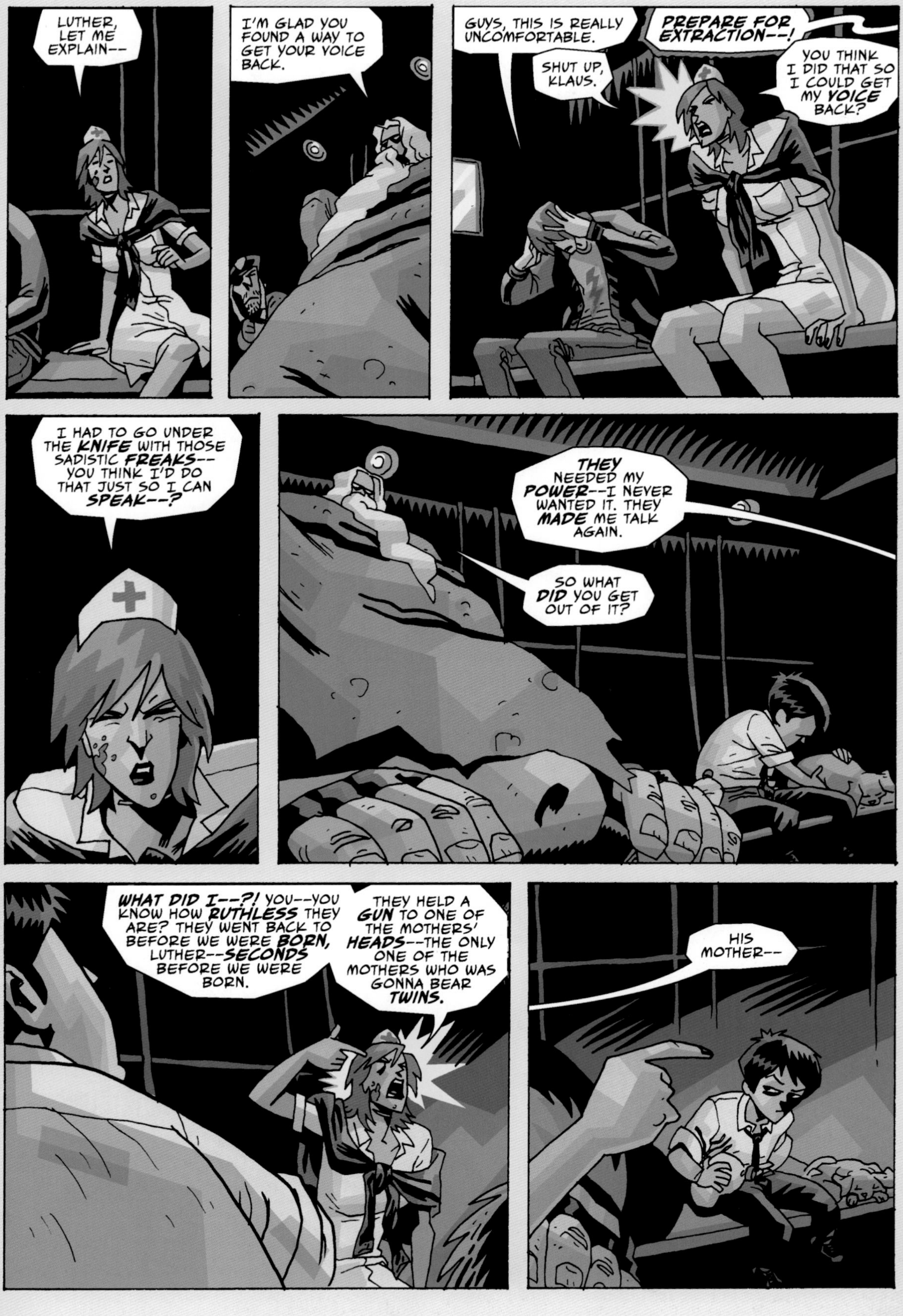
LUTHER, LET ME EXPLAIN--
I'M GLAD YOU FOUND A WAY TO GET YOUR VOICE BACK.
GUYS, THIS IS REALLY UNCOMFORTABLE.
SHUT UP, KLAUS.
PREPARE FOR EXTRACTION--!
YOU THINK I DID THAT SO I COULD GET MY VOICE BACK?
I HAD TO GO UNDER THE KNIFE WITH THOSE SADISTIC FREAKS-- YOU THINK I'D DO THAT JUST SO I CAN SPEAK--?
THEY NEEDED MY POWER--I NEVER WANTED IT. THEY MADE ME TALK AGAIN.
SO WHAT DID YOU GET OUT OF IT?
WHAT DID I--?! YOU--YOU KNOW HOW RUTHLESS THEY ARE? THEY WENT BACK TO BEFORE WE WERE BORN, LUTHER--SECONDS BEFORE WE WERE BORN.
THEY HELD A GUN TO ONE OF THE MOTHERS' HEADS--THE ONLY ONE OF THE MOTHERS WHO WAS GONNA BEAR TWINS.
HIS MOTHER--

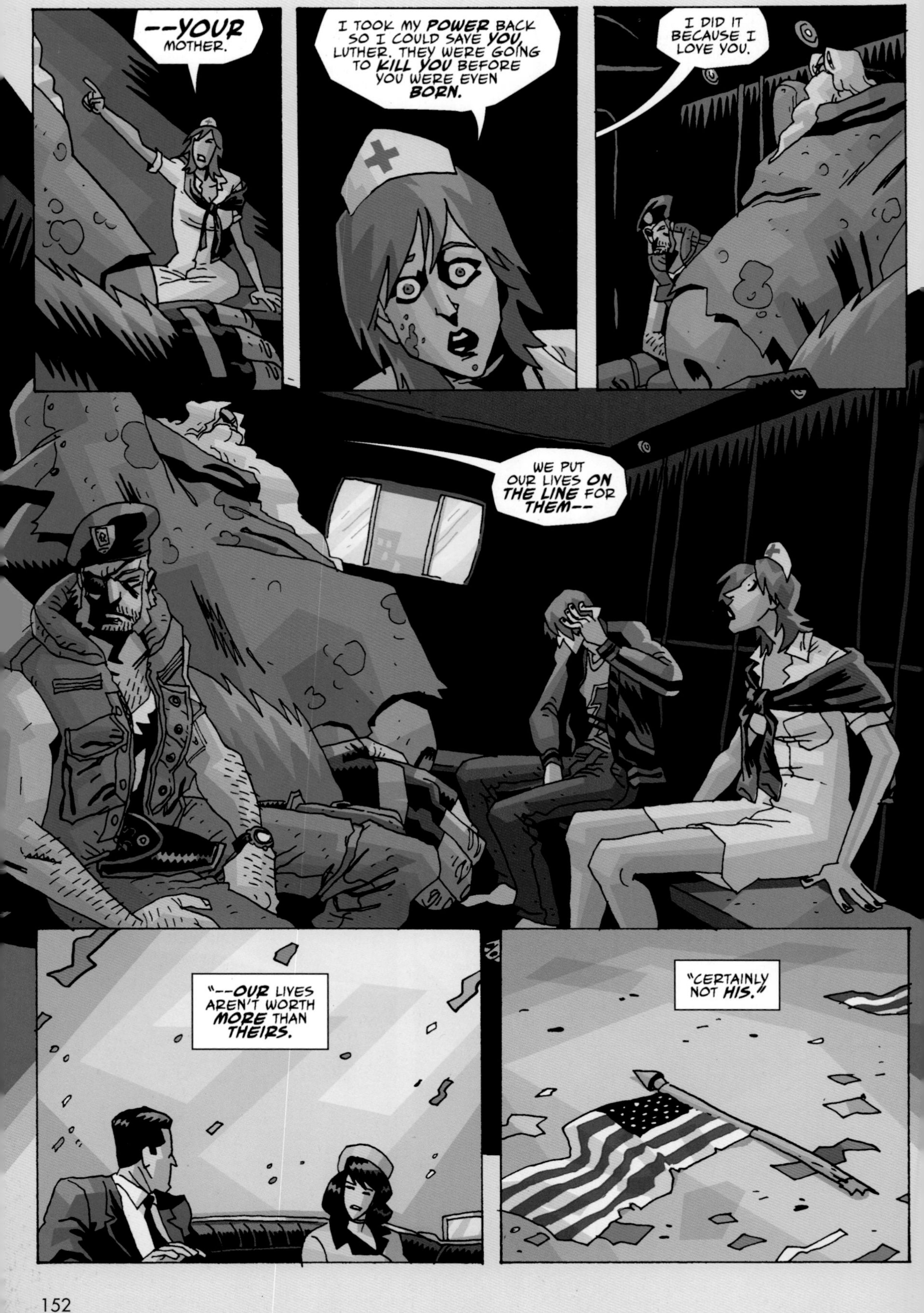
--YOUR MOTHER.
I TOOK MY POWER BACK SO I COULD SAVE YOU, LUTHER. THEY WERE GOING TO KILL YOU BEFORE YOU WERE EVEN BORN.
I DID IT BECAUSE I LOVE YOU.
WE PUT OUR LIVES ON THE LINE FOR THEM--
"--OUR LIVES AREN'T WORTH MORE THAN THEIRS.
"CERTAINLY NOT HIS."

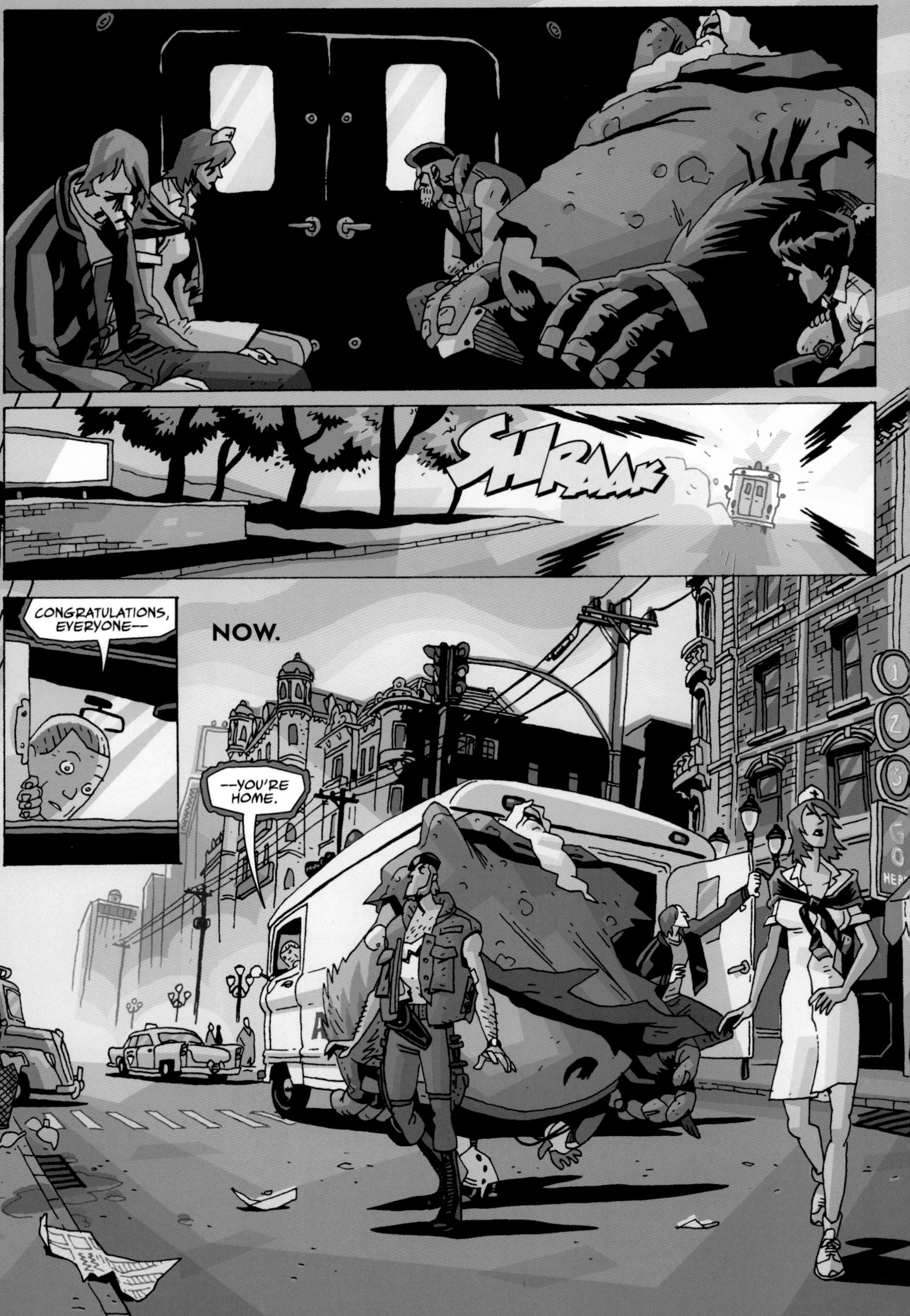
SHRAAK
CONGRATULATIONS, EVERYONE--
NOW.
--YOU'RE HOME.

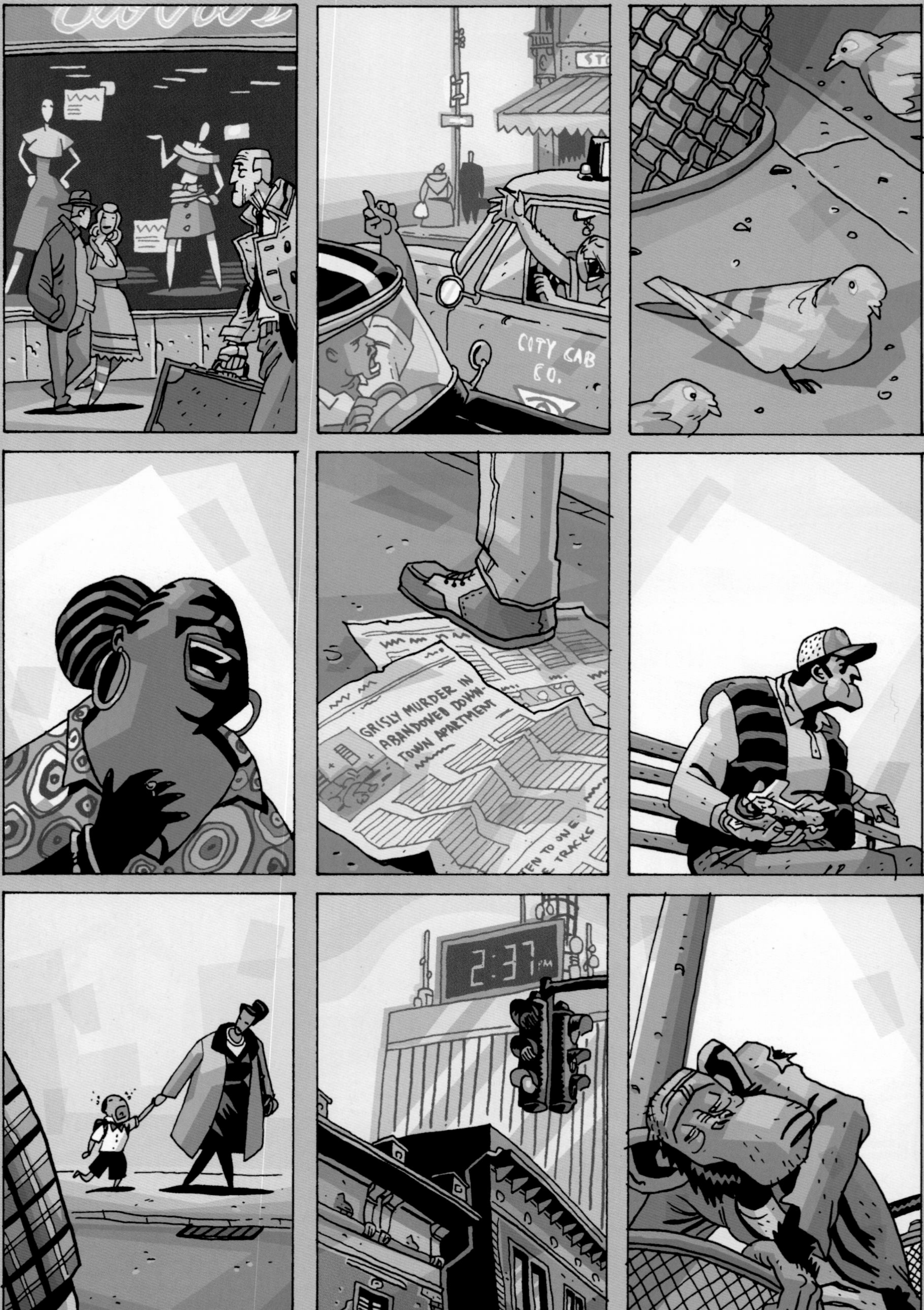
CITY CAB CO.
GRISLY MURDER IN ABANDONED DOWN-TOWN APARTMENT
2:37 PM

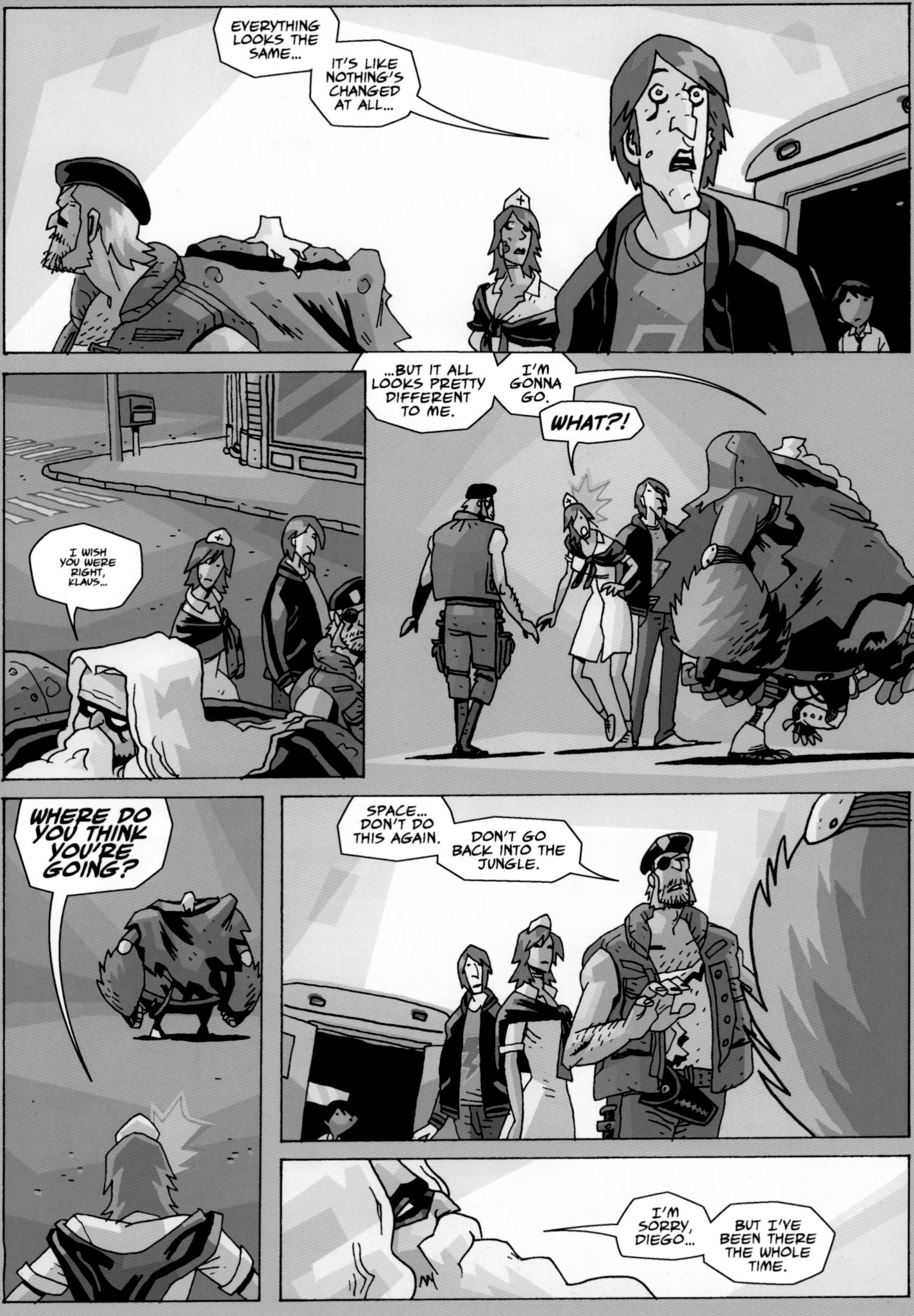
EVERYTHING LOOKS THE SAME...
IT'S LIKE NOTHING'S CHANGED AT ALL...
I WISH YOU WERE RIGHT, KLAUS...
...BUT IT ALL LOOKS PRETTY DIFFERENT TO ME.
I'M GONNA GO.
WHAT?!
WHERE DO YOU THINK YOU'RE GOING?
SPACE... DON'T DO THIS AGAIN.
DON'T GO BACK INTO THE JUNGLE.
I'M SORRY, DIEGO...
BUT I'VE BEEN THERE THE WHOLE TIME.

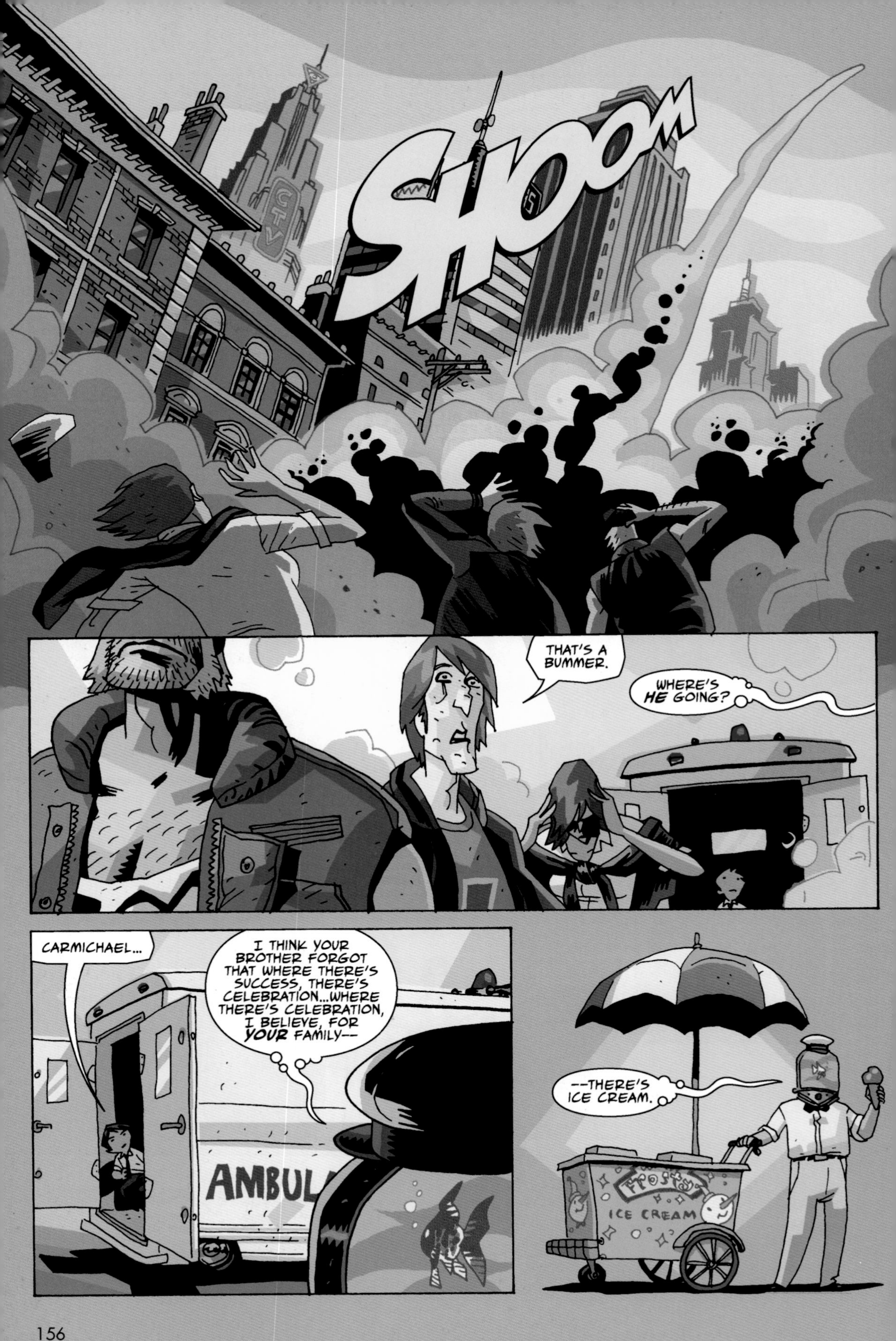
SHOOM
THAT'S A BUMMER.
WHERE'S HE GOING?
CARMICHAEL...
I THINK YOUR BROTHER FORGOT THAT WHERE THERE'S SUCCESS, THERE'S CELEBRATION...WHERE THERE'S CELEBRATION, I BELIEVE, FOR YOUR FAMILY--
--THERE'S ICE CREAM.
AMBUL
ICE CREAM

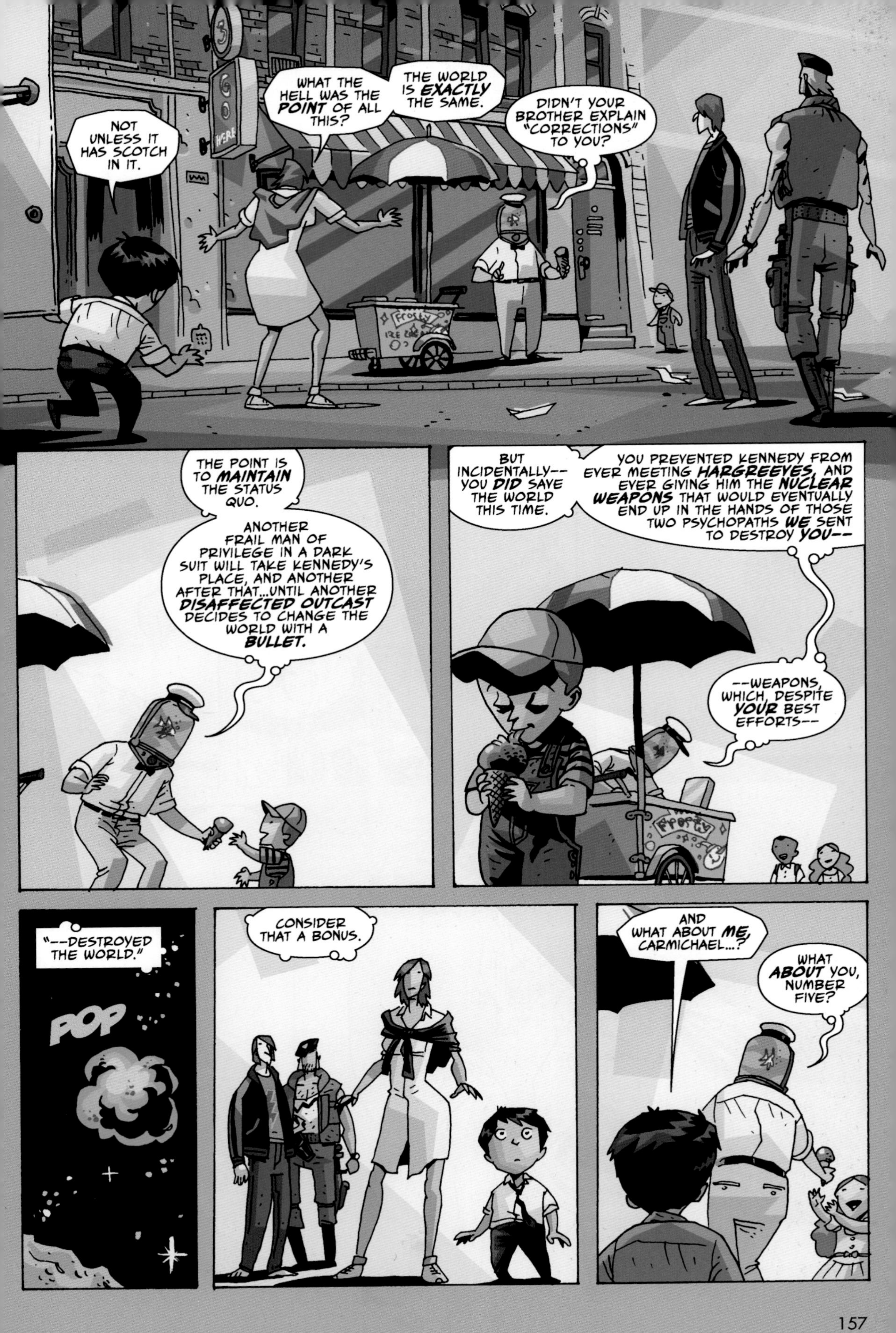

WHAT THE HELL WAS THE POINT OF ALL THIS?
THE WORLD IS EXACTLY THE SAME.
NOT UNLESS IT HAS SCOTCH IN IT.
DIDN'T YOUR BROTHER EXPLAIN "CORRECTIONS" TO YOU?
THE POINT IS TO MAINTAIN THE STATUS QUO.
ANOTHER FRAIL MAN OF PRIVILEGE IN A DARK SUIT WILL TAKE KENNEDY'S PLACE, AND ANOTHER AFTER THAT...UNTIL ANOTHER DISAFFECTED OUTCAST DECIDES TO CHANGE THE WORLD WITH A BULLET.
BUT INCIDENTALLY-- YOU DID SAVE THE WORLD THIS TIME.
YOU PREVENTED KENNEDY FROM EVER MEETING HARGREEVES, AND EVER GIVING HIM THE NUCLEAR WEAPONS THAT WOULD EVENTUALLY END UP IN THE HANDS OF THOSE TWO PSYCHOPATHS WE SENT TO DESTROY YOU--
--WEAPONS, WHICH, DESPITE YOUR BEST EFFORTS--
"--DESTROYED THE WORLD."
POP
CONSIDER THAT A BONUS.
AND WHAT ABOUT ME, CARMICHAEL...?
WHAT ABOUT YOU, NUMBER FIVE?

SMASH!

EEK!

AAH!

YOU CUT OUT MY *HUMANITY* WITH A *SCALPEL*--LIKE A *MALIGNANCY.*

I WAKE UP IN THE MORNING WITH THE *FINEST* IMPULSES KNOWN TO MAN--

AND THANKS TO *YOU*--I *SLAUGHTER* THEM.

EVERY--

--SINGLE--

--DAY.

EXCEPT TODAY.

GULP

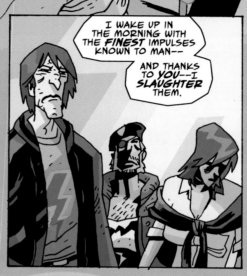

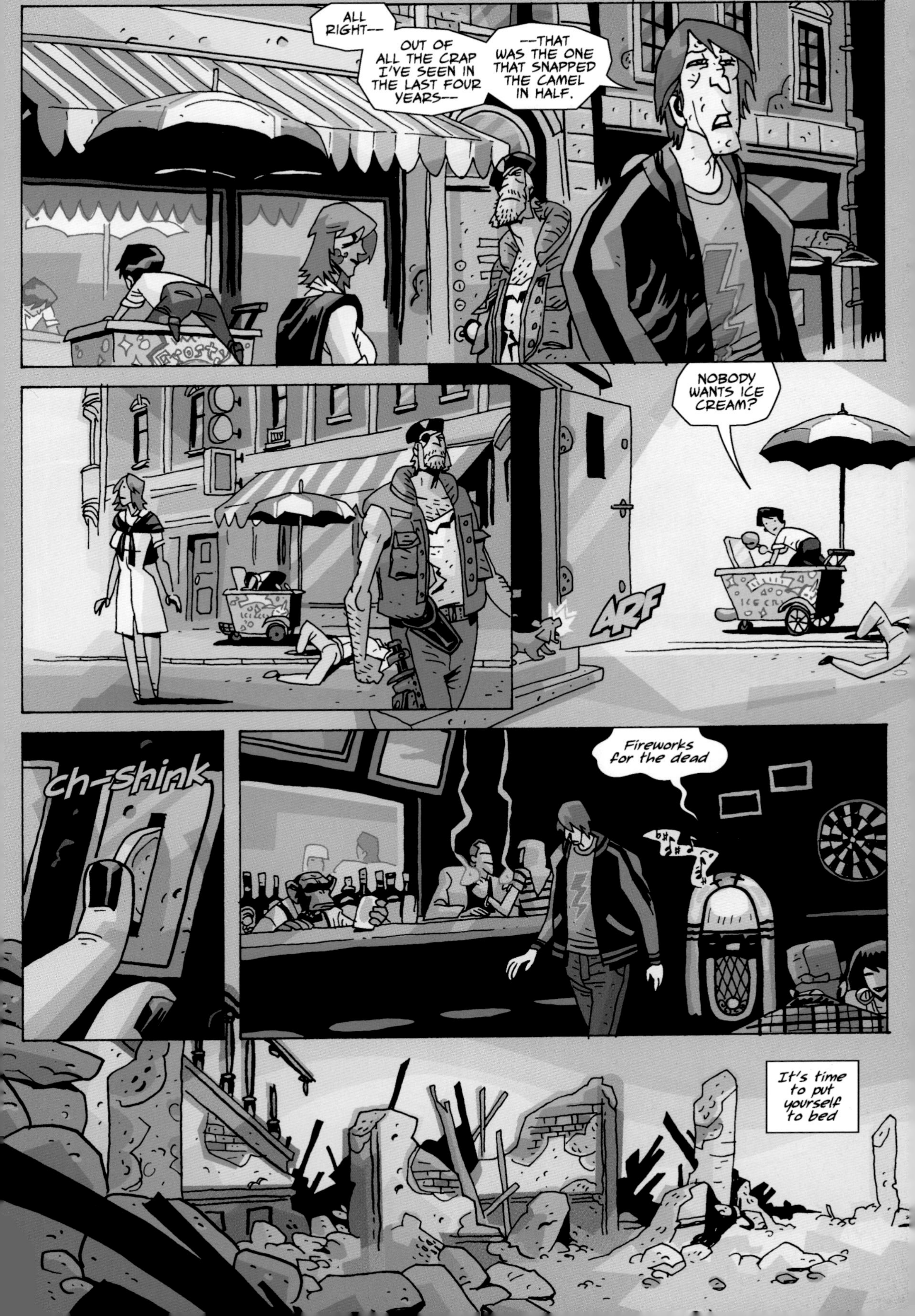
ALL RIGHT--
OUT OF ALL THE CRAP I'VE SEEN IN THE LAST FOUR YEARS--
--THAT WAS THE ONE THAT SNAPPED THE CAMEL IN HALF.
NOBODY WANTS ICE CREAM?
ARF
ch-shink
Fireworks for the dead
It's time to put yourself to bed

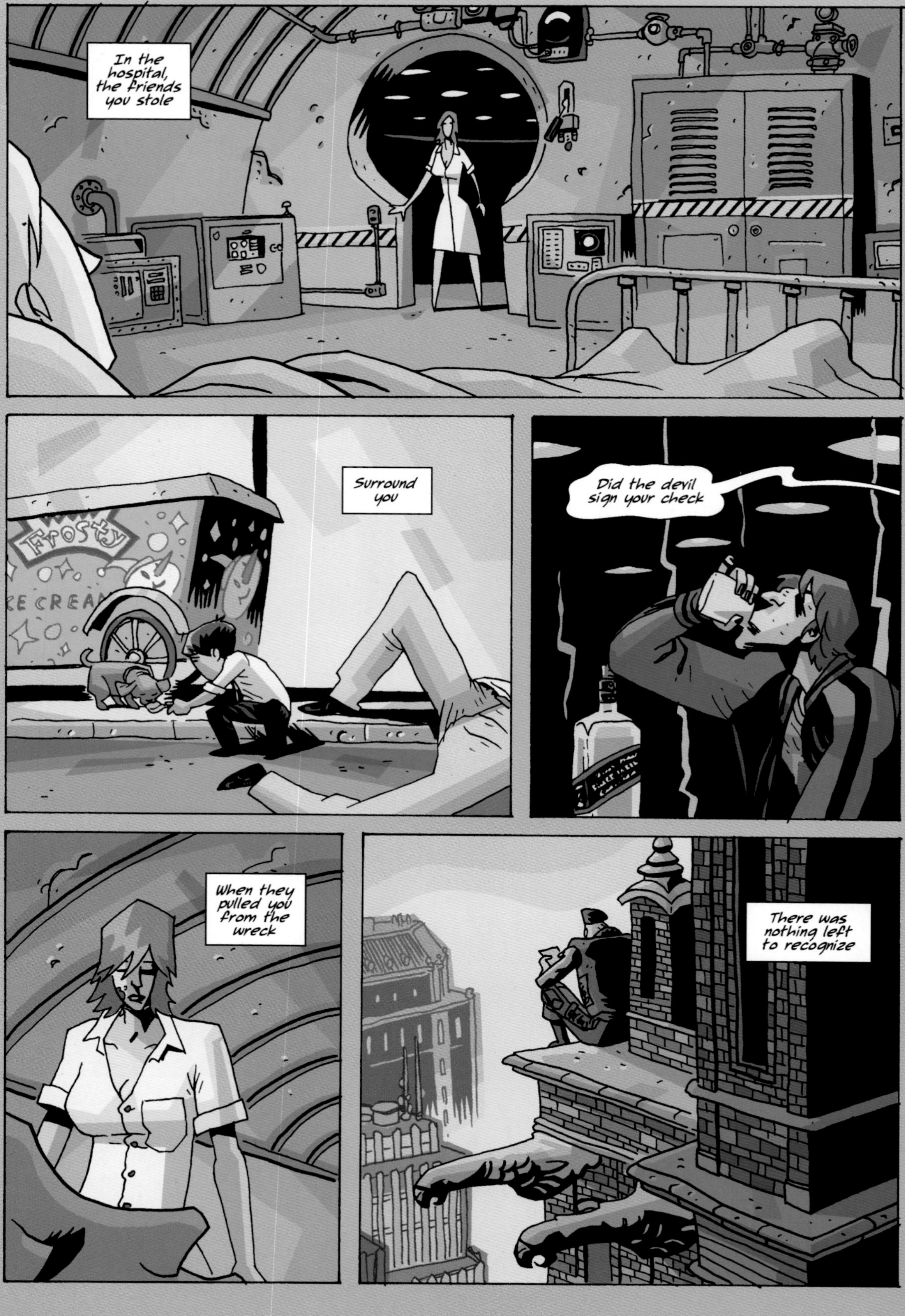
In the hospital, the friends you stole
Surround you
Did the devil sign your check
When they pulled you from the wreck
There was nothing left to recognize

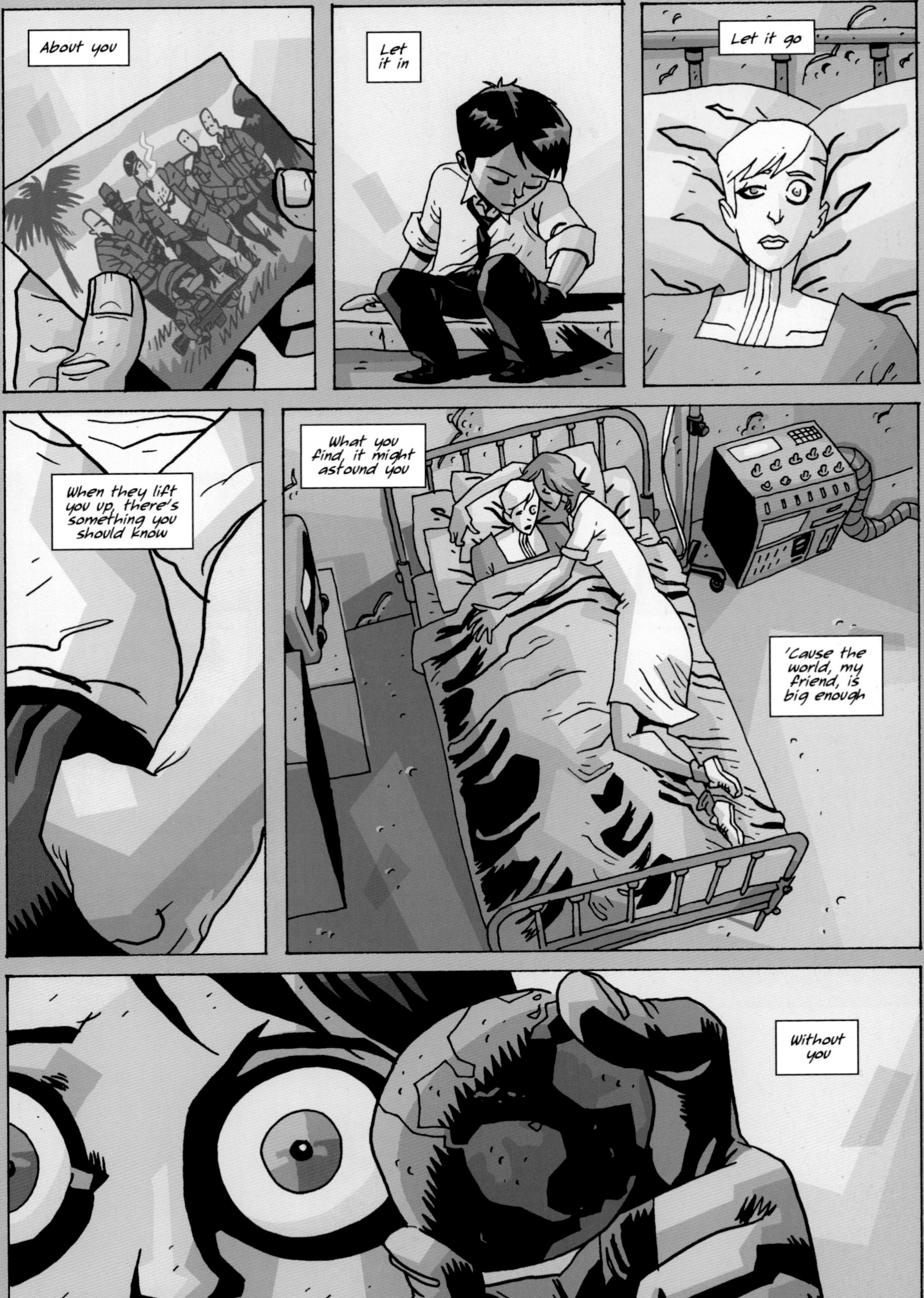
About you
Let it in
Let it go
When they lift you up, there's something you should know
What you find, it might astound you
'Cause the world, my friend, is big enough
Without you

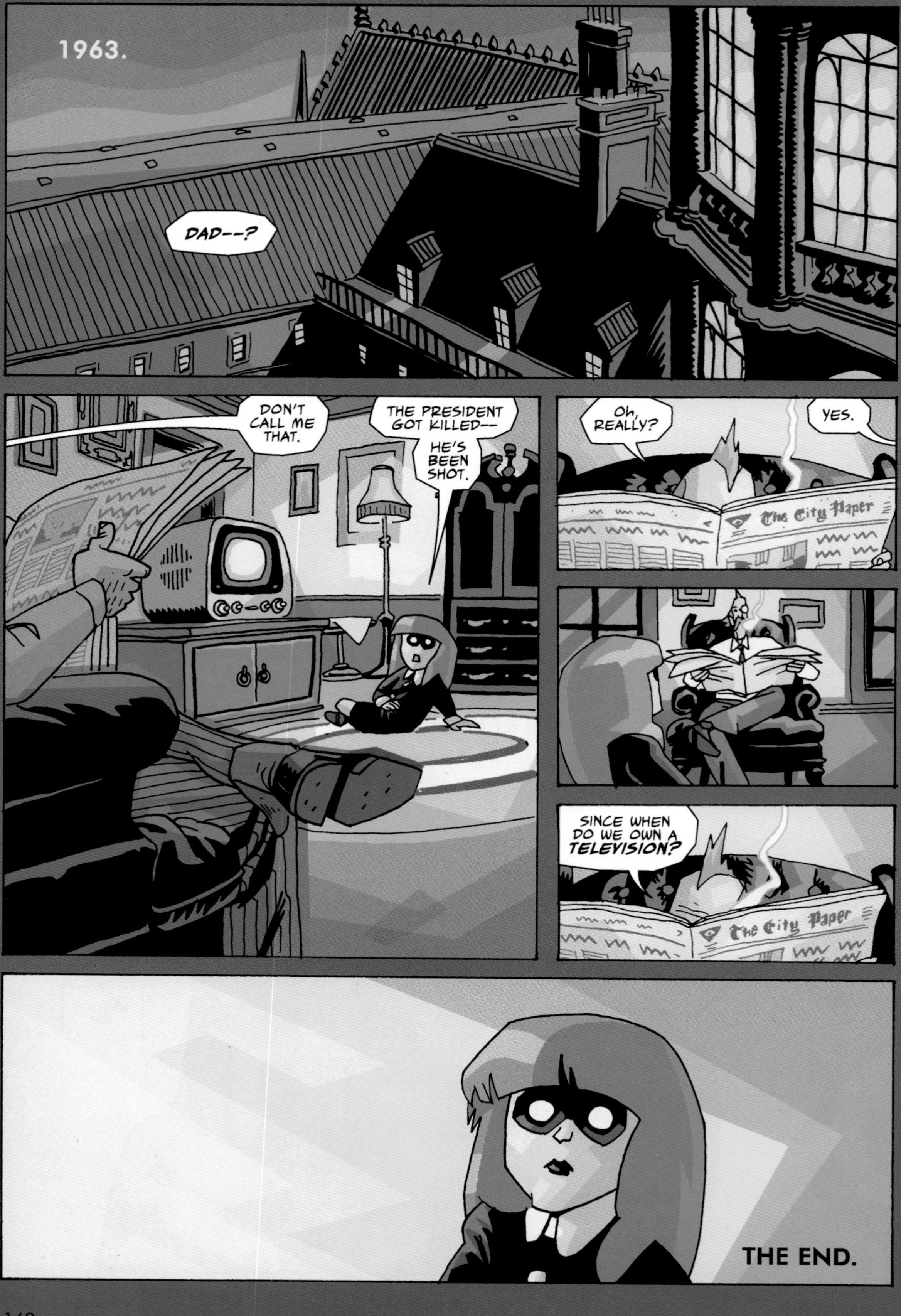
1963.
DAD--?
DON'T CALL ME THAT.
THE PRESIDENT GOT KILLED--
HE'S BEEN SHOT.
Oh, REALLY?
YES.
The City Paper
SINCE WHEN DO WE OWN A TELEVISION?
The City Paper
THE END.

TEXAS IS THE REASON

Reinventing The Umbrella Academy *through the rifle sight of America*

It was one of those really breezy California nights, and I was standing outside an upper level of the San Diego Convention Center, along with my wife, brother, family, and friends, exhaling carcinogens into what was an otherwise starry and mostly unspoiled sky.

Gabriel and I had just won the Eisner Award for Best Limited Series, and as the ceremony continued back in the darkened exhibit hall, I stood, dazed and oblivious to sound, cradling a very important hunk of metal, and wondering one thing:

What the hell were we going to do now?

It's the answer to this question that always makes me smile, but we'll come back to that later. Right then, and in the following months, I had a lot of thinking to do, and we had a new series to create.

The book you hold in your hands is the product of a lot of hard work, as most comics are, involving a lot of people. It's the result of not just the hours spent at drawing tables and keyboards creating *Dallas*, but also the hours spent executing *Apocalypse Suite*. You see, I like to think that *Dallas* is where our heroes' story really begins, and more importantly, what *The Umbrella Academy* as a comic book really *is*. What we accumulated over the course of the first six issues was an identity. Much like you, we really weren't sure who The Umbrella Academy was until we took the journey ourselves, created the sandbox in which to play, and made it as painless as possible for the reader.

So in a way, we were starting over. Only this time I didn't have a beginning.

You see, I had always planned *The Umbrella Academy* to run until its eighth or ninth series. I had mostly figured out the beginning, middle, and end, but it's the bits in between that I didn't have in my head. And though I knew I wanted the series to run for many years, I hadn't the slightest inkling of how to get there—which, as I have come to learn, is the nature of the book.

Dallas began as an idea for a single-issue adventure, like a great episode of *The Twilight Zone* or *Doctor Who*, or a crazy old *Challengers of the Unknown* adventure comic. I planned on telling this story where, by the end of the issue, our heroes, torn apart and lost in time, have succeeded or failed in their mission to either eradicate or save President John F. Kennedy. And naturally, in typical *Umbrella Academy* fashion, it ended up becoming six issues. The only major concern, or problem, was the question in my head:

How are we going to have our heroes *assassinate a president?*

The answer, and the real question, as our editor, Scott Allie, put it, is "How could we *not?*"

And he was right. It was, to all of us involved, the next logical progression of the book—an attempt to redefine and set new rules, while bringing the book's fearlessness into maturity. And its power to entertain or offend, given the harsh, violent, and borderline-insensitive subject matter, typified the ideals of the country it would be set in—America.

And that's exactly what *Dallas* is—a story about America. It's a story about guns, bombs, pie, television, disappointment, rebellion, and gods that look like cowboys. I had never planned on bringing the "children" to America, but this time that's exactly where they needed to be, because they needed a harsh dose of both fantasy and reality, and there's no better place to get your fix than the good old USA.

This time, working with Gabriel, Dave, Nate, Scott, and Sierra was exactly what it was supposed to be—old friends getting together to make something unique, which only they could make. Just when I thought Gabriel couldn't possibly get any better, any more daring, I would turn the page to be blown away again, and the best part to me was that it felt like we were only getting started.

Dallas was even more exhilarating to write because it had a much less rigid story line—it only had an ending. And as with the larger series as a whole, I found myself sticking my hand into a swirling vortex, grabbing the first thing I could, and pulling it out.

We traveled through time, we dressed up a chimp like Marilyn Monroe, we introduced two sugar-loving psychopaths and proceeded to kill them. We went from Vietnam to Dealey Plaza and we assassinated—

Well, we blew up the world.

So again, I'll ask myself, *What the hell are we going to do now?*

I have absolutely no idea.

And that's why I love this book so much.

GERARD WAY
Los Angeles
May 25, 2009

ROCK 'N' ROLL

It wasn't until my midtwenties that the "rock bug" really bit me for good. As a nerdy and shy kid in Brazil who loved movie soundtracks (*American Graffiti* was a top favorite, but I didn't really know then who all those bands were—it just sounded good), for whom rock was something between Elvis, The Beatles, and the Stones, a teenager who wasn't a rebel at all and didn't sleep in after parties, I spent all my early adult years studying in college, getting drunk at parties with friends, and drawing comics at home. Aside from two really bad car crashes, I didn't give my parents any trouble at all.

By the time I was twenty-one years old (I know, I know), I got to know Led Zeppelin, Jimi Hendrix, and the best Brazilian rock band ever, Os Mutantes. It was all over, bands and songs from a time before I was born, but it all made sense to me. That music and those lyrics and those distorted guitar riffs spoke to me for the first time then and there, and I really enjoyed that new language I was learning.

Three years later, I had my second rock breakthrough, when I discovered Blur, Pixies, Pavement, Weezer, Yo La Tengo, and so many more. That happened at the same time I discovered the rock scene in São Paulo, the small clubs, and all the independent rock bands. For the first time in my life, I had bars that I'd want to go to, music that I enjoyed listening to, and I loved the experience of discovering new bands, and young people like me who loved what they did just as much as I loved comics and who were trying to make their dreams come true the same way I was.

It all seemed like a train was passing through my eyes, and I was standing in the station. It had been passing for years, and I just realized that this was my time, my generation, my world that was passing and I was missing it. So I just jumped on the train, and since then I've had to catch up with all the stuff that had happened before that point, but at least I knew I was going to the right destination.

These bands and places have helped craft the world of stories I tell with my brother. There were songs that said the same things we wanted to say, about lost love, friendship, and loneliness. All the images that come to one's mind when watching a show, like drunk and mysterious looks across the bar, a romantic kiss right there on the crowded dance floor, a couple having sex in the tight, wet bathroom. A rock show has a mix between words and images that walks really close to what can be done in comics.

Rock has given me all the juice I need to tell my stories.

So imagine what joy it was when my rock-star writer gave me a story about the rebel days of Kraken and Vanya, when they had a punk-rock band and a gig in a small club in the shady part of town. It felt so right I thanked heaven once more that I was the artist of this series. It just gets better and better.

This story looks like the ones I usually write—small rock shows in cramped, smoky bars, people drinking, lots of weirdos walking all around—but I usually portray the perspective of the guy in the crowd. I've been to lots of shows of all sizes, and lots of back stages. I have a lot of friends who are musicians and have one or several bands, but I'm not a rock star, or a starving musician, or even that guy who loves rock but can't make rent at the end of the month. Well, Gerard is all those things, and that's why this story was great for both of us—the perfect marriage of our love for comics and music.

GABRIEL BÁ

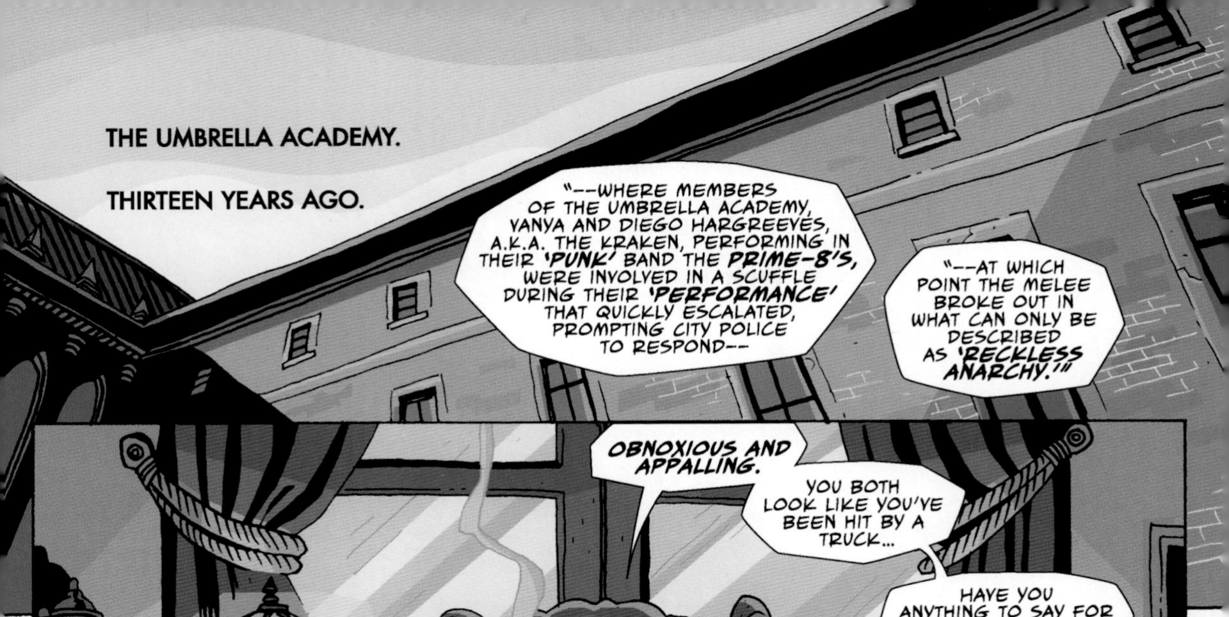
THE UMBRELLA ACADEMY.
THIRTEEN YEARS AGO.
"--WHERE MEMBERS OF THE UMBRELLA ACADEMY, VANYA AND DIEGO HARGREEVES, A.K.A. THE KRAKEN, PERFORMING IN THEIR 'PUNK' BAND THE PRIME-8'S, WERE INVOLVED IN A SCUFFLE DURING THEIR 'PERFORMANCE' THAT QUICKLY ESCALATED, PROMPTING CITY POLICE TO RESPOND--
"--AT WHICH POINT THE MELEE BROKE OUT IN WHAT CAN ONLY BE DESCRIBED AS 'RECKLESS ANARCHY.'"

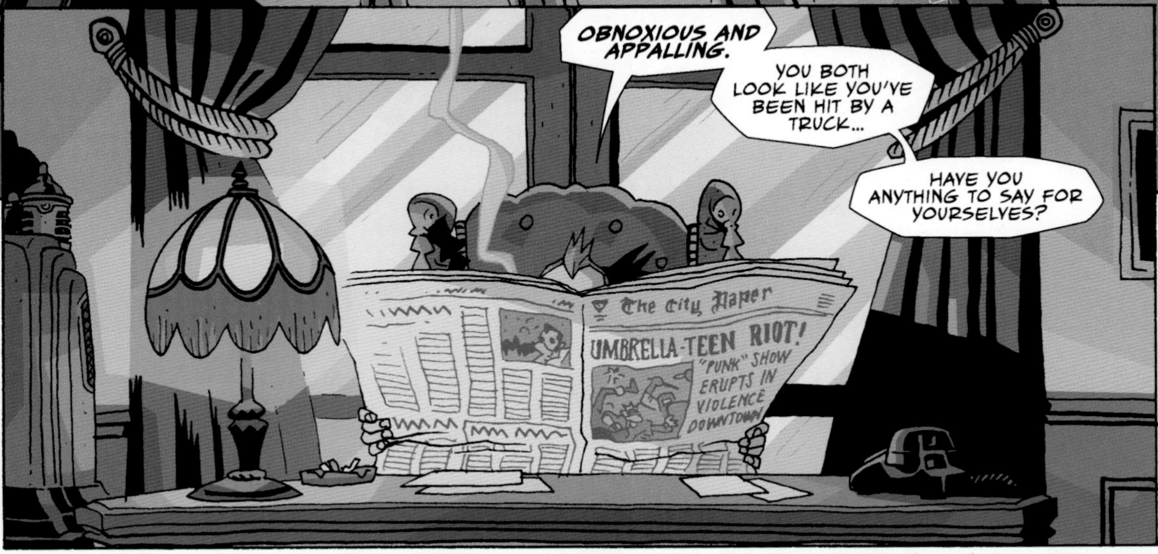
OBNOXIOUS AND APPALLING.
YOU BOTH LOOK LIKE YOU'VE BEEN HIT BY A TRUCK...
HAVE YOU ANYTHING TO SAY FOR YOURSELVES?
The City Paper
UMBRELLA-TEEN RIOT!
"PUNK" SHOW ERUPTS IN VIOLENCE DOWNTOWN

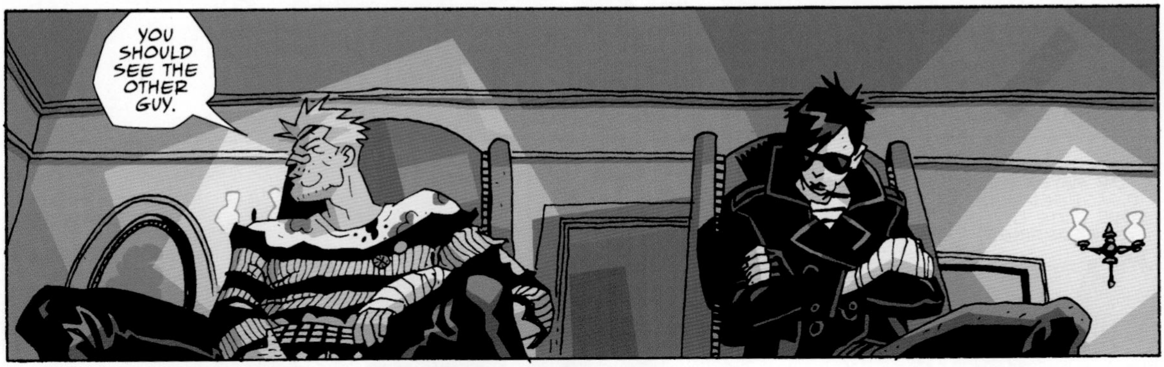
YOU SHOULD SEE THE OTHER GUY.

THE UMBRELLA ACADEMY
ANYWHERE BUT HERE

By Gerard Way & Gabriel Bá
with Dave Stewart and Nate Piekos

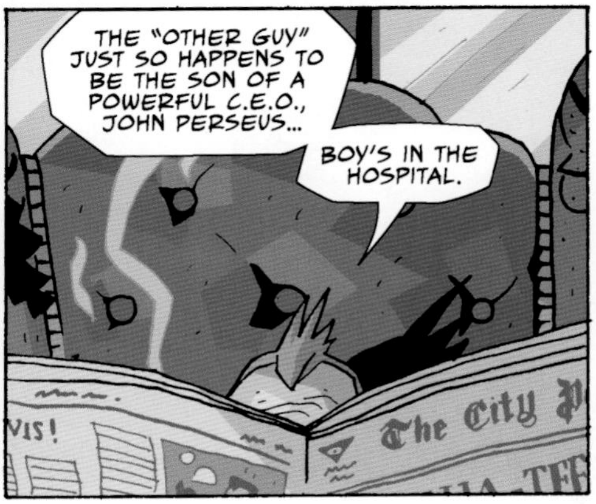
THE "OTHER GUY" JUST SO HAPPENS TO BE THE SON OF A POWERFUL C.E.O., JOHN PERSEUS...
BOY'S IN THE HOSPITAL.

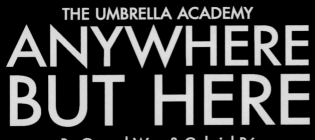

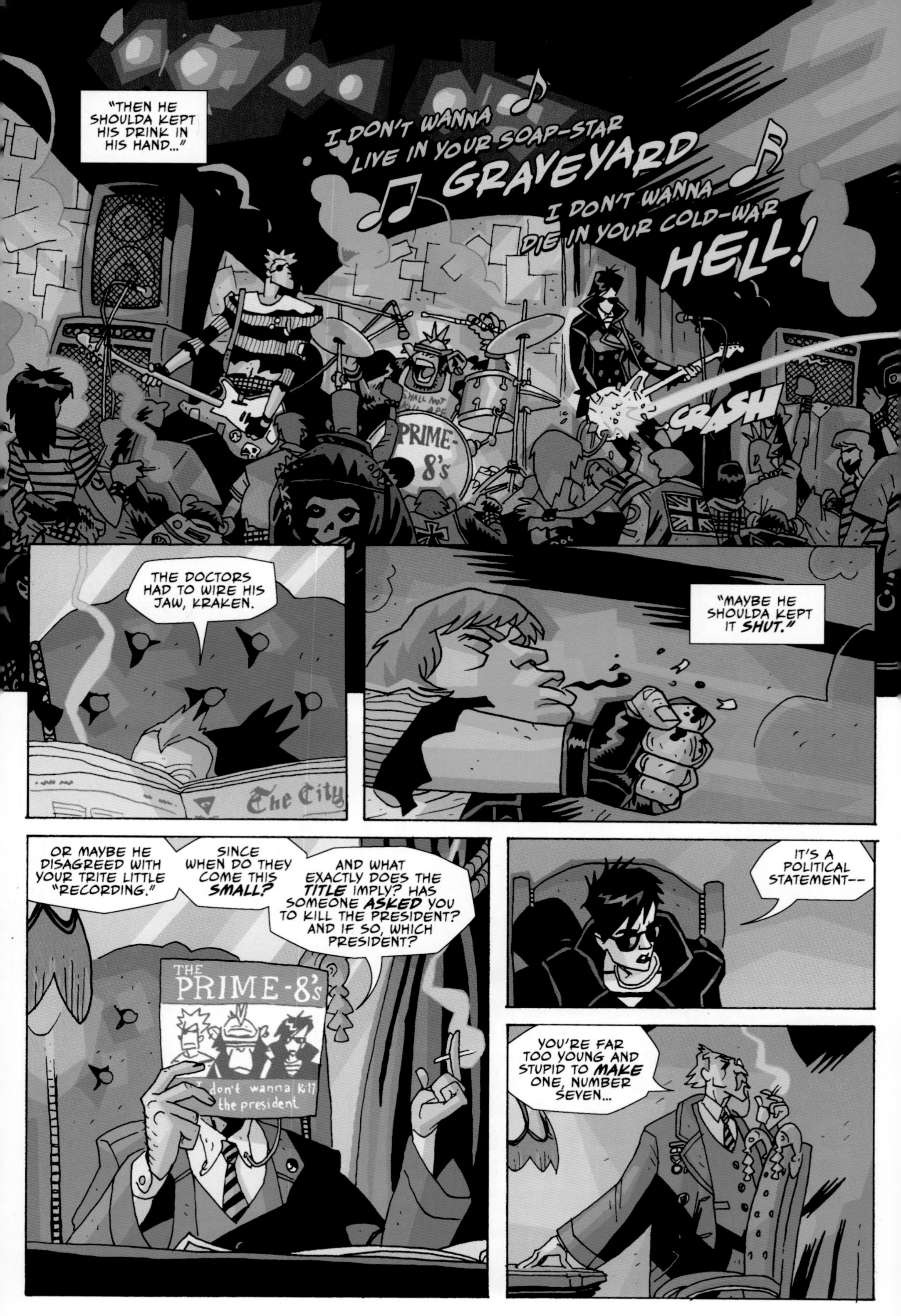
"THEN HE SHOULDA KEPT HIS DRINK IN HIS HAND..."
I DON'T WANNA LIVE IN YOUR SOAP-STAR GRAVEYARD
I DON'T WANNA DIE IN YOUR COLD-WAR HELL!
PRIME-8's
CRASH
THE DOCTORS HAD TO WIRE HIS JAW, KRAKEN.
The City
"MAYBE HE SHOULDA KEPT IT SHUT."
OR MAYBE HE DISAGREED WITH YOUR TRITE LITTLE "RECORDING."
SINCE WHEN DO THEY COME THIS SMALL?
AND WHAT EXACTLY DOES THE TITLE IMPLY? HAS SOMEONE ASKED YOU TO KILL THE PRESIDENT? AND IF SO, WHICH PRESIDENT?
THE PRIME-8's
I don't wanna kill the president
IT'S A POLITICAL STATEMENT--
YOU'RE FAR TOO YOUNG AND STUPID TO MAKE ONE, NUMBER SEVEN...

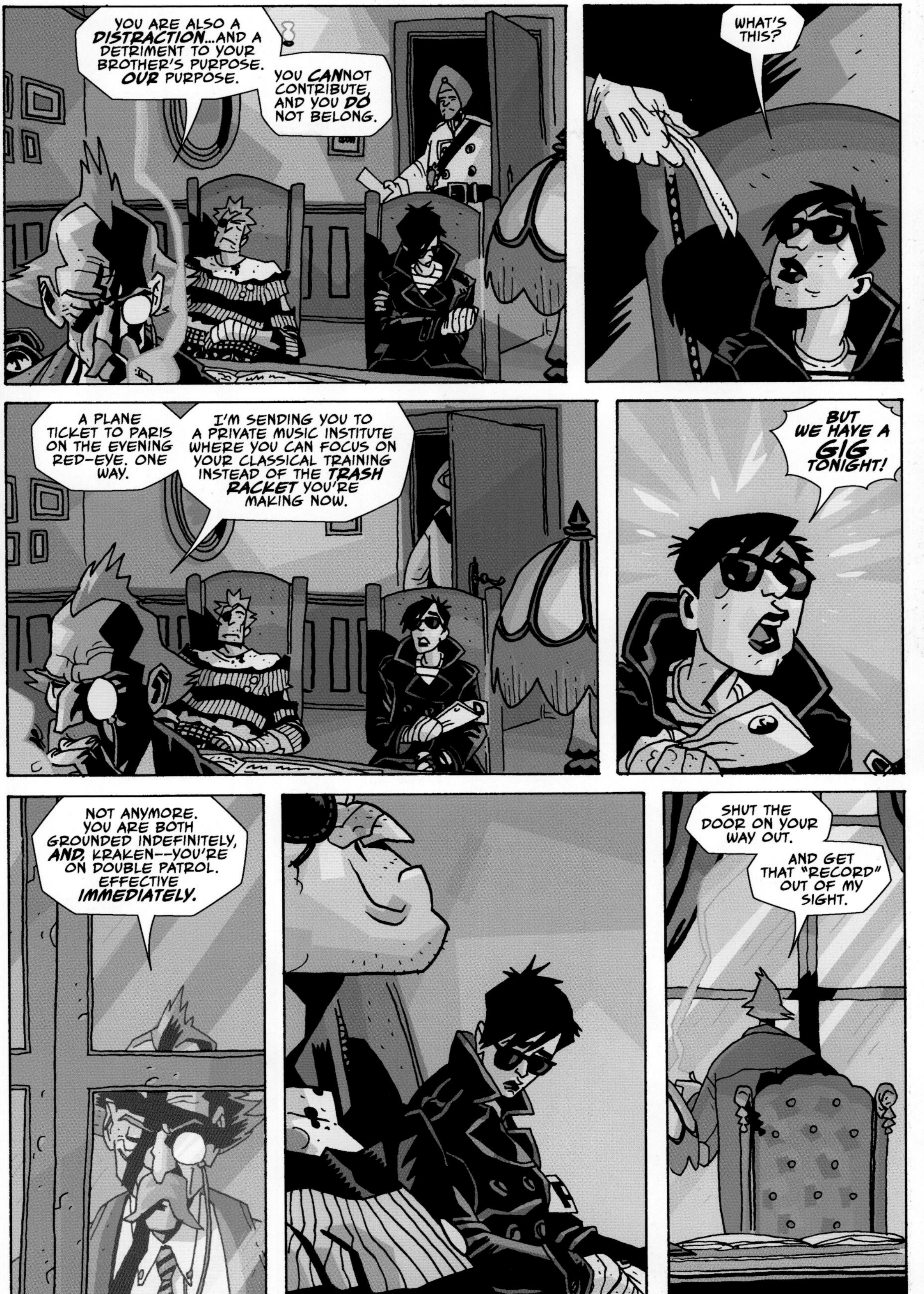
YOU ARE ALSO A DISTRACTION...AND A DETRIMENT TO YOUR BROTHER'S PURPOSE. OUR PURPOSE.
YOU CANNOT CONTRIBUTE, AND YOU DO NOT BELONG.
WHAT'S THIS?
A PLANE TICKET TO PARIS ON THE EVENING RED-EYE. ONE WAY.
I'M SENDING YOU TO A PRIVATE MUSIC INSTITUTE WHERE YOU CAN FOCUS ON YOUR CLASSICAL TRAINING INSTEAD OF THE TRASH RACKET YOU'RE MAKING NOW.
BUT WE HAVE A GIG TONIGHT!
NOT ANYMORE. YOU ARE BOTH GROUNDED INDEFINITELY, AND, KRAKEN--YOU'RE ON DOUBLE PATROL. EFFECTIVE IMMEDIATELY.
SHUT THE DOOR ON YOUR WAY OUT.
AND GET THAT "RECORD" OUT OF MY SIGHT.

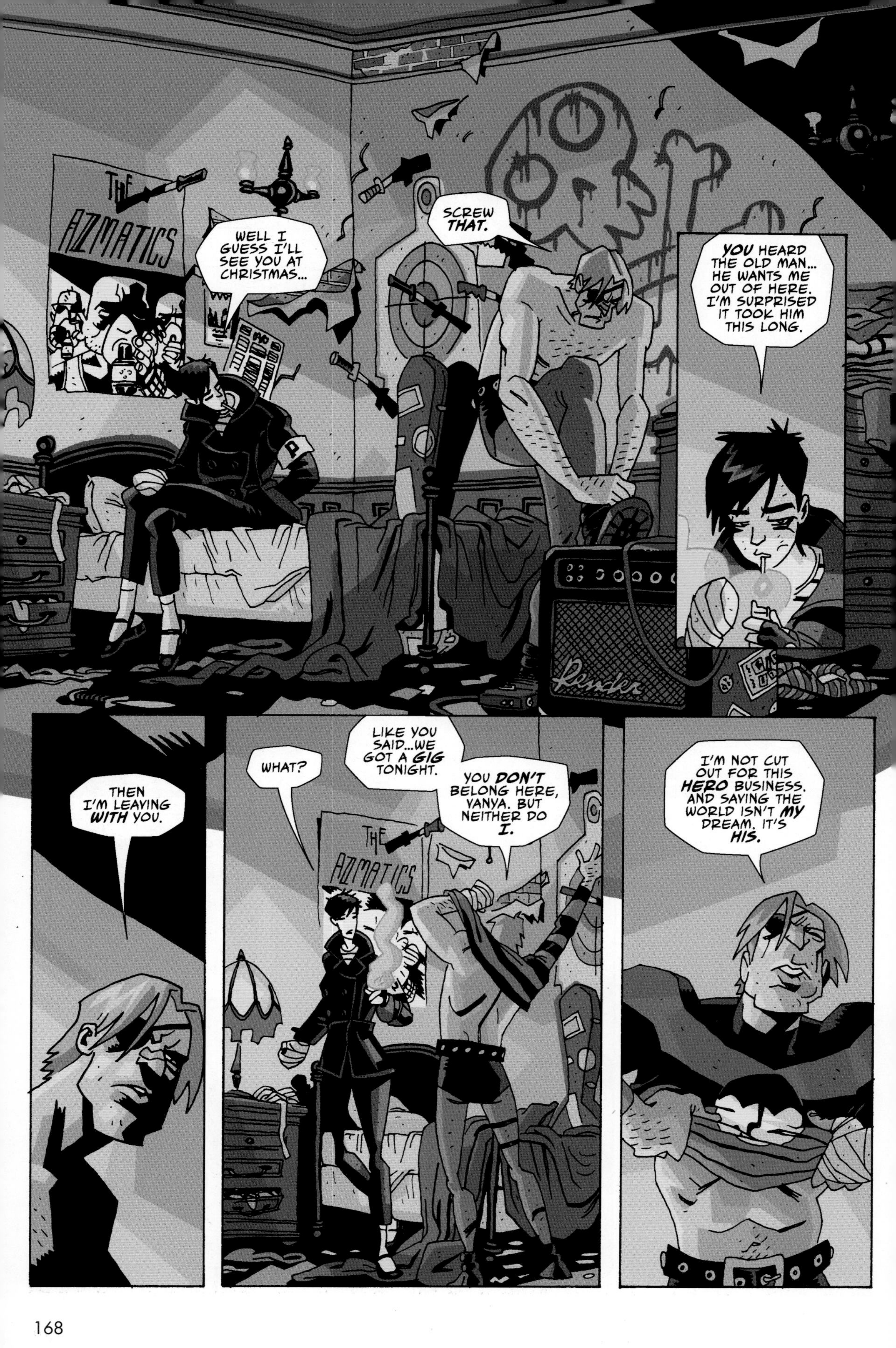
THE AZMATICS
WELL I GUESS I'LL SEE YOU AT CHRISTMAS...
SCREW THAT.
YOU HEARD THE OLD MAN... HE WANTS ME OUT OF HERE. I'M SURPRISED IT TOOK HIM THIS LONG.
Fender
THEN I'M LEAVING WITH YOU.
WHAT?
LIKE YOU SAID...WE GOT A GIG TONIGHT.
YOU DON'T BELONG HERE, VANYA. BUT NEITHER DO I.
THE AZMATICS
I'M NOT CUT OUT FOR THIS HERO BUSINESS. AND SAVING THE WORLD ISN'T MY DREAM. IT'S HIS.

THIS IS WHERE YOU BELONG.

THIS IS WHAT YOU'RE MEANT TO DO.

PLAYING GIGS, RAISING HELL, HITTING CITIES LIKE A SLEDGEHAMMER ALL OVER THE WORLD.

I'LL DITCH OUT ON PATROL AND MEET YOU AT THE CLUB. WE DO THE SHOW, GRAB THE CASH, PACK THE GEAR IN BODY'S VAN, HIT THE GAS--AND NEVER COME HOME.

PRIME
I don't wanna
the president

YOU WITH ME?

YOU GOT YOURSELF AN AXELADY, HOT-HEAD.

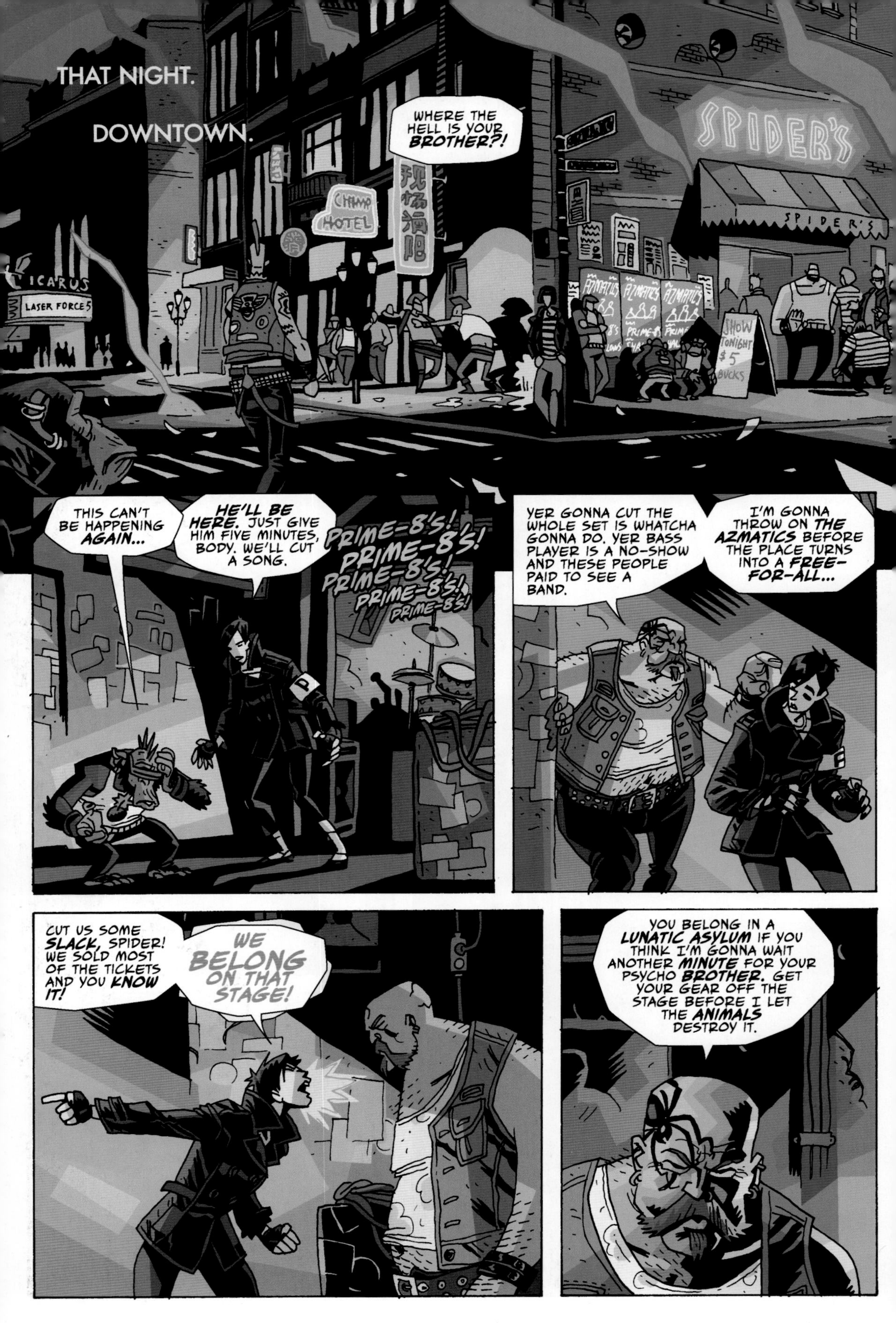

THAT NIGHT.
DOWNTOWN.
WHERE THE HELL IS YOUR BROTHER?!
SPIDER'S
CHAMP HOTEL
ICARUS
LASER FORCE 5
SPIDER'S
AZMATICS
SHOW TONIGHT $5 BUCKS
THIS CAN'T BE HAPPENING AGAIN...
HE'LL BE HERE. JUST GIVE HIM FIVE MINUTES, BODY. WE'LL CUT A SONG.
PRIME-8'S! PRIME-8'S! PRIME-8'S! PRIME-8'S! PRIME-8'S!
YER GONNA CUT THE WHOLE SET IS WHATCHA GONNA DO. YER BASS PLAYER IS A NO-SHOW AND THESE PEOPLE PAID TO SEE A BAND.
I'M GONNA THROW ON THE AZMATICS BEFORE THE PLACE TURNS INTO A FREE-FOR-ALL...
CUT US SOME SLACK, SPIDER! WE SOLD MOST OF THE TICKETS AND YOU KNOW IT!
WE BELONG ON THAT STAGE!
YOU BELONG IN A LUNATIC ASYLUM IF YOU THINK I'M GONNA WAIT ANOTHER MINUTE FOR YOUR PSYCHO BROTHER. GET YOUR GEAR OFF THE STAGE BEFORE I LET THE ANIMALS DESTROY IT.

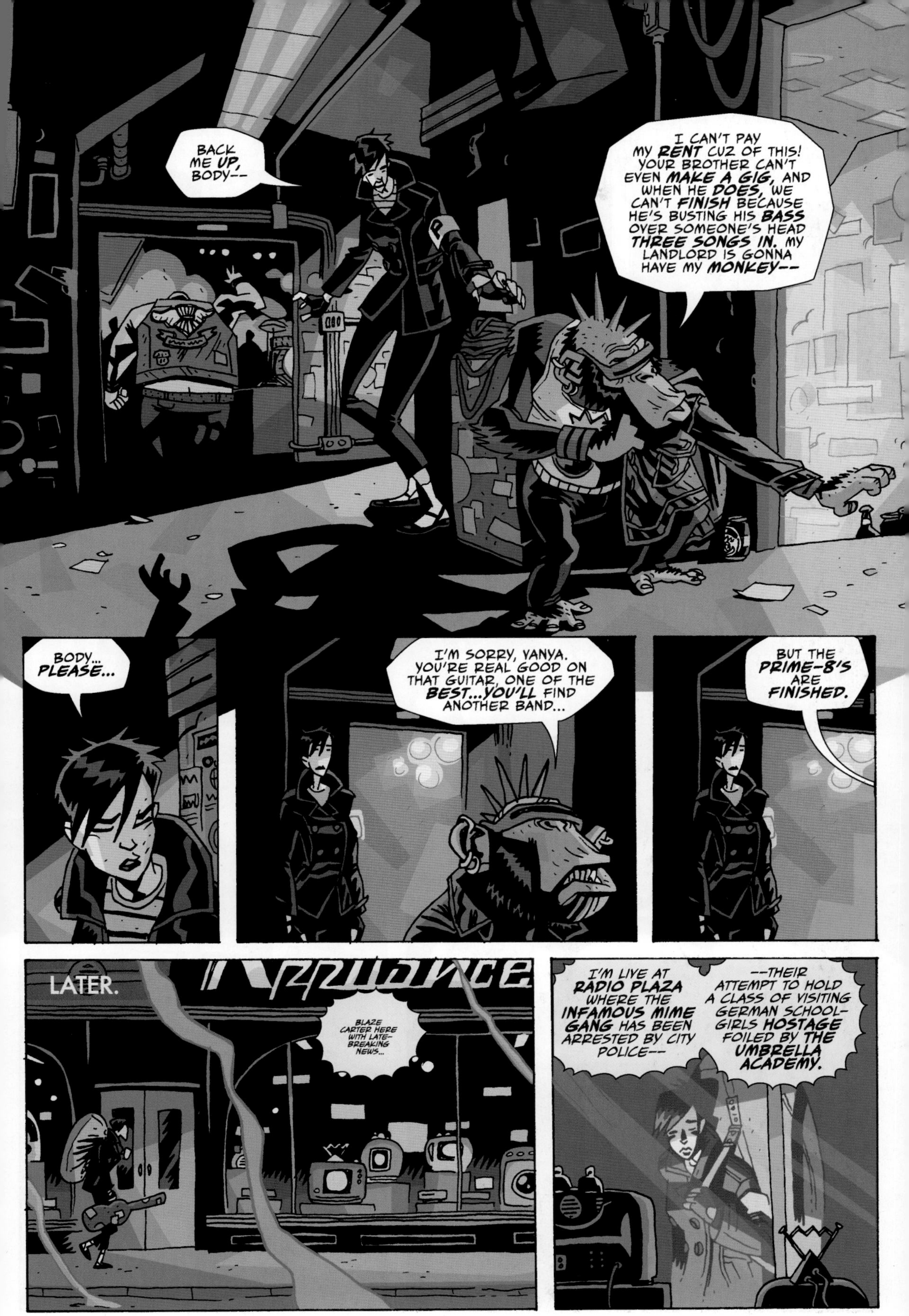
BACK ME UP, BODY--
I CAN'T PAY MY RENT CUZ OF THIS! YOUR BROTHER CAN'T EVEN MAKE A GIG, AND WHEN HE DOES, WE CAN'T FINISH BECAUSE HE'S BUSTING HIS BASS OVER SOMEONE'S HEAD THREE SONGS IN. MY LANDLORD IS GONNA HAVE MY MONKEY--
BODY... PLEASE...
I'M SORRY, YANYA. YOU'RE REAL GOOD ON THAT GUITAR, ONE OF THE BEST...YOU'LL FIND ANOTHER BAND...
BUT THE PRIME-8'S ARE FINISHED.
LATER.
BLAZE CARTER HERE WITH LATE-BREAKING NEWS...
I'M LIVE AT RADIO PLAZA WHERE THE INFAMOUS MIME GANG HAS BEEN ARRESTED BY CITY POLICE--
--THEIR ATTEMPT TO HOLD A CLASS OF VISITING GERMAN SCHOOL-GIRLS HOSTAGE FOILED BY THE UMBRELLA ACADEMY.

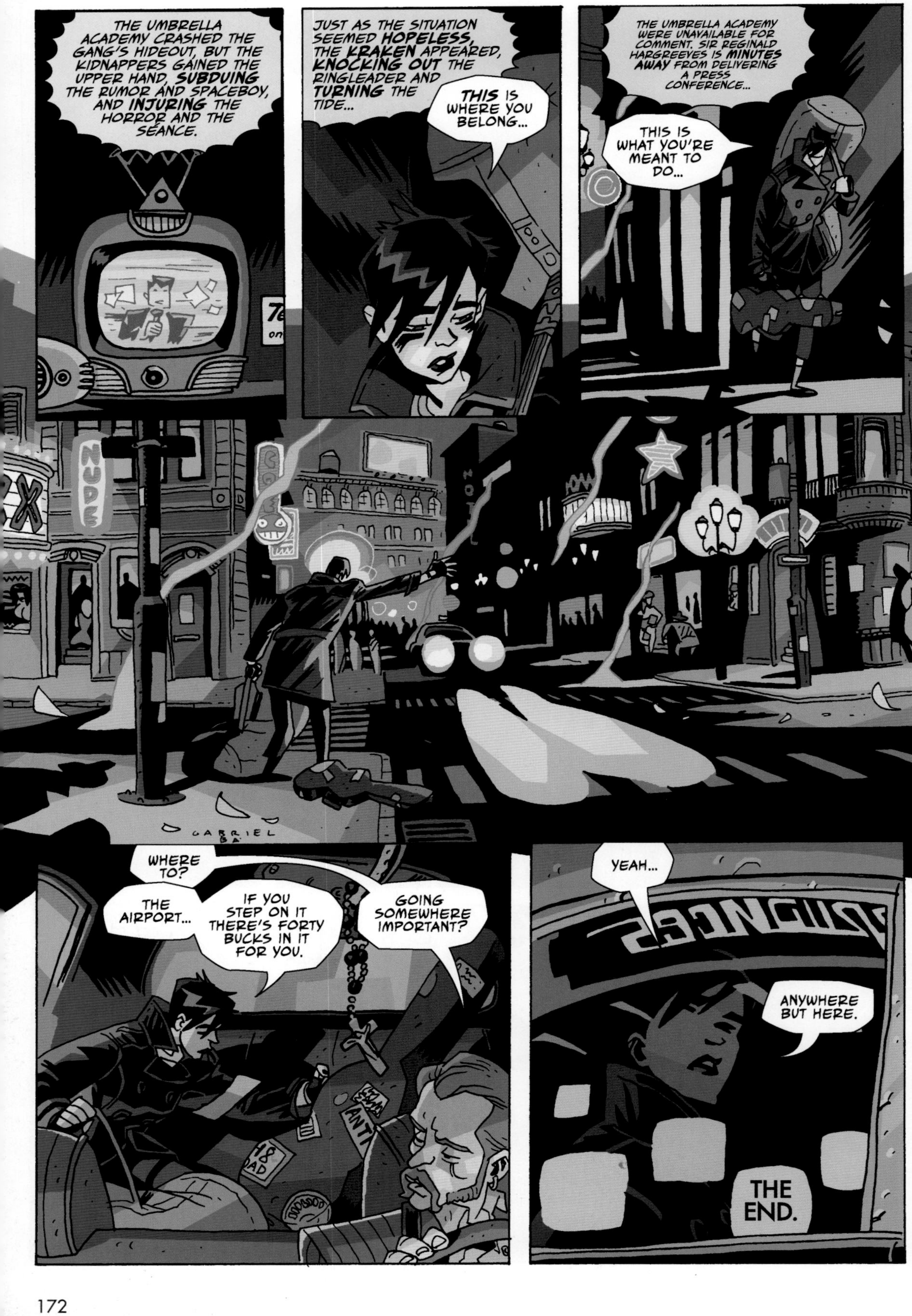
THE UMBRELLA ACADEMY CRASHED THE GANG'S HIDEOUT, BUT THE KIDNAPPERS GAINED THE UPPER HAND, SUBDUING THE RUMOR AND SPACEBOY, AND INJURING THE HORROR AND THE SÉANCE.
JUST AS THE SITUATION SEEMED HOPELESS, THE KRAKEN APPEARED, KNOCKING OUT THE RINGLEADER AND TURNING THE TIDE...
THIS IS WHERE YOU BELONG...
THE UMBRELLA ACADEMY WERE UNAVAILABLE FOR COMMENT. SIR REGINALD HARGREEVES IS MINUTES AWAY FROM DELIVERING A PRESS CONFERENCE...
THIS IS WHAT YOU'RE MEANT TO DO...
NUDE
GABRIEL BÁ
WHERE TO?
THE AIRPORT...
IF YOU STEP ON IT THERE'S FORTY BUCKS IN IT FOR YOU.
GOING SOMEWHERE IMPORTANT?
YEAH...
ANYWHERE BUT HERE.
THE END.

Designing THE UMBRELLA ACADEMY: DALLAS

Art by Gabriel Bá and Gerard Way

with Tony Ong and Dave Stewart

Notes by Scott Allie

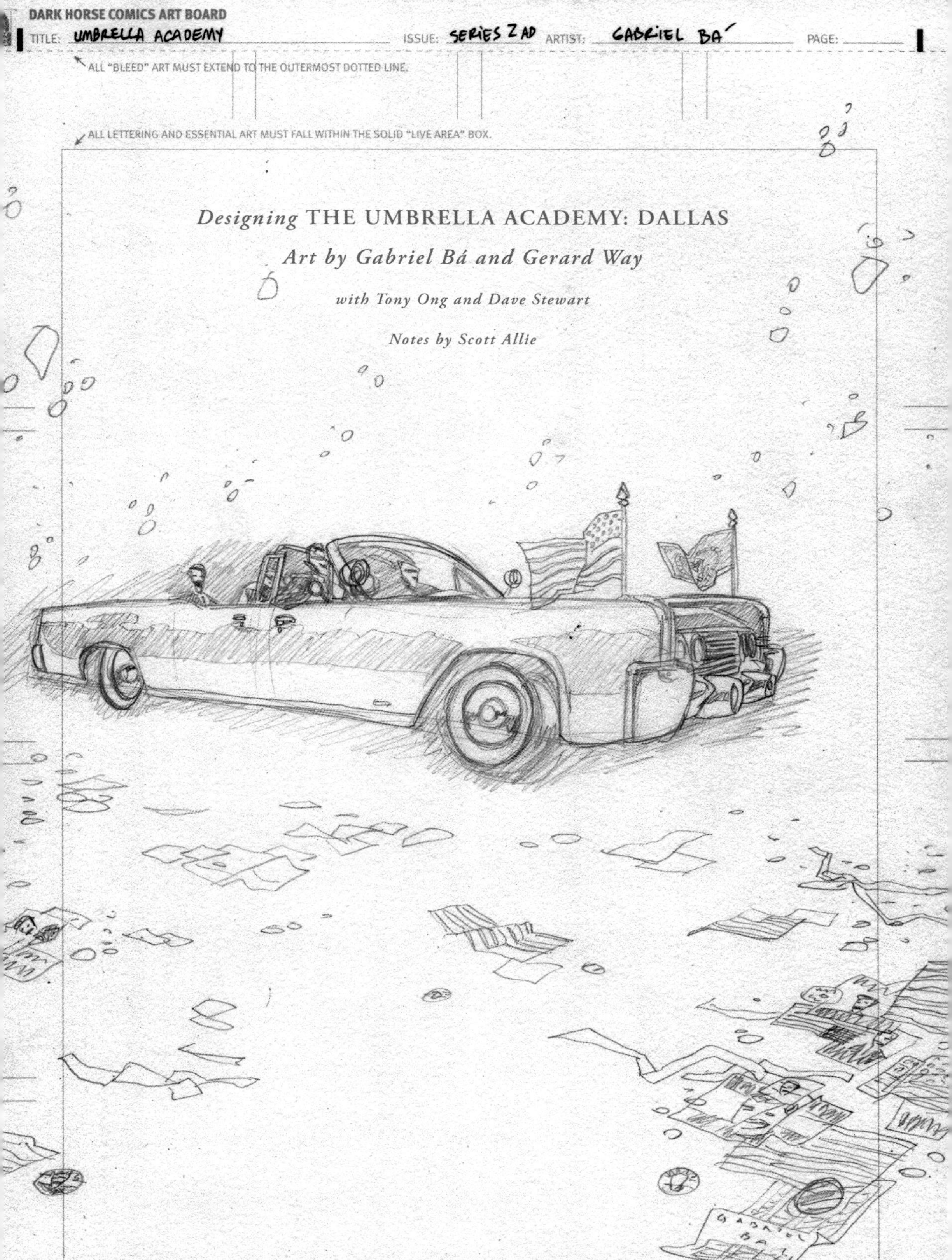
DARK HORSE COMICS ART BOARD
TITLE: UMBRELLA ACADEMY
ISSUE: SERIES 2 AD
ARTIST: GABRIEL BA´
PAGE:
ALL "BLEED" ART MUST EXTEND TO THE OUTERMOST DOTTED LINE.
ALL LETTERING AND ESSENTIAL ART MUST FALL WITHIN THE SOLID "LIVE AREA" BOX.
GABRIEL BA

We wanted an early teaser image for the series, and played on the fact that *Dallas* #1 would come out within days of the thirty-fifth anniversary of Kennedy's death. Compare to the finished image on page 2 of this volume.

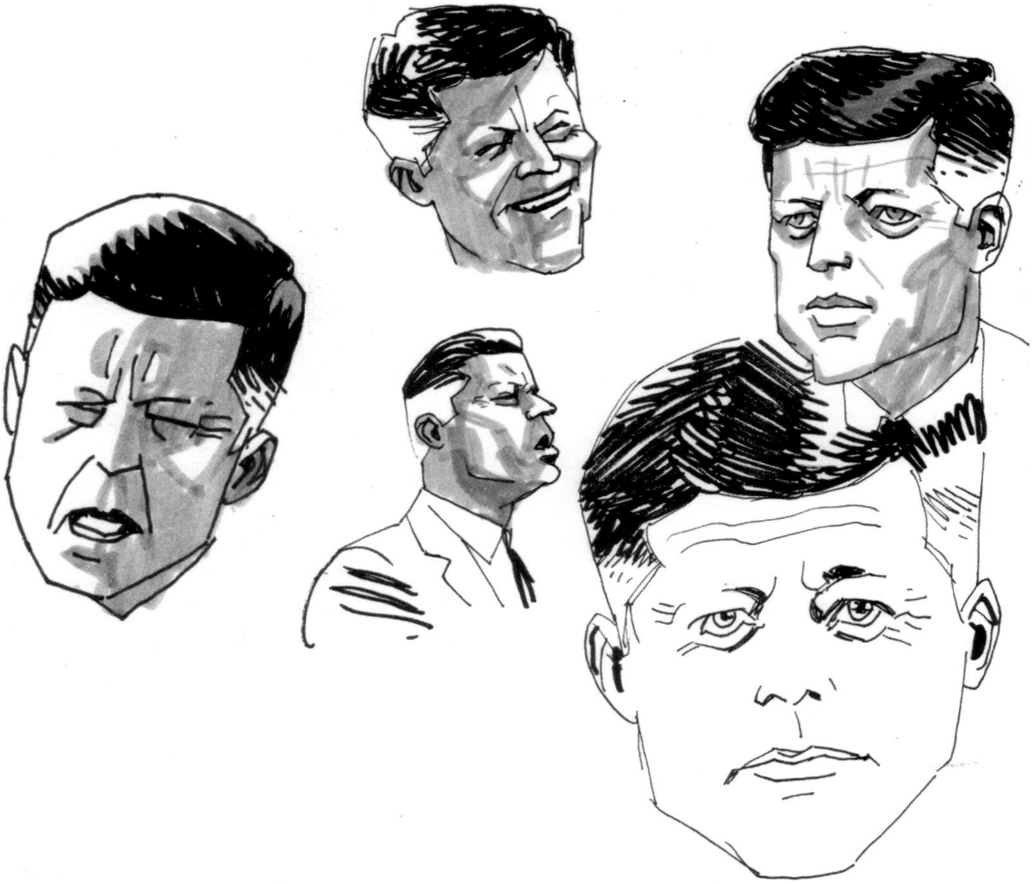

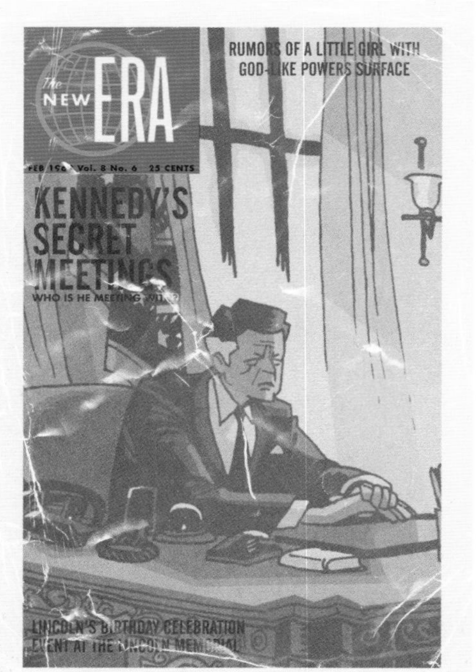
The NEW ERA
RUMORS OF A LITTLE GIRL WITH GOD-LIKE POWERS SURFACE
Vol. 8 No. 6 25 CENTS
KENNEDY'S SECRET MEETINGS
WHO IS HE
LINCOLN'S BIRTHDAY CELEBRATION

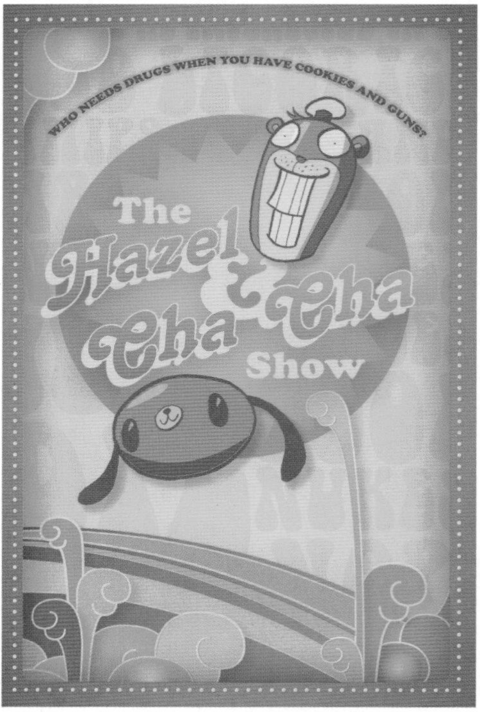
WHO NEEDS DRUGS WHEN YOU HAVE COOKIES AND GUNS?
The Hazel & Cha-Cha Show

Top: Gabriel practices on Kennedy. Bottom left: We loved Tony Ong's design work on the first series so much, we gave him more freedom this time. We suggested putting Kennedy on the back cover of *Dallas* #1, but everything else was his idea, including the text. Bottom right: Tony's *Dallas* #3 back cover.

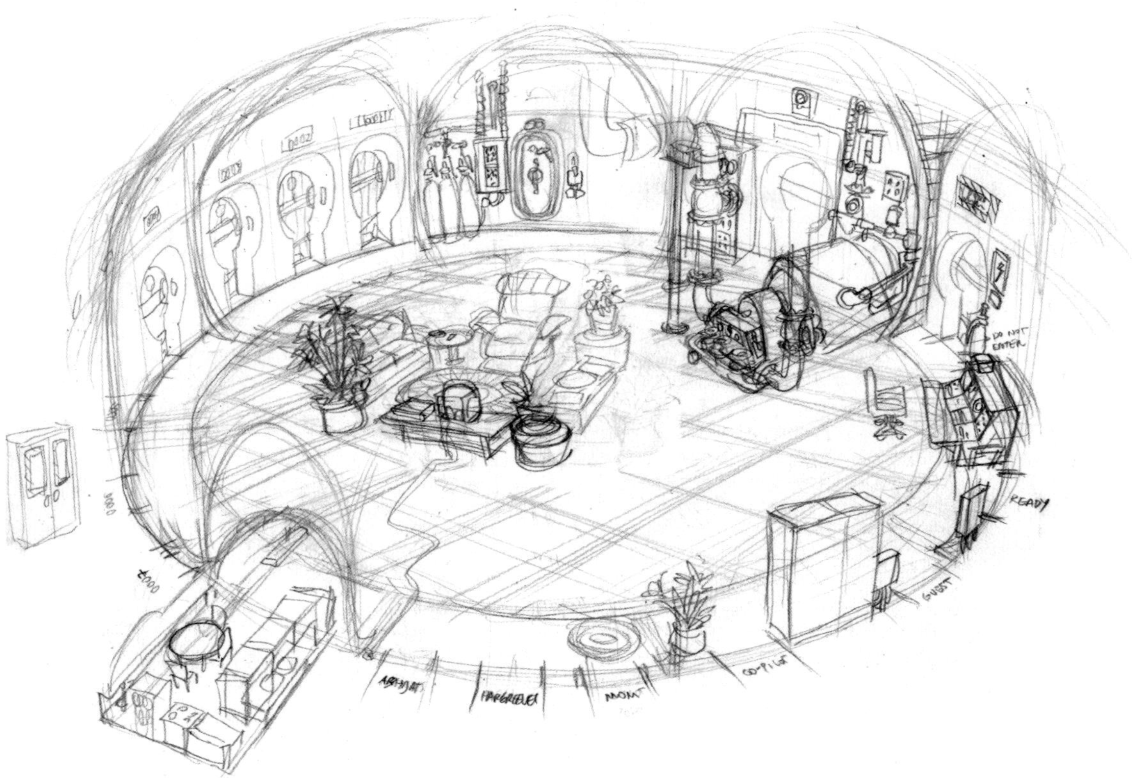
DO NOT ENTER
READY
GUEST
MOM

Above: Gabriel usually designs settings as he draws the page itself, but the basement of the Academy needed more forethought. Below: Gabriel works out Vanya's bedridden look.

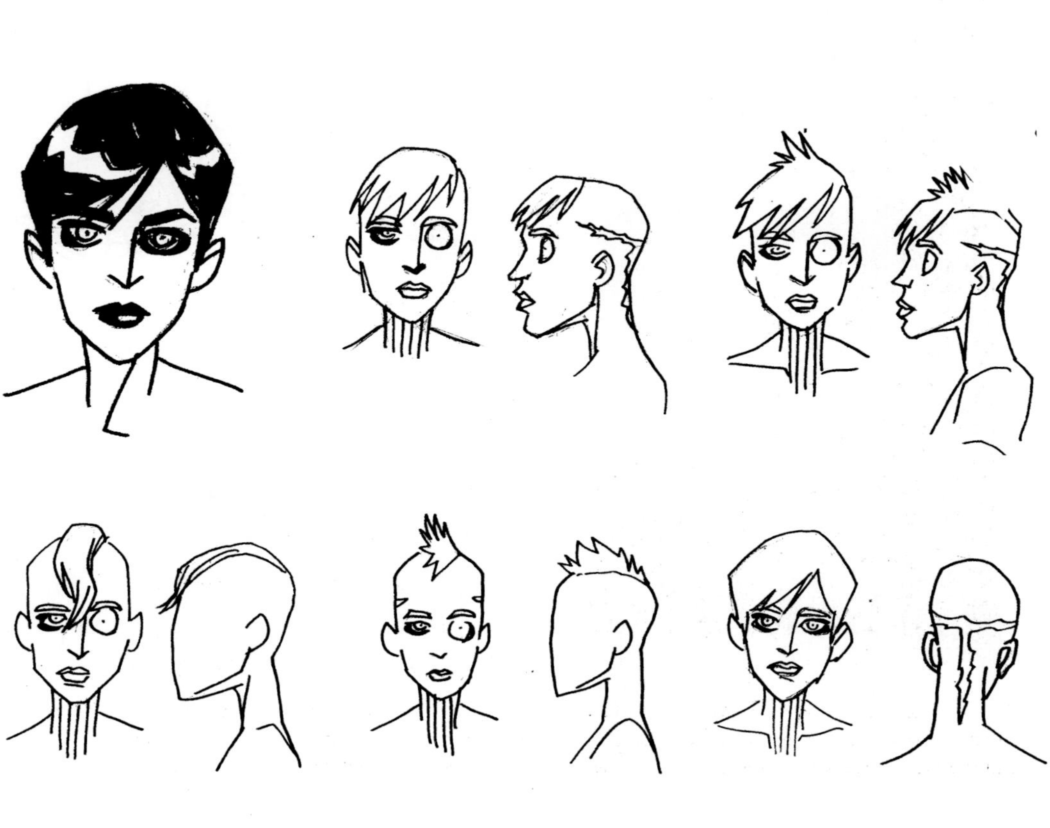

At first there was going to be a single hit man named Bruno, whose name would strike terror in Number Five. Gerard designed him (top left), but we would have been sued into oblivion. When Gerard came up with the names Hazel and Cha Cha, it had such a perfect ring we knew we needed Bá to design a duo, and wanted to stick with an insipid, vacant animal mask, deciding it was safer to go Banana Splits than Magic Kingdom. Bottom far left: Tony's back cover to *Dallas* #2.

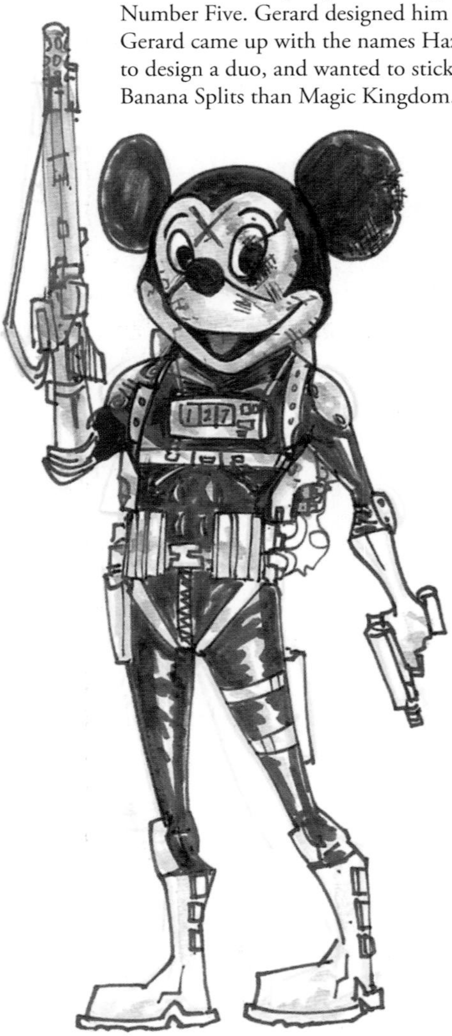

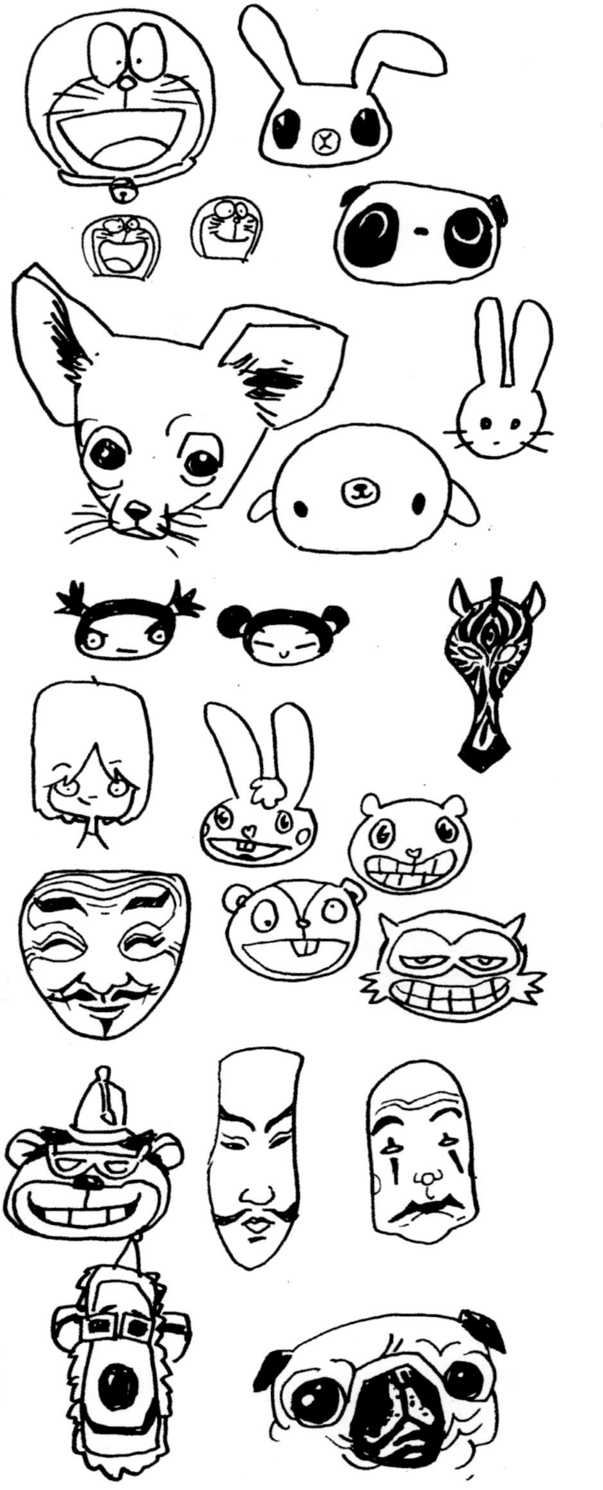

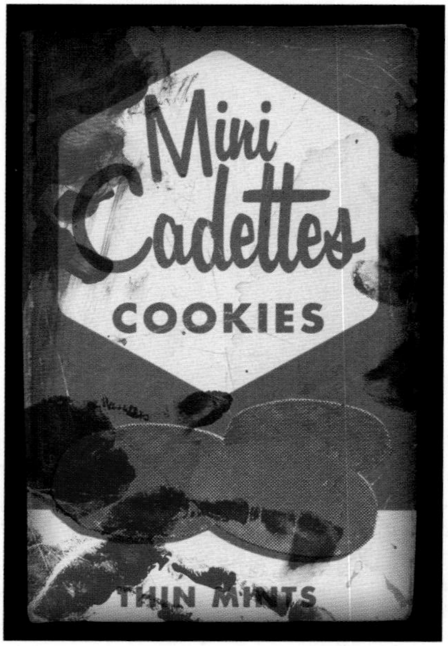
Mini Cadettes
COOKIES
THIN MINTS

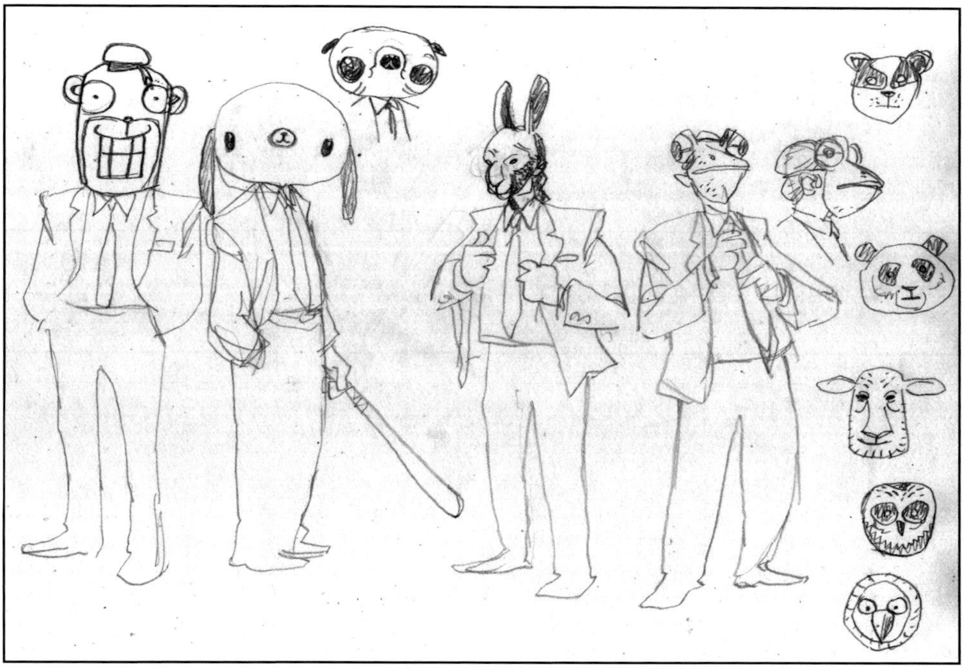

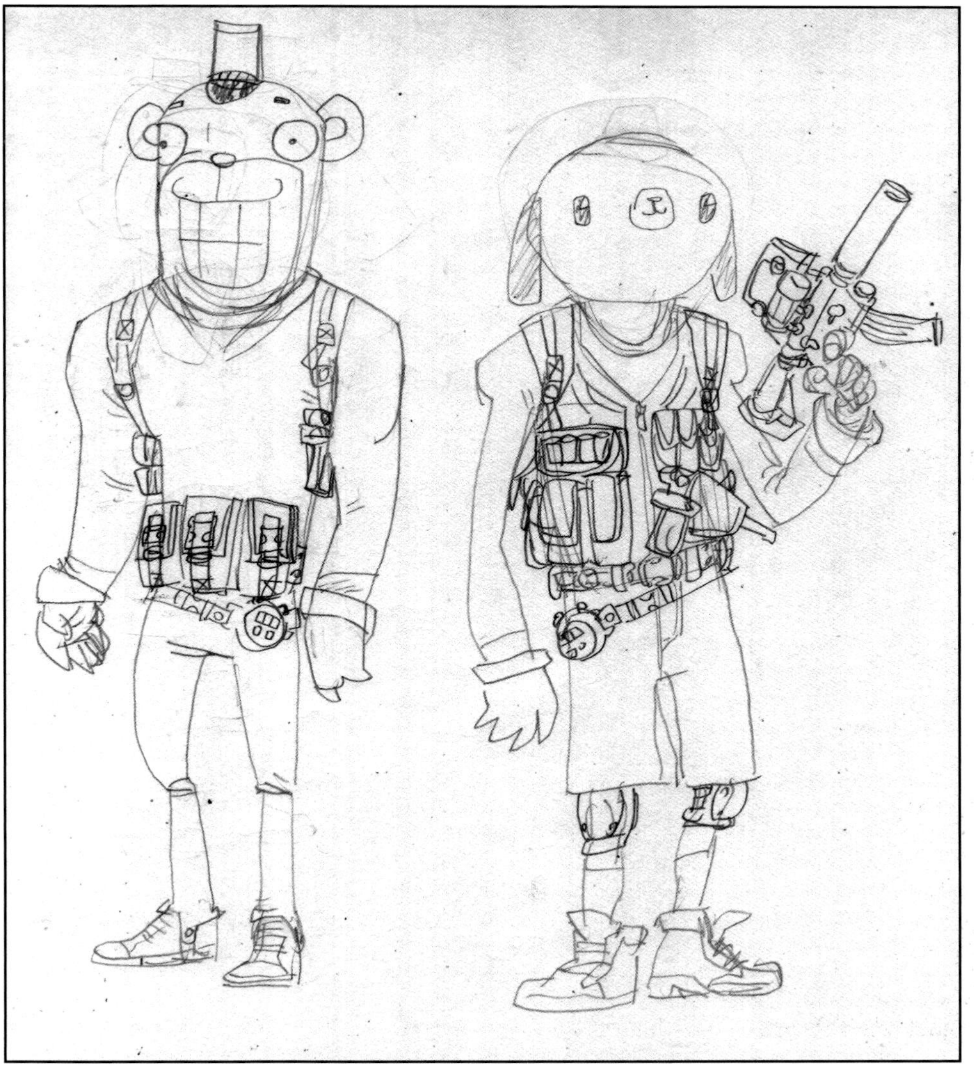

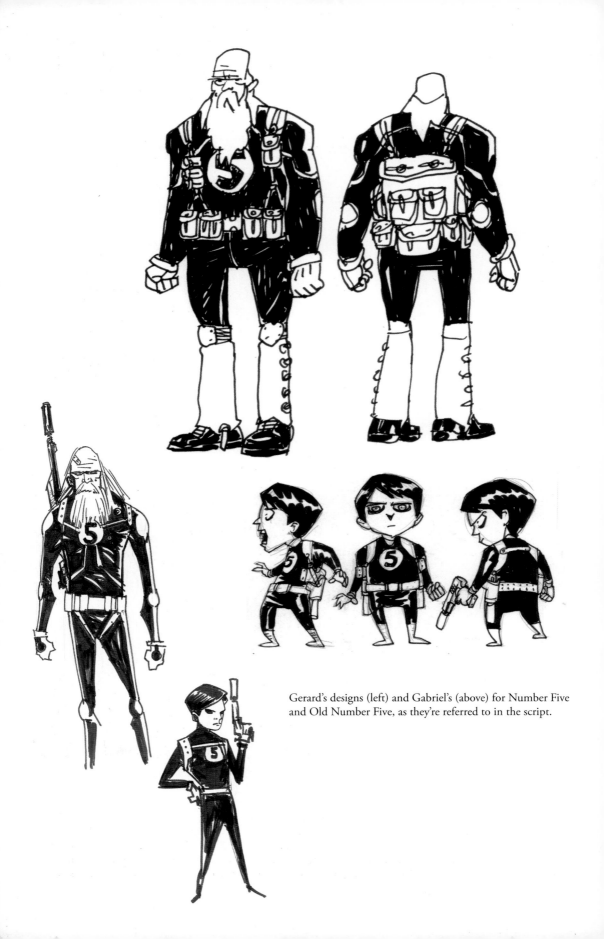

Gerard's designs (left) and Gabriel's (above) for Number Five and Old Number Five, as they're referred to in the script.

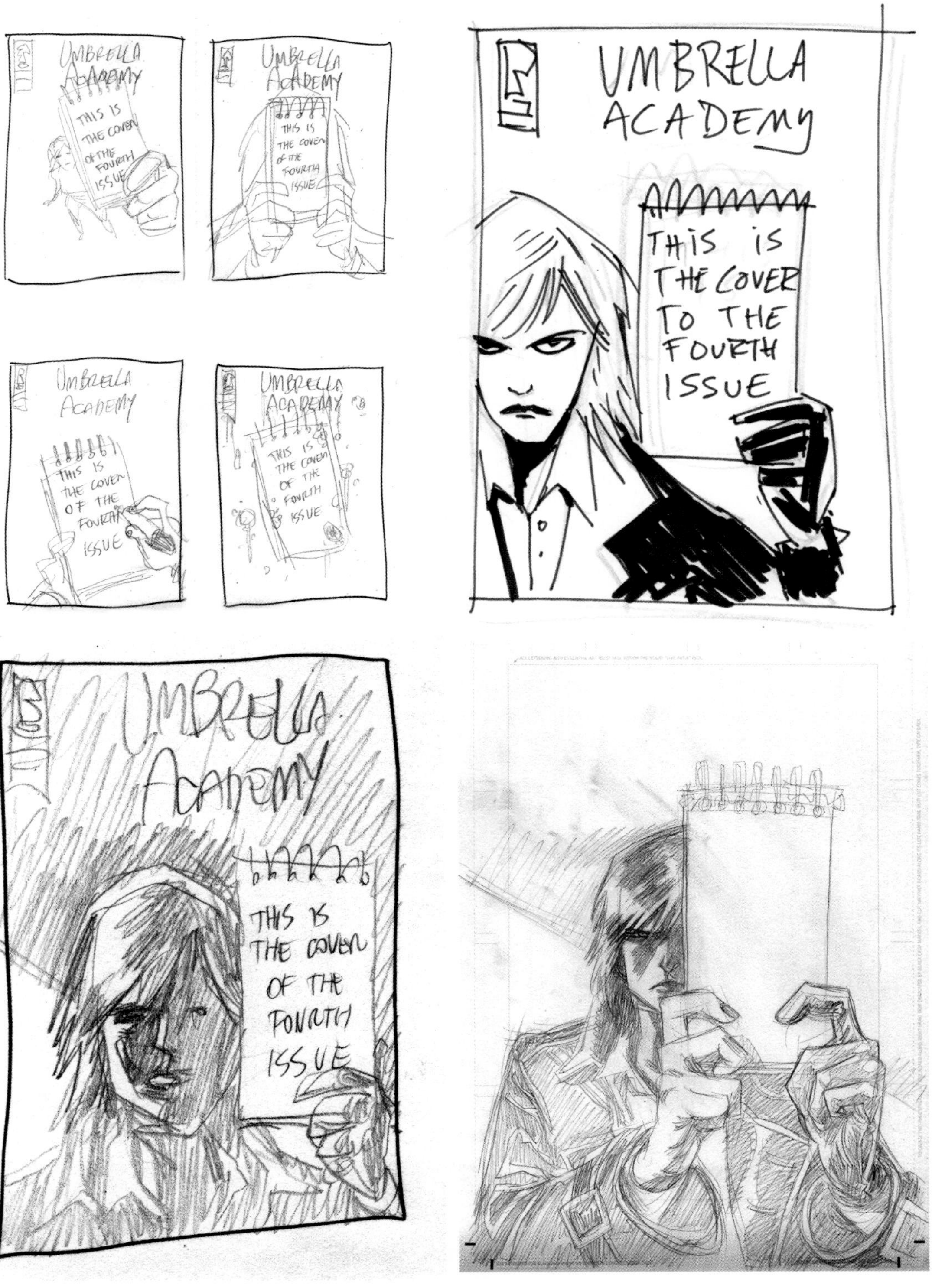
UMBRELLA ACADEMY
THIS IS THE COVER OF THE FOURTH ISSUE
UMBRELLA ACADEMY
THIS IS THE COVER TO THE FOURTH ISSUE
UMBRELLA ACADEMY
THIS IS THE COVER OF THE FOURTH ISSUE

The ending of *Dallas* was one of the first things we knew about the story, but there were a lot of things along the way we didn't have worked out. *Dallas* #4 was still wide open by the time we needed the cover. Gerard didn't know what to suggest for a cover, so Lindsey, his wife, offered this idea. Gabriel did a few rounds of sketches, but they weren't quite dull enough, so Gerard did a sketch (top right). Bottom right: Gabriel's final pencils. Compare to page 90. Some Dark Horse staff worried this cover would make readers and retailers feel like they were being mocked, but we think people got the joke.

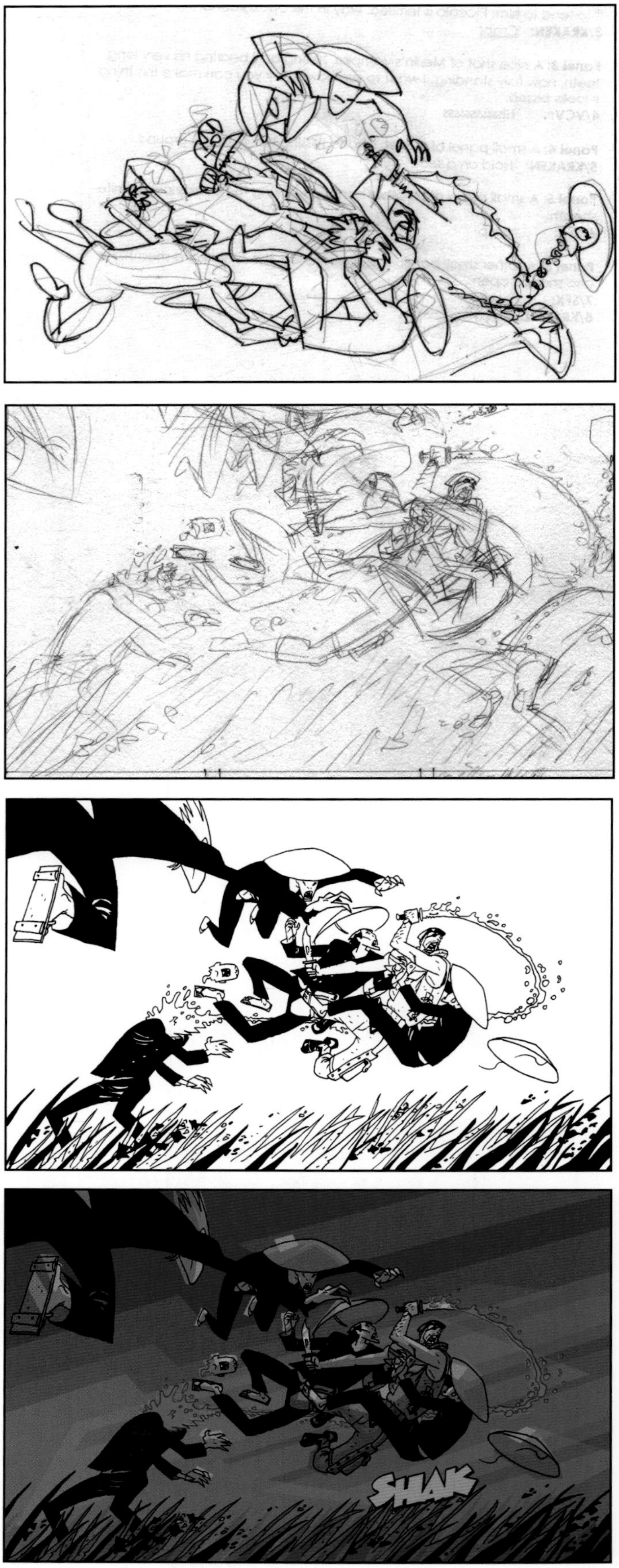
SHAK

Kraken's fight with the Vietcong vampires, from sketch to finishes. Compare to page 124.

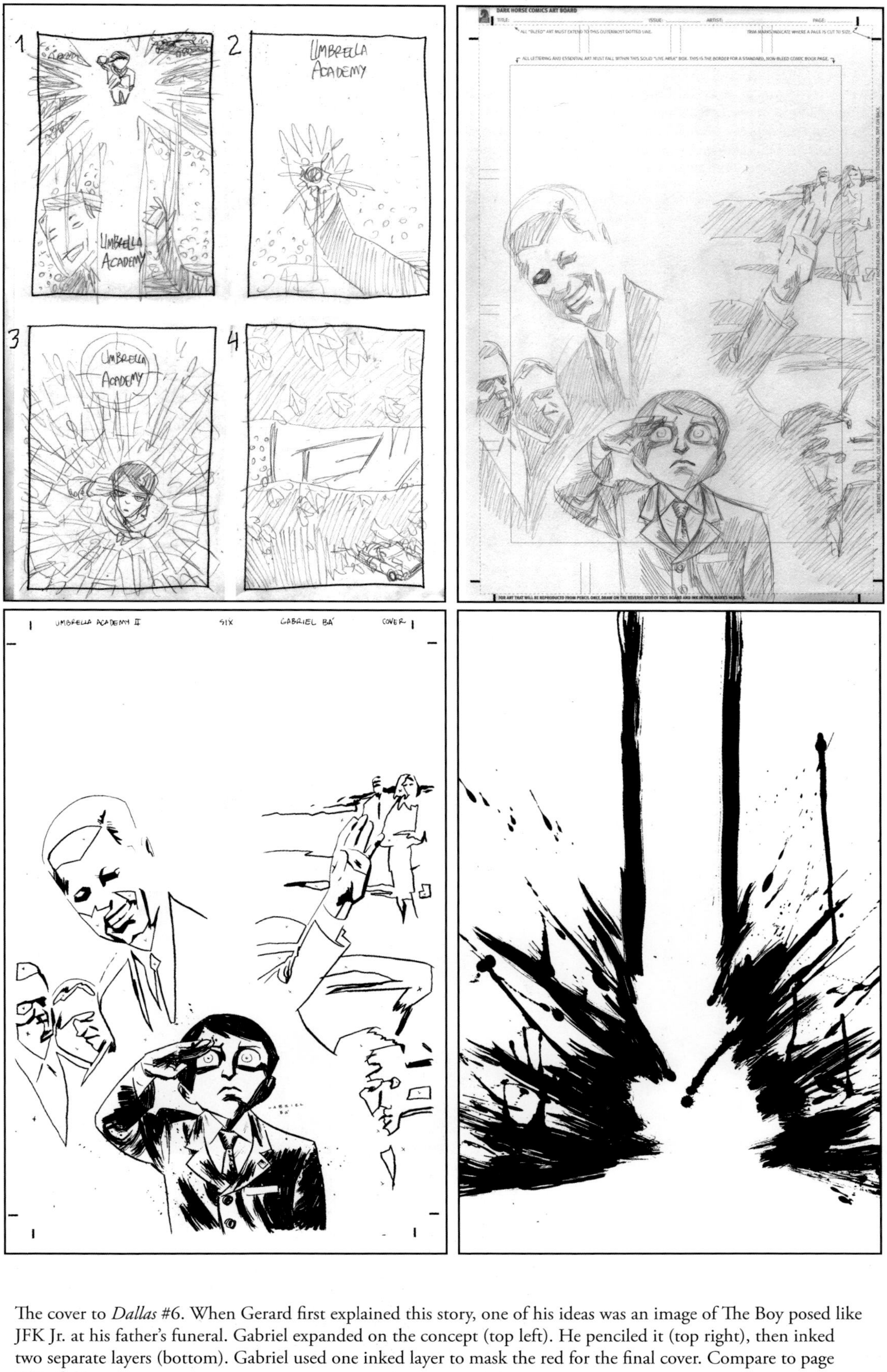
1
UMBRELLA ACADEMY
2
UMBRELLA ACADEMY
3
UMBRELLA ACADEMY
4
DARK HORSE COMICS ART BOARD
UMBRELLA ACADEMY II
SIX
GABRIEL BÁ
COVER
GABRIEL BÁ

The cover to *Dallas* #6. When Gerard first explained this story, one of his ideas was an image of The Boy posed like JFK Jr. at his father's funeral. Gabriel expanded on the concept (top left). He penciled it (top right), then inked two separate layers (bottom). Gabriel used one inked layer to mask the red for the final cover. Compare to page 138 of this volume.

GERARD WAY

Gerard Way won a prize, in the third grade, while enrolled at Number Four Elementary School in Belleville, New Jersey, for creating a drawing depicting a large playground filled with children, most likely his age, playing various sports that he himself had never played, such as badminton, archery, and field hockey. His depiction placed third, earning him a certificate and his photograph in the *Belleville Times*, though the reporting journalist misspelled his name as "Gerard Waigh." Despite this oversight, he was not discouraged from drawing and continues to do so to this day, along with his wife, Lindsey; their daughter, Bandit; and their French bulldog, Susan Michelle, in Southern California. *Photo by Chris Anthony*

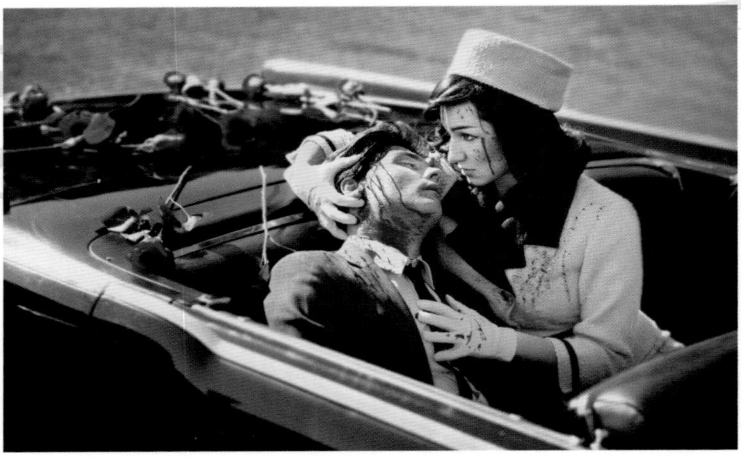

GABRIEL BÁ

Gabriel Bá has been creating comics for over ten years now, often collaborating with his twin brother, Fábio Moon, on stories that capture the essence of where he lives and plays—the megalopolis of São Paulo, Brazil—in books like *De:TALES* and *Daytripper*. His other collaborative efforts include *Casanova*, *Pixu*, and *B.P.R.D.: 1947*. *The Umbrella Academy* has marked Bá's first venture into the world of "superhero" comics; his artwork has garnered him much attention and praise, including the illustrious Harvey and Eisner Awards for Best Artist. *Photo by Alexandre Schneider*

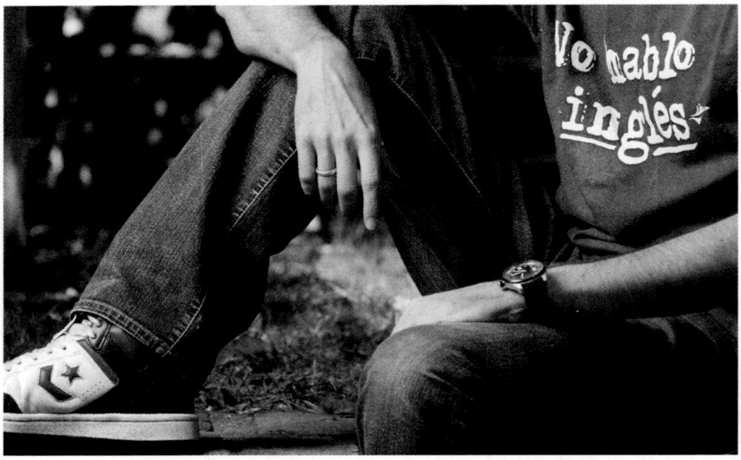
Yo hablo
inglés

THE UMBRELLA ACADEMY: APOCALYPSE SUITE

2008 Eisner Award for Best Limited Series

2008 Harvey Award for Best New Series

One of the Library Journal*'s Best Graphic Novels of 2008*

One of YALSA's Great Graphic Novels for Teens

One of Comic Book Resources' Best 100 Comics of 2008

2008 Scream Award for Best Comic Artist

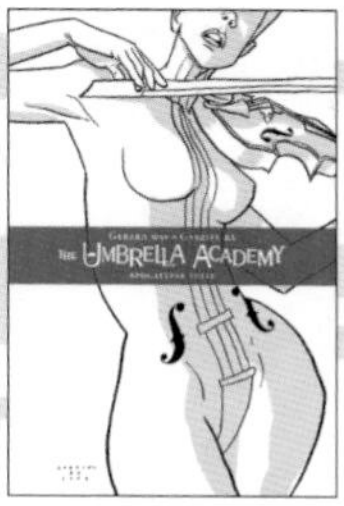
THE UMBRELLA ACADEMY

THE UMBRELLA ACADEMY VOLUME 1: APOCALYPSE SUITE
Gerard Way, Gabriel Bá, and Dave Stewart

In an inexplicable worldwide event, forty-seven extraordinary children were spontaneously born. Millionaire inventor Reginald Hargreeves adopted seven of the children; when asked why, his only explanation was, "To save the world." These seven children form The Umbrella Academy, a dysfunctional family of superheroes with bizarre powers.
$17.95/ISBN 978-1-59307-978-9

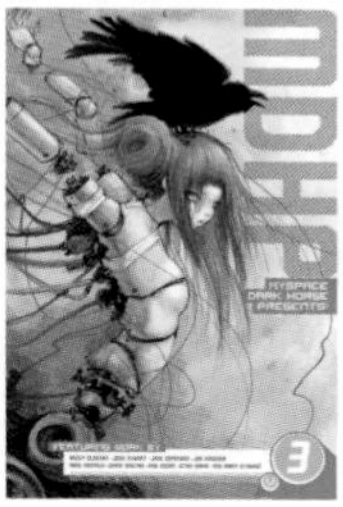
MDHP

MYSPACE DARK HORSE PRESENTS VOLUMES 1–3
Gerard Way, Gabriel Bá, Fábio Moon, Becky Cloonan, Mike Mignola, Joss Whedon, and others

The online comics anthology *MySpace Dark Horse Presents* sees print in these three volumes—each collecting six issues of the still ongoing series.
$19.95 each

Volume 1
ISBN 978-1-59307-998-7

Volume 2
ISBN 978-1-59582-248-2

Volume 3
ISBN 978-1-59582-327-4

RECOMMENDED DARK HORSE READING . . .

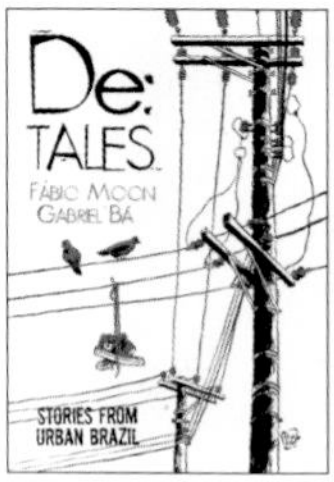
De: TALES
FÁBIO MOON
GABRIEL BÁ
STORIES FROM URBAN BRAZIL

DE:TALES
Fábio Moon and Gabriel Bá

Brazilian twins Fábio Moon and Gabriel Bá share an award-winning talent for comics and an abiding love of the medium. This collection of short stories is brimming with all the details of human life—the charming tales move from the urban reality of their home in São Paulo to the magical realism of their Latin American background.
$14.95/ISBN 978-1-59307-485-2

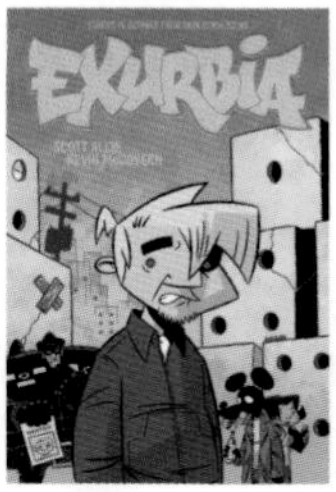
EXURBIA

EXURBIA
Scott Allie and Kevin McGovern

A disillusioned young man finds himself accused of a terrorist rampage that he's not nearly idealistic enough to have committed—while a doomed city looks to a talking, cigar-chomping rat for salvation. *Exurbia* paints a weird and hilarious portrait of a city on the brink of doom, with bizarre supporting characters constantly rising up to steal center stage from a protagonist who lacks the gumption to take charge of this Hitchcockian farce.
$9.95/ISBN 978-1-59582-339-7

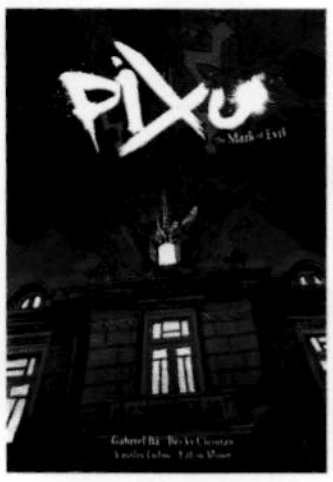
PIXU

PIXU: THE MARK OF EVIL
Gabriel Bá, Becky Cloonan, Vasilis Lolos, and Fábio Moon

This gripping tale of urban horror follows the lives of five lonely tenants—strangers—whose lives become intertwined when they discover a dark mark scrawled on the walls of their building. The horror sprouts from a small seed and finds life as something otherworldly, damaged, full of love, hate, fear, and power. As the walls come alive, everyone is slowly driven mad—stripped of free will, leaving only confusion, chaos, and eventual death.
$17.95/ISBN 978-1-59582-340-3

AVAILABLE AT YOUR LOCAL COMICS SHOP OR BOOKSTORE
To find a comics shop in your area, call 1-888-266-4226.
For more information or to order direct visit darkhorse.com or call 1-800-862-0052 • Mon.–Fri. 9 A.M. to 5 P.M. Pacific Time. *Prices and availability subject to change without notice.

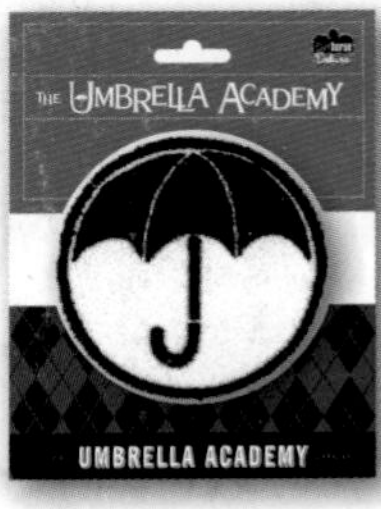
THE UMBRELLA ACADEMY
UMBRELLA ACADEMY

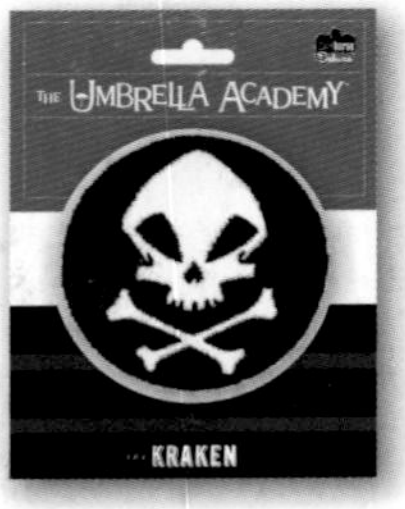
THE UMBRELLA ACADEMY
KRAKEN

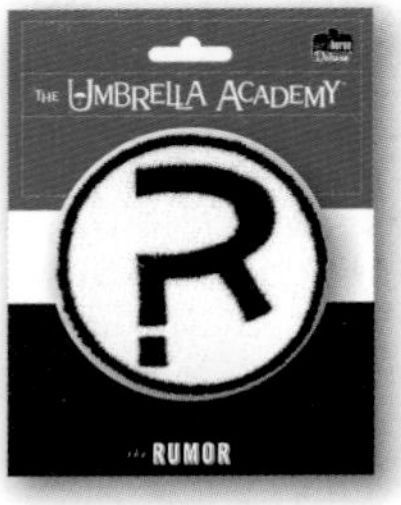
THE UMBRELLA ACADEMY
RUMOR

UMBRELLA PATCH
$4.99/978-1-59617-569-3

KRAKEN'S EMBLEM PATCH
$4.99/978-1-59617-567-9

RUMOR'S LOGO PATCH
$4.99/978-1-59617-568-6

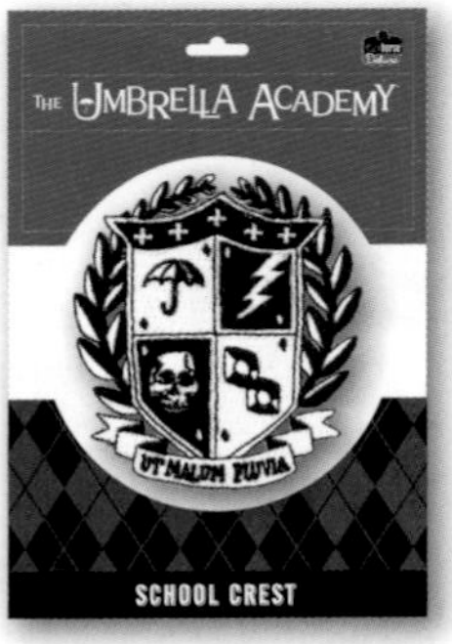
THE UMBRELLA ACADEMY
UT MALUM PLUVIA
SCHOOL CREST

CREST EMBROIDERED PATCH
$5.99/978-1-59617-570-9

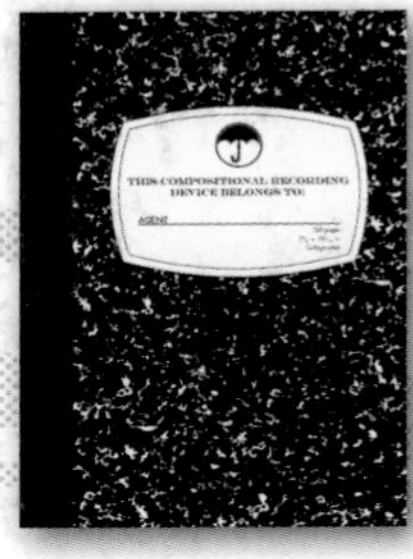

COMPOSITION BOOK
$6.99/978-1-59617-817-5

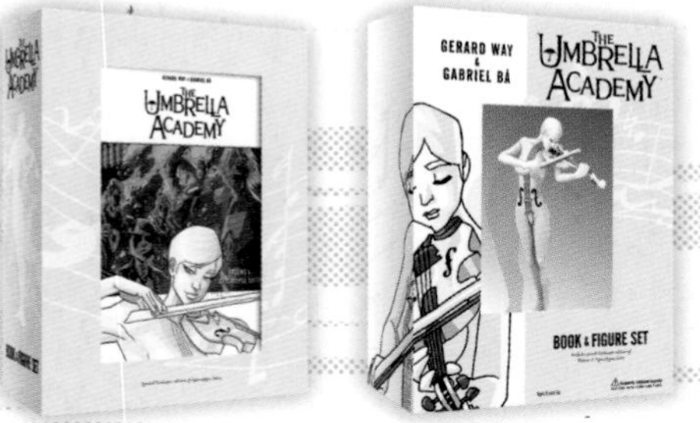
THE UMBRELLA ACADEMY
GERARD WAY & GABRIEL BÁ
BOOK & FIGURE SET

BOOK AND FIGURE SET
$24.99/978-1-59617-744-4

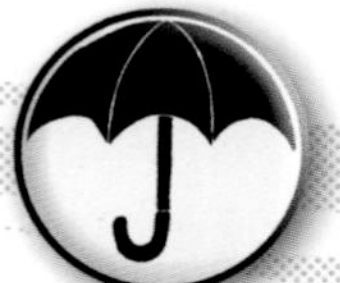

MAGNET
$4.99/978-1-59617-695-9

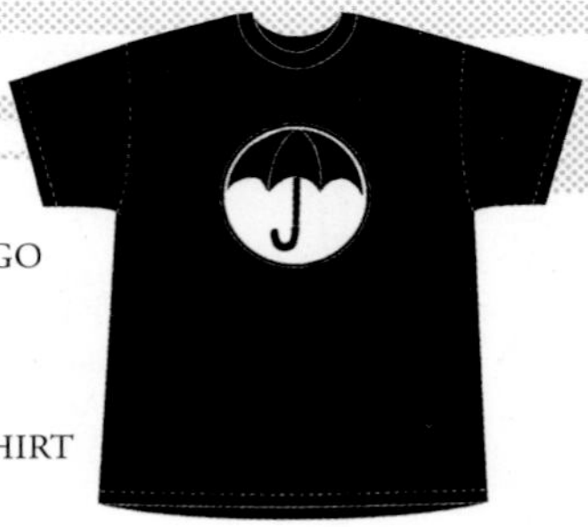

MEN'S LOGO T-SHIRT
$29.99

WOMEN'S LOGO T-SHIRT
$29.99

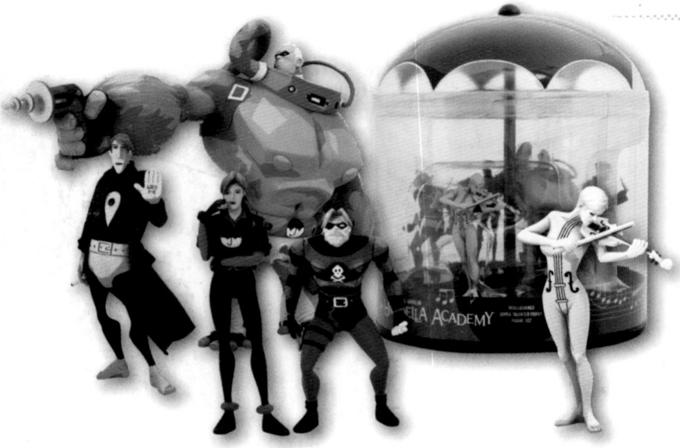

6-PIECE FIGURE SET
$39.99/978-1-59617-575-4

AND MORE OF THE UMBRELLA ACADEMY FROM DARK HORSE DELUXE . . .

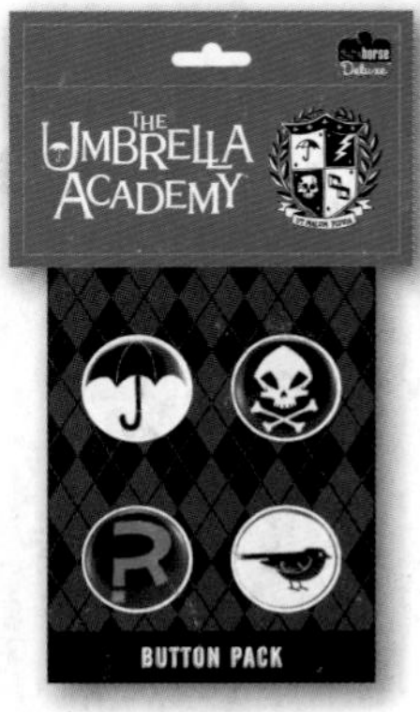
THE UMBRELLA ACADEMY
BUTTON PACK

BUTTON PACK
$5.99/978-1-59617-571-6

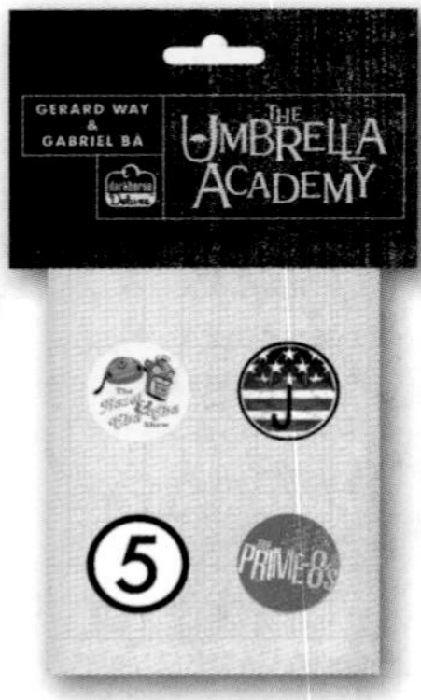
GERARD WAY & GABRIEL BÁ
THE UMBRELLA ACADEMY

BUTTON PACK #2
$5.99/978-1-59617-818-2

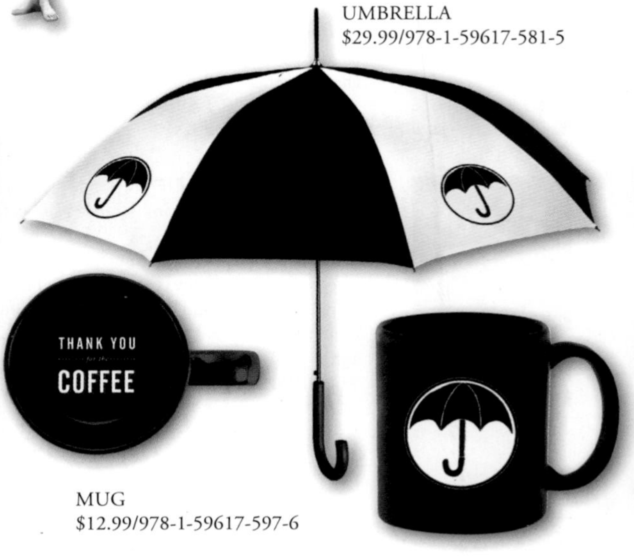

UMBRELLA
$29.99/978-1-59617-581-5

THANK YOU
COFFEE

MUG
$12.99/978-1-59617-597-6

AVAILABLE AT YOUR LOCAL COMICS SHOP OR BOOKSTORE
To find a comics shop in your area, call 1-888-266-4226.
For more information or to order direct visit darkhorse.com or call 1-800-862-0052 • Mon.–Fri. 9 A.M. to 5 P.M. Pacific Time. *Prices and availability subject to change without notice.